Sustainable Development – The Cultural Perspective

Gesellschaft – Technik – Umwelt
Neue Folge

15

Gerhard Banse
Gordon L. Nelson
Oliver Parodi (eds.)

Sustainable Development – The Cultural Perspective

Concepts – Aspects – Examples

edition sigma

Die Deutsche Nationalbibliothek: bibliographical data

Detailed bibliographical data from the
Deutsche Nationalbibliografie can be obtained at
http://dnb.d-nb.de.

Bibliografische Informationen Der Deutschen Nationalbibliothek

*Die Deutsche Nationalbibliothek verzeichnet diese
Publikation in der Deutschen Nationalbibliografie;
detaillierte bibliografische Daten sind im Internet
über http://dnb.d-nb.de abrufbar.*

ISBN 978-3-89404-945-4

Printing and binding: Rosch-Buch, Scheßlitz

Printed in Germany

Content

Preface

This volume is the eighth in a series based on workshops that have been organized as an International Forum on Sustainable Technological Development in a Globalizing World.

A brief discussion about the origin of the Forum is important. Two universities, Florida Institute of Technology (Florida Tech) located in Melbourne, Florida, and the Budapest University of Technology and Economics (BME) have cooperated together beginning in 2001, supported by a U.S. State Department CUAP Grant for three years in the field of environmental protection and environmentally sustainable technologies (environmental studies). The then Department of Innovation Studies and History of Technology at BME also had long periods of cooperation with the Institute of Technology Assessment and Systems Research at the Research Center of Karlsruhe (ITAS/Forschungszentrum Karlsruhe, Germany) (now the Karlsruhe Institute of Technology – KIT), with the University of Basque Country, and with the former head of the Research Evaluation Unit of DG Research of the European Committee, *Dr. Gilbert Fayl,* (he also became foreign secretary of the European Academy of Sciences and the Arts). When BME and Florida Tech personnel met, in June 2002, in the beautiful small Hungarian town of Eger to conduct a "Sustainable Tourismus" workshop, Professors *Gerhard Banse* (KIT) and *Imre Hronszky* (BME) explained their idea to Professors *Gordon L. Nelson* (Florida Tech) and *Nicanor Ursua* (University of Basque Country) to initiate and develop a process to provide for a (loose) organizational forum for discussing how technological development can be made sustainable. It was decided that these institutions would try to develop and realize an annual international workshop devoted to this goal. Professor *Imre Hronszky,* Vice-President, and Mr. *Peter Gresiczki,* Secretary General of the Hungarian UNESCO Commission promised that the Hungarian UNESCO Commission would also do its best to support the Forum.

Sustainability Ideas & Topics

Three main ideas for a forum were put into focus. One was that a continuous discourse between European and US institutes could make the discourse truly trans-Atlantic. To this was added the perspective of UNESCO, and through this the thought that the views and interests of less developed countries should also be represented. It was agreed that a continuous effort should be made so that the workshops would be multi and transdisciplinary as far as possible and would represent different research and participant perspectives, including not only scientific researchers but also students, representatives of companies, governments, and NGOs. The topic for the first year was chosen to be: Rationality in an Uncertain World, for the second year International Sustainability, and for the third a look at the social visions around so-called "Converging Technologies", based on recent and expected developments of the nanotech, biotech, infotech and cognitive sciences.

Meeting Logistics and First Forum

Based on the invaluable importance of trans-Atlantic discussion, the initiators decided on trying to realize yearly workshops alternately in Florida and in Europe. So, the first Forum was held in Budapest, with BME as the local organizer in December, 2003. The second Forum was realized in February, 2005, in a modified form in Melbourne, Florida, at Florida Tech, and a third was held at BME in Budapest in December, 2005.

The first workshop was organized by Imre Hronszky and Gerhard Banse with thirty participants from 13 countries and three continents. They were not only professors in their specialty, but also students and governmental specialists, including the EC. Natural science, technology, social science and humanities were represented in the presentations.

Second Forum

The second Forum held February 21–23, 2005, on the campus of Florida Tech was entitled "Sustainability's New Age, Preservation & Planning (SNAP)".

Sustainability means different things to different people. How do we know that an activity or product is truly sustainable and for how long? Sustainability assessment requires a detailed factual basis, i.e., a comprehensive scientific foundation. The Forum's annual mission encompasses the humanities, social sciences, sustainable development, economics, environmental sciences as well as legal and policy aspects as they broadly intersect with the theme of environmental studies.

The February, 2005 meeting focused on introducing European colleagues to a typical US understanding of sustainability problems in the context of the environmental issues, science drivers and practices used in Florida – where rapid development and one of the world's largest tourism industries impact a particularly sensitive environment.

Available funding provided travel expenses for ten, non-US participants with critical expertise from the Czech Republic, Hungary, Korea, Romania, the United Kingdom and the Ukraine. The meeting brought together both environmental and social sciences, involving experts (and graduate students) in the fields of Biology, Business Management, Chemistry, Ecology, Economics, Engineering, Policy Making, Politics, Science Education, etc.

Third Forum

The Third Forum held in Budapest in December, 2005, concerned the convergence characteristics of typical technological developments of today.

It was one of the goals for the Forum that a follow-on book be published. That book would not be a proceedings, but would capture the flavor of the Forum and move beyond it. As mentioned at the beginning of this Preface, the workshops were organized in the framework of a Forum on Sustainable Technological Development in a Globalizing World. The materials of the first Forum were published by edition sigma, Berlin, in 2005. Its title was "Rationality in an Uncertain World" (eds.: Gerhard Banse, Imre Hronszky, Gordon L. Nelson). The second workshop was published in a series funded for the yearly reports of the cooperation of Florida Tech and BME/Budapest with the title "Environmental Studies: Implications for Sustainability" (eds.: Gordon L. Nelson, Imre Hronszky), Arisztotelesz Publishing Company, Budapest, 2005. It is also available on Florida Tech's website at http://cos.fit.edu/documents/deanbook/Yearbook_2005_end.pdf. Materials from the third workshop were published in 2007 by edition sigma, Berlin. Its title is "Assessing Societal Implications of Converging Technological Development" (eds.: Gerhard Banse, Armin Grunwald, Imre Hronszky, Gordon L. Nelson).

Fourth Forum

The fourth international, interdisciplinary forum, "Sustainable Pathways: New Research and Practices" was held on the Florida Tech campus in Melbourne, Florida, on March 6–7, 2007. The forum was a collaborative effort of the Florida Tech College of Business and the College of Science, with active involvement by BME/Budapest.

The forum took a holistic approach for the 100 attendees (coming from as far away as the Philippines), looking at sustainability issues from business, science and socio-political viewpoints. It was designed to appeal to a varied audience and offered the latest academic research and perspectives for practitioners and public policy makers. The forum began with a look at developments in ecotourism. Former Florida Governor, Bob Martinez, passionate about sustainability in public policy, was the keynote speaker. The final day of the forum offered a panel discussion on smart growth and regional planning, coordinated by Brevard County Commissioner, Sue Carlson. Other sessions included "Sustainability, Technology and Innovation", and "Renewable Energy", led by speakers and panelists from Florida Tech, BME and the European Commission.

A book was published with the title "An International Forum on Sustainability" (eds. Gordon L. Nelson, Imre Hronszky), Arisztotelesz Publishing Company, Budapest, 2008. It is also available on Florida Tech's website at http://cos.fit.edu/documents/BOOK%20FINAL%20RECD%207-17-2008%20Forum%20on%20sustainability_changed_2008.pdf.

Fifth Forum

The Fifth Workshop entitled "Foresight, Roadmapping and Governance – Forum on Sustainable Technological Development in a Globalizing World" was held at BME in Budapest, December 7–8, 2007. Sponsors were BME, Florida Tech, KIT, and the Hungarian National Commission for UNESCO. There were 18 invited participants. There were 13 papers presented.

The 2007 Workshop concentrated on problems of relations of foresight, roadmapping, and governance of forefront technological development; methodological problems were concentrated upon. These included how trends solidify when some players are "overweight" in the dynamics, what the possible effects will be and how ethical assessment may help foresight and governance.

Work from the fifth forum has been recently published. It seemed worthwhile to unify Fifth Forum materials with selected presentations from a symposium on History of Prospective Technology Studies, in the framework of the XXII International Congress of History of Science and Technology, Budapest, July 2009. That symposium was actually organized by nearly the same persons who established the Forum. The publication will be a KIT-report (Karlsruhe 2011; eds.: Gerhard Banse, Armin Grunwald, Imre Hronszky, Gordon L. Nelson).

Sixth Forum

The 6th International Sustainability Forum was entitled "Sustainability 2009: The Next Horizon" and was held on the Florida Tech campus March 3–4, 2009.

As defined at a 1987 United Nations conference, sustainability is "Meeting present needs without compromising the ability of future generations to meet their needs." This ambitious and critical goal is an enormous global challenge. To share knowledge and demonstrate what's happening in this area, Florida Tech's College of Science and College of Business hosted the sixth international sustainability forum with partner BME. The conference was a showcase of Florida Tech's involvement as a global player in sustainability. Its focus was on practical solutions to emerging sustainability issues from business, science and social-political viewpoints. It was designed to appeal to a varied audience and to offer the latest academic research and perspectives for practitioners and policymakers. With 175 registered for lectures (some 30 in number, with presenters from seven countries), it was standing room only for some forum sessions. Participants filled the room to hear keynote presenter Michael Sole '86, Secretary of the Florida Department of Environmental Protection. He spoke on "climate change, the most significant challenge of our lifetime", and related it to what's happening in Florida. Sole discussed the Sunshine State's sustainability issues and how the state government has risen to meet the challenges. He has also been involved in efforts to, among other things, increase energy efficiency in buildings, reduce greenhouse gas emissions from motor vehicles and increase the production and availability of renewable transportation fuels.

> "Both our economy and our way of life depend on our ability to preserve and maintain a healthy and sustainable marine and terrestrial ecosystem for Florida's future generations", he said.
>
> "The economy is always a factor in the ability to attain sustainability. Where resources are few and people are poor, it's difficult to make the necessary investments. The need for sustainability is real; the question is can or will people pay for it?"

More than a dozen Florida Tech researchers presented their sustainability research. They presented their work on such issues as abrupt climate change; climate change and coral reefs; predicting climate in Florida; sustainable tourism; economic drivers of sustainability; opportunities in reclaimed asphalt pavement; and the legal and policy developments of the United Nations on climate change. From the conference came three keys to sustainability. The first is that everyone must have clean water. There can't be good health without it and we have to figure out how to make that happen. Second, sustainability is a global issue because everyone on the planet is affected by the decisions of individual countries. Third, sustainability involves new technology. We need to use it correctly and cost-effectively. Summing up a major conclusion from the forum was that you can have the best environmental science, but it's of no use unless you have the proper economic and political climate. The resulting book captured the essence of and follows on from the 2009 Forum and was published as Gordon L. Nelson, Imre Hronszky (eds.): Sustainability 2009: The Next Horizon, Melville, New York, 2009, AIP Conference Proceedings, volume 1157.

Seventh and Eighth Forums

This current volume is a result of the Seventh and Eighth Forums. The Seventh Forum was held June 9–12, 2010 in Berlin. The Karlsruhe Institute of Technology hosted the event, which was organized around culture and sustainability. What we each value as a society, as a country, in our culture, is what we want to protect. What is sustainable is only what we value. This applies all the more to sustainable development which is planned for long time scales and therefore to go beyond individual sustainable technology solutions as well as economic and political cycles. What we hold in high regard is the result of cultural influences. Consequently, we need cultural change in the sense of sustainable development in order to secure sustainability pathways in the long term. The key question arising is whether and how this change can be brought about. The following Introduction leads us into the specific discussion.

At the end of the Seventh Forum, participants concluded that more specific case studies would be useful and recommended that the Eighth Forum provide a focus for case studies. Since the remainder of the Eighth Forum, held March 8–10, 2011, in Melbourne, Florida, focused on Alternative Energy with oral papers not really appropriate as written papers, it was decided to include the case studies in combination with those papers from Berlin to provide a holistic discussion of culture and sustainability. That is the concept for this volume.

Ninth Forum

The Ninth Forum (10th Anniversary) has been scheduled for June 2012 in Eger, Hungary, where the Forum series began in 2002.

Karlsruhe and Florida, June 2011

Gerhard Banse
Gordon L. Nelson
Oliver Parodi

Introduction: "Culture" as a Challenge to Sustainability Research

Verena Holz, Barbara Muraca

Culture and Sustainable Development – a Debate both Scientific and about Everyday Culture

Globalization entails challenges to the way in which societies design their future. These challenges are being discussed also with regard to their cultural ramifications.[1] While there are some economists who now plead in favor of fully including social and cultural interests of individuals in indexing development and growth, artists and curators are designing exhibitions about the cultural consequences of climate change. Also in the world of the web, the interactions of sustainable development with culture have found their platforms: While the Goethe Institute runs a portal on "Climate Change and Culture" and even a corresponding facebook account[2], users all over the world debate "culture and sustainability" in numerous blogs specially installed for this purpose. These heterogeneous examples of discourses and activities of a variety of players reflect an interest in global development policy and its strategies which is increasingly being taken seriously and discussed also in scientific terms.

The scientific sustainability discourse is transdisciplinary by nature: It is located at the interface between interdisciplinary (theoretical and applied) scientific research, political objectives, and political decisionmaking processes as well as societal design, which requires the broadest possible participation of all players (cf., inter alia, Muraca 2010). This necessity is seen not only on a local and national level, but on a global plane. Ceasing to regard the cultural dimension of sustainable development as an "additive to sustainable development" and instead investigating and perceiving its functions as a structuring, modeling power has become a challenge in contemporary science.

Cultural Dimensions of Sustainability

This challenge has been taken up by scientists and scholars performing interdisciplinary and transdisciplinary work from twelve countries at the workshop on

1 An abbreviated version of the following text was in German published in: Technikfolgenabschätzung. Theorie und Praxis, Vol. 19 (2010), No. 3 (December), pp. 120–124.

2 Cf. http://www.goethe.de/ges/umw/prj/kuk/deindex.htm.

"Sustainability 2010: The Cultural Dimension". The event focused on the points of contact of sustainable development and culture as seen from the perspectives of the different disciplines and contexts represented.

The meeting constituted the 7th workshop of the "Forum on Sustainable Technological Development in a Globalizing World". The Forum was founded as an international research initiative in Budapest in 2002 by representatives of the Budapest University of Technology and Economics (BUTE; *Imre Hronszky*), the Florida Institute of Technology (FIT; *Gordon L. Nelson*), and the then Karlsruhe Research Center, now Karlsruhe Institute of Technology (KIT; *Armin Grunwald, Gerhard Banse*)[3] with the objective, among others, to organize annual multi- and transdisciplinary workshops combining different research perspectives and different participant perspectives, the former by inviting representatives of various scientific disciplines, the latter through the participation, for instance, of scientists, scholars, students, representatives of industry and NGOs, etc. Since 2003, scientists and scholars have attended annual meetings of the Forum organized alternately in Europe and in the USA to discuss, against the backdrop of sustainable development, perspectives and connections of innovations (including technical ones) in a changing social and cultural environment.[4]

The 7th workshop dealt with these key issues against the background of the respective (national) cultural and (scientific) disciplinary patterns:

- What is meant by sustainable development?
- Where are there points of contact between sustainable development and the "culture" area (irrespective of the interpretation of culture used)?
- What efforts are taken or to be taken to trigger sustainable development, and what are the obstacles / barriers hindering this effort?

Over a wide range of facets, and not always in consensus, cultural preconditions and prerequisites were discussed in this way as a requirement for embarking on the road to "sustainable development," i.e. the cultural connectivity of sustainable solution approaches. Cultural phenomena central to sustainable development in science and in practice as well as relevant areas of action were identified for this purpose.[5]

Armin Grunwald in his words of welcome emphasized that the implementation of sustainable development constituted a major challenge not only to politics and society. The way in which situations relevant to sustainability, the systems to be considered, the interactions among the different dimensions of

---

3 Cf. http://www.itas.fzk.de/tatup/041/itas-news.htm.

4 A survey of the activities and publications of the Forum is contained in Nelson 2009.

5 Participants in the meeting were distributed a copy of a book published for this meeting together with the documentation (cf. Parodi et al. 2010), which enriched the discussion.

sustainability, and the frequent occurrence of competing effects were cross-linked, made it impossible to use simple linear arguments to identify deficits in sustainability, determine their causes, elaborate measures and strategies for correction, and examine the consequences of these strategies. Scientific contributions to sustainable development often do not follow the classical approaches to knowledge and are not part of the traditional concept of science. The thesis is that strategic knowledge for sustainable development by far exceeds knowledge gained from explanation and observation. Instead, it comprises problem-oriented combinations of knowledge for explanation, orientation, and action. New ways must be found in generating and applying this strategic knowledge which, so far, have been visible only tentatively. Technological innovation is more than tools of human action, as *Imre Hronszky* emphasized in his introductory remarks. Instead, technology is a medium closely interconnecting people and, as such, isassociated with values, symbolic in nature and creating purpose. The increasing complexity of systems in which we move also requires a near-infinite number of perspectives of observation in which relatedness to culture and context represent an indispensable enrichment. This applies all the more to sustainable development which, according to *Gordon L. Nelson*, is planned for long time scales and therefore has to go beyond individual sustainable technology solutions as well as economic and political cycles. What we hold in high regard is the result of cultural influences. Consequently, we need cultural change in the sense of sustainable development in order to secure sustainability pathways on the long term. The key question arising was whether and how this change can be brought about.

In order to establish a system classifying the cultural preconditions, prerequisites, contexts and obstacles of and to sustainable development, the following sessions were established as a structural framework of the workshop on the basis of the three key topics identified at the beginning: "Meanings of Sustainable Development", "Cultural Diversity and Sustainability – Implicit Norms and Values", and "Sustainability – Political and Educational Implications". They informed the arrangement of the first three chapters in this book, which are preceded by an introductory text by *Robert Hauser* and *Gerhard Banse* opening up the field of culture and sustainability. Their contribution reflects on the term culture in particular and identifies possible relations (and impossible relations) between both culture and sustainable development. These conceptions and understandings are presented to create and offer a basis for further discussion of the two terms and their correlation, taking into account normative standards.

Following up the rather conceptual reflexions in the first three chapters, six case studies will illustrate the cultural interplay between local people and (un-) sustainable development in China, Hungary, India, Florida, Mesoamerica, Vietnam and Indonesia. These Case Studies were presented at the conference „Sustainability 2011: Is It Worth It?" in Melbourne, Florida, in March 2011 (cf. Banse/Parodi 2011).

Meanings of "Sustainable Development"

Given the existence of numerous definitions of sustainable development, some of them depending on research context and political framework conditions, cultural problems and perspectives were discussed first in relation to sustainable development. Culture as a dimension stands in the area of tension of nature, society/ies, values and value systems. Agreement existed more or less among the first speakers, *Gordon L. Nelson,* and *Medardo Tapia Uribe,* in their basic interpretation of culture as a structuring framework of shared attitudes, objectives, values, practices, and methods. Nelson dealt with the relations of growth and culture. The development of the U.S. state of Florida showed that the indicators used to describe "growth culture" had to be different ones in the future. Linear thinking on the basis of progress, in which technologies served as a means for achieving objectives, had to give way to self-critical holistic thinking taking into account ethical and axiological questions (providential principle, ability to anticipate and adapt, problems of orientation, etc.). Tapia Uribe referred to a concept of culture "freeing" human beings from nature forcing them into their limits – a concept which has been around in Europe etymologically since antiquity, idealistically even in the biblical history of creation, culminating in teleological assertions regarding human beings and their culture as the ultimate purpose of nature. With a view to society, culture could be understood as an overarching, structuring, organizing entity and as a social engine. Within this framework, it was also possible to interpret development paradigms. The classical theories of modernization, for instance, according to Uribe, reflected as part of culture the prevailing patterns of interpretation in a specific way of looking at things. Even if many of the objectives and ideals of these theories counteracted sustainable development, it was evident that sustainable development had to be analyzed within the context of these conventional development paradigms.

Following up on this, *Andreas Metzner-Szigeth* in his contribution emphasized that sustainable development in a field of tension of ecological, socio-cultural, economic, and politico-institutional interests could be achieved only if accompanied by integrative technology assessment integrating multiple vulnerabilities and failure potentials of the individual systems.

However, sustainability goals could not simply be transferred from the global and general level to the local level, as any context realization always implied interpretation and adaptation as well. A good example of these interpretation processes was presented by *Appukuttan N. Damodaran* for the case of India.

Besides the "grand traditions" establishing the prevailing cultural orientation also with respect to sustainability issues, there were numerous "minor traditions," which had become established on the spot as verified systems of handling natural resources and among the members of a community. These showed greater permeability to exogenous influences and were able in part, thanks to their higher adaptability, to establish a positive combination of elements of Western technology and culture with local traditions, and achieve an outcome positive for the community.

This perspective was reinforced by *Gabriele Tautscher:* For decades, cultural anthropology, among other subjects, has been dealing with the intercultural impact of projects within the framework of what is called development aid, and with the hegemonial meaning of the concept of development, which reflected Western ethnocentric assumptions; this could lead, among other things, to underestimating the resilience and dynamics of non-Western cultures and to "indigenization" of Western cultural imports. "Cultures" are permanently undergoing creative processes of constant change and negotiation, and cannot be fixed.

The contributions lead to the question of how far the ideas and values anchored in the sustainability concept are universal. The concept of translating into local contexts, interpretation systems and symbolic dimensions is followed by the question who will cope with this transfer and whether or under what conditions such translation can succeed. Is it also possible to recognize and incorporate the narratives and interests of subordinates? A paradigm of such global significance as sustainable development not only must take into account cultural differences, which by far cannot be identified with national or geographic borders only, but also must involve the question who, in these contexts of strategy development, actually has a say and a possibility to express an input.

In operationalizing the guiding principle of sustainable development, therefore, cultural specificities must be taken into account on a local level. Even within Europe, cultural differences are of immense importance. The establishment of a *Ne*twork for *S*ustainability in *S*outh *E*astern *E*urope (NESSEE) – thus *Ildiko Tulbure* – is a successful case of implementation of sustainability goals, with contexts taken into account, and inter- and multicultural aspects considered. The problem of "local interpretation" of general sustainability principles is in the focus of the "Risk Habitat Megacities" project, an application of the "Integrative Sustainability Concept" developed over ten years ago by the Helmholtz Association (cf. Kopfmüller et al. 2001) for megacities in South America. Three principles were derived from the Brundlandt "definition" of sustainable development (inter- and intragenerative justice, global perspectives, and anthropocentric approach), translated into three transdimensional objectives of sustainable development (securing human existence, preserving social productivity potential, and maintaining society's possibilities of development and action) and, in a third step, used as a basis for formulating substantive and instrumented rules allowing the concept to be operationalized. As emphasized by *Jürgen Kopfmüller* in this contribution, the project from the beginning faced the challenge of inter- and transdisciplinary and, above all, intercultural cooperation of partners from science, administration, and politics and society. Cultural aspects (especially with regard to cultural heritage and multicultural perspectives on the spot) were taken into account in the project under the heading of contextual "translation" of general principles.

Norms, Values, and Education

Sustainable development as a normative concept is aimed at achieving a societal change in values and awareness – and, at the same time, is confronted with value systems varying culturally worldwide. This is expressed in the controversies about "democracy", "human rights", and "growth" frequently used as a basis. The respective different expressions of the guiding idea of sustainable development as a normative objective and a regulatory ideal, respectively, have not been implemented so far, despite the definition of concrete instructions for action. As was shown by *Larissa Krainer* in referring to a variety of materials from the media, this is due, among other things, to their conflicts with the value systems prevailing in our culture. The basis was a culture of production and consumption, guided mainly by technical and economic values, which needed competition, profit maximization, acceleration, and the urge towards innovation. As values and value systems were contradictory even within one culture, dialectic treatment of conflicting values was needed. The process ethics developed by Krainer and Peter Heintel constitutes a basis for dialectic conflict management (cf. Krainer/Heintel 2010).

Also according to *Robert Hauser,* the normative concept of sustainable development contradicts other applicable normative concepts and value concepts at odds with intercultural connections. Norms generated patterns of action which created identity for cultural communities: Those who did not follow these patterns were perceived as outsiders. The category of normative was summarized under "axiological," and, according to Hauser, encompassed customs, ethical norms, and legal norms (including laws and ethical laws in the narrower sense), whose obligatory character was beyond negotiation.

Values and value systems have developed and established themselves throughout history. As was shown by *János Szlavik/Miklós Füle,* feedback to local value systems is indispensable to modernization projects in the sense of sustainable development. Historical values comprised aesthetic and ethical values as well as stratified experience in managing materials and things. The example of the use of water as a resource was cited by *Virender Sharma* to show that taking into account local environmental, cultural, and economic conditions plays a major role. Technical solutions needed integration with political measures in the health system, and their success depended on close cooperation with the partners on a local level.

Barbara Muraca/Lieske Voget-Kleschin in a first step of their contribution reconstruct the two approaches established in Germany which create a systematic-normative framework for sustainability (the so-called HGF approach and the theory of pronounced sustainability) and then, in a second step, critically analyze mainly the theory of pronounced sustainability from the perspective of the cultural dimension of sustainability. In doing so, they approach a "third" path between universally normative claims and culturally relativistic criticism.

Sustainability – Political and Educational Implications

This part focuses mainly on project cases, such as one example of "non-sustainable" patterns of production and behavior in the sector of potential waste avoidance and, on the other hand, on Education for Sustainable Development (BNE), which explicitly includes cultural and aesthetic questions in its concept.

Renate Hübner uses waste policy in Austria since 1990 to draw attention to contradictions and conflicting targets potentially arising in case of real waste avoidance. She indicates how these dilemmas took several years to culminate with respect to the environmental policy goal, namely waste avoidance, as a consequence of the systemic logics of societal subsystems. In this political area, considered to be a tool of sustainable development, systemic contradictions are explained which show the tremendous societal relevance of utilizing the capacities of systems and facilities as a phenomenon which could be the driver of our non-sustainable way of handling resources and material goods.

Oliver Parodi and *Verena Holz* in their contributions about BNE stress another subarea of culture: Aesthetics, symbolic orders and design possibilities of sustainable development are related to the learning individual and his or her function in society. The concept of education for sustainable development was not geared to any specific target group. Instead, the declared objective was to include the broadest possible group of persons in this subject in a participatory sense, and make available learning contexts to enable all participants to contribute actively in a common design of the future. This was exemplified, on the one hand, in the School of Sustainability, which is part of the House of Competence of the Karlsruhe Institute of Technology (KIT), and, on the other hand, by a transdisciplinary learning project implemented at the Leuphana University of Lüneburg, Germany, together with a Lüneburg elementary school and two artists. Unlike previous concepts (such as those within the framework of environmental education), aesthetic perception patterns and artifacts as well as cultural issues and interpretations are explicitly integrated into the processes of change of sustainable development, especially in order to emphasize the design potential of sustainable development instead of rules of behavior.

Sustainability among Cultures: Round Table Discussion at the Paul Loebe Haus

Part of the workshop, and a basis of further contributions to this book, was a round table discussion held at the Paul Loebe Haus of the German Federal Parliament, introduced by words of welcome by *Ulla Burchardt,* SPD Member of Parliament (reprinted at the beginning of this book). As chairperson of the Cross-sectional Group on Sustainable Development (1998–2002), she was instrumental from the beginning in the political implementation of "sustainable development" strategies. Burchardt points out that awareness of the cultural dimension of sustainable development was indispensable to understanding the idea proper underlying sustainable development, especially when it was a matter of incorporation into a variety of contexts and traditions in various regions of the world. In her function as chairperson of the Committee for Education, Research, and Technology Assessment of the German Federal Parliament (since 2005), Burchardt emphasized education and research as prime movers of innovation in our system of economy and society. For more than ten years, sustainable development had constituted the key normative orientation. Especially newly developed technologies for sustainable development had to consider economic, social, ethical, and cultural aspects. In this connection, she emphasized the importance of international research networks, such as the *Forum on Sustainable Technological Development in a Globalizing World,* which organizes its discussions of subjects and issues of sustainable development as a continuous process.

The discussion, moderated by Grunwald, subsequently focused on intercultural aspects of sustainable development. Cultural misunderstandings often arise from natural assumptions, not queried in any way, about one's understanding of key categories, such as time, space, relations, and change. In her introductory contribution, *Silja Graupe* emphasizes that, in Chinese and Japanese Buddhism, the basic concept of the world was based not on "things" but rather on relations and processes. Against this background, concepts like "preserve and store" were misleading. In India, there was also a different understanding of space and time: Time was infinite from a reincarnation perspective, and the obligations to future generations arose in a very different connection. In this sense, sustainable development had to be understood also as a process, not just as a goal. Civil society, with its manifold and complex structures, should play the key role in this process. Broad participation of all stakeholders was fundamental, as was shown by the example of opposition to specific forms of development and growth of the local indigenous population in Mexico. It was also emphasized that cultural pluralism was an indispensable resource at a local level which, so far, had not been managed in the right way ("culture of cultural pluralism"). However this should not be mixed up with a simplistic cultural relativism without common normative guide rails. In moving from the cultural dimension of sustainability to the sustainability of culture *(sustaining culture),* it could be stated that not every aspect of a culture per se should be preserved. However, to what extent do we have a right to determine what other countries are to do or not to do on their way to sustainable development or, in other words, to what extent they did not have the right to make mistakes of their own, is a difficult question, as was formulated in the joint discussion. Any contact with other cultures can become an opportunity for questioning one's own cultural background, too often taken for granted, and thus open up options for shifting or mediation without giving up cultural differences.

Armin Grunwald pointed out, that sustainability has become a major issue also in Technology Assessment (TA) giving scientific advice to political bodies. He briefly describes the work in this field, which has been done by the Office of Technology Assessment at the German Bundestag (TAB) at the occasion of TAB reports on different issues such as energy, tourism, and access to information. As a more cross-cutting issue a new TAB project on "Parliaments and Sustainability" will be introduced briefly. In most of the TAB studies on sustainability issues the cultural dimension is present but rather as a background. In the last-mentioned cross-cutting project, however, this will be different because there is a need to develop and implement a new "culture" of dealing with sustainability on the level of parliaments which is a challenge to political culture and to accordingly shaping political institutions.

Case Studies

The case studies, forming the second part of the book, were presented on a subsequent conference in Melbourne, FL, U.S. (March 2011), entitled "Sustainability 2011: Is It Worth It?". They do not refer explicitly to the contributions in the first part, however they pick up several questions and topics that came up in the more conceptual articles (cf. Banse/Parodi 2011). In the following we will give a short overview about the case studies.

In his contribution *Feng Yang* describes how China is gradually abandoning its traditional high energy consuming economic development by implementing renewable energies in its production. He points out how this transformation process also takes into account the relationship between humans and nature in terms of policies, regulations, communication and education.

Miklós Füle/János Szlávik frame a critic based on the principle of "Sustainable Growth", an economic philosophy of constant growth, that has managed to maintain its position over the logic of Sustainable Development. This latter philosophy, which focuses on the natural requirements of human life, has been steadily gaining a place in technological advances and applications during the last two decades. The result of this duel of socio-economic philosophies is that technologies supporting economic growth pose a constant level of threat on the one hand, and emergencies on a catastrophic magnitude on the other, affecting present generations on Earth. The case study depicts an ecologic catastrophe which took place in Hungary in Autumn 2010. It analyses the problematic circumstances and shows up potential measures to avoid or at least encounter such technological and ecological disasters.

It follows up *Appukuttan N. Damodaran's* case study about the Tsunami Sea waves that struck India in December 2004. It was an unforeseen calamity that could not be explained in terms of standard paradigms of disaster occurrence. The knowledge gap on the part of the "omniscient" State created a crisis of confidence about official machinery. His paper discusses the essence of local knowledge engendered in the wake of the Tsunami disaster by its victims and the gradual cognizance of these local insights by the State machinery. In the light of the field evidence on the Tsunami disaster, the paper advocates a bottom-up approach to framing policies for managing unforeseen natural disasters through robust damage prevention measures.

Jon Shenker describes a local approach to encounter overfishing in Florida, that could serve as a model for similar restoration programs in other regions. The project consists in developing a coordinated network of marine fishery enhancement centers around the coastline of the state that will combine habitat restoration and aquaculture production to enhance coastal and estuarine recreational fisheries.

Another contribution by *Eduard Müller* and *Kenyon C. Lindeman* discusses the problem of ignoring the crosscutting significance of Climate Change. For some scientists, practitioners and decision makers and the general public, climate issues usually lie even further down the scale of priorities. For many, it is still something that will happen at the poles and towards the end of this century. A primary focus of this article will consider the question: why do we have such high quality research and low quality decisions?

The case studies in the second part of the book will be completed by a paper of *Kien To,* who introduces the issues of community participation and Sustainable Communities (SC) with a focus on developing countries. He is exploring good SC approaches and initiatives in Vietnam and Indonesia, demonstrating local practices and experiences.

Concluding Remarks

It is instructive to learn that the authors do not, from the beginning, agree on one definition of culture. In the sense of inter- and transdisciplinarity, an informative process of defining "culture" and "sustainable development" can be observed. All participants agree, thus *Gerhard Banse* in his summary comments at the Berlin conference, that a next step is to elaborate a methodologically adequate description of the relation between sustainable development and the cultural dimension. The greatest challenge is posed by the fact that sustainability can be focused on only from a transdisciplinary perspective implying not only cooperation of various scientific disciplines and practices, but rather requiring rethinking of the concept of science. This can be achieved only through a common exchange but, at the same time, shows the need for scientific elaboration of the object of research. The concluding article of *Caroline Robertson-von Trotha/ Oliver Parodi/Robert Hauser* is informed by the impulses given by the different insights and points of view in this volume. It opens up the new perspective of a cultural dimension in the context of sustainable development in theory and practice, including norms, methodological questions and learning.

References

Banse, G.; Parodi, O. (2011): Sustainability 2011: Is It Worth It? Bericht vom "8th International, Interdisciplinary Sustainability Forum", Melbourne, Florida/USA, 8–9 March 2011. In: Technikfolgenabschätzung. Theorie und Praxis, Vol. 20/No. 1 (April), pp. 99–101 (in German)

Kopfmüller, J.; Brandl, V.; Jörissen, J.; Paetau, M.; Banse, G.; Coenen, R.; Grunwald, A. (2001): Nachhaltige Entwicklung integrativ betrachtet. Konstitutive Elemente, Regeln, Indikatoren. Berlin (in German)

Krainer, L.; Heitel, P. (2010): Prozessethik. Zur Organisation ethischer Entscheidungsprozesse. Wiesbaden (in German)

Muraca, B. (2010): Denken im Grenzgebiet. Prozessphilosophische Grundlagen einer Theorie starker Nachhaltigkeit. Freiburg (in German)

Nelson, G. (2009): Introduction. In: Nelson, G.; Hronszky, I. (eds.): Sustainability 2010: The Next Horizon. Conference Proceedings. Melville/NY, pp. vii–xiv

Parodi, O.; Banse, G.; Schaffer, A. (eds.) (2010): Wechselspiele: Kultur und Nachhaltigkeit. Annäherungen an ein Spannungsfeld. Berlin (in German)

Address of Welcome

Ulla Burchardt, MdB

Ladies and Gentlemen,

on behalf of the German Federal Parliament, the 'Bundestag', I would like to express a warm welcome to all of you. Most of you travelled over a long distance (f. i. from India, Mexico and the United States) to come to Berlin and to join the international workshop "Sustainability 2010: The Cultural Dimension". Sustainable development has, over a long time, been regarded mostly as an economic, a political or a technical challenge while the cultural dimension was recognized rather late. However, there is an increasing awareness that the cultural dimension of sustainability is crucial not only for the identification and implementation of measures and strategies but also on how to understand the very idea of sustainability and how to embed it into traditions in the different regions of the World.

The highly international composition of the participants of the conference shows the wide interest and will allow for really inter-cultural dialogue on sustainable development. I regard it as absolutely important that such conferences are not stand-alone or isolated events but are embedded in a lively and continuous process which allows building and developing stabile and fruitful networks. In this respect I was very glad to notice that your conference is already the seventh conference organised by the Sustainable Technological Development Forum which was founded in 2002.

The workshop 2010 concentrates on problems of relationships between sustainable development and culture. Step by step, the cultural perspective is becoming an aspect in the debates on sustainable development. Your workshop intends to provide a sound scientific contribution to that debate by opening up the subject of cultural sustainability in an interdisciplinary way without hasty restrictions or exclusions. Based on this principle, the subject is discussed in the conflicting fields of cultural heritage, globalization and technological change. You selected Berlin as location for debating these issues, and the Bundestag as the place for the Panel discussion this afternoon. Therefore, please allow me to say few words about activities at the Bundestag which might be of interest to your workshop.

This is the Paul-Löbe Haus of the Bundestag. It is the "Work Bench" of the Bundestag, the house of its committees including the meeting rooms – this is one of them –, offices and secretaries. The different committees debate political issues in their fields, inform themselves about ongoing activities, discuss reports and proposals form ministries and prepare laws.

I am chairwomen of the Committee for Education, Research and Technology Assessment. Education and research are essential preconditions for innovation in the economy and in society. It is, therefore, a highly important task of the political system to provide adequate boundary conditions and budgets for the research and education systems. The Committee for Education, Research and Technology Assessment debates mid- and long-term developments of the German research system and its impacts for society. The postulate of Sustainable Development has been a central normative orientation for guiding research policy for more than ten years. Several programmes of research for sustainable development have been designed which are now being executed by the ministry for education and research. The programmes of socio-ecological research and FONA („Forschung für Nachhaltigkeit“ – „Research for Sustainability“) are examples for this type of targeted research.

The Committee for Education, Research and Technology Assessment carries as third element in its title “Technology Assessment”. Technology Assessment is recognized by the Bundestag as an essential element of parliamentary policy advice. The Bundestag is funding its Office of Technology Assessment for now 20 years (Professor Grunwald will present the work of this office in some minutes). The Research Committee is acting as the supervisory body on behalf of the entire Bundestag. The idea of Sustainable Development motivated many reports of this office since its foundation (for example “Sustainable tourism” in 1996 already). In these TA reports mostly the relation between innovative technology and sustainable development is considered, in fields such as energy, transportation or agriculture. However, it is clear that considering technologies for supporting sustainability must also take into account economical, social, ethical – and cultural – issues.

Dealing with the challenge of sustainable development has a long-lasting tradition in the German Bundestag. In the 1990ies there were two Enquéte-Committees – committees consisting of Members of Parliament as well as of researchers and stakeholders – which took care about how to translate this challenge in to the “machinery” of the political system.

One of the results was to urge the Federal Government to establish a Council for Sustainable Development which is working since 2001, and to set up a National Strategy on Sustainable Development which was installed in 2002. Furthermore, criteria for a research policy dedicated to Sustainability were developed and applied in several fields – in some cases supported by TA studies provided by the Office of Technology Assessment.

As a further result of the work of these committees sustainability has been institutionalised in the Bundestag through the foundation of a Parliamentary Advisory Council on Sustainable Development. This Advisory Council had been called for by the CDU/CSU, SPD, FDP and ALLIANCE 90/The Greens in a joint motion. This motion stressed the necessity, against the background of the challenges posed by globalisation, for the Bundestag to make clear its commitment to sustainable development. The motion underlined the fact that the Parliamentary Advisory Council should serve as the advocate of long-term responsibility in the political process, should structure policy for future generations and support the work of the bodies created by the Federal Government.

The Parliamentary Council comprising 22 full members is intended to lend a parliamentary dimension to the national strategy on sustainability, play a role in developing goals, measures and instruments and defining them in concrete terms, present recommendations on medium and long-term planning, enter into dialogue with other parliaments, particularly in the European Union, and underpin the discussion within society on the subject of sustainable development.

A central element of its work was the implementation of a systematic sustainability assessment of political action. Political and legislative action and decision-making is a central place of determining future developments in modern societies. In contrast to considering only isolated political measures under aspects of sustainable development, a systematic sustainability assessment of political action could provide an occasion to orientate the entire political and juridical system and its outcomes to the idea of sustainability. Elements of such a sustainability assessment were added to the established Law Impact Assessment procedure (Gesetzesfolgenabschätzung) during the last election period.

Ladies and gentlemen, you see that the Bundestag is a place where ideas and problems of sustainable development are being debated, where decisions relevant to sustainable development are made, and where scientific input from sustainability research is urgently needed. I wish you and your conference great success in these days and in future at all the places where you're working.

Thank you for your attention!

Culture and Culturality

Approaching a Multi-faceted Concept

Robert Hauser, Gerhard Banse

1 Concepts of Culture – The Plurality of the Concept of Culture

As early as in classical antiquity, culture occupied a central position in occidental thought.[1] Culture, in its original classical meaning, i.e. the Latin *cultura,* refers to cultivating fields (cf. "agriculture"), meaning tilling, cultivating, planting, as well as mental care and education of intellectual capabilities (cf. Pfeiffer 1997, p. 743). In the Middle Ages, the term hardly played a role in the "Germanic" language area. Only towards the end of the 17th century culture, after having appeared in German texts in its Latin form, it became integrated into German, achieving greater significance as a concept (though with partly very different meanings).

This highlights the first difficulty when dealing with the concept of culture. As a consequence of its long tradition, the subdisciplines of the humanities and social sciences now feature a multitude of concepts of culture side by side, all of them defined and used in different ways (cf. Gerhards 2000, p. 16). As a consequence, the concept of culture is far from being sharply defined even in the literature of the field. Disciplines as different as philosophy, sociology, anthropology and interdisciplinary schools, such as "cultural studies", attempted to describe and characterize what "culture" means from their points of view. Epistemological research in this area is multi-faceted, historically speaking, and continues to grow.

This multiplicity is so pronounced also because, depending on the purpose, object and method of a study, it may make sense to opt for a different concept of culture. Generally, concepts of culture can be distinguished with respect to access (qualitative and quantitative or mixed forms) and level of a study (micro, meso, macro levels). However, even within specific disciplines, the concept of culture often remains vague and ambivalent. Theoretical difficulties begin with the many forms culture can assume, and they end with the paradoxes encountered invariably when looking at the phenomenon of culture from a scientific point of view.

---

1 This contribution is based in large parts on Hauser 2009.

It is especially three (seemingly) conflicting characteristics of culture which cause difficulties (cf. Demorgon/Molz 1996, pp. 43f.):

(1) *Continuity and change:* While culture, on the one hand, ensures the preservation of cultural heritage by means of tradition (holidays, memorial days, etc.), lasting new patterns, techniques and practices of culture keep arising, often as a result of specific influences.
(2) *Standardization and differentiation:* Culture is frequently described as orientation or standardization of values or patterns of behavior, thus as uniform; on the other hand, however, there are also individual variations, subcultures, and miniature collectives making cultures appear divergent.
(3) *Openness and boundaries:* Cultures, seen as national cultures, on the one hand, are open to other cultures and cultural patterns (which can also cause them to change) but, at the same time, also represent boundaries of a community: Only those knowing and understanding the common symbols, such as language, history, and institutions, can find orientation and behave accordingly. Behavior adequate to a culture indicates who belongs and who does not.

2 History – The Genesis of the Concept of Culture

While the classical concept of culture implied cultivation (of soil, plants) or education (of persons), it became broader and was redefined in part from the 17th century onward. Over the following periods of time, the concept of culture was related to the three major concepts of enlightened thought: culture/nature (cf. Pufendorf 2002/1686), culture/civilization (cf. Kant 1977/1784), and culture/life (cf. Freud 1989/1930) (cf. Reckwitz 2000, pp. 66ff; cf. also Hubig 2010). In its definition relative to those concepts, and in comparison with them, it acquires different meanings. The resultant definitions of culture may also be referred to as concepts of culture "in the narrow sense". They do not point to an ontic difference but merely to different aspects of the same object (cf. Janich 2005, p. 21).

In the period of Enlightenment, the concept was popularized by Immanuel Kant and Johann Gottfried Herder, becoming a buzzword in philosophical thought. The very civilizatory concept of culture can still be found in the everyday meaning of culture. To this day, the "achievements of civilization", such as theater, movies, or books, are referred to as cultural products or even high culture. This also reflects Western European thought of the late 19th century, when peoples were still judged by their civilizatory achievements, of course always against the backdrop of one's own "cultural achievements" for comparison: Accordingly, there were highly developed cultures and cultures which were less developed or not developed at all – as a rule, this referred to African or American aborigines. Those were not only devoid of religion, i.e. they were heathen, but also of culture, i.e. civilization.

While Kant "charged" the concept of culture normatively in connection with morals, coupling it to civilization, Herder used concepts of popular psychology to develop the historico-holistic concept of culture, thus recontextualizing it (cf. Herder 1989/1784/91):

> "The holistic concept of culture de-universalizes the concept of culture, contextualizing and historicizing it. Culture is no longer a distinguished form of life, cultures rather are specific ways of life of individual collectives in history, and the concept of culture logically occurs in the plural form, referring to the diversity of the totalities of human forms of life in various 'peoples,' 'nations,' 'communities,' 'cultural areas." (Reckwitz 2005, p. 95)

This makes Herder the first author to establish a broad understanding of culture related neither only to man and nature nor, chiefly in a normative way, to civilization:

> *"The culture of a people is the bloom of its existence through which it manifests itself in a pleasant but also frail way.* Like human beings coming into this world and knowing nothing – needing to learn what they want to know –, a crude people learns from practice for itself or through contacts with others. However, every kind of human knowledge has its own ambience, i.e. its nature, time, place, and period of life [...]" (Herder 1989/1784/91, p. 571; original italics. R.H./G.B.)

Culture as used by Herder refers, in a neutral way, to the totality of a historically specific contextualized way of life of a collective in contrast to other collectives. This becomes apparent also in the criticism of contemporary concepts of culture, where he complains: "Nothing is less defined than this word, and nothing is more delusive than its application to entire peoples and periods of time" (Herder 1989/1784/91, preface, p. 39). The concept of culture coined by Herder in this way had a special impact on the discipline of anthropology, which was still young at that time. In their studies of so-called natural peoples, anthropologists found that some of those not only had produced differentiated societies, but also had many rites, traditions, ceremonies, interpretations of the world, and "cultural products", such as carvings, or the like. Accordingly, they did have culture(s), even if those functioned by different mechanisms, and other values and norms influenced activities. The interpretation of culture began to change with these research findings.

The concepts of culture developed in anthropology, also influenced by the emergence of cultural studies, then more and more resembled the meaning of the Anglo-Saxon term "culture" – in the sense of "everyday culture" – thus establishing a broader concept of culture. To this day, this has incorporated everything of importance to human everyday life. Things mental and things material are regarded as culture or are influenced by culture. This enlarged concept of culture (referred to below as the "broader" concept of culture) is used epistemologically chiefly in a reflexive way, i.e., it serves primarily to compare everyday cultures. Culture as defined in this sense is what distinguishes people's ways of life. Accordingly, it is based mainly on the finding that people developed different ways of life by which they are distinguished (cf. Cappai 2005, pp. 50ff.; Reckwitz 2005, p. 95). This gives rise to a pluralistic concept of culture not referring to *culture* per se, but differentiating between equivalent, yet different cultures in contradistinction to civilizational/normative interpretations. Any culture in this sense seems to be anchored in three units:

> "[...] in a collective of persons (frequently thought of as a *community*), in a *shared* space – cultures are associated with geographic spaces – and in a continuity of time – cultures appear to be bound to a *historic tradition*." (Reckwitz 2005, p. 95; emphasis and brackets in the original, R.H./G.B.)

Parallel to the "narrow" and "broad" concepts of culture, a concept of culture developed in the 20th century according to theories of differentiation which strongly influenced especially the social sciences. As a full-blown systematic concept, this concept of culture was found for the first time in systems theory constructivism as described by Talcott Parsons in his evolution theory treatise about functional differentiation in modern societies (cf. Reckwitz 2005, p. 95). This shows culture as a functional societal subsystem, a "fiduciary system", institutionalized mainly in the arts and in education and with the duty of handing down and newly developing interpretations of the world (cf. Parsons 1977).

In the mid-20th century, the "linguistic turn" in linguistics was followed by the "cultural" turn: a move away from the narrow normative concept of culture towards a broader concept of culture focusing on associations of meaning. In everyday usage, a very narrow concept of culture can still be found (especially in the public and on the feature pages of newspapers), which is associated mainly with the representatives of culture and, in this way, cultural artifacts, such as books, movies, but also dramas, operas, etc. In this case, the concept of culture, following Kant's interpretation, is linked to civilization and the achievements of civilization, respectively.

In the humanities, this concept of culture was discarded around the middle of the 20th century. This break, which is seen in various scientific disciplines under different names, became apparent first in the linguistic papers by Ludwig Wittgenstein. His work shows him in an epistemological position between studies in the early period (cf. Wittgenstein 2003/1921) and the late period (cf. Wittgenstein 2001/1935/1949), expressed in linguistics in the term "crises of representation" (cf. also Mersch 1999). The fundamental difference lies in the fact that it had been recognized that words, as elements of linguistic systems, derive their significance not from any direct correspondence to the objective world to the elements of which they refer, but rather from their position and their relation with other elements of language. This major difference, which is considered the epistemological turnaround and later referred to as "linguistic turn" (cf. Rorty 1967), means that the meaning of words is detached from concrete representatives, instead emphasizing contexts and reference associations within a linguistic system.

This break also occurred with regard to the concept of culture and was expressed in the term "cultural turn" (cf. Reckwitz 2000, 2005, and others). This means that the concept of culture as civilization or high culture, which used to be associated with the material or immaterial products of these high cultures, is replaced by a concept of culture in which culture means context- or meaning-dependent practices of knowledge, communication and, thus, social and cultural practices, respectively (cf. Reckwitz 2005, p. 96). These practices interact with the environment of human life and existence.

3 Concepts of Culture – Cultural Concepts in Current Research Practice

Current research practice in cultural studies as well as in interdisciplinary and transdisciplinary research, provided that culture is interpreted as a concept, defines three methodological lines or types of concepts of culture of the "broad" variety according to Jürgen Bolten: *"Material" theories* of culture are mainly based semiotically on the totality of artifacts as meaningful real achievements of a society. Artifacts encompass monuments as well as factory buildings, tools or clothes (cf. Bolten 1997, p. 488). *"Mentalist" approaches,* employing cognitive anthropology (cf., e.g., Goodenough 1971), consistently consider culture immaterial. Their interest is devoted less to cultural "perceptus" than to cultural "conceptas".

> "'Conceptas' means collectively shared values, attitudes and norms which cannot be described directly as causes of actions and behavior, but require conclusions drawn, for instance, on the basis of observable reality. In a way, this is the 'cultural memory' or 'knowledge pool,' used by communicating parties to obtain interpretations by agreeing on something in the world." (Bolten 1997, p. 488; cf. also Reckwitz 2005, p. 97)

"Functionalist" theories of culture emphasize the aspect of "making oneself understood". This already denotes a functionalist perspective from which the meaning of the concept of culture again changes – culture is given a foundation in action theory. "Culture" in its functionalist interpretation consequently can be regarded as a system of orientation constitutive of, and necessary for, the social practice of a society, organization or group. This is closely related to the concept

of "normality" in the group: Only the existence of specific conventions of social action allows concrete everyday actions to invoke assumptions of normality which are presupposed without being queried (cf. Bolten 1997, p. 488).

The macrotheoretical approaches described above (provided they can be assigned unequivocally) can be summarized as type 3. On the other hand, the microtheoretical approaches tend to be type 2, relating culture to values and norms as interpretations of systems of symbols. The three variants of the broader concept of culture must not be considered mutually exclusive; on the contrary:

> "Nowadays, an integrating perspective is preferred in which culture is perceived as a system of interaction and orientation which can be described by 'perceptus' and explained as 'conceptas.'" (Bolten 1997, p. 489)

In scientific theory, the basic problem of the theory of culture in the humanities and social sciences lies in a precise definition of what precisely is to be understood by cultural differences in the light of existing historical circumstances (cf. Reckwitz 2005, p. 96). The question how to define differences conceptually can be answered only once the basis of comparison, i.e. the element to be compared, has been defined. According to Andreas Reckwitz, mainly three different discourses can be distinguished, which will be outlined briefly below as a summary and for classification (cf. Reckwitz 2005).

The *"social theory" discourse* tries to express the differences in "theories of culture" (cf. Reckwitz 2005, pp. 93ff.). These are mostly approaches of social constructivism formulating a general theory of the origins of social order in human thought and action (cf., e.g., Berger/Luckmann 2000). In this approach, action, thought and perception are based on symbolic orders which, at the same time, are constitutive to the perception of reality and, ultimately, also to the design of (social and cultural) reality. This group includes approaches from social phenomenology to Pierre Bourdieu, Michel Foucault, and symbolist ethnology to the systems theory constructivism of Parsons and Niklas Luhmann.

The methodological and *science theory discourses,* respectively, concentrated in particular on the specific conditions of, and obstacles to, external understanding of culture. Above all, the discussions in ethnology, especially the "writing culture" and post-colonialism debate (cf. Clifford/George 1986), and socio-philosophical hermeneutics provided important impulses.

In the context of *social science theory,* the question of cultural differences most recently has been studied especially in the theories of globalization (cf., e.g., Castells 2001; Giddens 1990). With regard to conditions in the Western world, cultural differences were shown also in theories of lifestyles (cf. Hradil 1997) and subcultures as well as gender identities. In the more recent post-Foucaultian cultural history these problems were addressed also with a view to cultural disruptions in history. The question about the differences of, and limits to, cultures is discussed in all these discourses, which cannot be separated clearly from each other, in connection with the abstract problem of the "essence of culture" and "what culture is made up of".

The concepts of culture in anthropology, which are based on the broader pluralistic concept of culture, exerted particular influence on the genesis of the concept of culture. Especially the arguments of the U.S. anthropologist, Florence Kluckhohn, exerted much influence, who thought that all cultures in the world concealed basic problems of human existence which could be summarized in dimensions and categories, respectively:

> "All cultures constitute [...] answers to essentially the same questions posed by human biology and by the generalities of the human situation. [...] Every society's pattern for living must provide approved and sanctioned ways for dealing with such universal circumstances as the existence of two sexes; the helplessness of infants; etc." (Kluckhohn 1962, pp. 17f.)

This definition by Kluckhohn was broad enough to be filled in different ways by different cultures. Macrotheoretical approaches, building on this principle, tried first to determine the most important dimensions of human existence and then show in various empirical studies by comparison that these dimensions are filled differently in different cultures, and that cultures vary within these dimensions, respectively.

4 Concepts of Culture at the Macro- and Microlevels

These approaches, which have remained influential to this day and are being used especially in empirical studies of culture or comparisons of cultures, will be briefly examined below for their epistemological potential in a comparison of cultures. The best known macrotheories of culture include those by Harry C. Triandis (cf. Triandis 1975, 1984), John Galtung (cf. Galtung 1988), Edward T. and Mildred Hall (cf. Hall 1969; Hall/Hall 1983, 1990), Geert Hofstede[2] (cf. Hofstede 1980, 1993), and Robert Hettlage (cf. Hettlage 1990). In these and other macrotheoretical approaches, the concept of culture typically is reduced to a few categories or dimensions. The reason frequently given is that culture (in the above comprehensive meaning of the broad concept) as a subject of research can hardly be captured completely because of its complexity (cf. Bolten 2001, p. 128). These dimensions or categories, thus the idea, are to make cultures comparable with each other. As a consequence, many macrotheoretical approaches try to develop various cultural dimensions and find epistemological reasons for the choice and weighting of the aspects dominating in a specific case. Although

2 For criticism of Hofstede, cf. Bolten 2001, pp. 130f., and Hansen 2003, pp. 281f.

these models seem to be quite appropriate in comparing cultures (which is what most of them were designed for), major objections can be raised against such concept of culture. Thus, critics frequently maintain that this kind of macrotheoretical model resulted in a high degree of stereotyping and, hence, simplification, which prevented many phenomena from being included (cf. Bolten 2001, p. 130).[3] In the attempt to force culture into a manageable number of categories or dimensions, merely part of the "surface" of cultures becomes visible as a function of the dimensions chosen. As a result of these macrotheoretical considerations, only abstract averages are obtained in most cases which say little or nothing about the specific actions of individuals (cf. Bolten 2001, p. 130). The relation between the individual and culture as part of everyday experience remains underinvestigated in this case, and the question often arises about the criteria by which the categories or dimensions were chosen.

The macrotheoretical perspective is contrasted with various concepts abstracting cultural characteristics from detailed analyses, i.e. proceeding deductively from the microlevel. These concepts therefore can be called micro-analytical and microtheoretical, respectively. They include concepts, such as the "Dense Description" by Clifford Geertz (cf. Geert 1987), which see culture as a "text" one must be able to "read," and the "Cross Cultural Psychology," inter alia in Alexander Thomas (cf. Thomas 1993), and the "Activity Theory"[4] and the "Cognitive Traits" concept developed in cultural studies. Other concepts of this type stem from the (cross-sectional) area of economics and are often summarized under the heading of "intercultural communication".

However, this perspective, too, entails ontological problems. Thus, deductive models often provide very little information, as findings based on them cannot be generalized. As Bolten puts it, the "more detailed the studies of (sub) cultures are, the less complex they may be if any information about them is to be produced at all" (Bolten 2001, p. 131). According to Bolten, such micro-analyses can be used optimally for intercultural coaching or mediation, but not to generate theories (cf. Bolten 2001). Often, approaches based on individual cases are unable to describe adequately cultural contexts in which the culturally specific elements appear, e.g. in the "text" (in the sense of culture as a text, see above) (cf. Bolten 2001). This entails the hazard that the broad context is neglected for assessments of cultural details. Another difficulty connected with micro-analytical approaches is seen in their emphasizing only the dynamic aspect of culture. For that reason, they tended to overemphasize the "change" pole (over "persistence" as the opposite pole) in the sense "that man could develop into anything, given the strong will to do so" (Demorgon/Molz 1996, p. 69).

---

3 For criticism of macrotheoretical concepts of culture, cf. Bolten 1997 and Demorgon/Molz 1996.

4 For the Activity Theory, see Engeström et al. 1999.

As has been shown in this brief summary and in the equally brief (and, because of that brevity, often sweeping) criticism, neither the macrotheoretical nor the microtheoretical concepts are able to describe culture in the most differentiated way possible and in as complex a fashion as necessary, at least for an empirical comparison of cultures. Hence, current empirical cultural research often shows mixed types of various macro- or micro-approaches. The anthropological theories of culture described above (cf., e.g., Hall/Hall 1983, 1989; Hofstede 1993; Kluckhohn 1962) are partly modified and expressed in different connotations, recontextualized, and arranged in a structure of meanings corresponding to current development. Mixing and combining different concepts of culture are meant to, if not repair, then at least diminish the deficits referred to above in both the macro- and the microtheoretical perspectives.

This technique of mixing various approaches is problematic, however, as it requires the systems to be greatly modified conceptually. It entails the hazard that the original intention of a concept may be lost. The consequence would be that many research projects which (ought to) deal with the concept of culture retract to an interpretation broad enough to encompass the variety of human actions in specific fields, such as communication, behavior, consumption, knowledge, technology etc., but then must try, by using props from other cultural models or conceptual building blocks, to adjust this concept of culture so as to match the actual object (cf. e.g. Paschen et al. 2002).

5 An Evolutionist Concept of Culture

Another branch of understanding culture, influenced mainly by anthropology, sees culture as a strategy of humans living in groups adapting to their environment. In this case, "environment" is not only the natural environment, nature, but also man-made social, material and symbolic environments. Also the evolution of social aggregations up to complex functionally differentiated societies consequently is a cultural act facilitating, or making possible, life and survival by adaptation. The "environments," in which people live and which they partly created by culture, show clear differences, as do the cultures which are in a dialectic relation to those environments.

This concept of culture is guided mainly by the praxeological concepts of culture which consider culture a "theory of practice" dependent on the environment and on knowledge – as described by Bourdieu and others (cf., e.g., Bourdieu 1979) – in which the social and symbolic environment is seen as a man-made cultural product and, at the same time, appears as knowledge-dependent, action- and awareness-related objectivity (cf. Schütz 1974 and, based on this, Berger/Luckmann 2000). Practical action and knowledge in this case depend on communication and its (partly technical) media which simultaneously are both the main prerequisite and the main function of cultures. In this concept, human beings develop cultural habits in line with their environment and knowledge which are useful in their closer or more distant living environments. This also includes the way in which technology is used.

Human beings as incomplete beings, "deficient beings", finding their way into life nearly without any instincts, compared to animals (cf. Gehlen 1941, pp. 34ff.), need to produce a technical culture in the sense of creation, i.e. an artificial world or environment (such as housing, roads, bridges) which holds symbolic meanings, but is made by means of technical artifacts (tools, equipment, machines, etc.), in order to survive under the natural conditions encountered and other environmental states (cf. Metzner 2002, p. 231). The huge flexibility this ensures in processes of adaptation to the environment in this case not only allowed human beings to penetrate nearly all over the world and develop new living space, but also, thanks to the feedback this produced of the different natural conditions encountered, led to a high contingency of cultural developments, such as different cultural practices and languages or, as far as socialization is concerned, manifold social structures. Cultures seen as "evolutionary" in this sense, therefore, in a first approximation, can be defined as follows: They are the outcome of the ways in which human beings cope with life and existence in a community of action and communication within a specific "environment" (cf. Banse/Metzner-Szigeth 2005, p. 33).

As a consequence of this evolutionist understanding of culture, culture can be considered an expanded context of human existence. This covers the whole range of human adaptation reactions. The contexts created in this way are too manifold and too complex to be transferred into a concept which could be operationalized. However, the most important contexts are condensed in three human products: language, history, and institutions. They must be considered functional because they allow groups of human beings to be distinguished by these categories. Consequently, a slightly more concrete, but still quite general, definition of culture can be formulated as follows: Culture becomes visible and plays a role when various groups of persons act differently and their reasons for doing so can be attributed to differences in history, language, and (social) institutions of these groups.

The concept of culture underlying this definition by Klaus P. Hansen (cf. Hansen 1995, 2003) will be described in greater detail below to show that culture, despite all conflicts and complexity, can be incorporated in a differentiated, operational concept (for empirical coverage) of culture(s).

6 The Difference-based Concept of Culture by Hansen

Culture is frequently described as orientation by, or standardization of, values or patterns of behavior, i.e. uniform or holistic. On the other hand, however, there is also room for individual variation, there are subcultures and miniature collectives which make cultures appear divergent (cf. Demorgon/Molz 1996, pp. 43ff.). Instead of considering culture a holistic entity, Hansen designs a concept of culture which is able to resolve the conflicting ideas of unity and differentiation of culture (cf. Hansen 1995). Consequently, his concept of culture is termed difference-based. Hansen explains it by the example of "Germany": Within German culture, one finds a multitude of different ways of life. Considering, e.g., the way a carpenter in Lower Bavaria lives compared to a manager working at the Frankfurt Stock Exchange, it would be difficult at first sight to find many common features in their everyday life. It would be easier, in fact, to describe the differences. Yet, although the ways of living and everyday activities of the two persons are so different, there are certain commonalities which characterize them as members of the very same culture. These commonalities, which Hansen refers to as "putty", promote cohesion within a national culture and delimit it towards the outside. These are the common history they experienced, or the history handed down, their common language, and the institutions they share (cf. Hansen 1995, p. 179).

These three constitutive elements of national culture and their importance as cultural dimensions within the framework of the difference-based[5] concept of culture will be described in more detail below. History constitutes a separate sphere of importance.

> "Human societies must be able to reproduce both materially and symbolically to guarantee their continued existence over time. Symbolic reproduction poses the problem for societies to absorb their cultural contents, practices, languages, institutions, norms, work of earlier generations and pass all of this on to the next generation. This requires not only the indispensable assistance of nature, but also personal 'cultural strategies of permanence'." (Assmann 1999, p. 88)

These "cultural strategies of permanence" are strategies of tradition. In the format of traditions and collective or individual histories handed down, history affects the reality of life, strongly influencing the thinking and action of the people identifying with these traditions. Accordingly, Aleida Assmann defines tradition as "a permanent cultural design of identity. This permanence must continuously be wrung from time as a dimension of destruction, forgetting, change, or relativation" (Assmann 1999, p. 90). A common history (historical facts) does not necessarily result in common views about that history, but constitutes the point

5 For more details about this concept, cf. Drechsel et al. 2000, pp. 16ff.

of departure and a common point of reference or framework of evaluation for and of these views (cf. Hansen 1995, p. 146).

Language is not just a medium of transmission enabling verbal communication to take place, but is closely connected to perception and reason. Every language community has its individual perception of the meaning of the reality of life achieved through its language (cf. Berger/Luckmann 2000, pp. 24ff.; Hansen 2003, pp. 73ff.). This promotes cohesion of this community and acts as the criterion of inclusion and exclusion. History and language are interdependent, on the one hand, because history is handed down by language and, on the other hand, because language also grew historically and is modified and formed by events in history. Despite their differences, cultures can be described by means of their language and their history as an entity in the sense of natural cultures. These natural cultures are a function not so much of national borders but rather of a common area of language and history (cf. Hansen 2003, p. 179), which can differ greatly from the area defined by national borders[6]. This constitutes a first background molding the individual, albeit "involuntarily" in most cases because it is defined by birth. At a later point in time (again mostly involuntarily), there is socialization of individuals. Socialization, i.e. education, teaches the individual his or her native language and something of the specific history related to the community in which he or she lives. Language, once learnt, plays a key role in this process. It provides the individuals newly born into a society or a communication space with "prefabrications" of objectified human experience, in this way simultaneously empowering the individuals socialized in this way to create their own objectivations (cf. Berger/Luckmann 2000, pp. 40ff.). Socialization also achieves the introduction to, and inclusion into, societal organization and its institutions.

The term institutions as used by Hansen was taken from Gehlen (cf. Gehlen 1962) and is defined very broadly. In the broadest sense, it means stabilized and, hence, institutionalized habits:

> "It is quite possible to say that animal groups and symbioses are held together by triggers and instinctive movements while humans achieve this by institutions and quasi-automatic habits, established therein, of thought, feeling, evaluation, and action which become specific, habitual and stable only when institutionalized. Only in this way can they be considered habitual and halfway reliable, i.e. predictable in their onesidedness." (Gehlen 1962, p. 79)

Consequently, our institutions are no longer seen as merely governmental or societal institutions but also as social and symbolic institutions, such as Christmas or birthdays. In the concept of institutions by Berger and Luckmann (cf. Ber-

6 National borders are arbitrary political structures which do not necessarily define cultural spaces, as can be seen in the Balkans or in Africa, for instance.

ger/Luckmann 2000), institutionalization processes can be described in steps. Institutions can be described epistemologically as objectivations of a higher order. Objectivation is at the beginning of institutionalization. This is achieved by language and action, respectively, habitualized by repetition. In a second step, these actions are further stabilized by typification of behavior (for instance in social roles). At the end of this process, there is standardization of typified behavior, which makes it institutionalized. Consequently, Berger and Luckmann offer this definition of institutionalization:

> "Institutionalzation occurs as soon as habitualized actions are typified reciprocally by types of players. Any typification achieved in this way is an institution." (Berger/Luckmann 2000, p. 58)

When a specific collective habitualizes a specific action, the players (as a community) and habitualized action (as a developing convention) reinforce each other (reciprocal typification), which means that action is institutionalized. The joint action of various institutions in a community develops and, at the same time, structures its type of organization. Although institutions are the outcome of collective action, they basically are opposites of the individual as objective facticities (unavoidably), exerting direct influence on everyday life (cf. Berger/ Luckmann, pp. 49ff.).

According to this concept of institution, also persons in the real world, imaginary or historical persons, can act as institutions. Such person may have the function of an institution if his or her importance, or the importance ascribed to him or her by others, as a result of him or her action or fate exerts a significant influence on areas of society or groups and thus, in a way, acts like an institution (such as Rudi Dutschke for the student movement in the 1960s). History, language, and institutions ensure continuity in a community through the process of socialization. They are the signs visible externally and thus detectable empirically of the action of culture(s). They are hallmarks of culture(s) and (functional) poles of identification for its members.

7 Areas of Standardization

The core of Hansen's concept of culture are standardizations which, in principle, can be considered conventions.[7] It subdivides the different cultural standardiza-

---

7 Although Hansen uses the term conventions but rarely, standardizations in principle can be seen as conventions. While the standardization concept may be more precise, but also too technical or too abstract, convention is more illustrative but not nearly well defined. For epistemological considerations it is therefore better to use the term standardization, while illustrations by way of example should use really existing conventions. For cultural conventions, cf. also Hauser 2007; for detailed criticism, cf. Altmayer 1996.

tions into four areas for analytical distinction: communication, thought, feeling, and behavior and action. Cultural standardizations or conventions are bound to collectives; on the other hand, collectives constitute themselves through standardizations. One exception to this rule are overarching collectives defined much more by a common language, history, and institutions. Initially, collectivity in a quite general sense can be taken as a feeling of community generated by living in line with common conventions which thus constitute a collective. The need to be part of a community, both physically but also psychologically (cf. Tomasello 2007), is one of the prime movers specifically of human living together, or even its source. In addition, collectives offer possibilities to individuals to identify, thus creating identity. This commonality of conventions makes communities confirm purpose; their members feel secure (cf. Hauser 2007, p. 682). In sociology, this is described by the term "assurance of expectation" (cf. Bonß 1995, p. 90).

This can be linked to Gehlen's concept of institutions, which relates to the removal of behavioral uncertainties by establishing norms of behavior (cf. Metzner-Szigeth 2004, p. 392). This results in more assumptions about the importance to collectives of cultural standardizations:

> "(1) Efficiency: Tried and tested behavior implies a lower risk of failure. (2) Acceptance: Standardized behavior entails no [or fewer; authors' comment – R.H./G.B.] negative sanctions. (3) Anticipation: Conformity makes my behavior and the behavior of others capable of anticipation. (4) Normality: Existing conventions simplify the complexity of the environment, thereby reducing the cognitive burden. (5) Creation of meaning: If several people behave the way I do, my behavior most probably is meaningful. (6) Collectivity: When I behave like others do, I feel a member of the group." (Hauser 2007, p. 682)

Establishing collectives thus has subjective and objective advantages for the individual. Various collectives can be distinguished by the standardizations encountered, which appear as common features of the individuals making up these collectives. This means that the subdivision into different collective relations (within one overarching collective) is derived directly from the range of the standardizations encountered in each case. Wherever similar standardizations occur there is probably also a collective relation (at the level of mono, multi or overarching collectives). The range of standardizations which, at the same time, marks the borders of collective relations, can be termed "degree of partiality" (cf. Hansen 2004) after Hansen. Thus, particular standardizations apply only within specific monocollectives, while other standardizations extend to the level of multicollectives or even global collectives. Consequently, there are universal standardizations which are global in scope and by means of which global collectives can constitute themselves.

However, as standardizations are subject to the change of times and to many influences both within collectives and external environmental influences, standardizations as such and their degree of partiality can change, and so can the borders of segmentation. Standardizations understood as conventions do not arise spontaneously, but develop over a specific period of time and under specific environmental or framework conditions as negotiating processes both within a collective and among several collectives. Communication, thought, action, and feeling of individuals therefore are determined not only by the collective or collectives in which these individuals participate, but also historically, linguistically, and institutionally, in summary, by "cultural spaces and thus understandable only against the cultural background" (Holz-Mänttäri 1984, pp. 32f.). However, the individual is aware of these cultural influences only in part, and they are controllable only to that extent. They have to be that way so that the individual may adapt (and thus participate) in different, or also new, collectives. The spectrum and the variance of the conventions managed in each case thus depend strongly on socialization of the individual, his or her education, and other environmental factors.

8 Culture and Sustainability

Without wanting to anticipate other contributions to this volume, a few general ideas and comments about the relation between culture and sustainability will be made in this last paragraph from a point of view of cultural studies. The first question arising is whether culture(s) is/are sustainable and can be sustainable at all. Cultures are sustainable first and foremost in the sense that they function very effectively and are extremely longlived. Cultural mechanisms are designed to promote stability and cohesion. Now, this would be an absolutely neutral concept of sustainability more in line with everyday thinking and often used in the media as well. However, if a normative concept of sustainability is used as a basis, such as the integrative sustainability concept of the Helmholtz Association (cf. Kopfmüller et al. 2001), in which desirable sustainable development can only be achieved when manifold normative indicators are met, cultures and cultural mechanisms cannot be sustainable *per se.* This problem will be illustrated by a brief example: The culture of a people living in unison with nature for centuries, and using natural resources only to such an extent that these can regenerate, can be considered sustainable if the value of resource protection and use, respectively, is used as a yardstick. For comparison, Western cultures are not sustainable because they claim or exploit natural resources to an extreme degree, pollute their environment, and thus increasingly destroy the basis of their life. However, if values such as life, infant mortality, nutrition, or the ability to adapt to changing environmental conditions are used as indicators of sustainability, the fictitious people living close to nature probably would not compare well with Western cultures. The answer to the question whether cultures are sustainable in a normative sense therefore very strongly depends on the concept of sustainability used. They therefore cannot be called sustainable per se. Applying yardsticks of value to cultures entails another problem: It cannot be harmonized with a contemporary concept of culture. Contemporary concepts of culture emphasize the very neutrality, in terms of value, of cultures in order not to end up in outdated Western hegemonial categories, such as civilization or high culture, putting their own culture above those of other peoples (cf. above for the "narrow" concept of culture).

Yet, thinking about the relation between culture and sustainability can be fruitful in two ways: *On the one hand,* it can be taken in such a way that the generation of normative sustainability concepts has given rise to a cultural trend which, as an institution (according to Hansen's concept), is part of the respective culture and influences it. The question how such trends or movements gradually gain ground as cultural institutions and become a determining element of culture, raises interesting aspects and questions of further research from the perspective of cultural studies. The *second* line – more relevant to this study – would be to ask how cultural aspects can be integrated into existing normative concepts of sustainability. This has hardly happened so far: Although the concept of culture often appears in the concepts as a relevant element of sustainable development, it very rarely is made explicit (see also the contribution by Jürgen Kopfmüller to this volume). The high relevance of cultural contexts to the establishment of problem solutions (e.g. of a technical or organizational type) which are to promote sustainable development has hardly been reflected upon in the specialized community of "students of sustainability". A brief look into cultural and technology studies would show that technical systems are embedded in cultural contexts and interact with them (cf. Hauser 2010). Examples from the field of technology transfer in particular show that, when these contexts are taken into account not at all or insufficiently, this frequently causes partial or complete failure of a technology (cf. Hermeking 2001). In a similar way, this certainly applies also to organizational structures, though this question has not yet been studied sufficiently well.

That cultural factors so far have emerged in sustainability concepts only as "spacers" may be due partly to the fact that the field of concepts of culture is too broad and the time of researchers is too limited. On the other hand, there have hardly been any convincing attempts so far to conceptualize culture in such a way as to make it operationalizable for integration into existing sustainability concepts. The concept of culture by Hansen presented in this article, and the conceptualization of culture as a context and as conventions of action, seem to offer better preconditions for this step. Yet, there is still an interdisciplinary job to be done, namely to integrate cultural aspects meaningfully into concepts of sustainability.

References

Altmayer, C. (1996): Rezension: Klaus P. Hansen. Kultur und Kulturwissenschaft. Eine Einführung. Rezensiert von Claus Altmayer. In: Zeitschrift für Interkulturellen Fremdsprachenunterricht [Online] 1(2) (URL: http://spz1.spz.tu-darmstadt.de/projekt_ejournal/jg-01-2/beitrag/altmeenh.htm; 26.10.2008) (in German)

Assmann, A. (1999): Zeit und Tradition. Kulturelle Strategien der Dauer. Cologne (in German)

Assmann, J. (2007): Das kulturelle Gedächtnis. Schrift, Erinnerung und politische Identität in frühen Hochkulturen (6.th ed.). Munich (in German)

Banse, G.; Metzner-Szigeth, A. (2005): Veränderungen im Quadrat: Computervermittelte Kommunikation und moderne Gesellschaft – Überlegungen zum Design des europäischen Forschungs-Netzwerks „Kulturelle Diversität und neue Medien“. In: Banse, G. (ed.): Neue Kultur(en) durch Neue Medien (?). Das Beispiel Internet. Berlin, pp. 17–46 (in German)

Berger, L.; Luckmann, Th. (2000): Die gesellschaftliche Konstruktion der Wirklichkeit (17th ed.). Frankfurt/M. (in German)

Bolten, J. (1997): Interkulturelle Wirtschaftskommunikation. In: Walter, R. (ed.): Wirtschaftswissenschaften. Eine Einführung. Paderborn, pp. 469–497 (in German)

Bolten, J. (2001): Kann man Kulturen beschreiben oder erklären, ohne Stereotypen zu verwenden? Einige programmatische Überlegungen zur kulturellen Stilforschung. In: Bolten, J.; Schröter, D. (eds.): Im Netzwerk interkulturellen Handelns. Theoretische und praktische Perspektiven. Sternenfels, pp. 128–142 (in German)

Bonß, W. (1995.): Vom Risiko. Unsicherheit und Ungewißheit in der Moderne. Hamburg (in German)

Bourdieu, P. (1979): Entwurf einer Theorie der Praxis (auf der ethnologischen Grundlage der kabylischen Gesellschaft). Frankfurt/M. (in German)

Bourdieu, P. (1987): Die feinen Unterschiede. Kritik der gesellschaftlichen Urteilskraft. Frankfurt/M. (in German)

Cappai, G. (2005): Der interkulturelle Vergleich. Herausforderungen und Strategien einer sozialwissenschaftlichen Methode. In: Srubar, I.; Renn, J.; Wenzel, U. (eds.): Kulturen vergleichen: Sozial- und kulturwissenschaftliche Grundlagen und Kontroversen. Wiesbaden, pp. 48–79 (in German)

Clifford, J.; George E. M. (eds.) (1986): Writing Culture. The Poetics and Politics of Ethnography. Berkeley/CA

Demorgon, J.; Molz, M. (1996): Bedingungen und Auswirkungen der Analyse von Kultur(en) und interkulturelle Interaktion. In: Thomas, A. (ed.): Psychologie interkulturellen Handelns. Göttingen, Bern, pp. 43–80 (in German)

Drechsel, P.; Schmidt, B.; Gölz, B. (2000): Kultur im Zeitalter der Globalisierung. Von Identität zu Differenzen. Frankfurt/M. (in German)

Engeström, J.; Miettinen, R.; Punamäki-Gitai, R.-L. (1999): Perspectives on Activity Theory. Cambridge

Freud, S. (1989/1930): Das Unbehagen in der Kultur. In: Freud, S.: Studienausgabe in zehn Bänden. Vol. 9. Frankfurt/M., pp. 191–270 (in German)

Galtung, J. (1988): The Peace Movement: A Structural-Functional Exploration. In: Galtung, J.: Transarmament and the Cold War. Copenhagen, pp. 322–342

Galtung, J. (1998): Frieden mit friedlichen Mitteln. Friede und Konflikt, Entwicklung und Kultur. Opladen (in German)

Geertz, C. (1987): Dichte Beschreibung. Beiträge zum Verstehen kultureller Systeme (5th ed.). Frankfurt/M. (in German)

Gehlen, A. (1941): Der Mensch. Seine Natur und seine Stellung in der Welt (2nd ed.). Wiebelsheim (in German)

Gehlen, A. (1953): Die Technik in der Sichtweise der Anthropologie. In: Merkur, No. 7, pp. 626–636 (in German)

Gehlen, A. (1956): Urmensch und Spätkultur. Bonn (in German)

Gehlen, A. (1962): Der Mensch. Seine Natur und seine Stellung in der Welt (7th ed.). Frankfurt/M. (in German)

Gerhards, J. (2000): Die Vermessung kultureller Unterschiede. Deutschland und USA im Vergleich. Opladen (in German)

Hall, E. T. (1969): The Hidden Dimension. New York

Hall, E. T.; Hall, M. R. (1983): Verborgene Signale. Studien zur internationalen Kommunikation: Über den Umgang mit Amerikanern. Hamburg (in German)

Hall, E. T.; Hall, M. R. (1990): Understanding Cultural Differences: Germans, French and Americans. Yarmouth

Hansen, K. P. (1995): Kultur und Kulturwissenschaft (1st ed.). Tübingen, Basel (in German)

Hansen, K. P. (2003): Kultur und Kulturwissenschaft (3rd ed.). Tübingen, Basel (in German)

Hansen, K. P. (2004). Die Kulturen der Beschäftigung mit Nationalkultur (URL: http://www.germanistentag2004.unimuenchen. de/abstracts/wslandeskunde/hansen.doc.; 13.06.2007) (in German)

Hauser, G. (2007). Ein Kulturmodell für Translatoren. In: Schmitt, P. A.; Jüngst, H. E. (eds.): Translationsqualität. Frankfurt/M., pp. 680–695 (in German)

Hauser, R. (2010): Technische Kulturen oder kultivierte Technik? Das Internet in Deutschland und Russland. Berlin (zugleich Dissertation. Karlsruhe [Universität] 2009) (in German)

Herder, J. G. (1989/1784/91): Ideen zur Philosophie der Geschichte der Menschheit. Frankfurt/M. (in German)

Hermeking, M. (2001): Kulturen und Technik. Techniktransfer als Arbeitsfeld der Interkulturellen Kommunikation. Beispiele aus der arabischen, russischen und lateinamerikanischen Region. Munich a.o. (in German)

Hettlage, R. (1991): Rahmenanalyse – oder die innere Organisation unseres Wissens um die Ordnung der Wirklichkeit. In: Hettlage, R.; Lenz, K. (eds.): Erving Goffman – ein soziologischer Klassiker der zweiten Generation. Bern, Stuttgart, pp. 95–156 (in German)

Hofstede, G. (1993): Interkulturelle Zusammenarbeit. Kulturen – Organisation – Management. Wiesbaden (in German)

Holz-Mänttäri, J. (1984): Translatorisches Handeln. Theorie und Methode. In: Annales Academiae Scientiarum Fennicae, Helsinki, B 226 (in German)

Hubig, Ch. (2010): Kulturbegriff – Abgrenzungen, Leitdifferenzen, Perspektiven. In: Banse, G.; Grunwald, A. (eds.): Technik und Kultur. Bedingungs- und Beeinflussungsverhältnisse. Karlsruhe, pp. 55–71 (in German)

Janich, P. (2005): Beobachter Perspektive im Kulturvergleich. In: Renn, J.; Srubar, I.; Wenzel, U. (eds.): Kulturen Vergleichen. Sozial- und Kulturwissenschaftliche Grundlagen und Kontroversen. Wiesbaden, pp. 18–37 (in German)

Kant, I. (1977/1784): Idee zu einer allgemeinen Geschichte in weltbürgerlicher Absicht. In: Kant, I.: Werkausgabe in zwölf Bänden. Hg. v. W. Weischedel. Vol. XI. Frankfurt/M., pp. 33–41 (in German)

Kluckhohn, C. (1962): Universal Categories of Culture. In: Tax, S. (ed.): Anthropology Today. Chicago

Kopfmüller, J.; Brandl, V.; Jörissen, J.; Paetau, M.; Banse, G.; Coenen, R.: Grunwald, A. (2001): Nachhaltige Entwicklung integrativ betrachtet. Konstitutive Elemente, Regeln, Indikatoren. Berlin (in German)

Mersch, D. (1999): Das Sagbare und das Zeigbare. Wittgensteins frühe Theorie einer Duplizität im Symbolischen. In: Prima Philosophia, No. 4, pp. 85–94 (in German)

Metzner, A. (2002): Die Tücken der Objekte. Über die Risiken der Gesellschaft und ihre Wirklichkeit. Frankfurt/M., New York (in German)

Metzner-Szigeth, A. (2003): Zwischen Systemkomplexität und Akteursverantwortung. In: Kornwachs, K. (ed.): System – Technik – Verantwortung. Münster, London, pp. 391–409 (in German)

Parsons, T.; Toby, J. (1977): The Evolution of Societies. Englewood Cliffs/NJ

Paschen, H.; Wingert, B.; Coenen, Chr.; Banse, G. (2002): Kultur – Medien – Märkte. Medienentwicklung und kultureller Wandel. Berlin (in German)

Pufendorf, S. von (2002/1686): Eris Scandica. In: Pufendorf, S. von: Gesammelte Werke. Ed. by W. Schmidt-Biggemann. Vol. 5. Ed. by F. Palladini. Berlin

Rammert, W. (1999): Technik. Stichworte für ein Lexikon (URL: http://www.hyperkommunikation.ch/literatur/texte/rammert_technik.htm; 22.11.2007) (in German)

Reckwitz, A. (2000): Die Transformation der Kulturtheorien. Zur Entwicklung eines Theorieprogramms. Weilerswist (in German)

Reckwitz, A. (2005): Kulturelle Differenzen aus praxeologischer Perspektive: Kulturelle Globalisierung jenseits von Modernisierungstheorie und Kulturessentialismus. In: Srubar, I; Renn, J.; Wenzel, U. (eds.): Kulturen vergleichen. Sozial- und kulturwissenschaftliche Grundlagen und Kontroversen. Wiesbaden, pp. 92–112 (in German)

Schütz, A. (1974): Der sinnhafte Aufbau der sozialen Welt. Eine Einleitung in die verstehende Soziologie. Frankfurt/M. (in German)

Thomas, A. (ed.) (1993): Kulturvergleichende Psychologie. Eine Einführung. Göttingen (in German)

Tomasello, M. (2007): Personal Communication. Leipzig (in German)

Triandis, H. C. (1975): Culture Training: Cognitive Complexity and Interpersonal Attitudes. In: Brislin, R. W; Bochner, S.; Lonner, W. J. (eds.): Cross-Cultural Perspectives on Learning. New York, pp. 39–77

Triandis, H. C. (1984): A Theoretical Framework for the More Efficient Construction of Culture Assimiliator. In: International Journal of Intercultural Relations, No. 8, pp. 301–330

Wittgenstein, L. (2001/1935/1949): Philosophische Untersuchungen. Kritisch-genetische Edition. Ed. by J. Schulte, H. Nijman, E. v. Savigny, G. H. v. Wright. Frankfurt/M. (in German)

Wittgenstein, L. (2003/1921): Tractatus logico-philosophicus. Logisch-philosophische Abhandlung. Frankfurt/M. (in German)

1.

Meanings of Sustainable Development

What is Green?

Gordon L. Nelson

1 Introduction

There are several related phrases worthy of our consideration:

- Culture & Sustainability;
- Culture of Sustainability;
- Cultural Dimensions of Sustainable Development.

There needs to be a culture of sustainable development and there likely needs to be a cultural change in the direction of sustainable development, if it is to occur.

Among the most widely used definitions of sustainability is "development that meets the needs of the present without compromising the ability of future generations to meet their own needs" (WCED 1987, p. 24, no. 27). Sustainability is grounded in science and deals with resources, technology and business but it is also grounded in consciousness and deals with morality, aesthetics and religion. Its tripartite-values – Environment, Equity, Economics – are a continuous circle, one of continuous feedback (cf. Marx 2009).

Culture is "the totality of socially transmitted behavior patterns, arts, beliefs, institutions and other products of human work and thought [...] considered with respect to a particular subject or group". The cultural dimensions of sustainable development include cultural heritage and historic patterns of activities. Sustainable development includes sustainable technologies, sustainable economics and sustainable government. Clearly, culture is the context. Culture determines what we value. Yet what we value is itself in constant change. Culture evolves (cf. Marx 2009).

In this discussion of culture and sustainability I want to use Florida as an example. Florida is larger than all but ten European countries in population and all but 14 in land area. It is only a bit smaller than Romania in population and land area. Florida has its own uniqueness in environment, economics, politics and culture.

The 5th Forum in Budapest was focused on forecasting and on the importance of an adequate range of forecast scenarios. Thus it is reasonable to begin by describing Florida and to try to put it into perspective, now and in the future.

2 Growth of Florida

The State of Florida is the fourth largest state of the United States in population (2005), with over 18 million residents, behind California (36.5 million), Texas (23.5 million), and New York (19.3 million). The population growth of Florida since 1950 is nearly a factor of seven. Projected growth from 2000 to 2010, official census years, was 25%. The population projection for 2060 is 36 million. The Florida economy is $ 729 billion (2005) and is expected to grow to $ 3.7 trillion in 2036 (cf. FMF 2007). As a result of this growth Florida has elaborate planning processes, both official and unofficial. Each county, the next smaller governmental division to a state, has a "Comprehensive Plan". Actions by county government must be consistent with its comprehensive plan. Growth in population impacts multiple areas of life. Transportation, schools, housing, shopping, jobs, recreation, to name but six, are all impacted by population growth. Public processes must anticipate needs and plan for necessary future infrastructure. *Florida has had a culture of growth.*

Growth of 25% in ten years is not the norm in the United States or in Europe. Hungary, our partner in this Forum, has a population of 10 million in an area of 35,919 sq. mi. (93,030 sq. km) (versus 65,758 sq. mi. [170,313 sq. km] for Florida). Thus Florida and Hungary have similar populations per unit area. However, the population of Hungary declined 18,000 in the period of January–May 2007. There were 39,000 births (down 3%) and 57,000 deaths (up 2.3%) in Hungary during this period. Marriages were 12000, down 10% from a year earlier. At the end of World War II the population of Hungary was 9.8 million. Projections have the population of Hungary falling below 10 million in 2011 and to be at 8.7 million in 2050. The population of 0–19 year olds may halve over the next 40 years. By 2050 the working age population of Hungary may be 75% of that of today. By that time perhaps 36% of the population will be over 65. Immigration is expected to be modest.[1]

3 Planned (Smart) Growth

As noted above, some projections have Florida's population reaching 36 million by 2060. Assuming current development patterns, roughly 7 million acres (2.8 million hectares) will be converted from rural to urban of Florida's 38.3 million

1 Cf. "Hungary" – www.infoplease.com; Budapestsun.com, July 24, 2007 ("Population Continues to Fall"); Budapestsun.com, October 2, 2003 ("The Downward Population Spiral"); Budapestsun.com, March 30, 2002 ("Government Looking To Boost Population").

acres (15.5 million hectares). This would include 2.7 million acres (1.1 million hectares) of existing agricultural lands and 2.7 million acres (1.1 million hectares) of native/wildlife habitat. Urban development would go from 6 million acres (2.4 million hectares) to 13 million acres (5.3 million hectares). Counties like my own, Brevard, would be built out before the end of that period. The I-75 and I-4 corridors (interstate highways) would be fully developed. Thus the pressure is for more sustainable development (cf. FoF 2006). There are multiple study efforts. One such effort is MyRegion.org. The MyRegion.org effort spent $ 1 million over 18 months in 2006–2007 to develop a shared 50 year vision for the seven counties of east central Florida. The work involved numerous public, private, and civic organizations, and some 20000 individuals through meetings and questionnaires. The author attended both meetings and submitted a questionnaire.

Central Florida's population was 400,000 in 1950, 1.6 million in 1980, and 3.5 million in 2005. It is projected that Central Florida will double in population from 2005 to 2050, to 7 million people. The region's population is diverse, representing a broad mix of cultures, races, ethnicities, and ages. The region created one million new jobs between 1980 and 2005. The economy blends traditional strengths in agriculture, tourism, space, and defense with emerging industries related to aerospace, photonics, and life sciences. The income brought into the region has nearly tripled, from $ 37 billion in 1980 to $ 107 billion (in 2005 dollars) in 2005 (cf. MyRegion 2007b).

If the current pattern of development was to continue the following issues are foreseen (cf. MyRegion 2007b):

(1) The region will consume as much land in 45 years – 670,000 hectares – as has been developed over the last 440 years.
(2) About 89,000 additional hectares of irreplaceable environmental lands and wildlife habitats will be consumed.
(3) Most new buildings will be single-story, single family homes on 1/3 to 1/2 acre lots (~2,000 square meters).
(4) Residents will continue to move further away from where they work, resulting in increased commute times and less time at home. The majority of new money spent on transportation will be spent on new roads. Even so, the average person will spend more than 90 minutes per day commuting, compared to about 30 (45–50 author) minutes today.
(5) The volume of carbon monoxide and other green house gasses produced in the region will more than triple, contributing to a decline in air quality and public health and increased contributions to global climate change.
6) Water consumption will increase by 70%, depleting the Floridian aquifer and raising questions about the availability of water for future generations.

In its final report, "How Shall We Grow?", August 2007, My Region.org elucidated six regional growth principles (cf. MyRegion 2007b):

(1) Preserve open space, recreational areas, farmland, water resources, and regionally significant natural areas.
(2) Provide a variety of transportation choices.
(3) Foster distinct, attractive, and safe places to live.
(4) Encourage a diverse, globally competitive economy.
(5) Create a range of obtainable housing opportunities and choices.
(6) Build communities with educational, health care, and cultural amenities.

The preferred alternative is a different approach to growth, in which the region preserves its most precious environmental and agricultural lands, focuses development in urban centers, and connects those centers with transportation corridors that provide more choices for how people travel, a more European lifestyle. Implementation requires some 86 municipalities and 7 counties to work together, to develop a regional "greenprint", to develop regional transportation corridors, to unleash creativity of developers and others, and to measure progress, and improve over the 45 year timeframe. The report "How Shall We Grow" was followed by a much more detailed "Comprehensive Economic Development Strategy", September, 2007 (cf. MyRegion 2007a). But all of the above is predicated on a consistent pattern of growth, which provides the economic underpinning for development. Similar studies exist for other regions of Florida and for the state as a whole, with similar results (cf. Report 2006; Thorner 2007). But how valid is the forecast for continued growth?

4 Issues Challenging Growth

In 2004 four hurricanes hit Florida (Charlie, Francis, Jeanne, Ivan) covering most of the state. Statewide damage totaled $ 24 billion. In my county, Brevard County, alone, damage was $ 1 billion. Most counties of the state experienced some damage. While damage is largely repaired, the four hurricanes of 2004 and Wilma in Florida and Katrina in Mississippi and Louisiana in 2005 raised hurricane awareness in other parts of the county. There were certainly Florida people who said that they did not wish to go through a hurricane experience again. For Francis and Jeanne I evacuated to St. Petersburg on the other side of the state. While I experienced little damage, on return the city was a "war zone" with National Guardsmen, with machine guns, in the streets directing traffic. One follow on result of the 2004 and 2005 hurricane seasons was that some major insurance companies such as Allstate and State Farm dropped thousands of Florida customers for homeowners insurance. Many homeowners had to scramble for alternatives or use the State as the insurer of last resort. Even those who did not need to find a new carrier saw their coverage increase in cost two or three fold. Fear of hurricanes and cost of insurance is the first issue.

The second issue involves the subprime mortgage financial crisis. The origin of the subprime financial crisis was the sharp rise in foreclosures in the subprime mortgage market that began in the United States in 2006 and became a global financial crisis in July 2007. Rising interest rates increased the monthly payments on newly-popular adjustable rate mortgages. Many sub-prime mortgages were in fact "balloon" mortgages, whose payments were fixed for two years and then rise sharply to a higher variable rate (in some cases double). This coupled with property value declines (20%–40% in some markets) as the US housing market bubble collapsed, left homeowners unable to meet financial obligations and lenders without a means to recoup their losses, since the property was now worth less than the mortgage alone. This resulted in a credit crunch threatening the solvency of marginal private banks and other financial institutions. This led to declines in the stock markets worldwide, several hedge funds becoming worthless, coordinated national bank interventions, contraction of retail profits, bankruptcy of several mortgage lenders and finally in September 2008 the global financial collapse.

Subprime lending is a general term that refers to the practice of making loans to borrowers who do not qualify for market interest rates because of problems with their credit history or the ability to prove that they have enough income to support the monthly payment on the loan for which they are applying. Down payments may be less as well. Subprime loans or mortgages are risky for both creditors and debtors because of the combination of high interest, bad credit history, and murky financial situations often associated with subprime applicants. Subprime debt was them repackaged into wider debt offerings called collateralized debt obligations, which were then resold on the global market. As mortgages are bundled and sold between institutions, mortgages were eventually held by bond holders around the world.[2] Since the mortgage was not to be held by the initial lender there was less scrutiny of the applicant.

It was reported that in 2007 there were 7.2 million households in the US with subprime mortgages, and more that 14 percent of those were already in default. It was projected that 20% of those loans issued in 2005 and 2006 would end in foreclosure, with 2.2 million families losing their homes. Ohio, California, Nevada and Florida were the state's most affected (cf. Christie 2007a, 2007b; McCarthy 2007). There were 1 million foreclosures in 2010 in the U.S. with a higher number forecast for 2011.

---

2 Cf. Subprime Mortgage Financial Crisis – URL: http://en.wikipedia.org/wiki/Subprime_mortgage_crisis.

With the rapid rise in home values in Florida, as homes sold, they took on the new value for property tax purposes. However, Florida has a “Save Our Homes” constitutional amendment which limits increases of assessed valuations of existing “Homestead” property to 3% per year. Thus a substantial tax differential resulted between owner occupied existing homes and recently sold homes, perhaps sited next to each other. This doubling of property taxes plus the doubling to tripling in insurance premiums resulted in Florida homes no longer being affordable. Florida property which had been below the national average for some 15 years had by 2006 become 20% higher than the national average. Florida home affordability (price, mortgages, taxes, and insurance) is a second issue along with mortgage availability (cf. Vittner 2007).

Then Florida Governor Charles Crist called a second special session of the Florida Legislature in October, 2007, to deal with a $ 1.1 billion budget shortfall brought on by flagging tax collections (sales and real estate transfer tax, Florida does not have an income tax) against a $ 71.9 billion budget. For fiscal year 2008–09 revenues were again expected to fall about $ 1.5 billion short of previous projections. While this is only 2%, the numbers are still in billions of dollars. The 2009–2010 Florida budget was $ 66.5 billion or 8% less than in 2007 (cf. Ash 2007; Cotterell 2007; Goodnough 2007).

Housing is clearly related to other markets. In 2006 16 percent of new car purchases in Florida were made with home equity loans versus only 7% nationally. Families relied on cash from mortgage refinancing in an up market coupled with low interest rates to finance major purchases. In spring 2006 nine of 20 metropolitan areas that saw the sharpest home price appreciation in the US were in Florida. Now consumer confidence in Florida has dropped markedly, especially willingness to buy expensive items. The consumer confidence index was 77 in November 2007 versus 93 in 2006 (cf. Ash 2007; Cotterell 2007; Goodnough 2007). By March 2010, it had dropped to 70 (cf. Index 2010).

5 Schools

For the fall of 2006 the Florida Department of Education (DOE) had forecast a 48,853 (51,000 average 1989–2004) increase in the school population (K-12). It turned out to be only 477. There are 2.64 million students in Florida schools. The 2006–2007 actual was the largest anomaly in DOE student projections in 20 years (cf. Dukes 2007, Figure 2). Twenty-nine of 67 counties showed declines in enrollment, including eight of the ten largest school districts. The top ten school districts declined 19,000 students. Similar results occurred for the 2007–2008 school year; from Fall 2005 to Fall 2009 the top ten school districts lost almost 40,000 students (see Table 1).

Table 1: Annual Enrollment Change in Florida[a]

District	0506 Fall Count	0607 Fall Count	0910 Fall Count	Δ Fall 2005 to Fall 2009
Miami-Dade (4th Largest in US)	362,033	353,783	345,766	- 16,267
Broward	271,470	262,726	256,175	- 15,295
Hillsborough	193,669	193,460	193,239	- 430
Orange (12th Largest in US)	175,307	175,155	173,021	- 2286
Palm Beach	174,911	171,429	173,025	- 1886
Duval	126,535	125,171	122,649	- 3886
Pinellas	112,127	109,880	105,176	- 6951
Polk	89,483	42,873	94,577	+ 5094
Brevard ($ 1.2 Billion Budget)	75,160	74,791	72,402	- 2758
Lee	75,579	78.980	80,470	+ 4891
				- 39,774

a – Annual Enrollment Change for Florida's ten most Populous Districts; State Aid $7,300
Source: After Comparison 2010; Dukes 2007

Because of the lower than expected growth some school districts delayed or cancelled building projects. State aid ($ 19 billion) is distributed to school districts on the basis of the number of students (FTE), about $ 7000 per student (cf. Chamblis 2007; Rushing 2007). Thus for a school district to lose 1,000 students means a loss in revenue of $ 7 million direct to budget. The result is loss of teachers and other staff. Education constitutes 34% of the overall Florida state budget. The piece of good news is that it is easier to find teachers to meet the state mandated class size limits. Overall Florida needs to fill 17,000–20,000 teacher positions each year. In 2006–2007 Florida employed 168,181 teachers plus 29,097 instructional personnel (guidance counselors, librarians, etc.) (cf. Teachers 2007). If one had been watching carefully, the 2005–2006 school year actually showed the lowest growth since the 1984–1985 school year (cf. Public School 2006). School year 2005–2006 also showed the largest enrollment decline October to February in a decade (cf. Public School 2006). Thus overall school enrollment has stalled in Florida, meaning that population growth for the young family segment of the population has stalled.

6 Economy

Indeed estimates of population growth for Florida showed a 57,000 loss for April 1, 2008–April 1, 2009. This was the first annual loss of population for Florida since WWII: Estimates for April 1, 2009–April 1, 2010 show a gain of 23,000 to 18,773,000, so the actual 2000–2010 decade growth was 17.5% not 25% as forecast as late as 2005 (cf. Harrington 2010).

Such discussion does not consider foreign immigrants. South Florida (cf. Arthur 2007) growth is largely due to foreign immigrants, some 400,000 between April 2000 and July 2006. While domestic migration was negative since mid-2005. It is said that one-quarter of Florida's population growth since 2000 is due to foreign immigrants.[3]

Between the fall of 2007 and the fall of 2009, Florida lost 800,000 jobs and unemployment rose from 4 to over 12% (cf. Index 2010), remaining at 11% in mid-2011.

7 Culture of Growth?

For decades Florida had a pattern of extensive growth. It can be argued that that growth was based upon sunshine/beaches, low cost housing, low taxes, low living expenses, and ample jobs (low wage). Housing, taxes, insurance, living expenses are now higher than states such as Texas, Tennessee, and North Carolina. Salaries have not changed to reflect living expenses. The hurricanes have served as a reminder of dangers and of quality of life issues. Crime in some areas has become a problem. Little (no) polling is done to determine the attitudes of people in other parts of the US toward moving to Florida. Yet, the scenario of no growth is not on the planners list of options. Will sunshine and beaches be a sufficient magnet for growth in the absence of low costs and with low wages in the future? How long will the present situation last? Will growth of 200,000 people per year begin in 2013 or 2014 as forecast now by planners? Or is there a no growth scenario which in fact will last for decades (cf. Harrington 2010)?

8 Survey Results

If Florida has had a culture, economics and politics based on growth, how has the stalled growth and deep global recession of 2008–2009 changed attitudes towards the environmental and towards sustainability. Conveniently there were three related surveys of Florida done by the same methodology and done by the

3 Cf. Immigrant impact: Florida. – URL: http://www.fairus.org.

same national polling agency, McLaughlin and Associates in 2007 and 2009. Surveys were of 600 likely general election voters, conducted via phone by professional interviewers. Interview selection was random within predetermined election units. Those units were constructed to correlate with actual voter turnout. Accuracy is ± 4.0% at a 95% confidence level. There was a statewide survey conducted February 10–11, 2009, an energy survey conducted during the same period, and a survey conducted July 28–29, 2007. Surveys were conducted and published by the Associated Industries of Florida.[4]

In 2009 voters were asked whether the current direction of Florida was in the right or wrong direction; 31% answered – right direction, 55% – wrong direction, with 14% giving no answer. In Table 2, one finds the issues of most interest to voters in 2009 and 2007. The change in economic fortunes between 2007 and 2009 clearly changed voter's perceptions. The issue of improving the economy/creating jobs/reducing unemployment went from 6% in 2007 to 29% in 2009.

Table 2: What One Issue do You View as the Most Important to the State of Florida?

	2009	2007
ECONOMIC	58	51
Improve Economy	15	6
Create Jobs/Reduce Unemployment	14	
Reduce Property Taxes	9	10
Cut Wasteful Government Spending	8	5
Hold Line on State Taxes	6	18
Lower Cost of Home Insurance	6	12
SOCIAL	31	29
Improve Education	15	12
Fight Illegal Immigration	8	–
Health Care Afford-Access	8	11
Protect the Environment	1	6
RESTORE HONESTY/INTEGRITY TO GOVERNMENT	3	–
CONTROL GROWTH/DEVELOPMENT	2	6
FIGHT CRIME AND DRUGS	2	9
NOT ANSWERED	4	6

Source: See footnote 4

4 Cf. AIF Poll: Floridians Concerned About Energy Issues. – URL: http://aif.com/polling/2007/070808energypoll.htm. AIF Statewide Survey. – URL: http://aif.com/state_survey.shtm; Results of AIF Energy Poll. – URL: http://aif.com/state_survey.shtm.

An issue of more voter interest in 2009 versus 2007 was cutting wasteful spending. Of less voter interest was holding the line on taxes, cost of home insurance, affordability/access to health care, controlling growth, and (of most interest for this paper) protecting the environment, which went from 6% to only 1%.

Of voters in 2009, 90% felt that Florida was in a recession (66%) or depression (24%); 67% thought that it would take 2–5 years for recovery. Interestingly "if the governor and state legislature had to cut spending" the two top areas chosen from 7 identified for cuts were purchasing land for conservation (33%) and Everglades restoration (16%).

In 2009 voters identified the most important environmental issue facing Florida. Almost 40% who answered the survey identified water shortages or water pollution (32.5% did not know or answer the survey). Only 4.1% of voters who expressed an opinion picked global warming as the most important issue. All of the issues are shown in Figure 1. While Everglades restoration was identi-

Figure 1: "What Would You Say Is the Most Important Environmental Issue Facing Florida Right Now?"

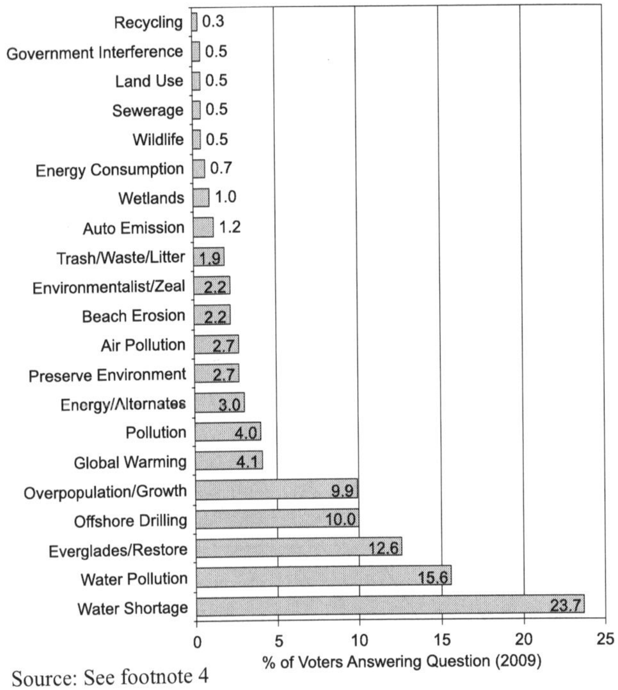

Source: See footnote 4

fied above for budget cuts, it was also the third most important environmental issue identified by voters.

In 2007 voters were asked what they felt was the most important energy issue facing Florida. They responded with energy costs (30%), followed by energy conservation 20%, and energy independence 19%. Energy's environmental impact was only cited by 14% of voters and energy reliability by 10%. In 2007 voters were asked whether they supported or opposed building more energy plants in Florida; 74% expressed support with 17% in opposition.

In 2007, 82% of voters supported the notion that the state government should spend more tax dollars to develop alternative, more environmentally friendly energy programs such as solar, wind and ethanol. However, by 56% to 38%, voters disapproved the notion that the state raise taxes on energy to encourage conservation. As to increasing production of oil by drilling off the coast of Florida that was approved 63% to 27%. But for 46% of voters that was only if oil drilling was at least 125 miles off the coast. In a 2009 poll of 625 Florida voters by Mason-Dixon Polling and Research (April 15–16) pollsters found that (cf. AIF 2008; Banfill 2009):

- 59% of Floridians support drilling off Florida's coast.
- 79% support drilling if it raises money for public education, health care and environmental protection.
- 83% support drilling if it will produce new jobs and stimulate the economy.
- 88% support drilling if it is environmentally safe.

What it means to be "environmentally safe" is of course key. With the 2010 oil event in the Gulf of Mexico, that support is likely to have declined markedly.

In 2009 voters were asked "Both the United States and Florida are considering a plan to address global warming which will impose limits on the amounts of greenhouse gases companies are allowed to emit. If a company emits less than that amount, they may sell the surplus to other companies. In general, do you support or oppose this plan?" (cap & trade). Voters were evenly divided 41% to 39.2% with 19.8% not answering the question. There was fear that such a "cap & trade" plan would increase costs or taxes or both (62.7% agreeing versus 24.2% disagreeing and 13.2% with no answer). Under current circumstances (uncertain economy, high energy prices) voters in 2009 were unwilling to pay more for electricity and gasoline (80.3% to 11.7%, with 8% no answer).

In 2009, voters felt that reducing reliance on foreign sources of energy was more important (65.8%) than addressing global warming (11.7%); 11% of voters identified both and 7.5% expressed no answer. When asked what they would be willing to pay each year in higher gasoline prices, higher electricity prices, or higher heating bills to deal with global warming, 47.5% did not answer the question and 32.8% answered $ 100 or less (the total 80.3% agreeing with the answer above). Only 3% indicated willingness to pay $ 500-$ 1000/year and 6.7% over $ 1000/year. Of voters, 32.2% said that there should be a moratorium on building coal-burning power plants until ways to capture and store emitted carbon are found versus 50% who favor continuing use of coal burning power plants.

Overall, as noted in the 2007 poll, when thinking about the environment, 85% of voters think of themselves as pro-environment (28% consider themselves active participants in the environmental movement who make significant lifestyle changes to conserve natural resources, and 57% care about the environment and do the best they can without necessarily changing their lifestyle to do things like conserve and recycle). Another 10% of voters think of themselves as someone who cares about the environment, but won't necessarily go out of their way to help the environment. Only 3% say they don't care much about the environment.

By 2010, the continuing global recession has had a further impact. A national Gallup poll (March 4–7, 2010) of 1014 American adults showed environmental concerns at the lowest level in ten years (cf. Gallup 2010). A Rasmussen poll reported April 7, 2010, only 17% of adults believe most Americans would be willing to make major cutbacks in their lifestyle in order to help save the environment, versus 65% "not the case" and 18% not sure. But 51% of adults believe major life style cutbacks are necessary in order to help the environment, while 32% disagree, with 16% undecided. Only 17% of Americans say it is at least somewhat likely that the next car they buy will be all-electric. By a 55% to 32% margin, most voters continue to believe that finding new sources of energy is more important than reducing the amount of energy Americans consume (cf. Report 2010).

In a March 19–21, 2010 poll by CNN/Opinion Research Corporation, when asked which statement do you agree with most – "Protection of the environment should be given priority, even at the risk of curbing economic growth", or "Economic growth should be given priority, even if the environment suffers to some extent" (501 interviews) (see Table 3).

Table 3: Level of Environmental Concern

	3/19-21/2010	6/26-29/2008	3/7-10/2005	4/3-9/2000
Environment	45	49	52	67
Economic Growth	51	44	37	28
Both Equally	3	6	6	2
No Opinion	1	1	4	3

Source: CNN 2010

Referring back to Table 2, one can see clearly that economic climates change voter priorities. Of importance in this discussion, protecting the environment is clearly not the top voter priority, although voters consider themselves to be highly pro-environment. While voters are perhaps willing to make some lifestyle changes, they are not willing to endure substantial cost increases for energy and are even willing to tee-up purchases of conservation lands and Everglades restoration for Florida state budget cuts if cuts are needed.

Two on campus examples show the dilemma. On February 5, 2009 we had a National Teach-In on Climate Change. There was no charge and 150 people crowded into a room holding 100. Four weeks later, for the 2009 Sustainability Forum, the initial public charge of $ 85 for a two day conference, with 30 quality papers from presenters from seven countries, including two lunches, breaks, etc, was viewed by numerous people as too expensive.

The dilemma for Sustainability is clear; Sustainability is for the long term. Sustainability requires sustained political agreement and will. It requires long term economics. Acceptable, sustainable, technologies are not enough. There are political cycles. Sustainability must have sufficient support to survive changes in the leadership political party. Sustainability must be able to survive economic cycles.

What we value is determined by culture. Cultural change in the direction of sustainable development is required. Will it happen? How can it be encouraged to happen?

References

AIF (2008): Floridians Want Oil Drilling. In: Orlando Sentinel, August 27 (URL: http://blogs.orlandosentinel.com/news_politics/2008/08/aif-floridians.html)

Arthur, L. (2007): South Florida's Population Booming Despite Challenges. In: Miami Herald, April 5

Ash, J. (2007): Budget Accord Trims $ 1.1 billion. In: Florida Today, October 9

Banfill, R. (2009): Florida Lawmakers Take Bold Step to Secure State's Energy Future. April 21 (URL: http://www.reuters.com/article/pressRelease/idUS224076+21-Apr-2009+PRN 20090421)

Chamblis, J. (2007): Polk School Enrollment Growth Tapers Off. In: The Ledger, November 14

Christie, L. (2007a): Foreclosure Filings: No Slowdown Yet. In: CNNMoney.com, November 14

Christie, L. (2007b): Home Prices Take Steeper Downturn. In: CNNMoney.com, November 27

CNN (2010): CNN Opinion Research Poll. March 19–21; For Release March 31

Comparison (2010): Five-Year Comparison of PK-12 Membership, Fall 2005 to Fall 2009. Florida Department of Education

Cotterell, B. (2007): Experts: Fla Economic Slump to Stick Around. In: Florida Today, November 13

Dukes, L. (2007): Florida Information Data Base Conference, 2007-2008 School Year. Florida Department of Education, June 18

FMF (2007): Florida & Metro Forecast, 2007-2036. June (URL: http://www.bus.ucf.edu/hitec/Forecasts.htm)

FoF – 1000 Friends of Florida (2006): Florida in 2060: Not a Pretty Picture? Executive Summary. December (URL: http://1000fof.org.)

Gallup (2010): Gallup Poll. March 4–7

Goodnough, A. (2007): Housing Slump Pinches States in Pocket Book. In: New York Times, April 7

Harrington J. (2010): After One-Year Blip, Florida's Population to Grow Again. In: St. Petersburg Times, March 3

Index (2010): Florida Consumer Confidence Index. March 30. Gainesville (UF Survey Research Center, University of Florida)

Marx, St. (2009): The Culture of Sustainability (2). Address to Focus the Nation II. In: Cal Poly, February 5

McCarthy, J. (2007): Seeds of Foreclosure Sown in Boom. In: Florida Today, October 7

MyRegion (2007a): East Central Florida – Comprehensive Economic Development Strategy. MyRegion.org, September

MyRegion (2007b): How Shall We Grow? MyRegion.org, August

Public School (2006): Public School Enrollment Trends, Economic and Demographic Research. Florida Department of Education, October 18

Report (2006): Charting the Course: Where is South Florida Heading? Report, March (URL: http://www.soflo.org)

Report (2010): 65% Say Americans Not Willing to Make Major Lifestyle Changes to Help Environment. In: Rasmussen Reports, April 7

Rushing, J. T. (2007): Eyes on School Funding Formula. In: Florida Times Union, April 2

Teachers (2007): Projected Numbers of Teachers Needed in Florida Public Schools. Florida Department of Education (Office of Evaluation and Reporting), February

Thorner, J. (2007): Stacking Up Our Future. In: St. Petersburg Times, May 19

Vittner, M. (2007): Florida Economic Outlook. Wachovia Bank, March 22

WCED – World Commission on Environment and Development (1987): Our Common Future. Oxford

Culture, Ethics and Sustainable Development

Medardo Tapia Uribe

Let us begin with the definition of the three central concepts of this essay: culture, ethics and sustainable development. This will be useful not only for being more precise with respect to the meaning of these concepts, but as a way to identify the cognitive relationship between them.

It is a paradox for example, that during the age of enlightenment, culture was defined as a human need that freed themselves of nature and religious tutelage (cf. Thurn 1976). In this definition, culture was a collective process by means of which men become independent of any external influence, like a natural force. A theory of development, like sustainable development for example, can be considered as culture and not only as a descriptive map considered true by scientists. It falls into the definition of culture because it is validated as a kind of truth within a certain context; it becomes a morally correct view of development because it agrees with certain predominant values in that particular society or that particular social context. Theories of sustainable development as part of a culture of development feed or reciprocally create a social reality with rules and institutions to be followed compulsively. Such theories tell us, culturally, how to grow the proper speed for growth, and the instructions on how to grow. The theory and culture of sustainable development tell us, in different principles or milestones, the canonical way to grow; a theory of sustainable development is not independent of its culture; such an idea is not wrong, it is absurd (cf. Brunner 1988, pp. 138f.). Culture can be defined as the knowledge, vision, set of beliefs and principles that guide our individual and social practices and, at the same time, allow society to create new ones. It is society's own model of creativity, not only of reproduction.

Ethics is also a part of any society's culture. Any social and economic system is built on ethical assumptions (cf. Leff 1998, p. 72). However, to be precise, we can define ethics as the discipline that studies the very nature, functions and values of moral judgments. We also need to define "moral" because it is very often confused with ethics. Moral judgments can be considered an individual's ability to freely evaluate the rightness of actions, situations, intentions, people and institutions. Ethics, however, is the origin or drive behind any human action. This characteristic is no accessory or a simple representation of how society works; nor is society a system defined exclusively by the exchanges within its environment. Society has the capacity to intervene upon itself. This is why Touraine considers ethics the true engine of social change, that unreachable mirror's image, in which we see ourselves, and then direct our actions towards progress and development.

This is why when we think about sustainable development, we need to recall the classic concepts that have been used in specialized literature – the two key concepts introduced by the Brundtland Commission in 1987 (cf. WCED 1987) and Agenda 21 as an action plan for sustainable development in 1992 (cf. Sitarz 1993) – as part of our culture. Behind the values and capacities of development and natural environment, we allow future generations to live and develop at least with equal or better opportunities and conditions than us. If we want to observe the problems of sustainable development as a cultural issue, we have to look at the beliefs, principles, values and criteria that justify or sustain them. We need to observe the way we work, the way we organize ourselves to function as individuals, as peasants, as an entrepreneur, as a community or as a nation. Studies similar to Max Weber's "The Protestant Ethic and the Spirit of Capitalism", are an attempt to reveal the ethic and cultural framework of a particular economic system: capitalism. Therefore there is not just one, but many cultures, as there are various kinds of co-existing human groups; there are even many cultures within a single nation. Mexico, for example, has been defined as a multicultural country.

Luis Villoro, a Mexican philosopher, asserts that in history there is a plurality of cultures, simultaneously or successively (cf. Villoro 2007, p. 139). Each culture represents a certain social group's way of life. Villoro also claims that any culture, as simple as it may be, fulfills several functions: it expresses emotions, hopes, ways of approaching the world; any culture also pinpoints values, allows the formation of preferences and the selection of means and ends; it also gives meaning to attitudes and behaviours. Therefore, it can be said that culture provides bonding within any group. It brings people together as a collective whole. Finally, culture determines the criteria to choose the proper means to fulfill certain goals and values. Any culture, adds Villoro, can be identified by the degree in which it fulfills the functions of expressing, providing meaning, bonding and determining the proper means to achieve certain goals. Villoro identifies two components of culture. On the one hand, he defines as the "value part of culture" the expressive and the meaning part of it. On the other hand, the "power value" of culture is the capacity to be successful in achieving its goals. Power, according to Weber, "is the possibility of imposing your own will within a social relationship, in spite of any resistance and whatever the foundation of such probability" (Villoro 2007, p 141). In every culture these two components are used, expressed or executed (cf. Villoro 2007, p. 140).

We can now understand how there can be rural or indigenous groups or communities that have different conceptions and values of development but might, most of the times, have no power, or not enough power before other groups, to achieve their goals. There also might be entire countries in such conditions. This is why we have to look at cultures in different countries or different groups within a country when we analyze development and sustainable development. We have to analyze these relationships in terms of values and power, as intercultural relationships, in response to the claim that there is a universal culture or ethics with respect to sustainable development. Of course, it would be morally wrong or unethical to ignore such a claim, however it can be seen as an imposition to the values and culture of a certain social group, having another's culture and values thrust upon them by claiming ethical and power superiority.

For example, one of the economically developed countries might protest against Brazil's Amazonian jungle management, defending the jungles' contribution to oxygen and to the world's environment. In contrast, on the same grounds, Latin America could present claims to the United States or to the European Union for their enormous levels of energy consumption and the per capita indexes of carbon dioxide thrown into the atmosphere. Latin America has an index emission of 3.08 tons of carbon dioxide into the atmosphere, almost half of the world average, 5.14 tons per capita. Nevertheless, 31% of Latin American territories and their biospheres are under threat, exposing their vegetable and animal species with extinction.

We, of course, have to consider development with this analysis of the cultural dimension of sustainable development. Some of the possible arguments would appeal to the important economic consequences of energy reduction consumption, because it will probably reduce, in a complex chain, economic activity, levels of employment, and surely create many other unpredictable economic and social consequences, including the increase in poverty levels. In contrast, a rural community or a group in a poverty situation might raise two kinds of arguments: "I 'choose' to use pesticides or cut down healthy trees from the forest or jungle because I have no choice, I have to make a living and survive." On the other hand, he might choose to defend his traditional way of farming because it is what he knows and happens to be sustainably right for the environment.

Culturally, it would not be easy to produce absolute or superior arguments to solve a debate we have had for more than a decade. Confusion would be one of the inevitable outcomes of this debate which does not mean a lack of meaning or culture, as it has been inadequately insinuated. The gap between a cultural ideal of sustainable development and its practice in society has been referred, since Durkheim and other classic works as those of Jürgen Habermas, as anomie (cf. Girola 2005, pp. 233, 300). Individuals and groups, accompanied by interests and affections, also, of course, exercise power to fill the gap in such debate. The players will surely use their culture value dimension to express powerful arguments and principles in order to defend their value position and their interests. In addition, it would not be less powerful for some rural or Indian group of the Amazon or for Mexico – or even an NGO – to express their cultural condition and goals before some CEO businessman than those arguments expressed by more powerful political authority or countries.

The disagreements between groups, communities or nations over different concepts, expressions, values and decisions over means and goals to take on development have been labeled as rights, cultural and legal rights. Under the assumption of the value of a cultural autonomy, it is said that freedom is a better choice than domination; that authenticity and identity are better for mankind than uniformity; that auto determination of means and goals is better than having your life goals and meaning be determined by someone else. This right to auto determination as a people *(pueblo)* – as an ethnic group or a community with a common history, a collective identity and a territory of their own – has been included in international law, although it has had problems within a nation state to be legally recognized as actual *pueblos* or simply as minorities. It has been debated and solved differently. The proper claims over a territory and deciding the way of life chosen for such territory are still under debate, like the choice of customs and practices are part of the legal rights being discussed. These kinds of rights we have to discuss to produce a global ethic and the possibility of establishing universal values for sustainable development. By means of these kinds of debates and agreements nation states have acquired responsibilities towards international agreements for worldwide sustainable development as those signed in the framework of the Brundtland Commission and Agenda 21. Mexico and the different Latin American countries have signed different kinds of international agreements in order to achieve such sustainable development. The agreements signed and their results show Mexico and Latin America's commitment and capacity to fulfill such goals.

A good way to reveal part of the beliefs, values, capacities (culture's power dimension) and commitment of Mexico and other Latin American governments to sustainable development is to examine their commitments and environmental performance in terms of the two components of culture according to Villoro, the "value part of culture" and "the power part of culture", as we referred above. We will do this comparison by examining the numbers of treaties signed by Mexico, Brazil, Argentina, Chile and Costa Rica and then by looking at two kinds of parameters, the number of treaties signed by these countries and the Environmental Performance Index (EPI). EPI replaced the Environmental Sustainability Index (ESI) in order to measure the results and practices more precisely rather than because of political will and the number of treaties signed by every nation. EPI and ESI measure success in a development process to improve environmental quality and quality of life. The first parameter would be "the value part of culture"; the second one would be "the power part of culture".

Mexico has signed almost every treaty in order to acquire an active environmental policy and reach the goals of Agenda 21 and it is ranked first in Latin America in signing these kinds of treaties (cf. Conte Grand/D'Elisa 2008). Nevertheless, when we look at Mexico's Environmental Performance Index (EPI), it is 14th place out of 29 American countries, two places above Canada and the U.S. In 2010, Iceland, Switzerland, Costa Rica, Sweden and Norway, out of 163 countries evaluated, were at the top of the EPI scores. Cuba (9), Colombia (10) and Chile (16) are also among the highest EPI scores worldwide.

Mexico has a population of 105.2 million people and the highest annual GDP per capita of all of these Latin American countries, $ 13,025 followed by Chile at $ 12,626, Argentina $ 11,615, Costa Rica $ 9,636, and Brazil $ 8,745. Only Brazil has a larger population than Mexico, with 190.1 million people and Costa Rica has the smallest population of these Latin American Countries with 4.4 million people.

Mexico has a global EPI of 67.3, larger than Brazil's 63.4 and Argentina's 61.0. However, Mexico's EPI is smaller than Costa Rica's 86.4 and Chile's 73.3. Of the two components of EPI, Environmental Health and Ecosystem Vitality, Mexico has the lowest index in its Ecosystem Vitality, 58.0, above Brazil's 55.1 and Argentina's 47.6; but significantly lower than Chile's 65.4, and Costa Rica's 90.6. Mexico's commitment to its Ecosystem Vitality and its capacity to manage is as low as Brazil and Argentina. Within this dimension of Mexico's Environmental Performance, its Ecosystem Vitality, Mexico manages with greater care its forestry, its fishing industry and its agriculture. In forestry, Mexico performs as well as Brazil and Argentina; of course below Chile and Costa Rica. Chile and Costa Rica performed at the top worldwide in terms of forestry.

In the fishing industry, we find a similar pattern between all the countries compared, except for Argentina whose index is half of that of the other countries, 48.0. It looks like Argentina does not value the fishing industry as much as other Latin American countries.

In spite of its Revolution and the fight for the land, Mexico, of the five Latin American countries compared, has in agriculture the lowest index. Mexicans do not value or adequately manage agriculture as well as its Latin American counterparts. All the five Latin American countries compared have the lowest indexes of their Ecosystem Vitality in two components:

(1) Air Pollution (effects on the ecosystem) and
(2) Biodiversity Habitat.

However, as it has been the pattern in this analysis, Costa Rica is at the top with 59.9 and 73.4 respectively and Mexico, Brazil and Chile, with 40.1, 39.3 and 42.2 respectively, seem to share a similar appreciation and handling of this problem. Since 1992, Chile, Brazil and Mexico have increased the emissions per kilowatt hour of energy produced, 112%, 20% and 6.7% respectively. In contrast, since 1992, Argentina and Costa Rica reduced those emissions with 6.8% and 48.6% respectively. This is why they perform better than the other three countries. Argentina, on the other hand, has the lowest index of these five countries in Biodiversity and Habitat, 31.2, and surprisingly, Chile has a much lower index than Mexico with 51.1, Brazil's 61.3, and of course Costa Rica's 73.4.

In Environmental Health, the other dimension of Environmental Performance, Costa Rica and Chile – at 82.1 and 81.2 – perform much better than the other three countries, while Mexico, Brazil and Argentina come out roughly at the same level, 76.6, 71.6, and 74.4 respectively. Again, this shows the larger appreciation and better handling that these two countries have over the other three, in spite of Mexico's largest GDP per capita. According to the indexes in this component, it is clear that Mexico does not value Water (effects on humans) due to Access to Sanitation, at 78.6, as much as Costa Rica, Chile and Argentina do, each with 95.5, 93.2, and 89.8, respectively. This outcome is surprisingly in spite of Mexico's larger GDP per capita and the fact that between 1990 and 2006 Mexico increased its Access to Sanitation by 44.6 percent. During the same period, Chile only increased its Access to Sanitation by 11.9 percent and Costa Rica only by 2.1 percent, and they both have much larger indexes.

This analysis disagrees with other research results that indicate that Mexico has achieved better results than, for example, Costa Rica and Chile (cf. Conte Grand/D'Elisa 2008, p. 115). In this report, Mexico has signed more treaties than any other country in Latin America and has achieved more goals of Agenda 21, by 84.21%, than any other Latin American country, including Costa Rica and Chile, 66.67% and 68.42%. This is not strange. Mexico has been accused, particularly the Environmental and Natural Resources Department (Secretaría de Medio Ambiente y Recursos Naturales: SEMARNAT), by NGOs of embracing environmental performance in theory rather than in practice, that is in terms of the value part of culture rather than the power part of culture. NGOs accused the Mexican government of having authorized developmental projects that put vegetal and animal species at risk (cf. Enciso 2010). If the research results referred to above were true, Mexico would be the Latin American country with the best environmental performance and with the best results on sustainable development. Unfortunately, although we would love to say it is true, it is not. The same research links environmental policies with other variables show some significant association with Human Development Index. We know that it is a statistical analysis; however, this is not the case with the other countries we compared. It is a similar case with Chile, which has the highest HDI and is at the EPI top with Costa Rica, but it is different from Argentina.

In sum, this is how Mexico and Latin America, exemplified by these five countries, are carrying out the actions agreed to in those treaties. Both the agreements as well as the obligations specified in them are more ethical or moral, that is, they express more "the value part of culture" than the judicial and "the power part of culture". because it is every country's responsibility to integrate sustainable development and decision-making; that is, to design policies and management strategies in order to provide an effective legal and regulatory framework; to make use of economic and market instruments as well as other incentives; to establish systems for integrated environmental and economic accounting. From a cultural analysis perspective, to integrate sustainable development and decision-making depends on the institutional and social capacity of a community, city, municipality or nation; in other words, its cultural power dimension to honour their values and beliefs. This is why it can be said that Costa Rica and Chile have a more powerful culture of sustainable development, because they are more culturally competent than Mexico, Brazil and Argentina to act and fulfill their goals.

As implied above, rather than posing some moral imperative categories that constitute "the ethics of sustainable development," it is the people, a community, a nation's cultural and – sometimes described as national and/or international – legal right to undertake a global ethic and the possibility of establishing universal values for sustainable development. Under this perspective, an intercultural dialogue becomes an ethical discourse or argument that has been sustained by Adela Cortina, Karl-Otto Apel, and Habermas. The parameters we will be using for this purpose are those proposed by Cortina and Emilio Martínez (cf. Cortina/Martínez 2001):

(1) Dialogue is the only reasonable way (of macro ethics) because there are no compulsory material ethical principles for all human beings and indoctrination is against human rationale.
(2) Ethics principles are really proceedings, meaning that they only indicate the norms for discussion, for those concerned over the rightness of a certain norm.
(3) Those concerned with a certain decision must have participated in it, in terms of rationality; that is, after a dialogue is carried out within the conditions of symmetry of the information and whose results are a product of the strength of the better argument rather than any other kind of coercion.
(4) Decision over the rightness of norms is always subject to be reviewed.
(5) There is a dialogic ethos behind every moral decision:

    – To express my position over an issue I know of the needs, interests and arguments of all of those concerned by a norm.

- We must gather as much information as possible by means of dialogue and inquiry.
- All participating in a dialogue must be willing to disclose their interests and needs to all concerned and offer their argument's proposals.
- There is good will for satisfying interests worthy of becoming universal.
- He/she is willing to assume the consequences of his/her decision.

(6) The rightness of the ethics of dialogic does not rest upon any kind of agreement that is reached by group consensus or by majority decision. The rightness of a norm is an issue to be solved by a person, who decides the obligatory nature of any norm as long as he/she is willing to listen, reply and decide based on satisfying interests worthy of becoming universal.

There will be two important cultural, ideal and practical, problems being addressed in the discussion of the ethics of sustainable development. Every person, community or nation concerned, affected or responsible in this debate must be recognized as communicatively competent and grounded or oriented to two communities. One of these communities is the peoples' historic or actual community; the community in which they were born, raised and socialized. The other community is an ideal one (cf. Cortina 1991), towards which he/she – they – aim in advance, a sort of imperative moral, that perhaps is unreachable or a utopian mirror image, our ethic, of future possible sustainable development. Unfortunately in Mexico, more than in the rest of Latin America, we seem to value sustainable development much more than the cultural and social capacity to reach such an ideal image. In other terms, our value part of environment and sustainable development is more powerful than our capacity to achieve, to live and to develop ourselves according to those values – the power part of culture –. I am certain that many Mexicans would passionately maintain that through our government, we are really only lying to ourselves, Mexicans; or perhaps, the Mexican government is simply culturally incompetent in both dimensions: the value and the power cultural dimensions of sustainable development.

References

Brunner, J. (1988): Actual Minds, Possible Worlds. Cambridge/MA

Conte Grand, M.; D'Elia, V. (2008): Problemas del Desarrollo [Problems of Development]. In: Revista Latinoamericana de Economía, Vol. 39/No. 154 (July–September), pp. 112–134 (in Spanish)

Cortina, A. (1991): Introducción [Introduction]. In: Apel, K.-O.: Teoría de la verdad y ética del discurso [Theory of Truth and Speech Ethics]. Barcelona, pp. 9–33 (in Spanish)

Cortina, A.; Martínez, E. (2001): Ética [Ethics]. Madrid (in Spanish)

Enciso, A. (2010): Sólo en el discurso, la defensa de la Semarnat al ambiente [Only in Speech, Federal Government Defense of the Environment]. In: La Jornada, Mexico City, May 31, p. 44 (in Spanish)

Girola, L. (2005): Anomia e individualismo. Del diagnóstico de la modernidad de. Durkheim al pensamiento contemporáneo [Lawlessness and Individualism. From the Diagnosis of the moderness by Durkheim to Contemporary Thinking.] Barcelona (in Spanish)

Leff, E. (1998): Saber ambiental. Sustentabilidad, racionalidad, complejidad y poder [Environmental Knowledge. Sustainability, Rationality, Complexity and Power]. México (in Spanish)

Sitarz, D. (1993): Agenda 21: The Earth Summit Strategy to Save Our Planet. New York

Thurn, H. P. (1976): Soziologie der Kultur. Stuttgart (in German)

Villoro, L. (2007): Los retos de la sociedad por venire [Society Challenges to Come]. Mexico: Fondo de Cultura Económica (in Spanish)

WCED – World Commission on Environment and Development (1987): Our Common Future. Oxford

Key Issues of Integrative Technology Assessment

Andreas Metzner-Szigeth

1 Introduction

This paper has been written with the intention to present some conceptual and programmatic considerations. The length of its complete title is therefore nothing less than an expression of the idea to pay attention to far-reaching and broad civilizational and paradigmatic connections instead of focusing on a single area of professional specialization.

In this way – and according to KISS, a well-known principle of great design that says "Keep It Simple and Straightforward" – four clusters of contents will be introduced and treated subsequently:

(1) "Progress", because it's shaping is indeed *the* central subject of governance of science and technology in general and of technology assessment (TA) in particular!
(2) "Vulnerability", because that is *the* very challenge of our times!
(3) "Sustainable Development", because *that* really answers the question of how to gain the future!
(4) "Governance of Science and Technology", because evidently *there* is some discrepancy between a growing demand for good governance of these issues and a lack of satisfying strategies and concepts of how to do it! Therefore – and because of the fact that technology assessment is of crucial importance for any ambitious governance approach – I would like to introduce a framework concept that I call "Integrative Technology Assessment" (ITA).

Moreover, and in order to develop my argument in a clear and understandable way, there will be composed four general theses on the line of the four points, one of each for "progress", "vulnerability" and "sustainable development" plus one for the concluding general thesis.

2 Progress

2.1 Progress and Enlightenment

European modernization has been – and in fact is – determined by the thought of "enlightenment" but also by the idea of "progress". Whereas one of them intends to foster human faculties for reasoning in the sense of independence and self-responsibility, the other one tries to examine and tame the forces of nature with the instruments and media of science and to develop and utilize them in form of technology. The promises of this civilizational initiative are "freedom", "wealth" and "security".[1]

2.2 Progress and (In-)Security

"No one should hinder progress!" So a popular speech reads. With this, a one-dimensional *apologetic* comprehension of progress comes to expression, which indeed conflicts most vehemently with – in the same way one-dimensional – the *apocalyptic* understanding of progress, which comprehends progress (under changed pre-signs) as an unstoppable all-engulfing "Juggernaut". But the deterministic, unilinear model of progress breaks much more systematically with an opinion that understands progress not *essentialistically* but *process-oriented* as an increase of design or shaping possibilities and development options.

In the sense of the last opinion, progress was and is and will be practice, a process powered by human actors and formed by them in mode and manner (cf., among others, Bijker et al. 1987; MacKenzie/Wajcman 1985). Therefore, and regardless of its past, present or future, progress is a socially shapeable process, which characterizes itself in so far, as it does not just reduce contingencies – thereby determining the direction and the further possibilities of development cumulatively – but multiplies contingencies, while opening up new options permanently.

Progress – a mixture of "chances" and "risks" – must therefore be ambivalent by its very nature: progress is creating securities, in so far as it contributes to the solution of existing societal problems, thus performing like "keeping-things-in-order" and stabilizing better living conditions; and progress is acting as an "insecurity generator", while multiplying options that are to be coped with as decisions under uncertainty, which are questioning the "status quo" permanently.

2.3 Progress, Reflexivity and Domination

In the circles of scientific-technological progress of course questions and doubts emerge: Do the strengths of the sciences suffice in order to cope with or compensate for the ensuing consequences and shaping problems of modernization? Or are the problem-generating potentials of science and technology greater than

1 See, among others, Berting 2006, pp. 39ff., for the complex interplay of cultural reasons of this transformation that are especially linked with the pair of secularization and rationalization.

their problem-solving capacities? Does it therefore go ahead? Or are we caught in a spiral?[2]

Trying to answer these questions Ulrich Beck, in his book about the "Risk Society", has introduced for that the terms of the simple and reflexive scientification[3]: The stage of the "simple scientification" is characterized by the application of science to the "original" ("virginal") world of nature, human beings and society. On the other hand, in the "reflexive stage", the sciences are dealing with a modified world, already altered by science and technology – and while doing so, they are confronted with the products, shortcomings, consequences and shifted problems of their own "success".

With the increasing necessity for overcoming or compensating for the after-effects, problems and risks that emerge within the relationship of human society and ecological environment, the characteristic pattern of scientific knowledge changes: Formerly, science was thought of as a producer of the instruments and remedies for an increasing "control of nature", (that was supposed to be) accompanied by a (more and more) rationally "planned development of society". Nowadays, that science has to dedicate itself to the problem of the successful appropriation of nature (as well as the successful ignition of society's modernization) – it has altered into a "reflexive science". This one is confronted more and more – so my subsequent thesis reads – with the task of "mastering the domination of nature" that comes to expression, for instance, in the ever-growing demand for the control of intervention consequences and not intended side effects.

The evolution of science and technology has become contradictory in itself, because it is – according to Beck – simultaneously a complementary cause, a definitional remedy and a source of solution for problems. Inter- and trans-disciplinary approaches, as they have been practiced for a long time in systems analysis and technology assessment, are therefore becoming year by year more necessary in order to shape scientific-technological progress. But their "business" becomes also ever more difficult.

2.4 Progress and Industrial Innovation Cycles

In order to achieve its contribution, the social scientific science-, technology-, environment- and risk-research is being required, not only to reflect the cultural (communicative, symbolic) reality of developed industrial societies, but to do

---

2 In a spiral of ever more new problems to solve, originating from earlier attempts to do exactly that, namely to solve problems.

3 Cf. Beck 1992 and further Beck 1999; for similar ideas and discussions cf. also Giddens 1990; Beck et al. 1994; Lash et al. 1996.

that in the context and in the inner connection with their material (substantial, infrastructural) reality.[4]

In what way that could be done, will be demonstrated now in the context of "industrial innovation cycles"[5]. The main ideas of the illustration presented in Figure 1 are: Each basis-innovation or key technology[6] (e.g. steam engine) releases a series of process innovations (in the example power and work machines) and finally condenses in a techno-industrial innovation cycle. The two "classical" innovation cycles I and II are indicated here as that of "coal & steel" and of "electrical engineering & synthetic chemistry". They are followed by two "neo-classical" cycles: III, which is yet in plain development, and IV, which is partly beginning to be indicated by fore-signs. Their direction of movement is: from "electronics" over the "information and communication technologies (ICT)" to the further basis innovations of "bio and gene technologies (BGT)" and the "microsystem and nano technologies (MNT)".

Moreover, and without yet being able to clear its systematic position in the context of the industrial innovation cycles just introduced, there is need to mention the concept of "converging technologies" (indicated by the cloud in Figure 1) that proposes some dynamic convergence between information technology (ICT), biotechnology (BGT), nanotechnology (MNT) and further very dynamic areas like brain research and psychopharmacology which are not only occasionally linked with visions of "human enhancement" (cf. Roco/Bainbridge 2004). The concept of converging technologies – also known as NBIC, an acronym for nanotechnology, biotechnology, information technology and cognitive science – has up to now been more programmatic than descriptive, but its relevance as a vision that already is on its way to guide or direct some branches of further techno-scientific development is of utmost importance (particularly when transcending a viewpoint interested in competitive advantages only) (cf., among others, ETAG 2006; Grunwald 2007; Nordmann 2004).

---

4 Cf. Metzner 2002, where this approach has been elaborated and proved to be worthwhile.

5 I am using this term that is inspired by the economical ideas of Nikolai Kondratieff and the works of Alvin Toffler because of its structural instructiveness in order to analyze patterns of development; cf. also Barnett 1998; Freeman/Louçã 2001.

6 The terms "basis innovation" and "key technology" are used more or less synonymously here because of some fundamental functional similarities, despite other important differences. Cf. in that context Godin 2006, who presents the strength and weaknesses of the linear model of innovation in the context of his analysis of its scientific-historical development. Other accentuations are expressed with "generic technologies", that promise new methods and innovative solutions, and "general purpose technologies" (GPT), which dominate whole areas of technical progress and growth, such as the steam engine, the electric motor, and semiconductors because of their pervasiveness and inherent potential for improvements (cf. Bresnahana/Trajtenberg 1995).

Figure 1: Industrial Innovation Cycles and their Consequences

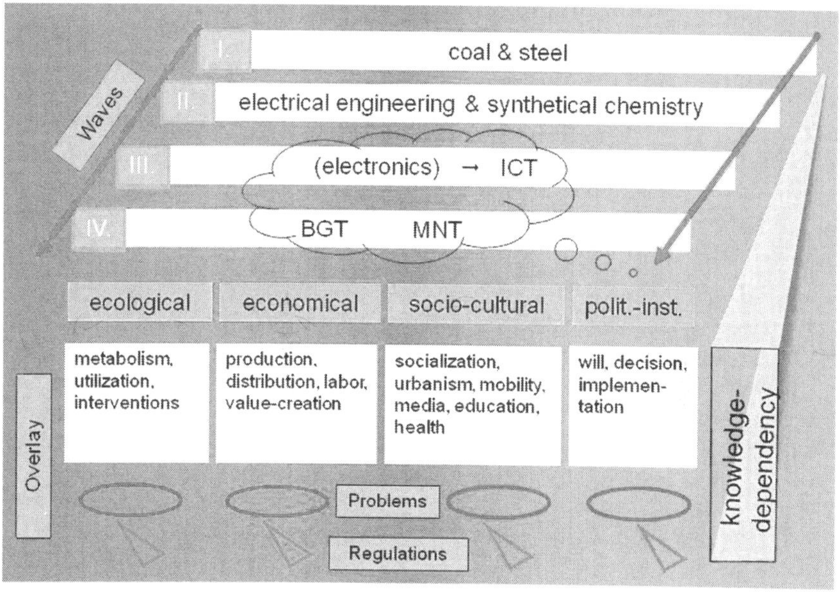

Author's archive

Each of these innovation-cycles provokes wide-range "transformations"[7], that are shaping the *"Gestalt"*, that is the configuration and the dynamics of industrial (and meanwhile post-industrial) society. The emerging consequences of these transformations are materializing subsequently and are together forming an overlay-zone, that is successively moving forward in time. This happens:

(1) in the profile of the metabolism with nature, including the quality and quantity of flows of energy and materials (cf. Haberl et al. 2004; Schiller 2009; Suh 2005), the form and degree of the utilization and charge of environmental goods and services, and the extension and intensity of manipulative interventions in the physical-organic world;

(2) with reference to the structure of the economic basis that is related to the configuration of productive forces, the allocation of resources, the distribution of wealth, the patterns of consumption, the organization of labor, or finally the form and length of product-life-cycles and value-creation chains;

---

7 Meant as something that is comparable in scope and range with that "great transformation" described by Karl Polyani; cf. Polyani 1944 and the review of Mayhew 2000; cf. also the next reference about "socio-ecological transformations".

(3) with regard to the socio-cultural patterns of society-building, of co-existence and individuation (that is, of living together in families and communities that are altering in scope, function and cultural meaning), as well as referring to the patterns of urbanity, mobility, informing and communicating with media or organizing education and public health;
(4) in relation to the organizational forms of public will-building and the political decision-making procedures that become mediated especially by those technologies and media that re-organize mobility and communication (cf. Banse/Metzner-Szigeth 2012; Castells 1996), and that includes also the administrative preparation and implementation of programs and actions.

These transformations – that already have been *presented* here separated according to the four dimensions of sustainable development – are obviously influencing each other.[8] They are not developing separated from one another, and are (besides their analytical distinction) pre-determined for being deciphered by some "systemic" approach (cf. Hjorth/Bagheri 2006; Metzner 1998; Spangenberg et al. 2002) because of their complex inter-dependencies. With respect to ecology – *for example* – the "classic" industrial society innovation cycles I and II that is being connected with the key sectors of coal and steel industry as well as with the branches of electrical industry, automobile production and synthetic chemistry, correspond with "problem-clusters" (pointed out in the Figure 1 by grey circles), that are characterized, on the one hand, by the charge of the environmental media (water, earth and air) with mass pollutants (as, for instance, phosphates, heavy metals and carbon dioxide) and, on the other hand, by the scarcity and imminent shortage of environmental goods or natural resources (above all those not renewable like fossil energy sources).

Mediated by these problem clusters are corresponding specific "regulation-approaches" (pointed out in the Figure 1 by grey triangles) with the innovation cycles and the transformations that have been released by them. In the example of the environment-related consequences of cycles I and II these are the strategies of the technical and the administrative environmental "protection" as well as the "recycling" of valuable resources.

The following innovation cycles III and IV are leading to transformations that are not only interacting with one another, but also with the states that have been built from antecedent that are foregoing transformations. An example for such a transformation – here with regard to the *economical* dimension – is the reconfiguration of production factors, value-creation chains and economical

8 The term of "socio-ecological transformations" (cf. Becker et al. 2000) gains considerably more analytical power when expanded and differentiated like in the fourfold scheme presented here.

sectors by the information and communication technologies (cf. Castells 1996; Hodgson 2000; Stehr 1994).

Moreover, Figure 1 indicates that in transition to the both "neoclassic" innovation cycles, there will be created not only altered problem clusters, but also an overload of the up to then developed regulation approaches. Examples for that are the appropriation and utilization rights of "genetic resources" (cf. Cassier 2002), that are conflicted intensely, as well as the "digital rights" (cf. David 2001), that are laying in midst of no less vehement struggles.

2.5 First General Thesis and its Explication

The first general thesis results from all considerations presented so far. It says: *The more the scientific-technological progress advances, the more dependent on knowledge and science becomes the task of its constructive shaping!*

In other words, more politically spoken, the same finding could be expressed as follows: The governance of science and technology becomes the more dependent on the contribution of scientific and professional experts, the more science and technology are moving forward. The governance of science and technology becomes therefore less and less a purely political issue that can be dealt with successfully by politicians alone. Either the (governing) politicians and their (not only executing) administrators as well as the (governed) citizens need to be well-informed in order to provide for good decisions by transparent and effective decision-making procedures. And, in the case of governance of science and technology, the state of being well-informed is not reachable without assistance (knowledge, competencies and assessments) of those scientific and professional experts whose working results are composing the subject at stake.

The essential points of the first thesis can be explained as follows: Together with the ongoing and increasing scientification of the techno-industrial procedures for producing ever more complex products, there grows also the knowledge and science dependency of the possibilities for the identification and regulation of the *consequences* of their production, application and disposal. An example for that is the general debate of the "pros" and "cons" of modified crops (cf. Rissler/Mellon 1996) and the particular discussion about the "monitoring" of the possible release and diffusion of genetically modified elements of plants (cf., e.g., Barton/Dracup 2000), e.g. of oilseed rape, because of their potential adverse effects especially for biodiversity. Moreover, there is to mention that this monitoring requires the application of molecular-biological diagnosis methods whose reliability is still not very clear because they share the same origin as the disputed newly developed techniques. The same example illustrates that together with the increasing knowledge dependency also the uncertainties of prospective knowledge – that is crucial for informed decision-making – are expanding.[9] In addition, there is the need to recognize the boosting of complexity due to the overlapping consequences of the transformations released by the successive innovation cycles. The regulation-knowledge of the various consequences must also be produced faster in order to keep up with the innovation speed.

Up to now – in Section 2 – we have examined the shaping problem of scientific-technological progress departing from the forces and consequences, which have been set in motion by progress itself. We are turning now into another perspective, in order to examine in Section 3, "Vulnerability", the shaping problem the other way round, departing from the "weakness" of the modern society and the need of scientific-technological creativity.

3 Vulnerability

3.1 Vulnerability: Levels, Components and Definition

"Vulnerability" has an external and an internal component. In general are – on the micro-level – the individual human being, or the single community (or livelihood) in which he or she lives, and – on the meso-level – the single city or region or the particular differentiated functional system, or finally – on the macro-level – complete societies exposed to existential hazards ("exposure"), and are to some distinct degree able to encounter this "being-exposed" either out of own strength or with assistance from others or third parties ("coping").[10]

In order to present an example that can illustrate the given argument we could contrast two coinciding cases:[11] In 2010, Haiti (on January 12) and Chile (on February 27) suffered from major earthquakes, with 7,0 (Haiti) and 8,8

9 Cf. Wehling 2006; Metzner-Szigeth 2009; especially with regard to uncertainties of climate prognosis and global environmental change scenarios.

10 With this adapted differentiation I am following the definition of Robert Chambers: "Vulnerability [...] is not the same as poverty. It means not lack or want, but defenselessness, insecurity, and exposure to risk, shocks and stress. [...] Vulnerability here refers to exposure to contingencies and stress, and difficulty in coping with them. Vulnerability has thus two sides: an external side of risks, shocks, and stress to which an individual or household is subject; and an internal side which is defenselessness, meaning a lack of means to cope without damaging loss. Loss can take many forms – becoming or being physically weaker, economically impoverished, socially dependent, humiliated or psychologically harmed" (Chambers 1989, p. 1; cf. also Watts/Bohle 1993).

11 An excellent source of further information that introduces simultaneously in methods of how to organize such a comparison is offered by The Learning Network of the New York Times (cf. http://learning.blogs.nytimes.com/2010/03/02/two-earthquakes-in-two-months-comparing-the-quakes-in-haiti-and-chile/).

(Chile) points on the Moment Magnitude Scale (MMS). Despite the fact, that the sheer amount of the released potentially destructive energy was considerably greater in the case of Chile, one can observe that the Haiti quake was far more destructive in terms of its outcome (number of killed persons and cumulated damages). An explanation for this finding is that the *exposure* to the quake was different in both cases due to a different configuration of decisive (physical and societal) factors. Moreover, in the case of Haiti the action capacities decisive for the autonomous *coping* capabilities of this society were already at ground level (for several other reasons) when the catastrophe occurred. The combination of both was inevitably leading into the following humanitarian disaster and might also be an explanation for the finding, that the attention of the global public to the Haiti case was considerably larger.

Anyway, we should try to understand the nature of vulnerability apart from single cases and isolated events. Following the idea of "glocalization" (cf. Robertson 1995; that combines the two seemingly contradictory trends of globalization and localization in one artificial expression) we can say here that we do have a "hybrid pattern" of local, regional and global vulnerabilities that are intertwined. A governance approach that aims to encounter "global risks" would therefore be misleading if and in so far as it would not recognize the nested character of these vulnerabilities. Neglecting that characteristic in favor of the primary attention to the global scale would force us to remain on the surface instead of analyzing the deeper structure and would therefore finally lead to the (of course not intended) consequence of missing to recognize the particular synergies caused by the dynamic interactions of the components of the nested systems.

3.2 Vulnerability: Overview on the Configuration of Interdependencies

Vulnerability is some kind of "fuzzy concept". Due to its association richness as well as to its convincing core idea it is, however, very instructive.[12] Its great value can be shown best while analyzing the whole complex of hazards and vulnerability in its interconnection with the ensemble of techno-industrial devices, systems and infrastructures (whose dynamic is driven by scientific-technological knowledge and competencies) and with regard to risk and the notions of prevention and resilience that provide for some mental tools that are serving simultaneously as regulative ideas and interventional concepts that we use in our trials to encounter the challenges that are emerging out of this complex (see Figure 2).

12 Even the positive meaning of vulnerability as analyzed by Bijker 2006 in the contexts of technological culture and innovation dynamics can show this.

Figure 2: Vulnerability and its Implications

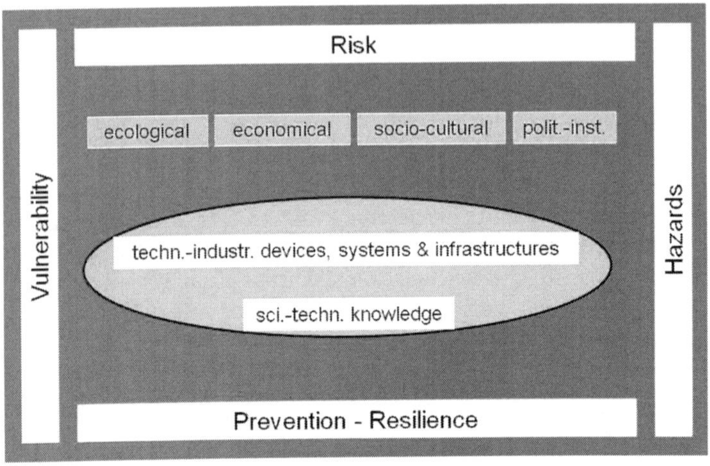

Author's archive

Figure 2 shows on the right a bar with the denomination "hazards".[13] These are to be classified according to different subsets:

(1) Epidemics, as for instance AIDS, BSE[14], bird flu or (the official declared pandemic of) H1N1 (that stayed out fortunately);
(2) "Natural"-disasters, including those that have some causal nexus with global environmental and climate changes, and are therefore hardly any more natural phenomena, but also of *anthropogenic* origin, as e.g. storms, landslips and avalanches, floods, droughts and earthquakes (cf. Abramovitz/Starke 2001);
(3) Techno-industrial accidents, that is essentially *man-made* incidents like that of the type "Seveso" (1976), "Bophal" (1984), "Chernobyl" (1986), "Exxon Valdez" (1989) or (most recently) the "Deepwater Horizon" (2010), but of course also those of "smaller" range (cf. Pidgeon/O'Leary 2000);
(4) Military struggles or civil wars, in whose consequence, for instance, oil fields are burning or once fertile regions are devastated (like in Iraq or Dafur);
(5) Terrorist attacks and acts of sabotage, above all insofar as they are suitable to provoke massive losses of human lives and/or the break-down of social infrastructures and function systems (like e.g. Internet-communication or

13 Further clarification about the definition and differentiation of the interrelated concepts of hazard, danger, accident and others could be found in Fisher 1994.

14 Bovine Spongiform Encephalitis, better known as "mad cow syndrome".

the world-wide electronic stock-market or the trans-regional power supply). Examples for that are the („9/11") attack on the "World Trade Center" or the recent attack on a hydroelectric power plant in the Russian city of Baksansk (in July 2010) but also – less spectacular – the seasonal "computer-viruses" and "software-worms" or the – in the public widely unknown – "cyber attack" (cf. Barletta 2008) on Estonia in 2007.

To the left we see a bar with the denomination "Vulnerability". There could be assigned a whole line of factors to it that can be divided at least in two categories:

(1) Factors of *general nature,* as e.g. the increasing density of interactions, the increasing networking-degree, the growing population, the increasing interdependencies between more and more specialized and differentiated systems, with services and productive units that are necessarily bound to a permanently running stream of transactions between them that leads to a growing sensitivity to interruptions and disruptions, and particularly – united with "globalization" – the "de-limitation" of large-scale and space-crossing cause-and-effect-chains (cf. Beck 1999a, 1999b; Held 2000; Lubbers/Koorevaar 2000; Young et al. 2006);
(2) Factors of *particular nature,* that are constituting "weak points" that could destabilize whole systems if they are exposed to "critical events" as e.g.
   - related to the ecological environment: the charge or degradation of freshwater ecosystems or mountain landscapes;
   - related to the economy: the dependency on single key resources, the rate of sources of income, or the quota of indebtedness;
   - related to the socio-cultural dimension: the knowledge and faculties of the people in relation to their access to education and other reservoirs of knowledge (catch word "digital divide");
   - related to the political-institutional dimension: the possibilities to participate (actively) in processes of decision-making and to receive the information necessary in order to do so.

In sum: The quantity and quality of governance faculties and management competencies are decisive parts of the entire self-organization capacity that is equal to the degree to which a society is capable to regulate itself (while referring simultaneously to internal alterations and structural shifts as well as to external turbulences and changing environmental conditions) and to perform intentionally caused reforms that change central parameters or the complete pattern of its operational self-processing and systemic reproduction.

In addition, there are factors that make sense with regard to techno-industrial devices, systems and infrastructures, as e.g. the factors of "high complexity" and "dense coupling", marked by the risk researcher Charles Perrow, that are above all problematic, if they are occurring together (cf. Perrow 1984); as well as the – by the complexity-researcher John Casti emphasized – "adaptability" of technical systems towards variable or even turbulent environments and critical events (cf. Casti 1994); the degree of "error-friendliness" or "reliability" of processes; the "robustness" of installations; the "singularity" of structures of the built-environment, as for instance bridges, tunnels, fill dams for purposes of territory-crossing supply; or (in contrast to the decentralized architecture of the highly complex but still robust Internet; cf. Willinger/Doyle 2002) the "centrality" of infrastructural networks (if, for instance, all subway lines are going through one "main station").[15]

As a rule, scientific-technological knowledge is meant to be used for serving "constructive" ends.[16] We know that this does not always succeed, and that vested interests are trying to influence science and technology, or simply to misuse them. Nevertheless, presumably all persons acting in "science, research and development" are dealing with the question of how could it be reached best (... to serve constructive ends) – *at least* in the context of the particular tasks and disciplinary issues that they are working on as a result of the division of labor in the whole society and within the sciences. The general occupation with the question of how this could be reached best, also with attention to the various goals that are linked with the four dimensions of sustainable development, is, however, the original and proper area of Science/Technology-Governance and TA.[17]

The upper bar with the denomination "risk" does not stand by chance between vulnerability on the left and hazards on the right. This should demonstrate

15 Cf. also the "large technical systems"-approach (e.g. Joerges 1996).

16 Here it may make sense to add a longer reference with regard to the utilization of scientific and technological knowledge for "destructive" purposes also, as for instance, weapons. One argument against the proximate objection that therefore it might be better not to use that term could be to make a distinction between the legitimate and the illegal production and application of these devices. Another argument is to mention the ambivalence of the term "constructive", especially in connection with another use of that term in engineering (cognitive) and humanities (normative), and to make use of that ambivalence. The verb means for the former ones an activity to build an artefact and for the latter ones an activity to perform in a problem-solving manner. Against the background of the two sides of this distinction grows the chance to argue that the intention of my introduction of the term "constructive" (especially as used in the propositions of the four general theses) figuratively "lives" from this twofold meaning because the notion not only highlights simultaneously the productive tension between that two poles but brings to expression that the settling and shaping of this tension is essentially what governance of science and technology needs to achieve.

17 Cf., among others, Grunwald 2004, who highlights the "need for reflexivity and learning at the interface between science and society".

that the measure of being-exposed-to-hazards related to the scale of damage on the one hand and the probability of occurrence on the other, is to be seen in correlation with both, either with the (potential) hazards as well as with the (latent) vulnerability.

Something similar is true for the (inter-dependencies of the) bar at the bottom with the denomination "prevention and resilience".[18] In case of prevention the subject is, to limit damages and to reduce the probability of their occurrence, *before* the risks are manifesting themselves as events. In case of resilience the subject is in adverse, to provide assistances and to be able to achieve compensations, *after* the risks in question have realized themselves in events. Whether enough has been done (also with regard to the alternate but interrelated strategies of climate change adaptation, CCA, and disaster risk reduction, DRR) can be judged in both cases only in relation to the potential hazards and the latent vulnerability.[19]

3.3 Second General Thesis and its Explication

Now we are coming to the second general thesis. It says: *The less it succeeds to shape the scientific-technological progress constructively, the more vulnerable becomes modernity!* And that means, more politically spoken: Modernity becomes more vulnerable, the less it succeeds to perform an excellent governance of science and technology.

Betrayed like this it makes no sense any more to claim that modernity quasi automatically becomes more and more exposed to "global risks" that are meant to be essentially "out of control"[20] or to promote the suggestion that it might be sufficient to blame (cf. Douglas/Wildavsky 1988) certain social actors (like industry) or particular social activities (like technology). Instead, this view recommends to recognize the apparent problems as outcomes emerging from inher-

---

18 For the original context of resilience cf. Holling 1973, 1994; in contrast to Morone/Woodhouse 1986 I prefer to take prevention and resilience as complementary strategies instead of oppositional alternatives.

19 For a more elaborated and proven concept cf. the BBC-model (from Janos Bogardi, Jörn Birkmann and Omar Cardona) as described in Birkmann/Wisner 2006, especially p. 22 and fig. 8. That model also links vulnerability explicitly to three spheres of sustainability, instead of four, like in my approach, which nevertheless has come to coinciding findings despite its independent development. The BBC-model is based on theoretical considerations, i.e. how social, economical and environmental dimensions of human security can be integrated with existing hazard and risk concepts. It follows the paradigm shift from a hazard-orientated research towards integrative risk reduction perspective as discussed by Bogardi/Birkmann 2004; for a resume cf. Birkmann 2006.

20 Cf. Winner 1977, for the ancient "technics out of control"-theme that seems to be an "evergreen" of political thought.

ent qualities of modern societies that are deeply rooted in their genesis, dispersed over the whole societal system and embracing either its material as well as its mental infrastructure[21]. Evoking an image where modernity is inevitably drifting into some kind of terminal catastrophe is not only a doubtful legitimization of the widespread feeling of living within a "State of Fear" (Crichton 2004) but draws attention away, energies and resources from still existing opportunities to better the situation, to solve the crisis and to redirect development. In contrast, that image involuntarily favors some species of common sense fatalism.

The second general thesis can be explained as follows: The higher the (grade of) sustainability of the four dimensions, the lower their (grade of) vulnerability, and the higher simultaneously is their ability for prevention and resilience, in order to limit occurring damages or impairments in their scale, to reduce them in their probability of taking place or "to get up again", that is to overcome vast consequences and to recover from severe events. In reverse that means: The greater the "non-sustainability", the comparatively more vulnerable, less prevention-capable and resilient is a society. From this follows: All that we are doing – particularly with the instruments of technology assessment and the more general governance actions – in order to utilize the techno-scientific knowledge "constructively", in order to design techno-industrial systems favorably with regard to their consequences for the sustainability of the four dimensions, is a contribution to reduce the vulnerability of society and to increase simultaneously its faculties for prevention and resilience. In reverse it is valid, unfortunately, that modernity becomes the more vulnerable, the less it succeeds, to do exactly this.

For the illustration of these theses serves the notice, that a decentralized system of supplying electric power with regenerative energies is more favorable with regard to some dimensions of sustainability than a few major mega-power-plants with overland transmission lines. Moreover, the decentralized system is more resilient, could therefore be repaired after catastrophes faster and with simpler means, while in reverse the mega-power-plants (above all naturally that of nuclear type) could be a much more worthwhile target for terror actions, than, for instance, a wind energy park.[22]

---

21 One of the characteristics of that mental infrastructure most important here are the open horizons of uncertainties that are – for better or for worse – accompanying the wide space for individual self-realization, experimental endeavors, creative explorations and free entrepreneurship that was opened up in modern societies; cf. Giddens 1990.

22 Cf. also the recommendations of Perrow, who emphasized that "instead of focusing on preventing disasters and coping with their aftermath – which we must continue to do – we should *reduce the size of vulnerable targets.*" (Perrow 2007, p. 1, emphasis in the original)

After we have so far examined the shaping problem (of the scientific-technological progress) so to say "from inside" (Chapter 2) and "from outside" (Chapter 3), it should now be tackled (in Chapter 4) in relation to the guiding model of "sustainability".

4 Sustainable Development

4.1 Conventional Model of Wealth and Essentials of SD

Sustainable Development (SD) is no "utopian" vision – it is a "pragmatic" concept. SD offends nobody, can be proclaimed everywhere, and establishes, however, a tension arch that is distinct enough in order to be able to re-direct on-going practice.

Departing from the 1987 published results of the "World Commission for Environment and Development" (also well-known as "Brundtland-Report") we can observe in politics, economy, science and the public that there is a spreading and growing insight, that the conventional model of growth and prosperity of the "western hemisphere"[23] could neither be temporally prolonged forever, not even for some centuries, nor could it be spatially expanded for all, that is, for the whole planet. It hurts either on the input- as on the output-side upon limitations, in the form of reclining resources (that get increasingly expensive) and the finite or exhausted charging capacities of ecological systems (cf. WCED 1987).

"Sustainable Development", the new paradigm suggested by the commission, aims consequently at guaranteeing the economic development ability forever (leastwise virtually), by coupling it with the moment of the preservation of the ecological environment and its usability.[24] The question "how" both moments could be combined with each other in order to achieve exactly this in practice, does not answer the guiding model, however.

4.2 Third General Thesis and its Explication

Thereby we are moving to the third general thesis. It says: *The re-direction of a system that is developing non-sustainably is the need of the constructive shaping of the scientific-technological progress!* And more politically spoken that means:

23 This model has been for long the paradigm for the efforts of developing and threshold countries because it raises the suggestive idea, that it might be sufficient to copy its instructions in order to realize the same successful strategy of creating common wealth by forced industrialization within a scenario of a catch-up modernization of their economies and administrations.

24 Nevertheless, there do exist some diverging interpretations of this very idea that are often distinguished as "strong" or "weak" sustainability; cf., e.g., Neumayer 2003.

The governance of science and technology is of crucial importance for entering a future-capable and durable pathway of societal (or even civilizational) development.

Figure 3: Sustainable Development and Problems of Governance

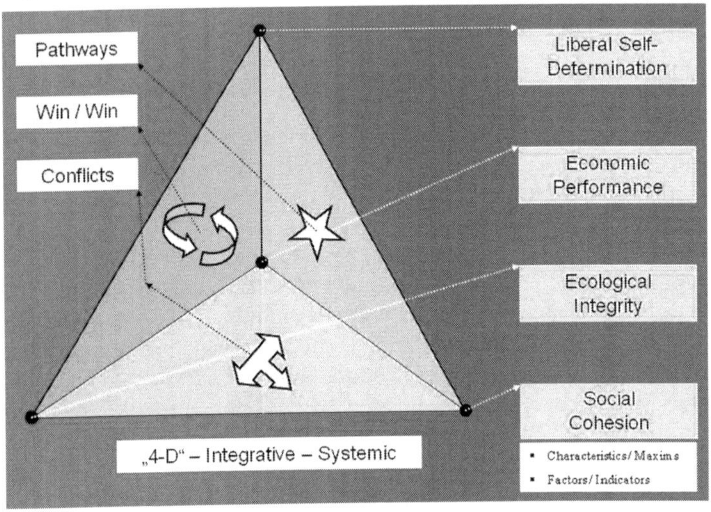

Author's archive

Essentially, as illustrated in Figure 3, the third general thesis can be explained as follows: The guiding model "sustainable development" unfolds its very sense of promoting some "future-capable" "development" under no circumstances in some "only" environment-related interpretation (aiming at its "protection") or in some interpretation that is „only" related to social affairs (interested in questions of the "distribution of wealth"[25]), but with rather (1.) multi-dimensional, (2.) integrative and (3.) systemic understanding (cf., e.g., Grunwald 2005; Grunwald et al 2001; Kopfmüller et al. 2001), that is by using a concept that

(1) takes equally serious environmental, economic, socio-cultural and political-institutional problem clusters and requests;
(2) does not comprehend the optimization of the common welfare as some kind of zero-sum game of (more or less) justified distributions of the produced prosperity, but instead as some kind of positive-sum game, in which variant contributions are to be accumulated dynamically, without one target of optimization being ignored or neglected in favor of any other one;

25 For some review of the concept of social sustainability cf. Littig/Grießler 2005.

(3) must be suitable for the purpose, not only to register interactions and target conflicts between the dimensions, but to analyze them with a view to possible win/win-constellations, positive synergies und dynamically stabilizing pathways of development.

Such a concept becomes all the more necessary as it is a matter of fact that "if all goes on like always", the delicious "cake" of wealth will not remain equally great but must shrink. That is like that, because our society represents a system whose steady state is that of accelerating "non-sustainable" processes of development.[26] "To redirect" this system is nevertheless possible, above all by using the means of shaping the scientific-technological progress (for example with help of combined efficiency-, sufficiency- and consistency-strategies; cf. Huber 2000; Walz/Kuhlmann 2005) – but there is no way that would allow simply "stopping" it.

Sustainable development, in terms of its dependency on knowledge and communication, consequently involves many requirements, because it is considerably more demanding than any non-sustainable path of progression. The reasons for this are, among other things:

(1) Systematically optimising societal use, i.e. including social and ecological "costs" of the budgeting in the calculations and decision-making processes of the particular economic units and social actors instead of selectively maximising it, requires greater scientific and technical knowledge, but, above all, also considerably more contextual knowledge, and more intensive and extensive information, communication and negotiation processes between a growing number of units and actors taking part or affected.
(2) Finding solutions for social problems that do justice to the complete set of the diverse rules of sustainable development (as represented e. g. in the "Integrative Approach" of the "Hermann von Helmholtz Community of German Research Centres"[27]) and consider all dimensions of sustainability in terms of their individual characteristics and peculiarities, is a highly coordinated process, which, for its part, demands in each case for one's own knowledge that it should be considered, communicated and put to the most diverse tests to the same extent as that of other social actors.
(3) The depth of intervention and consequence effectiveness of industrial activities in the structure and processes of nature grown out of industrial-tech-

26 According to the assessment of lots of experts, we are actually doing nothing more than reducing the acceleration and are far from becoming slower or to reach the turning-point where processes of sustainable development would be generally supported by the momentum of the whole system.

27 Cf. Kopfmüller et al. 2001, where this integrative approach is formulated.

nological development is only the other side of the coin; the change in form of ecological consequences finds its equivalent in the social consequences; for these, too, the temporal and spatial expansion, shift and change in emphasizing consequences of decisions is characteristic, as well as the confused, uncertain scattering of probabilities and risks; to comply with this development, to assess it and to even be able to properly regulate it, demands a corresponding intensification and acceleration of the acquisition of knowledge and its communicative distribution and imparting.

(4) Innovation cycles, as for instance the one of coal and steel, of electric engines, of petrochemical processes, etc., or that of ICT, BGT and MNT (as introduced in Section 2.4) were and are leading to far-reaching modifications of the metabolism with nature, and they were and are leading to revolutions of the economical production structures of industrial societies. These social-ecological transformation processes are characterized by modified models of stress upon environmental goods and services as well as altered clusters of use competitions and shifting distribution conflicts about them. Due to the increasing science and knowledge dependency of technological-industrial innovations, also the conditions of the possibility for the identification and regulation of their social and ecological results become increasingly knowledge-dependent.

Having considered the question of the *"how"* of the shaping of the scientific-technological progress in three different respects, (in Section 2) departing from the options and consequences, that progress produces itself, (in Section 3) by means of the requirements, that are produced by the complex vulnerability of modern society, and (in the just finished Section 4) with regard to its suitability for implementing the alternate course of sustainable development, we are coming now (in Section 5) finally to speak about the „instruments“, that are supposed to help deal with the problem of *"how"* it might be possible to shape science and technology as best as possible, namely the more general governance approach in connection with a more particular concept of technology assessment.

5 Improving Governance by Integrative Technology Assessment

Essentially the task of *governing*[28] and doing the *governance* of global risks is for a notable part identical with that of governing or organizing the governance

28 The most significant difference between both of them is, that governance includes the participation of citizens also in decision-making processes whereas governing, that is the performance of political authorities, is dependent on citizens participation in the representative way only; cf. also the common difference between politics and policy; more characteristics are discussed by Türke 2008.

of science and technology (cf., among others, Petschow et al. 2005; Renn 2008; Renn/Walker 2008; Voss et al. 2006). This argument is reasonable, because the latter one constitutes the most important factor in order to influence the whole process of societal shaping of the techno-industrial progress – including the consequences, uncertainties and risks that are accompanying and following this development – in an active and intentional way according to principles like, e.g., the one of sustainable development.

Regarding the elements for shaping the outcomes of science and technology there are, in general, two indispensible kinds of action: (1.) forecasting developments, and (2.) evaluation of choices. Both are of crucial importance for the enhancement of decision-making procedures, and that is, on its part, a precondition for shaping the scientific-technological progress effectively (cf. Funtowicz/Ravetz 1992; Rosa 1988). In order to do so, we have to ask either for the expertise of academics and professionals (top down) because of the considerable (and still growing) knowledge-dependency, as well as for the participation of citizens (bottom up) because of the diversity of value-orientations.[29]

The importance of technology assessment as a requirement for a successful governance of science and technology is more than evident, especially whilst taking into account the accelerating speed of the techno-scientific development. Consequently the on-going work of technology assessment needs to have approaches, concepts and models that should be getting more powerful together with the expanding tasks TA is confronted with (cf. Grunwald 2010). Therefore, I would like to introduce finally a framework concept that tries to take into account all the factors tackled so far.

5.1 Guidelines for an Integrated TA

Under "Integrative Technology Assessment" (ITA) I understand basically, that the dimensions of the environmental, economic, socio-cultural and political-institutional conditions and consequences of technologies are dealt with systematically, and in connection with some four-dimensional, integrative and systemic concept of sustainable development, which, as an analytically enriched "civilizational guiding-model", provides an excellent framework for differentiating and balancing and therefore well-justified evaluation of "options for progress" (at least in so far as they are mediated by science and technology).[30]

---

29 As a consequence of the overlapping processes of globalization and individualization we also face growing multiplicity in cultural orientations, value-judgments and ethical preferences; cf. the implications of "networked individualism" as described by Manuel Castells (cf. Castells 2001; cf. also Bora/Hausendorf 2006; Ladikas 2009).

30 Understanding the complexity of different systems as well as analyzing the interactions between them (cf., e.g., Holling 2001) is, in this sense, a precondition for gaining the

ITA, as presented here, is only a framework concept that tries to offer inspiring heuristics, not an operative model that gives precise methodological prescriptions of how to carry out TA procedures and investigations.[31] From its design it is predestined to approach the ability to embrace different TA-models, which for their part prescribe different modes of how to realize the work to be done methodologically correct and effective. The objective of its proposal is therefore nothing more – but also nothing less – than to contribute to the expanding discourse on the conceptual foundations of TA.

In order to prevent misunderstandings: If sustainability is constitutive for a concept of ITA, then this requires dealing with all four dimensions of sustainable development with equal attention ... in the framework concept (!) – but not in every single project. If therefore in some project, for instance, the focus is on investigating "electronic governance", then, obviously, political-institutional issues are standing in the foreground. The advantage of such a framework concept is, to be prepared for reacting in a flexible but competent way on particular calls for project funding and emerging demands for investigating issues that are on the ever-changing public agenda, without having to refrain from processing the results of various projects also synthetically, in order to build up one's own theoretical, methodological and professional capacities for the acquisition and elaboration of further projects "step by step".

ITA, a "holistic" concept, requires more than an expansion of a multitude of single research areas. ITA cannot thrive by doing science studies or innovation research (that is by analyzing probable or desirable innovations with the intention of paving the way for the realization of economic benefits by their promotion). In order to fulfill its cross-sectional task, TA must – even for complexity reasons (cf. Bechmann et al. 2007) – transcend an understanding of its subject that is "only" oriented to economics and the social sciences. TA can moreover not achieve its ends simply by "co-opting" natural scientists' and engineering competencies. Instead, the decisive point is, from an inter- and transdisciplinary comprehension (cf. Decker/Grunwald 2001; Gallopín et al. 2001), the possibility to depart from different disciplinary backgrounds and similarly developed professional competencies in order to analyze and assess the *heterogenous* conditions, consequences, and choices of technology, and to enhance these working perspectives (or strategies of knowledge elaboration and capacity building) mutually within a common framework for problem-driven investigation. Integrative TA is therefore extraordinarily dependent on teamwork.

---

abilities that are necessary in order to navigate successfully towards sustainable development (cf., e.g., Hjorth/Bagheri 2006).

31 For some similar endeavor cf. Liebert/Schmidt 2010; a well thought-out idea of how to direct our attention comes from Decker/Fleischer 2010; cf. also Schot/Rip 1997.

In the purview of ITA the central task is:

(1) to *combine competencies,* namely above all those of the various sciences, and, moreover, those of professionals from several fields of practice, and those of citizens or so-called lay-persons;
(2) to *process problems* departing from the changing perspectives of science, economy, politics and the public; and
(3) to *provide solutions,* approaches and criteria, in order to advise societal actors (both in politics and policy).

Not least comes into play, however, a function that matters concerning the sciences themselves: namely *to achieve a contribution to their consolidation.* This is all the more important as any TA institution, be it an academy of science or university, a (public) research centre or (private) enterprise, must have a *vital* interest in its own consolidation, as well to its outside, in front of the public, the economy, and the politics, as to its inside, in the relationship of its scientific disciplines and its particular institutes or working-units.

For ITA the research field of the "new" "key technologies" is of utmost importance, because they are particularly aligned to or generally associated with considerable expectations of growth and progress. Their importance from the viewpoint of a sustainable development of economy and society is thereby not at all to estimate lesser, than under the pre-sign of a conventional course of modernization (cf., among others, Fleischer et al. 2001).

An important element of integrative TA is to identify and localize possible targeting-conflicts that should be resolved or settled, and probable win/win-constellations that should be promoted because they are promising some concrete "added value". An example of this, that simultaneously makes us recognize the often conflict-laden character of the requests that TA becomes more and more confronted with in the field of the "new" key technologies, is the opportunity to substitute processes of the chemical synthesis of substances by bio-technological procedures (cf. Willke/Vorlop 2004). Following the economic principle of "creative destruction" thereby comes under pressure an "older" industrial branch – including its jobs – for the benefit of a "younger" one that is promising more prosperity (cf. Reinert/Reinert 2006). Considered ecologically, these procedures are offering ambivalent opportunities. On the one side, they indeed do have potentials for *ameliorating the charge* of the environment, either regarding the side of their input (referring to the grade of making use of energetic and material resources), and also concerning the side of their output (with regard to the possible reduction in the release of environmental chemicals and mass pollutants). On the other side are to register, however, the *risks* and uncertainties of the release of bio-active substances and trans-geneous organisms.

ITA offers no panacea. It can process, however, highly complex problem bundles, whose judgment – as just shown – is normally leading to complications in an organized and differentiating manner, that is refined according to the distinct purposes of decision-making.[32]

5.2 Fourth General Thesis, and its Explication

Thereby we are coming to the fourth, concluding, general thesis. It says: *In order to master the challenges, (the shaping of) science and technology becomes confronted with by the present problems, it is essential to make use of a framework concept like ITA!*

And traduced into a more political language, that is to say that the governance of science and technology could not be done sufficiently well without approaches that allow for overview and orientation. The task of regulating and optimizing the techno-scientific and (post-)industrial development that is currently creating the options of the shape and configuration of our societal and environmental future cannot be achieved successfully while performing no more than some kind of "muddling through"-strategy.[33] Because of the need to develop applicable strategies in order to restore and maintain a future-capable pattern of development there does exist a great demand for integrated approaches and wide framework concepts.

The fourth general thesis, as indicated by Figure 4, can be explained as follows: "ITA" is an instructive approach that is meant to be used for opening up the problems of the increasing knowledge and science dependency (I.) of the complex vulnerability of modern societies (II.) and of the practical achievability of sustainable development (III.), in order to structure, as optimal as possible, the preparation, realization and reworking of TA-projects and -procedures aiming at informing not only governing bodies and affiliated parties but all kinds of social actors (including NGOs) that participate in governance activities.

32 Another requisite to foster "sustainable" decision-making procedures is strengthening foresight and scenario approaches especially with reference to the mentioned problem of growing uncertainties; cf., among others, Guimaraes Pereira et al. 2007; Newman 2006; Stirling 2006.

33 With reference to the further implications of the "muddling through"-strategy it should be said that "incrementalism", as the underlying political steering idea this strategy is based upon, is endangering the realization of long-term goals because of its prevalence for giving attention to short-term goals.

Figure 4: Integrated Technology Assessment and its Challenges

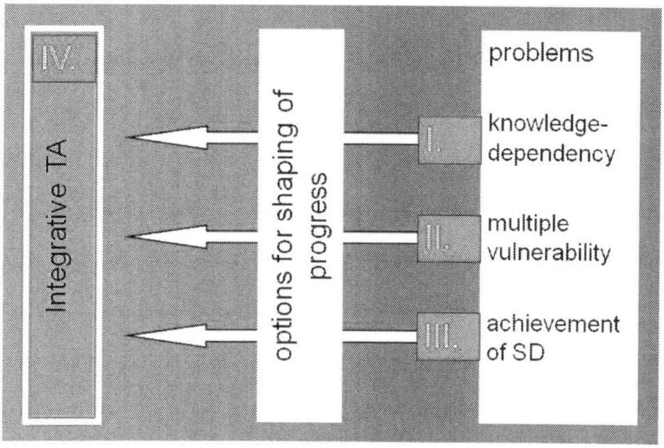

Author's archive

A little more detailed, these three points indicate the following claims:

(I) ITA provides for both, for an analytical separation of the shaping conditions and implementation consequences of the scientific-technological progress (with reference to economic, ecological, socio-cultural and political-institutional interdependencies), as well as for the synthesis of the investigation results (with regard to key technologies, innovation cycles and industrial society transformations).

(II) ITA provides for the opening up of questions of the shaping of the scientific-technological progress in the interrelationship of hazards, vulnerability, risks, prevention and resilience, problem-sensitive and solution-oriented: ... on the micro-level of single humans or households that could be affected, on the meso-level of single communities, companies, social systems as well as on the macro-level of complete societies.

(III) ITA provides for (re)directing innovation processes to the resolution or settling of target conflicts, to the utilization of win-win-constellations and to walking along stable pathways of progressive development.

6 Outlook

With the new millennium we face tremendous challenges. Limited actions like governance of science and technology in general, and technology assessment in particular, are hardly *sufficient* in order to master them – but it is, however, *necessary* to contribute all that they *can do,* in order to provide for some constructive shaping of scientific-technological progress. I would like to close therefore with a saying of Antoine de St. Exupéry: "One must require from everyone what he could achieve!"

References

Abramovitz, J.; Starke, L. (eds.) (2001): Unnatural Disasters. Washington/D.C. (Worldwatch Institute)

Adriaanse, A.; Bringezu, St.; Hammond, A.; Moriguchi, Y.; Rodenburg, E.; Rogich, D.; Schütz, H. (1997): Resource Flows. The Material Basis of Industrial Economies. Washington/D.C. (World Resource Institute)

Ayres, R. U.; Simonis, U. E. (eds.) (1992): Industrial Metabolism. Restructuring for Sustainable Development. Tokyo a.o.

Baker, S. (2000): The European Union. Integration, Competition, Growth – and Sustainability. In: Lafferty, W. M.; Meadowcroft, J. (eds.): Implementing Sustainable Development. Strategies and Initiatives in High Consumption Societies. Oxford, pp. 303–336

Banse, G.; Metzner-Szigeth, A. (2012): Cultural Diversity and New Media – their Interaction as an Element of European Integration. Elaborating an European Research Network. In: Rothkegel, A.; Ruda, S. (eds.): Communication on and via Technology. Berlin (in print)

Barletta, W. A. (2010): Cyberwar or Cyber-Terrorism. The Attack on Estonia. In: Westby, J. R.; Wegener, H.; Barletta, W. (eds.): Rights and Responsibilities in Cyberspace. Balancing the Need for Security and Liberty. New York: East West Institute/Geneva: World Federation of Scientists, pp. 11–15 (URL: http://www.ewi.info/system/files/Rights_and_Responsibilties_Web.pdf)

Barnett, V. (1998): Kondratiev and the Dynamics of Economic Development. London

Barton, J. E.; Dracup, M. (2000): Genetically Modified Crops and the Environment. In: Agronomy Journal, Vol. 92/No. 4, pp. 797–803 (URL: http://dx.doi.org/10.2134/agronj 2000. 924797x)

Bechmann, G.; Decker, M.; Fiedeler, U.; Krings, B.-J. (2007): TA in a Complex World. In: International Journal of Foresight and Innovation Policy, Vol. 3/No. 1, pp. 6–27

Beck, U. (1992): The Risk Society. Towards a New Modernity. London

Beck, U. (1999a): What is Globalization? Cambridge

Beck, U. (1999b): World Risk Society. Cambridge

Beck, U.; Giddens, A.; Lash, S. (1994): Reflexive Modernization. Politics, Tradition and Aesthetics in the Modern Social Order. Cambridge

Becker, E.; Jahn, Th.; Stiess, I. (1999): Exploring Uncommon Ground. Sustainability and the Social Sciences. In: Becker, E.; Jahn, Th. (eds.): Sustainability and the Social Sciences. A Cross-Disciplinary Approach Integrating Environmental Considerations into Theoretical Reorientation. London, pp. 1–22

Becker, E.; Jahn, Th.; Schramm, E.; Hummel, D.; Stiess, I. (2000): Social-Ecological Research. Conceptual Framework for a New Funding Policy (Synopsis of the Report for the German Federal Ministry of Education and Research). Frankfurt/M. (ISOE)

Beer, T.; Ismail-Zadeh, A. (eds.) (2003): Risk Science and Sustainability. Science for Reduction of Risk and Sustainable Development of Society. Dordrecht a.o.

Berting, J. (2006): Europe: a Heritage, a Challenge, a Promise. Delft

Bijker, W. E. (2006): The Vulnerability of Technological Culture. In: Nowotny, H. (ed.): Cultures of Technology and the Quest for Innovation. New York, pp. 52–69 (URL: http://arno.unimaas.nl/show.cgi?fid=14863)

Bijker, W. E.; Hughes, T. P.; Pinch, T. J. (eds.) (1987): The Social Construction of Technological Systems. New Directions in the Sociology and History of Technology. Cambridge/MA, London

Birkmann, J. (2006): Measuring Vulnerability to Promote Disaster-resilient Societies. Conceptual Frameworks and Definitions. In: Birkmann, J. (2006): Measuring Vulnerability to Natural Hazards. Towards Disaster Resilient Societies. New Delhi, pp. 9–54

Birkmann, J.; Wisner, B. (2006): Measuring the Un-Measurable. The Challenge of Vulnerability. Bonn (URL: http://www.ehs.unu.edu/file/get/3962)

Bogardi, J.; Birkmann, J. (2004): Vulnerability Assessment. The First Step Towards Sustainable Risk Reduction. In: Malzahn, D.; Plapp, T. (eds.): Disasters and Society. From Hazard Assessment to Risk Reduction. Berlin, pp. 75–82

Bora, A.; Hausendorf, H. (2006): Participatory Science Governance Revisited. Normative Expectations Versus Empirical Evidence. In: Science and Public Policy, Vol. 33/No. 7, pp. 478–488

Bresnahana, T. F.; Trajtenberg, M. (1995): General Purpose Technologies “Engines of growth”? In: Journal of Econometrics, Vol. 65/No. 1 (January), pp. 83–108 (URL: http://dx.doi.org/10.1016/0304-4076(94)01598-T)

Cassier, M. (2002): Private Property, Collective Property, and Public Property in the Age of Genomics. In: International Social Science Journal, Vol. 171, pp. 83–98

Castells, M. (1996): The Information Age: Economy, Society and Culture. Vol. I: The Rise of the Network Society. Malden, Oxford

Castells, M. (2001): The Internet Galaxy. Reflections on the Internet, Business, and Society. Oxford

Casti, J. L. (1994): Complexification. New York

Chambers, R. (1989): Editorial Introduction: Vulnerability, Coping and Policy. In: IDS Bulletin, Vol. 20/No. 2, pp.1–7

Crichton, M. (2004): State of Fear. London

David, P. A. (2001): Tragedy of the Public Knowledge “Commons”? Global Science, Intellectual Property and the Digital Technology Boomerang. In: Research Memoranda, Maastricht Economic Research Institute on Innovation and Technology – MERIT (URL: http://edocs.ub.unimaas.nl/loader/file.asp?id=208)

Decker, Michael (ed.) (2001): Interdisciplinarity in Technology Assessment. Implementation and its Chances and Limits. Berlin

Decker, M.; Fleischer, Th. (2010): When Should there be which Kind of Technology Assessment? A Plea for a Strictly Problem-oriented Approach from the Very Outset. In: Poiesis & Praxis. International Journal of Technology Assessment and Ethics of Science, No. 7, pp. 117–133

Decker, M.; Grunwald, A. (2001): Rational Technology Assessment as Interdisciplinary Research. In: Decker, M. (ed.): Interdisciplinarity in Technology Assessment. Implementation and its Chances and Limits. Berlin a.o., pp. 33–60

Douglas, M.; Wildavsky, A. (1988): Risk and Culture (2nd ed.). Berkley/CA a.o.

ETAG – European Technology Assessment Group (2006): Technology Assessment on Converging Technologies. Brussels (European Parliament)

Fakete, A. (2010): Assessment of Social Vulnerability for River-Floods in Germany. Bonn: University (Doctoral Thesis) (URL: http://hss.ulb.uni-bonn.de:90/2010/2004/2004.pdf)

Fischer-Kowalski, M. (1997): Society's Metabolism. On the Childhood and Adolescence of a Rising Conceptual Star. In: Redclift, M.; Woodgate, G. (eds.): The International Handbook of Environmental Sociology. Cheltenham, pp. 119–137

Fischer-Kowalski, M.; Haberl, H. (1993): Metabolism and Colonisation. Modes of Production and the Physical Exchange between Societies and Nature. In: Innovation in Social Science Research, Vol. 6, pp. 415–442

Fisher, H. W. (1994): Response to Disaster: Fact Versus Fiction and Its Perpetuation. The Sociology of Disaster. Lanham/MD

Fleischer, T.; Fugger, W.-D.; Grunwald, A.; Karger, C.; Poppenborg, A. (2001): Nachhaltigkeitspotenziale von Schlüsseltechnologien. In: Grunwald, A.; Coenen, R.; Nitsch, J.; Sydow, A.; Wiedemann, P. (eds.): Forschungswerkstatt Nachhaltigkeit. Auf dem Weg zur Diagnose und Therapie von Nachhaltigkeitsdefiziten. Berlin, pp. 267–290 (in German)

Freeman, Ch.; Louçã, F. (2001): As Time Goes By. From the Industrial Revolution to the Information Revolution. Oxford

Funtowicz, S. O.; Ravetz, J. R. (1992): Three Types of Risk Assessment and the Emergence of Post-Normal Science. In: Krimsky, Sh.; Golding, D. (eds.): Social Theories of Risk. Westport/CT, London, pp. 251–273

Gallopín, G. C.; Funtowicz, S. O.; O'Connor, M.; Ravetz, J. (2001): Science for the Twenty-First Century: From Social Contract to the Scientific Core. In: International Social Science Journal, Vol. 53/No. 168, pp. 219–229

Giddens, A. (1990) The Consequences of Modernity. Stanford/CA

Giddens, A. (2009): The Politics of Climate Change. Cambridge

Godin, B. (2006): The Linear Model of Innovation. The Historical Construction of an Analytical Frame-work. In: Science, Technology & Human Values, Vol. 31, pp. 639–667

Graham, J.; Amos, B.; Plumptre, T. (2003): Principles for Good Governance in the 21st Century. Policy Brief, No. 15 (Institute on Governance, Ottawa) (URL: http://iog.ca/sites/iog/files/policybrief15_0.pdf)

Grossmann, W. D. (2001): Entwicklungsstrategien in der Informationsgesellschaft. Mensch, Wirtschaft und Umwelt. Berlin a.o. (in German)

Grunwald, A. (2004): Strategic Knowledge for Sustainable Development: The Need for Reflexivity and Learning at the Interface Between Science and Society. In: International Journal for Foresight and Innovation Policy, Vol. 1/No. 1–2, pp. 150–167 (URL: http://dx.doi.org/10.1504/IJFIP.2004.004619)

Grunwald, A. (2005): Rationality in an Uncertain World. The Vision of Sustainable Development as an Adequate Answer? In: Banse, G.; Hronszky, I.; Nelson, G. (eds.): Rationality in an Uncertain World. Berlin, pp. 11–35

Grunwald, A. (2007): Converging Technologies: Visions, Increased Contingencies of the conditio humana, and Search for Orientation. In: Futures, Vol. 39/No. 4, pp. 380–392 (URL: http://dx.doi.org/10.1016/j.futures.2006.08.001)

Grunwald, A. (2010): Technikfolgenabschätzung. Eine Einführung (2nd, completely rev. and ext. ed.). Berlin (in German)

Grunwald, A.; Coenen, R.; Nitsch, J.; Sydow, A.; Wiedemann, P. (eds.) (2001): Forschungswerkstatt Nachhaltigkeit. Auf dem Weg zur Diagnose und Therapie von Nachhaltigkeitsdefiziten. Berlin (in German)

Grunwald, A.; Grin, J. (eds.) (1999): Vision Assessment. Shaping Technology in 21st Century Society. Berlin a.o.

Guimaraes Pereira, A.; Schomberg, R. von; Funtowicz, S. (2007): Foresight Knowledge Assessment. In: International Journal of Foresight and Innovation Policy, Vol. 3/No. 1, pp. 53–27 (URL: http://dx.doi.org/10.1504/IJFIP.2007.011421)

Haberl, H.; Fischer-Kowalski, M.; Krausmann, F.; Weisz, H.; Winiwarter, V. (2004): Progress Towards Sustainability? What the Conceptual Framework of Material and Energy Flow Accounting (MEFA) Can Offer. In: Land Use Policy, Vol. 21/No. 3 (July), pp. 199–213 (URL: http://dx.doi.org/10.1016/j.landusepol.2003.10.013)

Held, D. (ed.) (2000): A Globalizing World? Culture, Economics, Politics. London

Heng, Y.-K.; McDonagh, K. (2009): Risk, Global Governance and Security. The Other War on Terror. Milton Park

Hinterberger, F.; Luks, F.; Schmidt-Bleek, F. (1997): Material Flows vs. "Natural Capital". What Makes an Economy Sustainable? In: Ecological Economics, Vol. 23/No. 1, pp. 1–14

Hjorth, P.; Bagheri, A. (2006): Navigating Towards Sustainable Development. A System Dynamics Approach. In: Futures, Vol. 38/No. 1, pp. 74–92 (URL: http://dx.doi.org/10.1016/j.futures.2005.04.005)

Hodgson, G. M. (2000): Socio-economic Consequences of the Advance of Complexity and Knowledge. In: OECD – Organisation for Economic Co-operation and Development (ed.) (2000): The Creative Society of the 21st Century. Paris (OECD), pp. 89–112

Holling, Crawford Stanley (1973): Resilience and Stability of Ecological Systems. In: Annual Review of Ecology and Systematics, Vol. 4, pp. 1–23

Holling, C. St. (1994): Simplifying the Complex. The Paradigms of Ecological Function and Structure. In: Futures, Vol. 26/No. 6, pp. 598-609

Holling, C. St. (2001): Understanding the Complexity of Economic, Ecological, and Social Systems. In: Ecosystems, Vol. 4/No. 5, pp. 390–405

Huber, J. (2000): Towards Industrial Ecology. Sustainable Development as a Concept of Ecological Modernization. In: Andersen, M.; Massa, I. (eds.): Ecological Modernization. Journal of Environmental Policy and Planning, Special Issue 2, pp. 269–285

IPCC – Intergovernmental Panel on Climate Change (2007): Climate Change 2007. Synthesis Report. Contribution of Working Groups I, II and III to the 4th Assessment Report of the Intergovernmental Panel on Climate Change (Core Writing Team, Pachauri, R. K.; Reisinger, A. eds.). Geneva: IPCC (URL: http://www.ipcc.ch/pdf/assessment-report/ar4/syr/ar4_syr.pdf)

Jaeger, C. C. (1994): Taming the Dragon. Transforming Economic Institutions in the Face of Global Change. Amsterdam, Singapore

Jaeger, C. C. (1998): Risk Management and Integrated Assessment. In: Environmental Modeling and Assessment, Vol. 3/No. 4, pp. 211–225

Joerges, B. (1996): Large Technical Systems and the Discourse of Complexity. In: Ingelstam, L. (ed.): Complex Technical Systems. Stockholm (Swedish Council for Planning and Coordination of Research), pp. 55–72

Johnston, P. (ed.) (2002): Visions and Roadmaps for Sustainable Development in a Networked Knowledge Society. Report of a Workshop Co-chaired by the Presidents of the Brussels EU-Chapter of the Club of Rome and the "Factor 10 Institute". Brussels: European Commission, DG – Information Society Technologies (URL: http://www.clubofrome.at/cor-eu/archive/dl_seminar.pdf)

Kleine, A. (2009): Operationalisierung einer Nachhaltigkeitsstrategie. Ökologie, Ökonomie und Soziales Integrieren. Wiesbaden (in German)

Klinke, A.; Renn, O. (2002): A New Approach to Risk-Evaluation and Management. Risk-Based, Precaution-Based, and Discourse-Based Strategies. In: Risk Analysis, Vol. 22/No. 6, pp. 1071–1094 (URL: http://directory.cip.management.dal.ca/publications/A%20new%20approach%20to%20risk%20evaluation%20and%20management.pdf)

Kondratieff, N. D. (1926): Die langen Wellen der Konjunktur. In: Archiv für Sozialwissenschaft und Sozialpolitik, Vol. 56, pp. 573–609 (in German)

Kopfmüller, J.; Brandl, V.; Jörissen, J.; Paetau, M.; Banse, G.; Coenen, R.; Grunwald, A. (2001): Nachhaltige Entwicklung integrativ betrachtet. Konstitutive Elemente, Regeln, Indikatoren. Berlin (in German)

Ladikas, M. (ed.) (2009): Embedding Society in Science & Technology Policy. European and Chinese perspectives. Luxembourg: Office for Official Publications of the European Communities (URL: http://ec.europa.eu/research/science-society/document_library/pdf_06/european-and-chinese-perspectives_en.pdf)

Lash, S.; Szerszinsky, B.; Wynne, B. (1996): Risk, Environment and Modernity. Towards a New Ecology. London

Liberatore, Angela (1998): The Management of Uncertainty – Learning from Chernobyl. Amsterdam, Singapore

Liberatore, A.; Funtowicz, S. (eds.) (2003): Democratising Expertise, Expertising Democracy. In: Science and Public Policy, Special Issue, 30 (2), June

Liebert, W.; Schmidt, J. C. (2010): Towards a Prospective Technology Assessment. Challenges and Requirements for Technology Assessment in the Age of Technoscience. In: Poiesis & Praxis. International Journal of Technology Assessment and Ethics of Science, Vol. 7/No. 1–2, pp. 99–116 (URL: http://dx.doi.org/10.1007/s10202-010-0079-1)

Lindblom, Ch. E. (1959): The Science of "Muddling Through". In: Public Administration Review, Vol. 19, pp. 79–88

Lindblom, Ch. E. (1979): Still Muddling, Not yet through. In: Public Administration Review, Vol. 39, pp. 517–526

Littig, B.; Grießler, E. (2005): Social Sustainability. A Catchword between Political Pragmatism and Social Theory. In: International Journal of Sustainable Development, Vol. 8/No. 1–2, pp. 65–79

Lubbers, R.; Koorevaar, J. (2000): Primary Globalisation, Secondary Globalisation, and the Sustainable Development Paradigm. Opposing Forces in the 21st Century. In: OECD –

Organisation for Economic Co-operation and Development (ed.): The Creative Society of the 21st Century. Paris (OECD), pp. 173–190

Luhmann, N. (1989): Ecological Communication. Chicago

Mappus, St. (ed.) (2005): Erde 2.0. Technologische Innovationen als Chance für eine nachhaltige Entwicklung. Heidelberg a.o. (in German)

Masera, M. (2005): Systemic Challenges for Critical Information Infrastructure Protection. In: Kowalik, J. S.; Górski, J.; Sachenko, A. (eds.): Cyberspace Security and Defense. Research Issues. Dordrecht a.o., pp. 57–74

Masera, M.; Gheorghe, A.; Weijnen, M.; Vries, L. de (2006): Critical Infrastructures at Risk. Securing the European Electric Power System. Dordrecht a.o.

Mayhew, A. (2000): Review of Karl Polanyi "The great transformation. The Political and Economic Origins of Our Time". In: EH.Net Economic History Services, June 1 (URL: http://eh.net/bookreviews/library/polanyi)

Metzner, A. (1993): Probleme sozio-ökologischer Systemtheorie. Natur und Gesellschaft in der Soziologie Luhmanns. Opladen (URL: http://sammelpunkt.philo.at:8080/1812/) (in German)

Metzner, A. (1998): Constructions of Environmental Issues in Scientific and Public Discourse. In: Müller, F.; Leupelt, M. (eds.): Eco Targets, Goal Functions and Orientors. Berlin a.o., pp. 312–333

Metzner, A. (2002): Die Tücken der Objekte. Über die Risiken der Gesellschaft und ihre Wirklichkeit. Frankfurt/M., New York (in German)

Metzner-Szigeth, A. (2009): Contradictory Approaches? On Realism and Constructivism in the Social Sciences Research on Risk, Technology and the Environment. In: Futures, Vol. 41/No. 2 (March), pp. 156–170 (URL: http://dx.doi.org/10.1016/j.futures.2008. 09.017)

Metzner-Szigeth, A. (2010): Kultur & Technik als Medien menschlicher Selbstverwirklichung. Überlegungen zur philosophischen Anthropologie und Gesellschaftstheorie. In: Banse, G.; Grunwald, A. (eds.): Technik und Kultur. Bedingungs- und Beeinflussungsverhältnisse, Karlsruhe, pp. 143–162 (URL: http://www.itas.fzk.de/deu/lit/2010/bagr10a.pdf) (in German)

Morone, J. G.; Woodhouse, E. J. (1986): Averting Catastrophe. Strategies for Regulating Risky Technologies. Berkeley/CA

Neumayer, E. (2003): Weak versus Strong Sustainability. Exploring the Limits of Two Opposing Paradigms. Northampton/MA

Newman, L. (2006): Change, Uncertainty, and Futures of Sustainable Development. In: Futures, Vol. 38/No. 5, pp. 633–637 (URL: http://dx.doi.org/10.1016/j.futures.2005.09.011)

Nordmann, A. (2004): Converging Technologies. Shaping the Future of European Societies (Report of the High Level Expert Group "Foresighting the New Technology Wave"). Brussels (European Communities)

Nowotny, H.; Scott, P.; Gibbons, M. (2001): Re-Thinking Science. Knowledge and the Public in an Age of Uncertainty. London

OECD – Organisation for Economic Co-operation and Development (2003): Emerging Risks in the 21st Century. An Agenda for Action. Paris: OECD (URL: http://www.oecd.org/dataoecd/20/23/37944611.pdf)

Orwat, C.; Grunwald, A. (2005): Informations- und Kommunikationstechnologien und nachhaltige Entwicklung. In: Mappus, St. (ed.) (2005): Erde 2.0. Technologische Innovationen als Chance für eine nachhaltige Entwicklung? Berlin a.o., pp. 242–273 (in German)

Perrow, Ch. (1984): Normal Accidents. Living with High-Risk Technologies. New York

Perrow, Ch. (2007): The Next Catastrophe. Reducing Our Vulnerabilities to Natural, Industrial, and Terrorist Disasters. New Jersey

Petschow, U.; Rosenau, J.; von Weizsäcker, E.-U. (eds.) (2005): Governance and Sustainability. Sheffield

Pidgeon, N.; O'Leary, M. (2000): Man-made Disasters. Why Technology and Organizations (Sometimes) Fail. In: Safety Science, Vol. 34, pp. 15–30 (URL: http://dx.doi.org/10.1016/S0925-7535(00)00004-7)

Pinch, T. J. (1991): How Do We Treat Technical Uncertainty in Systems Failure? The Case of the Space Shuttle Challenger. In: La Porte, T. R. (ed.): Social Responses to Large Technical Systems. Control or Anticipation. Dordrecht, pp. 143–158

Polanyi, K. (1944): The Great Transformation. The Political and Economic Origins of Our Time. Boston (2nd ed. 1957)

Reinert, H.; Reinert, E. S. (2006): Creative Destruction in Economics: Nietzsche, Sombart, Schumpeter. In: Backhaus, J.; Drechsler, W. (eds.): Friedrich Nietzsche 1844–2000. Boston, pp. 55–85

Renn, O. (2008): Risk Governance. Coping with Uncertainty in a Complex World. London

Renn, O.; Keil, F. (2008): Systemische Risiken. Versuch einer Charakterisierung. In: GAIA, Vol. 17/No. 4, pp. 349–354

Renn, O.; Walker, K. D. (eds.) (2008): Global Risk Governance. Concept and Practice Using the IRGC Framework. Dordrecht

Rissler, J.; Mellon, M. (1996): The Ecological Risks of Engineered Crops. Cambridge/MA

Robertson, R. (1995): Glocalization: Time-Space and Homogeneity-Heterogeneity. In: Featherstone, M.; Lash, S.; Robertson, R. (eds.): Global Modernities. London, pp. 25–44

Roco, M. C.; Bainbridge, W. S. (eds.) (2004): Converging Technologies for Improving Human Performance. Dordrecht

Rosa, E. A. (1988): Metatheoretical Foundations for Post-normal Risk. In: Journal of Risk Research, Vol. 1/No. 1, pp. 15–44

Schiller, F. (2009): Linking Material and Energy Flow Analyses and Social Theory. In: Ecological Economics, Vol. 68, Issue 6 (April 15), pp. 1676–1686 (URL: http://dx.doi.org/10.1016/j.ecolecon.2008.08.017)

Schomberg, R. von (2002): The Objective of Sustainable Development: Are We Coming Closer? Brussels (European Commission, DG Research)

Schot, J.; Rip, A. (1997): The Past and Future of Constructive Technology Assessment. In: Technological Forecasting and Social Change, Vol. 54/No. 2, pp. 251–268 (URL: http://dx.doi.org/10.1016/S0040-1625(96)00180-1)

Solana, J. (2003): A Secure Europe in a Better World. European Security Strategy (Document proposed by the EU High Representative for the Common Foreign and Security Policy and adopted by the Heads of State and Government at the European Council in Brussels on December 12, 2003). Paris: The European Union Institute for Security Studies (URL: http://www.iss.europa.eu/uploads/media/solanae.pdf)

Souza Porto, M. F. de; Freitas, C. M. de (2003): Vulnerability and Industrial Hazards in Industrializing Countries. An Integrative Approach. In: Futures, Vol. 35/No. 7, pp. 717–736 (URL: http://dx.doi.org/10.1016/S0016-3287(03)00024-7)

Spangenberg, J.; Mesicek, R.; Metzner, A.; Luks, F. (2002): Sustainability Indicators for the Knowledge-based Society. Measuring the Sustainability of the Information Society. In: Futura, Vol. 21/No. 2, pp. 85–95 (URL: https://www.doria.fi/handle/10024/22994)

Stehr, N. (1994): Knowledge Societies. London

Stern, N. H. (2007): The Economics of Climate Change. Cambridge

Stirling, A. (2006): Precaution, Foresight and Sustainability. Reflection and Reflexivity in the Governance of Science and Technology. In: Voß, J.-P.; Bauknecht, D.; Kemp, R. (eds.): Reflexive Governance for Sustainable Development. Cheltenham, pp. 225–272

Suh, S. (2005): Theory of Materials and Energy Flow Analysis in Ecology and Economics. In: Ecological Modelling, Vol. 189, Issue 3–4 (December 10), pp. 251–269 (URL: http://dx.doi.org/10.1016/j.ecolmodel.2005.03.011)

Thompson-Klein, J.; Grossenbacher-Mansuy, W.; Häberli, R.; Bill, A.; Scholz, R. W.; Welti, M. (eds.) (2001): Transdisciplinarity: Joint Problem Solving among Science, Technology, and Society. An Effective Way for Managing Complexity. Basel a.o.

Toffler, A. (1980): The Third Wave. New York

Türke, R.-E. (2008): Governance. Systemic Foundation and Framework. Heidelberg

UN – United Nations (2007): Indicators of Sustainable Development. Guidelines and Methodologies (3rd ed.). New York

Voss, J.-P.; Bauknecht, D.; Kemp, R. (eds.) (2006): Reflexive Governance for Sustainable Development. Cheltenham

Wajcman, J.; MacKenzie, D. A. (eds.) (1985): The Social Shaping of Technology. How the Refrigerator Got its Hum. Milton Keynes

Walz, R.; Kuhlmann, St. (2005): Nachhaltigkeitsinnovationen in systemischer Perspektive. In: Mappus, St. (ed.): Erde 2.0. Technologische Innovationen als Chance für eine nachhaltige Entwicklung. Heidelberg a.o., pp. 278–310 (in German)

Watts, M. J.; Bohle, H. G. (1993): The Space of Vulnerability. The Causal Structure of Hunger and Famine. In: Progress in Human Geography, Vol. 17/No. 1, pp. 43–67

WBGU – German Advisory Council on Global Change (2000): World in Transition. Strategies for Managing Global Environmental Risks. Annual Report 1998. Berlin a.o.

WCED – World Commission on Environment and Development (ed.) (1987): Our Common Future. Oxford

Wehling, P. (2006): Im Schatten des Wissens? Perspektiven der Soziologie des Nichtwissens. Konstanz (in German)

Willinger, W.; Doyle, J. (2002): Robustness and the Internet – Design and Evolution. Pasadena (URL: http://netlab.caltech.edu/pub/papers/part1_vers4.pdf)

Willke, Th.; Vorlop, K.-D. (2004): Industrial Bioconversion of Renewable Resources as an Alternative to Conventional Chemistry. In: Applied Microbiology and Biotechnology, Vol. 66/No. 2, pp. 131–142 (URL: http://dx.doi.org/10.1007/s00253-004-1733-0)

WEF – World Economic Forum (2010): Global Risks 2010. A Global Risk Network Report. Geneva

Young, O. R.; Berkhout, F.; Gallopin, G. C.; Janssen, M. A.; Ostrom, E.; Leeuw, S. van der (2006): The Globalization of Socio-ecological Systems. An Agenda for Scientific Research. In: Global Environmental Change, Vol. 16/No. 3 (August), pp. 304–316 (URL: http://dx.doi.org/10.1016/j.gloenvcha.2006.03.004)

Sustainability Ideas in Indian Culture

Little Traditions and Post-modern Adaptations

Appukuttan N. Damodaran

1 Introduction

Robert Redfield's pioneering paradigm of the "Little Tradition and Great Tradition" (cf. Redfield 1956), offers a rich approach towards the understanding of the cultural dynamics of local communities in terms of their adaptation to the precepts of great traditions. Redfield attempted to explain the process by which great traditions were internalized by local or village level communities. This framework is adopted here to explain sustainability trends in local spaces in India that include village communities, and local communities specializing in Indian systems of medicines.

The Great traditions of India as exemplified in the sacred texts, notably the Puranas, the Gita and the Indian Philosophical Streams, emphasized the principle of diversity as the basic principle of viewing nature. According to the Puranas the earth is composed of eight Continents namely "Bhuloka", "Jambudvipa" (or Rose Apple Land), Plaksha (Fig Tree), Salmala (Silk-Cotton Tree), Kus (Grass), Kraunca, Saka (Teak Tree) and Puskara (Blue Lotus) (cf. Dimmit/Buitenen 1998). As would be seen this categorization of continents is based on the type of vegetation donning different continents. What is more is the description of the "pre-heaven" formation, in the sacred texts, namely the Meru mountains which are at a height of 84,000 leagues and are nourished by forces of nature (cf. Dimmit/Buitenen 1998), the holy river Ganges that flows directly from the heavens above the Meru mountains and around the city of gods (cf. Dimmit/Buitenen 1998).

The point is not about the scientific veracity of this schema of categorization. The real point is that the sacred texts, which form the Great traditions of Indian civilization, visualized nature as a diverse entity, comprising mountain, rivers and terrestrial systems. India's traditions of forest management as reflected in the great traditions were also presaged on the principle of maintaining diversity, which was at variance with the principle of specie selectivity implicit in scientific forestry that was introduced during the British colonial period in the 19th century (cf. Damodaran 1992).

Indeed the "Gita", the sacred text of the Hindus says that a person is an embodiment of both virtues and vices. These are Satvik (virtuous, industrious, free from vices, good at heart), Rajasik (emotional and passionate) and Tamasik (indolent, dismal, dull). Each of these attributes are contrary to each other. The main proposition is that any modernity project that attempts to fashion out an ideal human being is bound to be counter-productive.

Leaving aside the Puranas, and looking at the Indian Schools of philosophical thought, it is seen that the principle of diversity and primacy of nature has been equally emphasized in the Nyaya Vaishesika and Dvaita schools of thought (cf. Nadkarni 2008).

To a large extent, this diversity principle implicit in India's Great Traditions, is reflected in the country's ethno-cultural diversity (cf. Kapoor 2004). Indeed it is argued that the combination of traditional thinking, anti-colonialism, and socialist policies that had guided India in the post-independence period correlated with the country's extremely slow rate of economic growth between 1950 and 1990 (cf. Kapoor 2004). Such arguments are situated in the paradigm of modernity that emphasizes economic growth. In such scheme of things, the natural capital costs of economic growth does not assume significance.

2 The Great Traditions and the New Geometry of Rural India

Traditionally, land surveys in India that were part of the great tradition texts, were not based on modern geometrical principles. A unit of land was measured in terms of the spread achieved by a handful of seeds thrown in a circular manner by a person. The boundaries of traditional village communities that focused on a village as a self-contained ecological unit, had a complement of various land forms and multiple water sources.

The little traditions were tuned to this thinking as well. Each village had a combination of cultivated lands which were proprietary while at the same time co-existing with common property resources. Commons have been the feature of village communities in Europe as well. The unique point about Indian village societies has been the mutual inter-changeability of common property resources and private property resources. While, during the main rainfall seasons, (the Indian monsoons), cultivated lands functioned as crop lands and common pastures were utilized for livestock grazing, in the post harvest season, privately owned lands were opened to grazing by community livestock. Community cattle grazed on the stubbles or leftovers of crops in the harvested fields. The regular commons were given rest from livestock during this period. Similarly common lands provided biomass and water resources for private use, though this was carefully regulated by the community.

A concomitant of such patterns of natural resource use was the interchangeability of the concepts of "community" and "society". The village as a society was different from the village as a community. While a village as a society, represented differences and was based on caste based social stratification that in turn guided social organization of production activities in a village, it was the village as a community that maintained common property resources. Community rituals for the upkeep of commons and community incantations for bringing in rainfall were based on collective efforts, whereby all social differences were forgotten. The type and method of organizing community rituals follow the great tradition precepts laid down in the Atharva Veda. Community rituals had a galvanizing impact in unleashing the collective consciousness of a village community.

The most important fall-out of the traditional system of land and natural resource management systems was sustainability. The balance of common and private property resources and the dialectic of the society-community relationship were responsible for village communities maintaining a diverse set of natural resources within their boundaries (see Figure 1). These diverse natural resources in turn, enabled village communities to be resilient to droughts and climate related vagaries.

Figure 1: Natural Resources Status in Semi-arid Agroecosystem – Pre 1980s

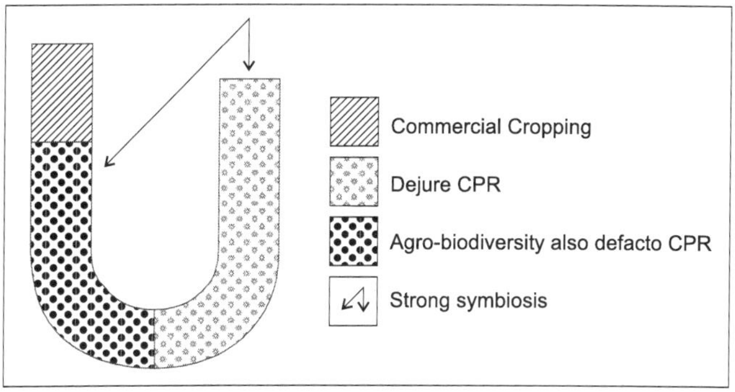

Source: Damodaran 2001, p. 54

The traditional system of land survey changed in medieval India with the introduction of new systems of land measurement systems to assess land revenue. However the principle of modern land survey did not get established until after the advent of British Rule in India. In British India the system of theodolite survey was introduced for land survey, whereby the focus was on measuring angles (horizontal and vertical) in combination with triangulation (cf. Anonymus w.y.). Analytical geometry principles made it easier for surveyors to calculate angles and distances that enabled them to start from a given point and return to the same point. This was the new geometry in rural India in the 19th and 20th centuries.

The new geometry enabled the positioning of the District Collector as the new fulcrum of political and administrative power in British India which cognitively displaced the centrality of village community in rural India. The new geometry also created a class of surveyors who like the Central European Kafkian surveyors, believed in a social and political order that was based on discrete, measurable landforms. The old anarchy of non-symmetric village boundaries that did not obey the laws of triangulation had to be changed and replaced in order to set up the new order. Great traditions were thus undermined by the forces of modernity. However at the village level, the little traditions practised sustainable traditions while formally respecting the modern survey and demarcation systems. These local communities selectively internalized modern technologies while de-facto continuing with their traditional resource management systems sharing systems based on common property-private property interchangeability (cf. Damodaran 2001, p. 53). However there were interesting adaptations by little traditions when it came to community rituals. This was in tune with changing times and the advent of modern technologies.

In the 1980s, the advent of bore well irrigation in Karnataka villages in South India, with its promise of copious ground water supply, changed cropping patterns from "traditional" drought hardy cereal crops to irrigation requiring horticultural crops. Bore-wells extracted ground water from hard rock formations, through an advanced drilling process. There were aided by geo-physical surveys. However bore-wells were not easy to come by, as it depended on the chance of locating a suitable fracture in the sub-terranean rocks. Besides, bore-wells by promoting excessive ground water extraction formed an unsustainable alternative to traditional sustainable management practices. While a few farmers were successful in locating a copious water yielding source, there were many wells which failed. In the year 1984, when droughts hit the villages in Bangalore District of Karnataka many community rituals were conducted to get over the difficult situations. The emphasis changed with changing times and changes in the "technology-scape". The advent of technologically superior bore-wells in the dry villages of Karnataka in India in the 1980s, radically changed their fortunes when it came to availability of water. A farmer with a copious water yielding borewell had no reason to be bound to the ecological limitation of water scarcity. However bore-wells had their "un-predictability". The probability of a bore well succeeding in yielding a "water bonanza" was not high. Cases of failed bore wells were abundant as most of the wells were not successful in tapping the right geological fracture that was capable of yielding copious water supply. Cultural vehicles provided a cushion against uncertainty.

3 Case of Adaptation to Great Tradition: A Semi Arid Village in Karnataka

In a village by name Mundur in rural Bangalore, community rituals to propitiate the "rain-gods" were a regular feature whenever droughts hit the village. Mundur was a semi-arid village agricultural ecosystem in Karnataka in South India prone to droughts. Villagers typically practised rainfed agriculture as they had no dependable irrigation facilities. During droughts, villagers typically lost their crops and livestock. Villagers of Mundur practiced rituals to appease Varuna, the rain-god and Parjanya, the weather deities. Both are pantheons of the Vedas, the Great Tradition text of India. The rituals followed the Vedic traditions but were adapted to local conditions. The description of the ritual was as follows:

> "Early in the morning on the day of the ritual, the village drummer beat his drum, inviting villagers to congregate at the temple dedicated to god Shiva.Within an hour, the villagers gathered outside the temple. The priest offered prayers inside the temple's inner sanctum for an hour. Meanwhile, outside the temple two donkeys stood, with bright red velvet cloth adorning their backs. Two sacks containing live frogs were also placed on the donkeys' backs. After his prayers, the priest came out and offered a camphor flame to the devotees. One of the village's core leaders applied sandal paste and *kumkum* (a red powder) to the donkey's foreheads, while another leader poured water into the sacks of frogs. The leader of the less privileged castes in the village secured the wet sacks on the donkeys' backs and then led a procession of enthusiastic and excited villagers dancing, drumming and chanting around the temple. The ritual was complete after three circumambulations of the temple. The symbolism of the ritual is this: The donkey being a beast of burden, is supposed to carry the village community's, burden of guilt for displeasing the weather gods. The croaking frogs are the harbingers of rain, which would relieve the village from its drought. After the ritual, the procession moved to an improvised dais away from the temple, where one of the leaders spoke about the circumstances that led to the ritual. The resultant heightened community consciousness led to a massive, unpaid, community effort to desilt the village ponds and other surface water sources as a follow-up to the ritual. The atmosphere triggered by this community effort had a salutary impact on community owned natural resources such as the water storing structures, which were repaired and rehabilitated." (Damodaran 2001, pp. 51f.)

However in the 1980s the advent of the borewell technology with copious water supplies changed the focus of the villagers from traditional surface water tanks to wells. In 1985 the ritual turned different with the village headman proclaiming to his fellow community members "Till now we prayed for rains from above. Let us pray for rains from below" (cf. Damodaran/Roe 1998). The little tradition was clearly adapting to modernity in imaginative ways

Though an interesting adaptation, the community ritual undertaken in 1985, was not conducive to the maintenance of traditional ecosystem practices. Traditional rituals that prayed for rains were coupled to community efforts to de-silt large surface water holding structures like "tanks", that not only yielded surface water supplies, but also recharged aquifers that formed the sources of ground water supplies.

Sustainability as a concept, requires utilization of a resource to be matched by efforts to re-create the resource, through careful husbanding and conservation measures. This was what community rituals and their associated community labour attempted to adhere to in the past. By ignoring this fundamental precept in 1985, the village community was moving away from its sustainability traditions. This was not a desirable adaptation to modernity by a "Little Tradition".

4 Post-modern Adaptations of Little Traditions in the 20th Century: The Case of Ayurveda

Ayurveda, the renowned Indian System of Medicine is part of the Great Tradition of India. The Ayurvedic texts of the great masters of this Indian System of Medicine, namely, Charaka and Sushruta, constitute the grand narratives on the hoary system of medicine. However different regions of India developed their own Little Traditions of Ayurveda. A case in point is the Kottakkal Ayurveda Sala, considered to be the premier Ayurvedic establishment in India today. It is the 'adaptation experiment' of Kottakkal Arya Vaidya Sala that saved Ayurveda from the onslaught of modern medicine in the 20th century. The Great Tradition of Ayurveda ordained that Ayurveda keep away from surgery and dissections of animals and human corpses. As the Indologist Arthur Llewellyn Basham observed, "the keep-off attitude" from surgery, denied Ayurveda the much needed insights into the (mal) functioning of the "brains" and the "lungs" i.e., organs covered by bones, which could only be uncovered for studies through dissections. To the outside world of modernity, the reticent Vaidyas appeared to be a closed community – old fashioned, unyielding and perhaps non-innovative (cf. Damodaran 2003). Vaidyaratnam Varier, the founder of the Kottakkal Arya Vaidya Sala changed these Great Tradition precepts. He picked up the intricacies of anatomy and surgery. Conceivably this served to improve the repertoire of Ayurveda and closed the knowledge gap, which had till then existed between Ayurveda and modern systems of medicine. Varier translated great works in English on Anatomy and Physiology into the local vernacular for benefit of students of Ayurveda, thus revolutionizing Ayurveda. He also took care to give a strong impetus to the Arya Vaidya Samajam Conferences, wherein scholars freely interacted on different aspects of Ayurveda uninhibited by the old Caraka dictum of "control over one's words". This further enhanced the repertoire of Ayurveda. Subsequently, Varier's establishment started a major movement for specialized production of Ayurvedic medicines on a large scale with the aid of modern technology (cf. Damodaran 2003). This adaptation has elevated the Kottakkal Arya Vaidya Sala into India's leading Ayurvedic establishment. Today, the Kottakkal Arya Vaidya Sala is in the forefront of Intellectual Property protection and maintains a herbarium of medicinal plants to conserve the disappearing flora of rare medicinal plants from natural forests.

Clearly this is a case of positive adaptation of Great Tradition precepts by a Little Tradition. This adaptation has today raised the international credibility of Indian System of Medicine as a pro-nature, pro-biodiversity conservation oriented traditional system of medicine that has kept with the positive tenets of modernity.

5 Larger Lessons

The most interesting aspect that is brought out from the preceding cases from India is that while Great Traditions have influenced Little Traditions, they have not imposed themselves on the latter. The influence of modernity has also not been total in large segments of traditional India. Modernity has not undermined well entrenched little traditions of sustainability in rural India. Rather little traditions have adapted their traditional ways to modernity. Some of them have been conducive to sustainability while certain others have not been. Either way these adaptations have created interesting post modern trends in India's rural and even urban areas (cf. Damodaran 2010). The post modern order has created new relevance for local spaces – some of them have enabled India's little traditions to be sustainable in a non traditional ways. This raises new challenges for policy makers grappling with sustainability in the country.

References

Anonymous (w.y.): Surveying & Triangulation (URL: www.survequip.com/surveying-triangulation/)

Damodaran, A. (1992): Local Self Governments and the Geometry of Biodiversity Conservations: Roots of the Incompatibility. In: Economic and Political Weekly, Vol. 27/No. 6 (February), pp. 419–424

Damodaran, A. (2001): Towards an Agro Ecosystem Policy for India. Lessons from Two Case Studies. New Delhi (Centre for Environment Education)

Damodaran, A. (2003): Ayurveda in the Age of IPRs. In: Varier, C. A. (ed.): Centenary Celebration Commemoration Volume. Kottakkal Arya Vaidya Pharmacy. Vol. 2. Kottakkal, India, pp. 197–200

Damodaran, A. (2010): Encircling the Seamless: India, Climate Change and Global Commons. New Delhi

Damodaran; A.; Roe, E. (1998): Theorizing to Explain and Triangulating to Explain Away? The Art and Non-Art of Multi-method in Policy Research. In: Economic and Political Weekly, Vol. 33/No. 1–2, pp. 55–62

Dimmit, C.; Buitenen, J. A. B. van (eds.) (1998): Classical Hindu Mythology. A Reader in the Sanskrit Puranas. Delhi

Kapoor, R. (2004): Plural Dreams: India in the 21st century. In: Futures, Vol. 36, pp. 637–653

Nadkarni, M. V. (2010): Approach to Knowledge. Contribution of Bhagavatgita and its Relevance to Holistic Social Science Research. In: Journal of Social and Economic Development (Institute of Social and Economic Change, India), Vol. 12/No. 1, pp. 26–42

Redfield, R. (1956): Peasant Society and Culture. An Anthropological Approach to Civilization. Chicago

Cultural Sustainability

Anthropological Perspectives

Gabriele Tautscher

1986 I travelled from Austria to Nepal to undertake a classical anthropological field study based on participatory observation for my doctoral theses. I went to live in a remote village (Chayarsaba) in the Nepalese middle hills inhabited by the Tibeto-Burmese Tamang community. My aim was to study their social relations based on kinship and prescribed marriage rules closely linked to their religious belief and ritual practice (cf. Tautscher 1993). At that time anthropological research in Nepal by foreign anthropologists often focused on ethnographic studies on a traditional community's social, religious, political and economic organization, e.g. on a "culture" very distinguished from our European own. In the 1980s in mainstream anthropology a concept of culture still prevailed which presumed distinct socio-cultural groups, with distinct cultural traits, shared ideas, values, and a code of moral behaviour. Traditional cultures were studied on how they were transmitted from generation to generation, perpetuated through ritual and linked to specific economic and political organization. In short: "culture" then was more seen as a constituted complex whole, rather than as an ongoing and societal process (compare with Riegler 2003; Wicker 1996). The 1980s was also the beginning of ethnic movements in Nepal who as indigenous minorities aspired towards an ethnic and cultural identity and demanded equality in the state. Thus a new protest movement emerged in Nepal based on culture.

The people of Chayarsaba in the mid-1980s were unaware of the changing political environment at the political centre Kathmandu. It took three days to reach the village – one day bus ride, two days walking – and the Tamangs of Chayarsaba in the "remote" mountain valley still lived the traditional life taken over from their elders. Never the less, what I had observed then, too, was an increasing influence on the villager's life by the state and international development programs, which in Nepal had started in the 1960s. These clearly unsettled the villagers and they met them with great uneasiness and scepticism. My research on the Tamang mountain farmers in the 1980s also revealed a new and growing economic struggle, due to loss of community lands and rights of utilization (like pastures and forests), decline in price of grain, and a growing population. These problems partly were caused by new "reforms" implemented through a modern administration (then the village Panchayats), a new land tenure based on private property (before it was based on rights of land use inherited within kin groups) and a modern school education (instead of oral tradition and learning under guidance). Their inheritance rules with regard to land, rights to pastures, and even their knowledge on their environment based on experience and their values became uprooted through these "modern" changes – changes, which, too, were initiated and supported by international "development" programs. The villagers of Chayarsaba – as most traditional remote villages of the world with a subsistence economy and tools instead of sophisticated technical equipment – gradually had become pushed into an "underdeveloped" and "backward" corner and at the same time were confronted with growing economic difficulties. The people from Chayarsaba themselves said at that time, "we live in the corner, where nobody can see us, not even the king can see us. Those who take pity on us, see us".[1]

In the 1980s, contrary to the anthropological concept of "culture", the "modern" West perceived culture more as a product of intellectuals, religions, arts, or medias. Culture has become segregated from the rest of social life, but somehow is accorded to influence systems of values and social acts (influenced by Talcott Parcons, cf. Parsons 1961). Typical for this perception of culture is the distinction between producers and consumers of culture, and that culture is being "created" – a definition of an industrialized world with an "art market". The modern West had also brought forth the idea of development based on rationality (the "Enlightenment") and technical and material progress. A dichotomy between developed modern and underdeveloped traditional, between centre and periphery, had become the reality for those engaged in development aid but also for the people of Chayarsaba.[2] In addition, the idea of "culture" became linked to a value-laden meaning of culture associated with a hierarchy of ways of living, therefore the idea to develop from primitive culture to a more progressive "Western" culture and way of life (cf. Skeleton/Allen, p. 4). What the people of Chayarsaba became confronted with – without given any clue to what and why these changes have been introduced and the chance to take part in decision-making, or even to realize its consequences – were the development interventions which in Nepal (but also worldwide) had begun in the 1950's with the aim to make the newly "independent" "Third World" "modern" and productive within an international political environment and market. Development discourse, at its beginning, had a very practical connotation with little theoretical reflection. It rather was accompanied with the "ideal" assumption to do "something good" for the people. According to Frederick Cooper and Randall Packard the new independent states (like India, the influential neighbour of Nepal) also became a

1 Interview with Luku Tamang in Chayarsaba (60 years old recorded in 1986).

2 Detailed discussions and analyses by anthropologists on development and culture cf. Skelton/Allen 1999.

stake within the "Cold War" – that is of high interest for both the American and Russian governments (cf. Cooper/Packard 2005, p. 132). Development Aid – as in Nepal – until the 1980's was state oriented to promote national economic growth in an international environment with the following set of operating assumptions: To see foreign aid in favourable terms, to promote transfer of knowledge and technique, to make measures to promote education and health, and that economic planning would lead impoverished countries to be able to become "normal" market economies (Cooper/Packard, p. 111). Studies and reflections on the impacts of the development interventions on social structure and culture, herein, were given very little room. Moreover, Cooper and Packard describe the 1950's and 1960's as the heydays of modernization theory, with the aim to create all people into a new sort of person – rational instead of superstitious, oriented towards achievement rather than status. The flip side of the modern, or those who did not make the transition, became the "indigenous people", the traditional, the community, the village, and the "local". Citing Cooper and Packard:

> "The goal of development was growth; the agent of development was the state and the means of development were the macro-economic policy instruments. An imagined future and a repudiated past, rather than a carefully spelled out analysis of the present are the starting point of development constructs." (Cooper/Packard 2005, p. 107)

Translated onto the then Hindu kingdom of Nepal – which opened itself only in 1950 to the outer world and economically had become dependant on the new government of India – an entirely new administrative system based on the model of Great Britain was implemented, education through "modern" schools was introduced in the rural areas, and the most radical change of all, the land became private property (cf. Regmi 1963/1968). By 1992, when Nepal became a democracy, all villages had become defined as "underdeveloped" and their village councils were named "Village Development Committees".

The village Chayarsaba – in other words – has become integrated into a new economic, political and administrative system, irrespective of their actual needs, let alone including their own customary law and debates. In spite of (or rather because of) the "modernization" and democratization[3] they had not only lost economic resources, or their voice within their own tribal (local lineage) context, but also started to lose control over their next generation. The loss of their traditional land rights meant that their inheritance rules became upset, through this their rules of marriage alliances (cross-cousin marriage rule) became disturbed, which were fundamental to their social and economic exchange and survival. In fact these formed the basis for their cultural life, like religious

3 Until then the various governments in Nepal were authoritarian, but still committed the local communities relative autonomy.

and social rituals, and constituted their traditional communal forms of social and economic security. Their children now became educated in schools with new subjects, in the state language Nepali with a Hindu ideology and an emphasis on progress. But what, too, had become crucial for the villagers, was a creeping adoption of the idea – especially among the youth –, that Western modern life is better than that of their parents, which for them had become stigmatized as "backward".

When I lived with the people in Chayarsaba in the 1980s they still tried to resist these changes: They had not registered all their lands to maintain their user rights and for fear of land losses to an upcoming literate class of bureaucrats. And they refused to send their children to school, because the elders feared to lose control over the next generation. The parents needed their sons and daughters as a security in old age. And what I had observed then in the Tamang village, too, was the deliberate destruction by the village elders of a water-line built by the Swiss Development Aid (at that time called SATA) throughout the valley. As a result the women and children had to carry again the heavy water jars to their houses from a far-away spring. For the people of Chayarsaba the acceptance of the water which came through the new solid iron pipes had meant a growing dependency on the neighbouring higher Hindu castes (who then actually were the local bureaucrats) through whose lands their new tab-water now was coming from. The Tamangs of Chayarsaba stuck to their own water sources and preferred to turn down a technical improvement, which clearly could have made their women's life much easier.

The case of the Tamang village Chayarsaba – although it is just a small case – shows clearly how little local social and cultural aspects, local knowledge or let alone the people's concerns are included within development programs, which too have had an effect on their (until one generation before well functioning) subsistence economy. Their refusal of the water pipe may depict how tradition among development workers wrongly may serve as an explanation to hinder a well-meant development project. The villagers have never learned (and never had the opportunity) to express their own interests within the development strategies, neither could the development workers communicate with them due to the language barrier. The answer to their refusal of the water pipe would have been simple.[4]

---

4 I agree with Emma Crewe and Elisabeth Harrison in the article "Seeing Culture as Barrier", that little or no attention is paid to explaining why and how in particular situations beliefs and actions are labeled by actor's themselves as traditional (cf. Crewe/Harrison 2008), or with James Ferguson (cf. Ferguson 2008) that both, the World Bund and Third World Governments, are content with development as a process which depoliticizes and dis-empowers local populations, both portray poverty as "aboriginal"

25 years later the situation in the Tamang village Chayarsaba has changed completely to the reverse. Since 2007 the road has arrived nearby the village. Most of the young generation, men and women, fly to work in Dubai, Quatar or Malaysia. The parents spend what little they have on school education of their children, hoping for their "better" future, in spite of the high unemployment rate in Nepal of the newly educated youth. The other side of the coin is that the one-clan Tamang community of the village is disintegrating more and more, their rich ritual life slowly is being abandoned. Most of all: The young don't see their future in the village, nor in their community or Tamang culture (on this topic cf. De Sales 2001). In fact a radical Maoist Movement attracts many young people in rural Nepal. It promised them to be part of the modern global world and denies its traditional past.

The people from Chayarsaba, as many rural people in Nepal, no longer want to resist the changes induced through development, but are thriving to become part of a "global" modern society. Moreover, they have discovered that they have become part of a larger system in which they have become poor and marginalized. They want to come out of their "corner" and participate in the new global market, be it through cheap labour in the new labour markets. Culture and ritual – even though they still may practice it – is not what they esteem as an answer to a sustainable development; it is money in form of wages for labour, which now as commodity has become most relevant!

Let us turn back to the debate on "culture": Since the 1980s the perspectives in social sciences have changed: With a so-called "cultural turn" in social and anthropological theories social structures, social behaviour, etc. began to be explained by cultural phenomena (e.g. Michel Foucault, Jacques Derrida, Pierre Bourdieu, Jürgen Habermas; compare with Riegler 2003; Wicker 1996). Ideologies become accentuated again in social theories and symbolic orders and ideological meanings are not merely considered as superstructure, but as necessary symbolic codes.

Since the 1980's, began the period when national and international control over capital movements were removed and the power of the state for development became drastically diminished. A policy to strengthen "market forces" (income generation, etc.), i.e. capital at the expense of the state especially in the Third World became the goal of development agencies – hand in hand with a newly declared respect for "culture" in development policy.[5]

---

disconnected from history which gave rise to unequal rights to resources; both are content with an expertise-driven structure of development; both are reinforced by failure as much as success.

5 For example in UNESCO Universal Declaration on Cultural Diversity 2001: "[...] culture as the set of distinctive spiritual, material, intellectual and emotional features of

What conclusions may be drawn from the brief retrospective analysis on Chayarsaba?

In the last five decades the villagers had been confronted, also indirectly, with varying development strategies and a multitude of concepts of "culture" linked to different parameters – including mine as anthropologist and that of Nepal's ethnic activists.

The term "culture" has been thoroughly studied in its various historical and contextual aspects (cf. Parodi et al. 2010; Riegler 2003; Wicker 1996). In a similar way, varying concepts of culture in the globalized context have been (and will be) effective simultaneously in one locality (as in the village Chayarsaba) and also change over the years. Cultural aspects one time are highly valued and at other times disregarded – be it by the development workers, politicians or even the villagers. In a cross-cultural context culture can only be referred to as a conceptual framework for investigations into various cultural ways of life (compare with Skeleton/Allen 2005, p. 4). The diversity of culture must be respected and reflected and not ignored as in the case of Chayarsaba – the people of Chayarsaba by the development interventions literally have been turned against their own culture. An understanding of the culture (in the case of Chayarsaba this would mean an understanding of heritage rights with its linkage to marriage rules and social security, of customary user rights of natural resources) of the people concerned must be imperative for far-reaching reforms (as land tenure) or development interventions (as water pipes). Further, the created dichotomy between traditional culture versus modernity is misleading, since it often conceals many social processes – e.g. how social and cultural phenomena are continually re-created, negotiated, and changed.

I, too, agree with the statement of Cooper and Packard (cf. Cooper/Packard 2005): The point is not that development – any more than a list of universal human rights – itself offers an answer, but that it shapes possibilities for political mobilization that cross differences of culture, nationality and geography. Only, the term development I would rather exchange for a more "neutral" term like "change" to avoid the notion of development as a historically and evolutionary formulated concept linked to relations of power.[6] The term change gives more justice to other and as traditional defined living forms who may incorporate new techniques for e.g. a more comfortable life. Technological interventions – if they are carried out among the currently impoverished and marginalized groups –

society or a social group, and that it encompasses, in addition to art and literature, lifestyle, ways of living together, value systems, traditions and beliefs" (http://portal.unesco.org/culture/en/ev.php).

6 Cf. hereto also the opinion expressed by Skeleton/Allen, 2005, p. 2.

have to lead to a better possible life but in their own terms and with more right to self-definition and self-reliance, with ensured rights to their natural resources. Only interventions not dislocated from the local context and the people it concerns can lead to a sustainable quality of lively-hood with a rich self-determined culture.

References

Cooper, F.; Packard, R. (2005): The History of Politics of Development Knowledge. In: Edelman, M.; Haugerud, A. (eds.): The Anthropology of Development and Globalization. Chichester a.o., pp. 126–139

Crewe, E.; Harrison, E. (2005): Seeing Culture as Barrier. In: Edelman, M.; Haugerud, A. (eds.): The Anthropology of Development and Globalization. Chichester a.o., pp. 232–234

De Sales, A. (2000): The Kham Magar Country, Nepal: between Ethnic Claims and Maoism. In: European Bulletin of Himalayan Research, No. 19, pp. 41–72

Ferguson, J. (2005): Anthropology and Its Evil Twin: "Development" in the Constitution of a Dsicipline. In: Edelman, M.; Haugerud, A. (eds.): The Anthropology of Development and Globalization. Chichester a.o., pp. 140–154

Parcons, T. (1961): Theories of Society. Foundations of Modern Sociological Theories. New York

Parodi, O.; Banse, G.; Schaffer, A. (eds.) (2010): Wechselspiele: Kultur und Nachhaltigkeit. Annäherungen an ein Spannungsfeld. Berlin (in German)

Regmi, M. C. (1963/1968): Landtenure and Taxation in Nepal (4 vols.). Berkeley, Los Angeles

Riegler, J. (2003): Aktuelle Debatten zum Kulturbegriff. In: Working Papers der Kommission für Sozialanthropologie der Österreichischen Akademie der Wissenschaften, Reihe A: Lokale Identitäten und überlokale Einflüsse (URL: http://www.oeaw.ac.at/sozant/images/working_papers/band002.pdf) (in German)

Skelton, T.; Allen, T. (1999): Culture and Global Change. London, New York

Tautscher, G. (1993): Meme Khor – Kreis der Ahnen. Gesellschaft und soziale Reproduktion der Tamang von Chayarsaba, Nepal. PhD Thesis. Vienna: University of Vienna (in German)

Wicker, H.-R. (1996): Von der komplexen Kultur zur kulturellen Komplexität. In: Wicker, H.-R. (ed.): Das Fremde in der Gesellschaft. Migration,Ethnizität und Staat. Zürich, pp. 373–392 (in German)

Considerations Regarding Cultural Differences when Operationalising Sustainability on a Regional Level

Ildiko Tulbure

1 The Concept of Sustainable Development

Starting with the '70's the world began to realize the dangers and undesired effects of human activities, especially industrial ones. After the Conference for Environment in Stockholm in 1972 and the first report of the Club of Rome "The Limits to Growth" (cf. Meadows et al. 1972) was understood that besides wanted effects of technological progress, undesired and negative effects can appear. After this time the environmental awareness in the Western world began changing. It was clear that regional and global environmental problems are very serious and need to be solved. Nowadays are we confronted with several global problems, which can be grouped in three categories: world population growth, growth of energy and natural resources consumption, and environmental pollution (cf. Jischa 2005; Tulbure 2003 – see Figure 1).

Discussions on political, scientific and social levels began worldwide a long time ago in order to find solutions for the globally complex problems confronting humanity (cf. NRC 2000). The idea was to find solutions which could be applicable with respect to regional differences, to the developed as well as to the developing countries. The Brundtland Report of the World Council on Environment and Development represented a result of these world wide political discussions (cf. WCED 1987). The concept of *sustainable development* was defined in the Brundtland Report 1987 and accepted as a possible solution for the global complex ecological, economic, and social problems. The concept of sustainable development was very much discussed during the Conference for Environment and Development in Rio de Janeiro 1992 in the closing document Agenda 21 as well as in 2002 in the follow-up Conference Rio+10 in Johannesburg, South Africa.

Many actions after this time emphasise that the evolution of technical, social and ecological systems has to be analysed in synergetic relation (cf. Tulbure 2003). At this point several events can be mentioned, for instance, the Western Cape Sustainable Development Conference 2005 in Cape Town, South Africa,[1] as well as the World Summit on the Information Society (WSIS), held in two

1 Cf. http://www.capegateway.gov.za/eng/your_gov/406/events/101218.

phases, 2003 in Geneva, Switzerland, and 2005 in Tunis, Tunisia.[2] In this context should be mentioned also the Club of Rome Anniversary Conference in the year 2008 having the title "Strategies for a Sustainable Planet" held in Rome, Italy.

Figure 1: Global (Environmental) Problems and the Concept of Sustainable Development

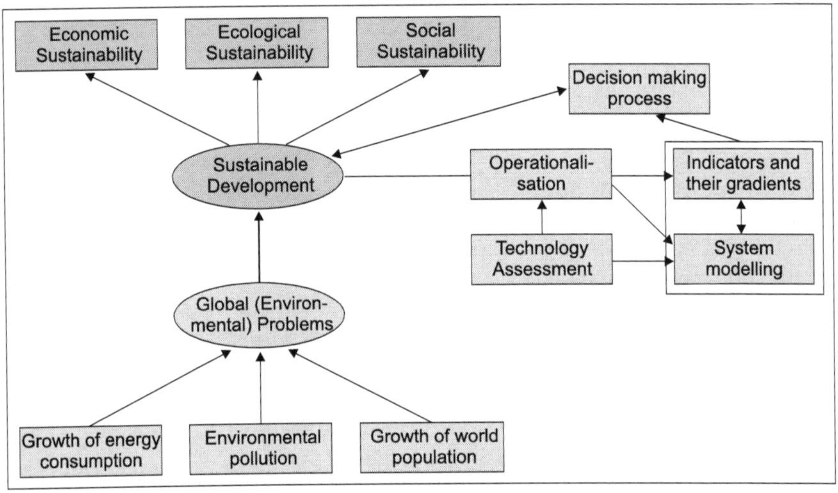

Author's archive

Sustainable development has become a widely used term today. However, looking in the literature dealing with this topic, the impression arises that there are as many definitions of sustainable development as there are users of the term. In order to make this concept more understandable, rules, strategies and principles of sustainable development have been defined (cf. Jischa 2005; Tulbure 2003; Voss 1994). The general Brundtland definition has been accepted world-wide, but together with the rules, strategies and principles, it does not give a concrete methodology, how to apply it to real concrete situations, especially on local or even production process levels (cf. Banse 2007; Tulbure 2003).

2 Operationalisation of Sustainable Development

The operationalisation of the concept of sustainable development means the transformation or translation of its goals into political measures and controlling

---

2 Cf. http://www.itu.int/wsis.

instruments. When studying the worldwide published literature about how to apply sustainable development on different levels, one can distinguish two strategic possibilities:

- establishing goals on global or national levels, the measures to achieve these goals being prepared on global or national level and applied on national or regional levels;
- establishing goals on a regional level, the measures being prepared on regional or local levels; the effects of these measures are evaluated on national and global levels, too.

As an application example of the first strategy studies in the form of scenarios could be mentioned, for instance with the goal of finding future sustainable energy supply systems with minimal effects on the environment. Such a project has been realized at IIASA (International Institute for Applied Systems Analysis) in Laxenburg/Vienna "Global Energy Perspectives" (cf. Nakicenovic et al. 1998) and another one was carried out in Germany, IKARUS, with the goal to deliver a concrete instrument to reduce pollutant emissions in the air (cf. VDI 1993). On this point international and national scenario studies could be mentioned, which try to find sustainable ways for future national development in a global context. The mentioned studies based on mathematical models to describe industrial and economic processes and their impacts. With the help of databases, which describe economic, social and political frames, simulations have been carried out and different development scenarios have been gained. The goal is to find the right ways for the proposed aims and to help with concrete measures as the decision making process on a political level.

The second strategy is illustrated by many actions in the form of Local Agendas 21 led especially in Western European countries after the Rio-Conference in 1992. Studies concerning regional future energy supply systems in the context of analysing economic, environmental and social impacts can be mentioned here, like many studies about withdrawal from the nuclear energy program.

A general methodology for operationalising sustainable development can be materialized in following steps (cf. Tulbure 2003):

- defining the sustainability problem;
- establishing the space and time scales;
- systemic approach of the region by modelling the interactions;
- establishing concrete aims for the studied case;
- developing concepts and measures by establishing priorities;
- developing evaluation and control instruments, indicators;
- verifying the possible results, which could be obtained after introducing the proposed measures, comparing different scenarios;
- applying in practice the developed concept.

The operationalisation is only possible, when for an individual problem-case concrete aims are established and from these aims concepts to achieve them are developed. Sustainability is to be newly defined for each different case. The space and time scales are to be established for each case. For its operationalisation technology assessment can be used, especially by engineers when developing new technologies (cf. Grunwald 2002; Jischa 2005).

Evaluation and control instruments are sustainable development indicators. These indicators permit one to formulate quantitatively the proposed objectives and goals of sustainable development (cf. Mitchell 1996). After applying the proposed measures, the degree of realization can be controlled and verified by calculating these indicators and by comparing to reference values. The possibility to make corrections is assured in this way. On the other hand indicators serve as an instrument which helps to better understand the possible effects of measures and to inform the general public.

In the last time there is consent among political economists and engineers that the gross national product (GNP) alone does not represent a measure for the quality of life of a nation. It gives information about national economies, but it does not consider many parameters which influence the quality of life, as for instance: environmental pollution, irreversible use of fossil fuels, social aspects, etc.

A lot of attempts to define indicators for sustainable development are known in the whole world (cf. Mitchell 1996). In the development of sustainable development indicators three directions are to be observed:

- defining one single aggregated indicator;
- defining a set of indicators for measuring sustainable development;
- defining partial aggregated indicators for each component of sustainable development, for the ecological, economical and social ones.

To illustrate the first direction I want to name as aggregated indicators the Human Development Index HDI[3], the Index of Sustainable Economic Welfare (ISEW)[4], and the Ecological National Product (ENP; cf. Dieren 1995). The second direction is represented by a system of indicators to measure sustainable development. In order to exemplify studies in this direction I want to mention the indicators system used in the German region Baden-Württemberg or the indicators system for the town Jacksonville (cf. Dieren 1995).

The third possibility is given by the modular design of SDI. Each of the three significant components of the concept of sustainable development is described by an indicator (cf. Tulbure 2003 – see Figure 2). When we want to get

3 Cf. http://hdr.undp.org/statistics/indices/about_hdi.cfm.

4 Cf. http://www.foe.co.uk/campaigns/sustainable_development/progress/templates/story-intro.html.

one single indicator, then we have to solve the aggregation problem of the three components. There are many aggregation methods, for instance by calculating mean values. As simple as the method is, it is based on the restriction, that all components have the same weight by the aggregation. Other methods are bases on weight coefficients, where establishing the way of such coefficients has to be clarified. In our department in Germany at the Clausthal University of Technology[5] we developed an aggregation method based on fuzzy logic, which assures a transparent aggregation and eliminates the negative aspects of other methods (cf. Ludwig 1995; Tulbure 1997).

Figure 2: Aggregation Levels for a Possible Sustainable Development Indicator

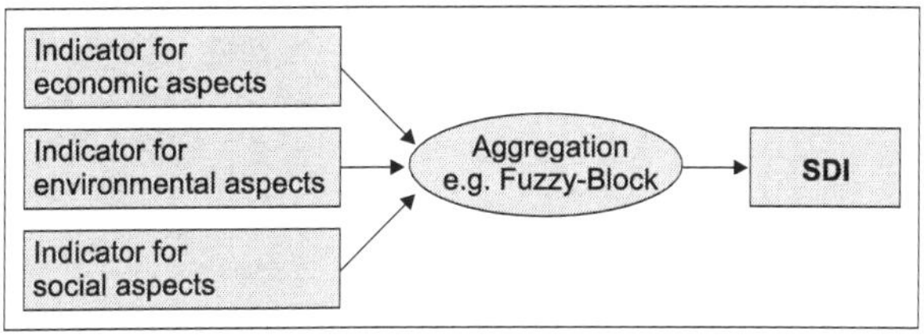

Author's archive

3 The Need of Transnational Co-operation for Assuring Sustainable Development

In order to assure sustainable development on a regional level among neighbouring countries and for its operationalisation there is a real need for successful transnational co-operation, this means that neighbouring countries should cooperate in order to achieve this common goal. The strategies for a successful transnational co-operation should try to combine the interests of individual countries, economic, ecologic and social ones with the goal of achieving at the end a regional sustainable development also by taking into account cultural differences from one society to another (cf. Banse 1998).

In the meantime it became very clear, that the operationalisation of the concept of sustainable development has to take into consideration the specific regional conditions (cf. Banse 2007; Tulbure 2003). It means differently if the concept of sustainable development is applied for an African country or for a country of Western Europe or South-Eastern Europe. There is a need to know very well, first of all, the regional conditions.

5 Cf. www.tu-clausthal.de.

With the goal of starting a successful transnational co-operation several institutions and networks have been established on global level as well as on regional/transnational level. At this point I want to mention the International Kick-off Conference of the Network for Sustainability Monitoring, Strategies and Management in South Eastern Europe NESSEE, which took place February 23–25, 2006, at the University "1 Decembrie 1918" at Alba Iulia, Romania. The foremost goal of this conference was to present the most critical problems connected with environmental protection and sustainable development in South Eastern Europe and to find appropriate solutions for the recognised problems. The launched regional network, having the name "NESSEE" (*NE*twork for *S*ustainability in *S*outh Eastern *E*urope), was to help find the best strategies in this direction (cf. Tulbure/Jischa 2006).

For the success of this kick-off-conference it was very important to recognise and to use the different cultures and management styles of the conference participants from different European countries. It was very useful to try to connect different national identities and cultural goals with the same goal of successfully working in the context of two projects:

1. Sustainability monitoring and strategies in South Eastern Europe
2. Education for Sustainability on university level in South Eastern Europe

It has been very much debated the managerial approach through project management and the management of multicultural teams, like in the context of this network (cf. Tulbure/Jischa 2006).

It was clear that with the goal of solving such major problems regarding assuring the sustainability in different parts of the world transnational co-operation is asked. Specific international institutions and networks, established on global and regional level have to help the realization of a real transnational co-operation, as the case of this Network for Sustainability in South Eastern Europe (cf. Tulbure/Jischa 2006).

This regional network for sustainability has to help the work on concrete projects in multicultural teams and find the best strategies in this direction. With the goal of launching this network, besides partners from our country and other neighbouring countries, scientists from Germany have been present at this event and helped with their experience the successful start of the network. In the context of this kick-off-conference it was very useful to have the experience of KIT/ITAS (Karlsruhe Institute for Technology/Institute for Technology Assessment and Systems Analysis) from Germany by the active involvement of *Gerhard Banse,* which assured the successful start of this network.

The network defined its work especially in the context of two projects in the field of sustainable development in our world region, one in the field of Sustainability Monitoring and Strategies in South Eastern Europe and the second one in field of Education for Sustainability in South Eastern Europe.

Institutionalising sustainability is nowadays another theme, which has been very much debated during different conferences. It is clear that there are attempts to make progress in each South Eastern European country, for example in Bulgaria, Macedonia, Slovenia, and Romania. There are still a lot of questions on how to improve the situation in the field of institutionalising sustainability, so to create institutions which should work in the field of sustainability, not at last because of cultural differences in these societies.

There are several transnational organizations, which are helping in a direct or indirect way the transnational cooperation for assuring the sustainable development of our human society. At this point I would like to mention the well-known global organization The Club of Rome[6] as well as its forum for the young generation, tt30. The Club of Rome is a global think tank and can be understood as a catalyst for change, being known for its long-term thinking, as well as its interdisciplinary and holistic approach. The first Club of Rome report "The Limits to Growth" was published in 1972 (cf. Meadows et al. 1972) and represented at that time an incubator for the environmental movement. The Club of Rome defined the "World Problematique", which is actually a complex set of interdependent challenges the world is facing.

At the same time, tt30 – the young think tank of the Club of Rome – was founded in 2001 during the kick-off meeting in Hamburg, Germany. It had about 30 participants, with an age between 25 and 35 years having diverse backgrounds (academia, business, politics, NGOs). tt30 provides the perspective of the young generation on the World Problematique, which is called "Web of the Problematique", because of the use of ICTs by describing the set of challenges the world is facing. There are three fundamental dimensions in the Web of the Problematique, which are: unequal access to goods, information and technology, conflicts and disruptions of value systems, as well as lack of good governance. The idea is to deliver a contribution to "Resolutique" with concrete requests and proposals for solutions in the form of certain international projects for finding solutions to these problems (cf. Lengsfeld et al. 2003).

By the activities of such transnational organisations also transnational cooperation is actually assured, which is necessary for operationalising sustainable development, even if there are cultural differences, as the members in these organizations have different backgrounds, are coming from different countries and have different mentalities.

---

6 Cf. www.clubofrome.org.

4 Holistic Education for Sustainable Development

For assuring in the future the sustainable development of our human society there is a need that the young generation knows well all the aspects related to global problems and which are possible solutions. This means that the young generation should learn in school or universities about the concept of sustainable development, assuring in this way a holistic education of the young generation for Sustainable Development (cf. Banse 2007; Tulbure/Jischa 2006). In other words, the holistic education of the young generation is the key issue for the world sustainability. In his book "Continuity, Innovation and Change", His Royal Highness Prince El Hassan bin Talal, former President of the Club of Rome, pointed out the need for education as a key issue for achieving these three human goals: continuity, innovation, and change. These are the fundamentals of sustainable development of our society. Three dimensions of education are recognised: *infrastructure, methodologies* and *values*. All these three dimensions of education are of crucial importance for the educational process regardless about which region we are talking about. *Frameworks* (economic, politic, social, cultural) are the bound elements between these dimensions. This *holistic education for sustainable development* should prepare the young generation to have the provocation to think about the future and to assure a Sustainable Future.

Institutionalising sustainability is an important step in making progress in the field of operationalising sustainability by assuring a proper education for sustainability of the young generation (cf. Tulbure/Jischa 2006). In South Eastern European countries it is not the same situation in each country and there are still a lot of question marks on how to improve the situation in the field of institutionalising sustainability, so to create institutions which should work in the field of sustainability.

5 Challenges Regarding Cultural Differences

Understanding the way of what it means to assure a sustainable development of society is influenced by the general economic and socio-political conditions, which are varying more or less from one region to another one. In this regard cultural aspects have an important influence as well (cf. Lengsfeld et al. 2003).

The many experiences after building up the Network for Sustainability in South Eastern Europe NESSEE, trying to operationalise sustainable development on a regional level, demonstrates that there are big cultural differences among societies even in Europe. These cultural differences have not always a very positive impact in relevant activities regarding the project work in similar groups (cf. Tulbure/Jischa 2006).

In each society, traditions are influencing cultural aspects very much. This means that there is a real need to analyse first of all existing traditions in each society, in order to understand cultural differences and then to conclude in which way traditions can influence applying sustainable development (cf. Lengsfeld et al. 2003; Tulbure/Jischa 2006). Just to give an example, in these Eastern European societies, a question of tradition is the fact that – per se – the older generation has the most important role regarding the "decision power" in society. But in most of the cases the older generation has not deep knowledge regarding the concept of sustainable development. As a result they are more or less stopping real attempts to concretely apply this concept in practice.

On the other side traditions represent the base for cultural differences. Actually there is another understanding way of everyday life in Eastern Europe compared to Western Europe or other parts of world, as for instance in the Arabic world. This is not always bad, it depends on each situation. But in these societies there is a mixture between professional life and personal, familiar life, not always having very positive impacts on a professional life. It is very interesting to analyse the impact of these cultural differences even on personal level. So, the question is how it looks like a "sustainable family" in Western Europe and how it looks like one in Eastern Europe. There are curious things in understanding family relations, let alone understanding ways of what "sustainability" mean in different parts of the world.

6 Conclusions

Sustainability has to be defined for each concrete situation on a regional level. For applying this concept there is a need to evaluate systems in an integrated way, from technical, economic, environmental and social points of view. There are different major problems regarding sustainability in different parts of the world.

A successful transnational co-operation is assured by specific international institutions and networks, established on global level as well as on regional/transnational level. The Club of Rome/tt30 is acting by its great innovation potential on assuring sustainable development of our world. NESSEE is a network acting on a regional level, in South Eastern Europe, with the foremost goal to develop a multicultural and interdisciplinary network, which should activate achieving Sustainability in South Eastern Europe by finding appropriate solutions for the recognised problems and to define strategies how to overcome these. The launched regional network has to work on concrete projects in multicultural teams and has to find the best strategies in this direction.

For assuring regional Sustainable Development there is a real need for a successful transnational co-operation, which happens very well in the context of multicultural organisations. Also education for sustainable development of the young generation does play an important role in this attempt and is also the driving force for a successful transnational co-operation. Cultural differences are influencing a lot the way of concretely applying sustainable development into practice. By a proper education humanity has to learn to accept and to successfully deal with such cultural differences from different societies in the world. At the end it is actually a nice reality that we are living in a world with so many cultural differences and it would be good to recognize the many advantages offered by these cultural differences.

References

Banse, G. (ed.) (1998): Technikfolgenbeurteilung und Wissenschaftsethik in Ländern Ostmitteleuropas. 2 Vols. Bad Neuenahr-Ahrweiler (Europäische Akademie zur Erforschung von Folgen Wissenschaftlich-Technischer Entwicklungen) (in German)

Banse, G. (ed.) (2007): Technological and Environmental Policy. Studies in Eastern Europe. Berlin

Dieren, W. van (ed.) (1995): Taking Nature into Account. New York a.o.

Grunwald, A. (2002): Technikfolgenabschätzung. Eine Einführung. Berlin (in German)

Jischa, M. F. (2005): Herausforderung Zukunft (2nd ed.). Heidelberg (in German)

Lengsfeld, T.; Tulbure, I.; Vali, A. (2003): Exploring a Worthwhile Future for All. A Report of tt30 of the Club of Rome. Valencia (Spanish Chapter of the Club of Rome)

Ludwig, B. (1995): Methoden zur Modellbildung in der Technikbewertung. Doctorate Thesis (TU Clausthal). Clausthal-Zellerfeld (CUTEC-Schriftenreihe, No. 18) (in German)

Meadows, D. H.; Meadows, D. L.; Randers, J.; Behrens III, W. W. (1972): The Limits to Growth. New York

Mitchell, G. (1996): Problems and Fundamentals of Sustainable Development Indicators. In: Sustainable Development, Vol. 4/No. 1 (March 1996), pp. 1–11

Nakicenovic, N.; Grübler, A.; McDonald, A. (eds.) (1998): Global Energy Perspectives. Cambridge

NRC – National Research Council (2000): Our Common Journey. A Transition toward Sustainability. Washington/D.C.

Tulbure, I. (1997): Zustandsbeschreibung und Dynamik umweltrelevanter Systeme (State and Dynamic Analysis of Environmental Systems). Doctorate Thesis (TU Clausthal). Clausthal-Zellerfeld (CUTEC-Schriftenreihe, No. 25) (in German)

Tulbure, I. (2003): Integrative Modellierung zur Beschreibung von Transformationsprozessen (Integrative Modelling to Describe Transformation Processes). Habilitation Thesis (TU Clausthal) Düsseldorf (VDI-Fortschrittsberichte, Series 16, No. 154) (in German)

Tulbure, I.; Jischa, M. (2006): First Report on Activities of the Network for Sustainability Strategies, Monitoring and Management in South-Eastern Europe (NESSEE). Alba Iulia

VDI – Verein Deutscher Ingenieure (ed.) (1993): Instrumente zur Minderung energiebedingter Klimagasemissionen IKARUS. Düsseldorf (VDI-Berichte, No. 1043) (in German)

Voss, G. (ed.) (1994): Sustainable Development. Leitziel auf dem Weg in das 21. Jahrhundert. Köln (in German)

WCED – World Commission on Environment and Development (ed.) (1987): Our Common Future. Oxford

The Integrative Sustainability Concept of the Helmholtz Association

The "Risk Habitat Megacity" Project as a Case of Application

Jürgen Kopfmüller

1 Sustainable Development: Basics and Challenges

Based on and focusing on post World War II development debates and policies, and addressing still existing environmental and social problems at the global, national and local level, the discussion about the sustainable development vision and its political implementation basically started with the World Commission on Environment and Development (so called Brundtland Commission) and its final report "Our common future" (cf. WCED 1987). Although this report was criticised for instance for its growth and technology optimism, it pushed the sustainability debate beyond the scientific frame by emphasising the basic tensions between development aspirations/needs and environmental protection and by making the according challenges and a basic development orientation transparent to a broader political and societal audience.

According to the still widely accepted definition of this report, "Sustainable development is development that meets the needs of the present without compromising the ability of future generations to meet their own needs" (WCED 1987, p. 24, no. 27). The report provided a key orientation for the United Nations Conference for Environment and Development in Rio 1992 (cf. UNCED 1992), where important initial sustainability documents such as Agenda 21 and the Rio Declaration where adopted being formative for the Rio follow-up process and for instance the Rio+10 Conference 2002 in Johannesburg.

While the 1970's and 1980's marked a first and foremost abstract episode in the sustainability debate, where efforts were mainly directed to conceptualize the term, Agenda 21 gave commencement to a new episode where focus was set on how to make sustainable development operational, i.e. on how to translate the concept into actual policy and planning. Agenda 21 set a milestone in this line by proposing concrete actions for actual implementation. It called into question many "traditional" paradigms about economic growth, the quality of development, environmental protection, public participation and the role of the State; and it called for new political processes based on inclusion, public participation and discourse, and creating alternative structures of governance to address existing problems (cf. UNCED 1992).

It is widely accepted today that sustainable development is to be associated with some crucial new (or recalled) perspectives: a comprehensive, holistic "view on the whole thing" considering complexities of social, economic, environmental, cultural etc. development dimensions and their interdependencies; the crucial role of distribution issues (regarding environmental and financial resources, development risks and opportunities, advantages and burdens from political measures, etc.); the global perspective which means setting goals at the global level and taking into account the national, regional and local level for implementation and implications; the longer-term orientation, e.g. in distinction from the political practice of parliamentary terms or the practice of company balances; and finally the idea of limits, with respect to economic growth, the use of finite resources, etc. For this, suitable sustainability concepts are required to sufficiently ground the idea in science, policy, planning, economy and society and to be able to provide appropriate orientation knowledge for societal decision makers.

Although there is a broad consensus about the idea in general terms and the basic perspectives mentioned above, controversies about its conceptual foundation and its precise definition as a basis for further operationalizing steps still prevail (cf. Ciegis et al. 2009; Gibson et al. 2005; Grabe 2010; Grunwald/Kopfmüller 2006; Kates et al. 2005). It is mainly the way of weighing the different dimensions ("pillars") – economic, ecological, social, institutional, cultural aspects, etc. – and of weighing the intra- and intergenerational justice perspective, being both the patterns for distinguishing existing sustainable development concepts and controversial issues. With respect to the pillars, basically three approaches can be differentiated, representing a trend towards increasing complexity over the past 20 years: initially, so called one-pillar-models, focusing on one of the dimensions – mostly on ecology, sometimes on economy were dominating, followed by the three-, four- or multi-pillar-models, depending on which dimensions are included, following the idea of equitable dimensions. These multi-pillar-models still represent the majority in sustainability research ad analysis. Mainly critisizing these models for their dimensional inside perspective on sustainable development neglecting interdependencies and potential conflicts between the dimensions, and for their inappropriate disciplinary view, trans-dimensional, integrative concepts were developed and applied – first by the Helmholtz Association (cf. Kopfmüller et al. 2001) and by the German Government in its sustainability strategy (cf. Bundesregierung 2002).

2 The Integrative Sustainability Concept of Helmholtz

The Integrative Concept was built on the ideas of the Brundtland report, the Rio documents and different international and national sustainability discourses. The aspiration and the claim was to overcome thinking in pillars and to provide both a theoretically well-founded approach to operationalise the sustainability idea as a normative goal orientation for development and an operable tool for current and future sustainability performance analyses. The concept has been (cf. Kopfmüller 2006) and currently is applied in various research and evaluation projects inside and outside the Helmholtz Association, in Germany and other countries.

In distinction from existing sustainability concepts, instead of the single dimensions the Integrative concept started from three constitutive elements (for details, cf. Kopfmüller et al. 2001):

(1) inter- and intragenerational justice, equal in weight;
(2) the global perspective regarding goals and action strategies;
(3) an enlightened anthropocentric approach, i. e. the obligation of mankind to protect nature out of a well understood self-interest to preserve the basics for living.

Accepting these elements, requires a comprehensive, integrative understanding of sustainable development, in particular as justice is a cross-dimensional issue.

These constitutive elements are operationalised in two steps: first, they were "translated" into three general goals of sustainable development, partly based on the Planetary trust theory of Edith Brown-Weiss (cf. Brown-Weiss 1989), being the condition precedent to sustainability:

- securing human existence;
- maintaining society's productive potential (comprising natural, man-made, human and knowledge capital);
- preserving society's options for development and action.

In a second and essential step, these goals are concretised by sustainability rules, which apply to various societal areas or to certain aspects in the relationship between society and nature (see Table 1). The concept distinguishes between substantial rules, identifying minimum conditions for sustainable development that ought to be assured for all people living in present and future generations, and instrumental rules, describing necessary framework conditions to realise these requirements. These rules – to be further concretised by suitable indicators – provide both the normative goal orientation for future development, and criteria to assess sustainability performances in different contexts.

Table 1: Sustainability Rules of the Integrative Concept

General Goals of Sustainable Development		
Securing human existence	Maintaining society's productive potentials	Preserving society's options for development and action
Substantial Rules		
Protection of human health	Sustainable use of renewable resources	Equal access for all people to information, education, occupation
Ensuring satisfaction of basic needs	Sustainable use of non-renewable resources	Participation in societal decision-making processes
Autonomous subsistence based on own income	Sustainable use of the environment as a sink	Conservation of cultural heritage and cultural diversity
Just distribution of chances for using natural resources	Avoiding technical risks with potentially catastrophic impacts	Conservation of the cultural function of nature
Reduction of extreme income or wealth inequalities	Sustainable development of man-made, human and knowledge capital	Conservation of social resources (tolerance, solidarity, etc.)
Instrumental Rules		
• Internalisation of external social and environmental costs • Adequate discounting • Public indebtedness • Fair global economic framework conditions • Promotion of international co-operation	• Society's ability to respond • Reflexivity of society • Society's steering ability • Self-organisation • Balance of power	

Source: After Kopfmüller et al. 2001, pp. 172, 174

In defining minimum requirements, the rules encompass by no means all desirable political, social and economic goals, but solely a certain welfare base *("Wohlfahrtssockel")*. Beyond that base, various other legitimate and desirable individual and societal goals may exist. Their realisation, however, is acceptable only to a degree that allows for the fulfilment of the sustainability rules. In principle, the rules are defined as a priori globally valid (i.e. independent from particular national or cultural contexts), but nevertheless they have to be adapted to the respective conditions, e.g. by determining according to indicators and target values. In terms of time, the system of rules is not infinitely valid, but rather serves as a kind of *"morale provisoire"*, i.e. a compass for sustainability assessments and relevance decisions, which does not preclude future changes and advancements.

The Helmholtz concept was developed to mark a well-founded answer to two fundamental critics in the discourse:

(1) to those who suspect an arbitrariness and degeneration of the guiding principle due to a lack of content and contour – by providing a clear, positive definition of sustainable development;
(2) to those who emphasize the problem of overcomplexity in a multidimensional, integrative approach – by defining the rules as minimum requirements.

2 The „Risk Habitat Megacity“ (RHM) Project: Implementation of an Integrative Research Approach

2.1 Background

Since the 1950's, urbanisation marks one of the basic trends in global development, 2008 being the first year where globally more people lived in cites than outside (cf. DSW 2009). Megacities, characterized by extreme size (more than five or ten million people), change dynamics and complexity, are places of accordingly extreme resource consumption and of highly concentrated economic and human capital as drivers of economic development and growth. Therefore, they play a key and continuously increasing role in the several global change processes and thus for the realisation of global sustainable development. Mega-urban agglomerations, in a sense being "laboratories" of global change processes, are both culprits and victims of these processes and anticipate trends with both regional and global consequences. They produce and have to deal with risks for sustainable development for instance in terms of earthquakes, climate change, air pollution, social exclusion, etc. At the same time, they provide opportunities to improve sustainability by using the possibilities of existing economic structures and dynamics, human capital, efficient design and use of supply infrastructures, etc.

Accordingly, megacities are currently a research topic with high priority, including a large array of both academic and popular publications so far focusing on classifications of megacites, their problems, self organising processes, or on urban governance basics and deficits. But, a particular perspective on the complexity of megacities, the interdependencies of thematic fields, temporal and special scales, and on different stakeholder perspectives has hardly been a distinct focus of attention previously (cf. Kopfmüller et al. 2009).

This was the starting point of the "Risk Habitat Megacity" research initiative of the German Helmholtz Association, beginning in 2005. The initiative conducted its studies in Latin America and for the initial case study in the Metropolitan Region of Santiago de Chile (MRS) for several reasons: Latin America is for a long time the most urbanised region in the world where existing problem constellations and previous experiences can be analysed. As a so called "primate city" (with 40–50% of national population and GDP), Santiago de Chile plays an important strategic economic and political role in Latin America. For a long time, the city experienced various problems representative of metropolises, applied political measures dealing with them, and thus provides the opportunity of learning and analysing the transferability of experiences to other (Latin American) megacities.

2.2 Objectives and Conceptual Approach of RHM

Against this background, the overall objective of the project was to develop and test a methodology that enables one to contribute to a better understanding of the complexity of megacities. Objectives in detail were to define sustainability goals of metropolitan development, to assess characteristic risks, to propose suitable risk and sustainability management strategies, and finally to integrate methodologies and project results into academic curricula and practice (cf. HA 2007). With this, the initiative aimed at both to work out basic scientific knowledge and, based on this, to provide suitable inter- and transdisciplinary orientation and action knowledge for regional decision makers. On the Chilean side, the initiative involved as partners the United Nations Economic Commission for Latin America and the Caribbean, the government of the Santiago Metropolitan Region, the most important Universities in Santiago de Chile and Valparaiso and engineering consultancies, on the German side several institutes in five Centres of the Helmholtz Association. Within this initiative, 20 PhD students worked both in Chile and Germany.

To implement this interdisciplinary and integrative research approach and to offer a common framework, the research initiative applied three theory-based analytical concepts: the concept of Sustainable Development defines the target dimension by using the Integrative concept; the Risk concept focuses on the extent and severity of problems and helps to analyse the threats to current and future sustainability; finally, the Governance concept concentrates on the actions to enhance sustainability and their implementation conditions. These three concepts were applied to several thematic fields typical for megacities: land use, socio-spatial differentiation, transportation, air quality and health, waste, energy and water. These issues illustrate the role of megacities as extensive resource consumers and producers of ecological and other negative externalities, and they point to crucial social aspects of mega-urban development processes.

The implementation of the integrative research approach with respect to the sustainability concept was mainly based on two tools representing an important distinct feature compared to other projects on megacity issues:

(1) the use of selected indicators to describe and assess the current and future sustainability performance, and
(2) the design and analysis of scenarios to consider and assess options for potential future development and action.

2.3 Sustainability and Scenario Analyses

Indicators are usually used to concretise the sustainability idea. In Santiago, to date there is no systematic application of sustainability indicators to orient urban and regional policies or to evaluate the effectiveness of planning instruments. In the RHM project, sets of headline indicators were selected for each of the thematic fields and for a field-independent level – based on the rules of the Integrative Concept – to measure and assess current and future sustainability performance. In this book contribution, only very few selected results can be presented (for detailed information cf. Heinrichs et al. 2011; Krellenberg et al. 2010).

At the field-independent level, the current sustainability analysis clearly revealed both strengths and weaknesses in the MRS (cf. Kopfmüller et al. 2011). Chile has made great progress since its return to democracy in 1990. In particular, poverty rates have fallen significantly (see Figure 1). Poverty is the principal factor that precludes people's capacity to meet their basic needs autonomously and live in human dignity – the basic sustainability goal at the individual level. Here, according to the definition of the National Planning and Cooperation Ministry, a person is defined as "living below the poverty line" if he/she is forced to live on a monthly income that is less than twice the value of the basic commodity basket (excluding public transfers). This decline in the poverty rate also implies improvements in related indicators, such as infant mortality (here defined as the risk of babies dying before the age of one), which halved between 1990 and 2007 (see Figure 2).

Figure 1: Percentage of People Living in Poverty

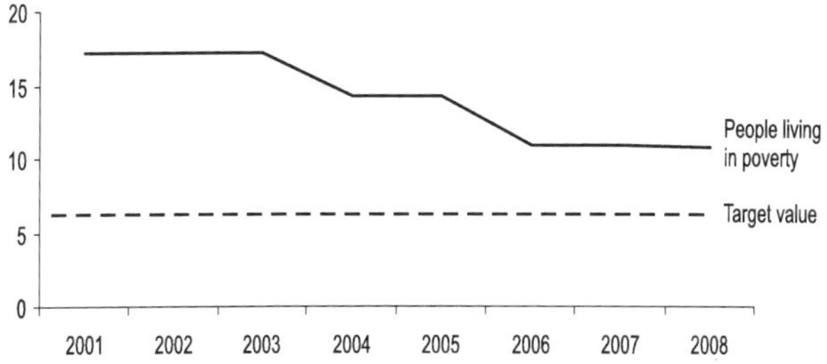

Source: After NSMI 2010

Figure 2: Infant Mortality Rate (per 1,000 life)

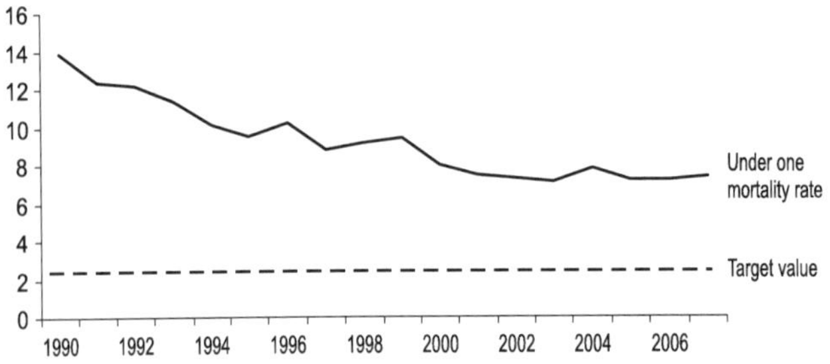

Source: After MoH 2008

These two variables reveal the close relationship between certain indicators. There is little doubt that strong economic growth rates at Chilean national and metropolitan levels, driven directly and indirectly by export revenues from copper and non-traditional agricultural products, have played a key role in the declining poverty rate, together with social policies. But still, considering target values based on organizations such as World Health Organisation and the UN Millennium Development Goals perspective shows that a further 50% reduction is imperative to be comparable to OECD countries standards.

Against these positive trends, concerns remain for instance about rising violent crime rates (see Figure 3). Personal security and its perception are critical to human well-being and quality of life. In the indicator used here, "serious crime rates" includes robbery with violence or intimidation, vehicle theft, theft, injury, manslaughter and rape. Delinquency and violent crime and fear about that remain the key preoccupations of urban inhabitants across social groups. Gated communities and private security companies in many areas of the city are a visible response to this process.

Income inequality generates according inequality of opportunities for a dignified human life. The Gini coefficient is one approach to measure distributional issues. It is defined as the proportion of the total population income that is cumulatively earned by the bottom x per cent of the population. It can range from 0 (complete equality) to 1 (complete inequality). The Santiago Metropolitan Region (see Figure 4) performs similar to the Chilean national level being among the ten per cent worst countries in the world regarding income distribution, constantly bearing Gini values above 0,5 (cf. UNDP 2009). An orientation in terms of the average for European countries would imply a target value of about 0,3. The minimum goal should be below the 0,5 line, which is regarded – for instance by the World Bank – as a threshold value for high inequality.

Figure 3: Reported Serious Crime Rate (per 100,000 people)

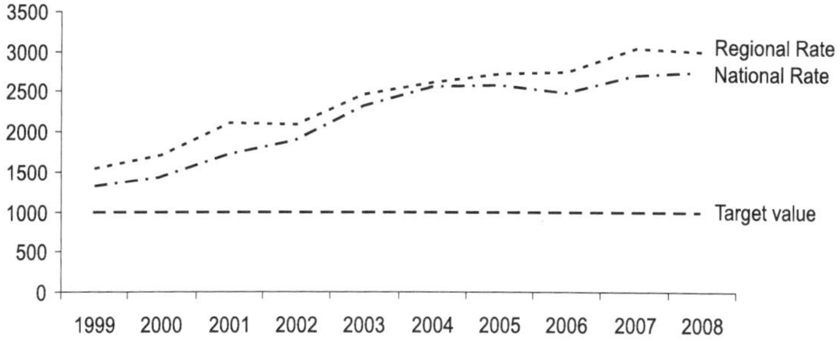

Source: After MoI 2009

Figure 4: Gini Coefficient

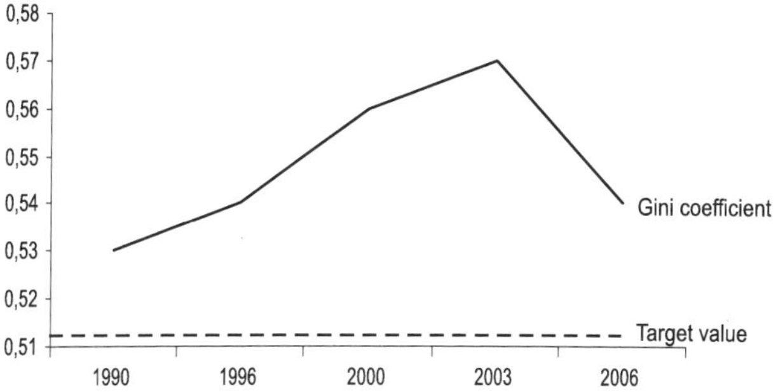

Source: MoP 2008

The second tool to implement the integrative research approach is the scenario method. The basic idea behind scenarios is not to predict future development, but to describe and analyse plausible alternative future options to appropriately deal with thematic complexities and future uncertainties to provide an improved knowledge base for decision makers.

In this project, a four-step approach was applied. In *step 1,* explorative framework scenarios were developed at the global level for the time horizon 2030, along a set of essential driving factors of societal development, such as economic development, demographics, technological development, or societal values.

Step 2 included a contextualisation of this framework for the Santiago/Chile level. For this, three alternative scenarios were developed. In short, the "Business-as usual" (BAU) scenario is characterised by a continuation of liberalisation and privatisation trends, persistence of strong market forces and weak public regulation activities. The basic idea of the "Market individualism" (MI) scenario is increasing individual freedom and freedom of action, markets dominating all societal transactions, and basic services and distribution being strongly subject to supply and demand. The "Collective responsibility" (CR) scenario is characterised by a stronger focus on social and environmental justice as goals of public regulation, stronger regulation of markets and increased public investments.

In *step 3,* these general scenarios were translated into the thematic field contexts by developing specific storylines for the three scenarios considering previous trends and future estimations for the most relevant driving factors.

Finally, in *step 4* quantitative and qualitative scenario analyses were carried out in all thematic fields, with respect to selected sustainability indicators and considering estimations for quantitative variables (population, GDP, household number, etc.) until 2030. The aim was to identify future strengths and problem "hot spots", mainly based on distance-to-target considerations, and to propose suitable measures addressing the most urgent problems within the scenarios.

The results indicate that the "Market Individualism" option includes more potential longer-term problems than the other two, and that the "Business-as-usual" option does not meet the demands that lie ahead for 2030 in the Metropolitan Region with then 8 million inhabitants (compared to currently 6.5 million). But also the "Collective responsibility" option is not a panacea, although it retains more positive outcomes, in particular reduced socio-spatial segregation and connected risks, and higher decoupling of demographics/GDP and resource demand. Apart from improvements in housing conditions, waste water treatment, or public transport, considerable challenges remain, for instance problems of socio-spatial segregation differing across the city, heavily influenced by access to education and housing policy instruments. Localisation of people and services are key elements to understand risks such as flooding, socioeconomic status is key to people's possibilities to successfully face these risks. It is evident that urban expansion did not consider socio-ecological risks and environmental justice issues. Localisation decisions also play a role for the shape of transport needs and associated health risks from emissions. Increased congestion and accordingly reduced accessibilities will require road pricing instruments as well as stronger public transport measures.

Rising population and income per capita will lead to a continued increase of water and energy demand. Due to expected climate changes, water stress will increase and new transfers will be required between sectors to maintain environmental services. To reduce emissions from waste collection, transfer and decomposition, existing options for processing the organic fraction of domestic waste need to be explored, involving informal workers appropriately to secure basic needs for vulnerable social groups. The considerably rising energy demand will require an increase in energy efficiency and renewable energies in order to move away from the current fossil fuel and big hydro power plant base.

The synergies across all thematic fields are evident, therefore more integrated, coordinated and consistent government and governance responses are required. Risks need to be identified in early stages of decision-making to ensure understanding of city-region dynamics and potential impacts. The intention to design a new regional longer-term development strategy with a time horizon 2021 (as opposed to previous short-term thinking) is a positive sign, but it should remain the road-map over time and across different heads of Regional Government or Regional Councils, to fulfil the claim of a longer-term perspective and to ensure consistency in decision-making towards more sustainable development.

Planning with existing tools such as the regional development strategy, the regional urban development policy, the inter-communal regulatory plan, or the local development plans will have to link much more with sectoral initiatives by public and private sectors on the one hand. On the other hand, these tools urgently need a review in terms of formulating goals and visions, a more systematic use of indicators, setting target values, and designing measures clearly oriented to these targets. These are crucial preconditions to implement a strategic metropolitan planning (cf., e.g., Hannemann 2008; Steinberg 2005) as a joint science-policy activity that should incorporate two basic ideas:

(1) an integrative approach, with respect to different societal sectors, political resorts, spatial and political levels or scientific disciplins, and
(2) a participatory approach, within scientific projects and in political decision processes.

The Risk Habitat Megacity project was conducted, including a continuous and broad involvement of relevant political and societal stakeholders, to provide suitable knowledge for regional actors and decision makers to enable them to implement such a strategic planning in the future.

References

Brown-Weiss, E. (1989): In Fairness to Future Generations. International Law, Common Patrimony and Intergenerational Equity. New York

Bundesregierung (2002): Perspektiven für Deutschland. Unsere Strategie für eine nachhaltige Entwicklung. Berlin (in German)

Ciegis, R.; Ramanauskiene, J.; Martinkus, B. (2009): The Concept of Sustainable Development and its Use for Sustainability Scenarios. In: Engineering Economics, Vol. 20/No. 2, pp. 28–37

DSW – Deutsche Stiftung Weltbevölkerung (2009): DSW Datenreport 2009. Soziale und demographische Daten zur Weltbevölkerung. Hannover (in German)

Gibson, R.; Hassan, S.; Holtz, S.; Tansey, J.; Whitelaw G. (2005): Sustainability Assessment – Criteria, Processes and Applications. London

Grabe, L. (2010): Das "Projekt Nachhaltigkeit". Zu den Grenzen des Nachhaltigkeitskonzepts aus kultureller Perspektive. Lüneburg (Cultura21 eBooks Series on Culture and Sustainability) (URL: (http://magazin.cultura21.de/_data/magazin-cultura21-de_addwp/2010/12/MA-Lisa-Grabe-c21-ebooks.pdf) (in German)

Grunwald, A.; Kopfmüller, J. (2006): Nachhaltigkeit. Eine Einführung. Frankfurt/M. (in German)

HA – Helmholtz Association (ed.) (2007): Risk Habitat Megacity. Sostenibilidad en Riesgo? A Helmholtz Research Initiative. Research Plan. Leipzig (URL: http://www.risk-habitat-megacity.ufz.de/index.php?en=14993)

Hannemann, A. (2008): Strategic Urban Planning and Municipal Governance: Within an Anglo-American Context. Saarbrücken

Heinrichs, D.; Krellenberg, K.; Hansjürgens, B.; Martinez, F. (eds.) (2011): Risk Habitat Megacity. The Case of Santiago de Chile. Berlin a.o. (in print)

Kates, R.; Parris, T.; Leiserowitz, A. (2005). What is Sustainable Development? Goals, Indicators, Values, and Practice. In: Environment, Vol. 47/No. 3, pp. 9–20

Kopfmüller, J. (ed.) (2006): Ein Konzept auf dem Prüfstand. Das integrative Konzept nachhaltiger Entwicklung in der Forschungspraxis. Berlin (in German)

Kopfmüller, J.; Brandl, V.; Jörissen, J.; Paetau, M.; Banse, G.; Coenen, R.; Grunwald, A. (2001): Nachhaltige Entwicklung integrativ betrachtet. Konstitutive Elemente, Regeln, Indikatoren. Berlin (in German)

Kopfmüller, J.; Lehn, H.; Nuissl, H.; Krellenberg, K.; Heinrichs, D. (2009): Sustainable Development of Megacities. An Integrative Research Approach for the Case of Santiago de Chile. In: DIE ERDE, Vol. 140/No. 4, pp. 417–448

Kopfmüller, J.; Barton, J.; Salas, A. (2011): How Sustainable is Santiago? In: Heinrichs, D.; Krellenberg, K.; Hansjürgens, B.; Martinez, F. (eds.): Risk Habitat Megacity. The Case of Santiago de Chile. Berlin a.o. (in print)

Krellenberg, K.; Kopfmüller, J.; Barton, J. (2010): How Sustainable is Santiago de Chile? Cirrent Performance – Furture Trends – Potential Measures. Synthesis Report of the Risk Habitat Megacity Research Initiative (2007–2011). Leipzig (UFZ-Report, No. 4/2010)

MoH – Ministry of Health (2008): Mortalidad por grupos programáticos (URL: http://deis.minsal.cl/deis/ev/index.asp)

MoI – Ministry of the Interior (2009): Informes anuales de estadísticas delictuales (URL: http://www.seguridadciudadana.gob.cl/ano_2002.html)

MoP – Ministry of Planning (2008): Encuesta CASEN: vivienda (URL: http://www.mideplan.cl/casen/Estadisticas/modulos/vivienda/2006/vivienda2006cuadro18.xls)

NSMI – National System of Municipal Information (2010): Selección de búsqueda (URL: http://www.sinim.gov.cl/indicadores/busq_serie.php)

Steinberg, F. (2005): Strategic Urban Planning in Latin America. Experiences of Building and Managing the Future. In: Habitat International, Vol. 29/No. 1, pp. 69–93

UNCED – United Nations Conference on Environment and Development (1992): Agenda 21: Earth Summit – The United Nations Program of Action from Rio. New York

UNDP – United Nations Development Programme (2009): Human Development Report 2009. New York

WCED – World Commission on Environment and Development (1987): Our Common Future. Oxford

2.
Cultural Diversity and Sustainability. Implicit Norms and Values

Ethics and Sustainability

Larissa Krainer

1 Introduction

There are three questions the organizers of our congress wanted to be answered:

(1.) How do you interpret sustainable development?
(2.) Where are the shared topics of sustainable development and culture (independent of the understanding you give to "culture")?
(3.) What are the efforts to promote sustainable development and what sorts of difficulties can be identified?

Let me take the first two questions together. When I speak about sustainable development, I am talking about a (political) need and an aim of our society. But at the same time I am talking about a cultural phenomenon and an ethical problem.

The ideas of sustainability and sustainable development cannot be seen as purely neutral demands. They are based on ethical values, focusing either on different "goods" (ecological, economical, social or cultural), or on various dimensions of justice (between cultures, generations and classes) or global fairness (trade, access to the media). And I really do think that our current culture does not promote sustainable development. Why? I would first like to offer two theses, then to formulate some consequences and to outline some answers from an ethical perspective.

2 Theses

(1) *To promote sustainable development many concepts have been proposed, mostly connected with proposals for action – on many levels from political through economical to private.*
However, very few of them, in fact, were ever put into practice. This can be explained as a matter of culture. Many authors do so, and some of them even claim a cultural change that should promote sustainable development in a better way (cf. Parodi et al. 2010) But: What is wrong with our current culture?
(2) *The dominant model of modern society follows technical and economical values that promote production and consumption, profit and competition, speed and innovation. It seems that our culture even works against sustainable development.*

So let's look for the central values within technical and economical concepts.

One slogan or motto says: *The new is the good.* It stands for technical development but equally for progress and the improvement of society. All in all it recalls the success story of western democracy. But at the same time it says: the old is the bad – throw it away! Do not repair or reuse the older things! If there is something new (for example a new generation of communication technology) go and buy it! This is one reason why millions of people living in poor circumstances (for example in states within the so called Third World countries) are motivated to want the same as we already have. What else should they do, if we are always running for technical development and if they want to make friends with us? I don't know why or how we should tell them that their push for technical development should be forbidden, in order to promote sustainable development instead. I would say we are not in a moral position to do so.

Another aspect of this motto is: If we call the new the best, we always have to devalue something else. Older things as mentioned before, but more and more it has been applied to older people as well. The elder generations are not seen as an important resource of knowledge and competences any longer but as a burden in different economic contexts: They earn too much (their human labour is too expensive), they live too long (their health insurance costs too much) and recently they spend most of their money before they die (their inheritance is not big enough anymore). Since we stopped looking after the knowledge and competences of elderly people, we are cutting through lines in our tradition and in fact we have to pay a lot to reconstruct what we had previously thrown out the door.

Another motto of our modern society is: *growth is good.* Even if we all know the prominent title of the Club of Rome's publication "The Limits to Growth", which back in 1972 already showed the consequences of a rapidly growing world population and finite resource supplies already in 1972, it seems that the economic mindset does not believe it. Our real economy but especially our public finance asks for profit and never for its limits. And since profit is the name of the game we do not even hesitate to make money from the collapse of countries which ought to be our partners in developing sustainability (like Greece for example).

A third motto – and I think one of the most problematic – is: *time is money.* And we can even turn it around and say: money is time. One important consequence of our modern society is speeding up and compression. First we agreed to measure human performance in work per time units. Then we found out that standstill is a step backwards. Finally we learned to become fast. Whatever we do, we try to do it fast, mostly faster than we ever did before. Our production became faster (on the market place the winner is always the one who presents a product first), and so did our travel system and our information system. On the one hand, this again can be seen as an improvement. On the other hand we all know that speed kills. We do not have enough time to examine the effects, to assess the technology and to reflect on the consequences. Our media system is forced to provide a running commentary which led to lots of mistakes in their reporting; Technology assessment should be done very quickly although it has become increasingly complex; to stop reflections means to prevent one of the most important questions of modern society: Do we like our world, our life and our circumstances like we have appointed them (cf. Heintel 1998)?

A final motto says: *politics should not interfere in the free play of forces of the market economy.* Again this idea is not so bad and especially Americans are well trained in this tradition through always fearing communism. But also again, it led to two problems. On the one hand our governments are unable to regulate the globalized public finance in order to prevent economic crises. One reason is that politics did not globalize in the same way as our money did. There is no powerful international cooperation to stop dangerous parts of public finance. Another well-known reason is that many powerful interests do their best to prevent politics from legislating against economic interests, as Robert B. Reich has shown impressively in his book *Supercapitalism: The Transformation of Business, Democracy, and Everyday Life* (cf. Reich 2008). On the other hand politics overall has become devalued (at least in many parts of Europe; in the USA there might be more "hope"). I don't know anybody who wants to become a politician, the younger generations even less so.

3 Consequences

The mottos I have described here can be seen as important, modern values. Each has its good sides but also very negative ones. Taking these to extremes means endangering ourselves. And that is what we have been doing for a very long time and it seems to be an ongoing danger. The idea that undefined intensification leads to a linear increase in success is wrong. The exact opposite is true.

If so, we should spend a little time on opposites in general. Ethical values are never unambiguous or completely clear. They are always contradictory. Even if some moral institutions taught us that just one thing, aim, believe or behaviour might be right, dialectic philosophy discovered that more positions than just one can be true or right and that there is always a thesis *and* an antithesis. Western democracy is based on the principle of government *and* opposition, and both might be right; we saw that the dominant values of modern economy (profit, growth, or speeding up) might be good *and* bad at the same time; they can lead to social progress *or* to economic disaster. The same goes for sustainability and sustainable development: it might be good *and* bad in the same time.

To set limits (on growth, on profit, on uninhibited speculation, on traffic and so on) might be good for sustainable development but it might also be a danger for freedom (of markets, globalization, travel and so on). And it offers inner contradictions. What might be good for social sustainability must not necessarily be good for economic sustainability as well. If employees earn (too) much a major corporation might go bankrupt. What might be good for ecological sustainability must not necessarily be good for social sustainability. If we have to pay lots of money for a clean environment we might become poor. And so on.

We live in a dialectic system standing in the tradition of enlightenment. If we agree to this result, we have to accept another conclusion: Dialectic systems need to process their opposites or contradictions in a dialectic way and not with the methods of logic. For example: If we agree that child labour is bad, we might come to a logical conclusion that says: don't buy things that are produced by child labour. But if we did so, we would get the children concerned and their families into big trouble, because many of them have to live off the income of these children, as the parents often don't get any work. So we first have to search for possibilities that offer an economic basis for families in all the parts of the world without child labour before we stop buying their products.

To use dialectic methods means to engage in conflicts, to handle and to process them, to weigh up the different possibilities against each other and finally to balance them. Most of the solutions are compromises. If just one side wins, both might lose. If we only push profit, we won't make much of a profit there. If we stop pushing profit, we also won't make much of a profit. So we have to be clever enough to handle our profit in a balanced way.

To organize a dialectic conflict management is a matter of time and finally a matter of money. We know: If the things are complex, so are the conflicts. All our systems have become enormously complex. Technology, Economy, Natural Science, science altogether. Politics cannot be seen as a simple area for taking decisions. And so, we need more time to analyze complexity within all these areas that are interconnected anyway (which makes it more complex). We have to analyze carefully and do it in interdisciplinary groups (which make it more complex again). We have to understand the arguments of our opponents (those who seem to work against sustainable development) the best we can in order to find solutions that have every chance of being converted into action or results. Most of the time we prefer to keep to ourselves, in an in-group of likeminded people standing for sustainable development. We won't find our opponents, if we don't move towards them. They won't search for us, because they prefer to achieve their goals with other methods than dialectic ones. They do not search for opposition. That is the reason why most of them dislike democracy. So: If we don't move – who will?

References

Heintel, P. (1998): Abendländische Rationalität. Welche Ethik für die Wissenschaften? Klagenfurt (unpublished; in German)

Parodi, O.; Banse, G.; Schaffer, A. (eds.) (2010): Wechselspiele: Kultur und Nachhaltigkeit. Annäherungen an ein Spannungsfeld. Berlin (in German)

Reich, R. B. (2008): Superkapitalismus. Wie die Wirtschaft unsere Demokratie untergräbt. Frankfurt/M. (in German)

Implicit Normative Settings in Concepts of Sustainability and Cultural Diversity

Solving the Antagonism

Robert Hauser

1 Culture and Sustainability

The concept of sustainable development is not the result of scientific research and is not descriptive; rather, it is normative and based in ethics. The term itself communicates a mental image of the world as it should be, particularly in regard to intergenerational (between generations) and intragenerational (distribution of wealth) equity. Concepts for sustainable development always involve implicit normative settings and, to a certain extent, the canonical values of the cultural context in which they originated. As in the area of technology, cultural "settings" have found their way into ideas about the "sustainable". Sustainability and sustainable development exert, therefore, a significant influence on behaviour; they are regulative "Wertideen" (concepts of value) in the sense of Immanuel Kant[1] (cf. Kant 1977/1781) or Max Weber (cf. Weber 1982/1904). In this way, they are not concepts that define (or name) an object of experience, instead, they are pragmatic and regulative principles, which create meaning: other well known examples for "Wertideen" are "freedom" or "justice". As principles that produce meaning, concepts of value exert a significant influence on our behaviour. Their interpretive task is therefore of crucial importance for producing activity. They have a distinct impact on human actions.

But what is the relationship between concepts of value and culture? What consequences does this relationship have for the application of these concepts of value when the context of global cultural diversity is duly considered?

2 The Constitutive Nature of Norms and Values for Cultural Communities

In order to better understand the dilemma surrounding the collision of implicit canons of values and norms and cultural diversity, it is helpful to reflect on the concept of culture and on the constitutive nature of norms and values for cultural

1 Kant uses in his "Critique of Pure Reason" the term "regulative Idee" (cf. Kant 1977/1781).

communities: Norms and values are considered to be constitutive for cultural communities. Cultural communities result from a common history of coming to terms with life and existence – a history maintained mainly through traditions, languages, and institutions.

Cultural communities develop over a long period of time as behavioural and communicative groups in a common geographic space and on the basis of specific norms and values that have been formed through the interaction of the community with and within a specific "environment" socially and natural, which represents a frame of reference (cf. Banse/Metzner 2005; Hauser 2010).

In this sense, cultures are a product of history; they have produced their own specific values and norms to guide behaviour, through an collective existential struggle. These values and norms provide the foundation for the creation and interpretation of symbolic systems, which, in turn, lead to specific social, economic, and technical structures and developments.

How do values and norms influence cultural existence?

3 Values and Norms in Theory

Cultural norms can be further differentiated. Klaus P. Hansen distinguishes hierarchically between norms of custom, norms of convention or decancy, and norms of law (cf. Hansen 2003). A community's value system, which is derived from implicit and explicit norms, can (to a limited extent) be deduced from the extent of sanctions, the degree of objectification or formalization, and the degree of institutionalization linked to nonconformity to norms. At the same time, there is a connection between the different kind of norms and the variance, range, and valence.

Norms of custom and convention can exhibit extreme variance within a given cultural community, sometimes in the form of a limited range (subcultures develop). Although not all members of that community may stick to norms of custom, they are familiar with them. Violations tend to be tolerated by the members of a community as a whole. To give an example: In Germany we usually don't have raw fish with cold rice and cold egg for breakfast (but Japanese do by the way). However, when I do eat this in Germany no body will detain me from doing so or even punish me.

Decency norms are likely to have little variety, limited range and may lead to social sanctions or can be punished by law depending on the cruelty of violation. This is handled differently in different cultures. Legal norms, on the other hand, are not only much more precisely formulated than other norms, above all, they are those norms which are institutionally anchored in constitutions and similar documents. They form a foundation of norms and values and are subject to change only over long periods of time. They possess a wide range normally the whole community or society, that is, they are valid for everyone and define in this way the boundaries of the cultural community. Violations are not tolerated and are typically also severely punished. In most societies, the assessment and the extent of the legal punishment are also formalised and institutionalized (courts, prisons, etc.).

Contrary to the norms discussed before, legal norms are essential for the existence and maintenance of social orders. Together with language, history and institutions are norms define generally the boundaries of communities, like that of most nations nowadays.

4 Norms and Cultural Practice: Micro-normative Standards

The constitutive power of norms and values in relation to groups is also revealed in their living manifestations. A collective's system of norms and values are negotiated over time and on the basis of a common existential struggle; furthermore, according to Hansen, they produce so-called micronormative standards or standardizations for the everyday life of the community (cf. Hansen 2003). These become observable in the form of conventions and patterns. These conventions and patterns can be illustrated in terms of four areas: in communication, in thought, in action, and in feeling and perception. These collective micronormative standards are highly conducive to the production of identity.

While anthropologists influenced by Arnold Gehlen (cf. Gehlen 1956, 1962/1940) and Clifford Geerts (cf. Geerts 1987) work with behavioural "patterns" and linguists work with the concepts of communicative or linguistic "standardizations", this concept may be little known within the disciplines concerned with sustainability. For this reason, it will be illustrated by a few brief examples: All of us are probably familiar with everyday standardizations of language: regional and group-specific greetings in the form of standardized phrases offer an obvious example. In Ireland you will hear "How are you?", in England, you are likely to hear "How do you do?", etc. Similar standardizations are to be found in all reasonably large language communities, including German (for example, between the Swiss and the Austrians or Germans and again within Germany). A further example is offered by specialist vocabularies, in which a particular term can possess a very specific meaning and usage, which differs from its use in everyday contexts or in other specialist vocabularies.

But there are also standardizations of thinking, which have a profound influence on our behaviour. Everyday activities offer any number of examples, such as separating our rubbish for recycling. Mr. X will only sort his rubbish if he is convinced that it is sensible to protect the environment and he values this goal. In this case, separating rubbish can be described as a behavioural norm that follows from a value held. Separation of garbage as norm of acting which follows the value of healthy and clean environment, as a standardisation in thinking, is in Germany and many other counties nowadays socially accepted by a majority of people and supported by politicians and law (at least as far as producers of packaging material are concerned) as well as local communities. One can say that it is already standardised as routine, meaning we no longer actively think about whether to separate garbage or not, only where to put a specific piece of garbage for some of our contemporaries still is a matter of its own. By identifying themselves with the patterns and conventions of a collective, by recognizing or applying them, individuals express their membership in a collective and a community; individuals that are unfamiliar with, or deliberately do not conform to, these patterns and conventions are perceived as outsiders or strangers. In this way social-cultural values exert a direct influence on behaviour and, as was just described, produce identity. This means a group is made up of individuals and groups shape individuals, who acquire their identities by reacting to collective standards'. In this way, groups and individuals find themselves in a continuous and reciprocal relationship, whereby the standardizations or conventions function as mechanisms for inclusion and exclusion (cf. Hauser 2010).

According to Kant and Weber, "Wertideen" (concepts of value) are particularly conducive to interpretation and creation of meaning. So what is the difference? Social values and their following norms define something that is adorable and how we should act to reach this valued goal but without an imperative. e.g. in some societies it is a value to be economical successful, the norms to reach this are for example diligence, be kind to your boss, etc. On the other hand it is imaginable that at the same time asceticism in the sense of abdication is a value which is followed by special norms again.

Contrary to the values we looked at so far, concepts of values or "Wertideen" are not only socially or societally desirable, but are categorical imperatives. For example "freedom" and "justice" are concepts of value in this sense, but ideologies or religions also ultimately represent concepts of value. They are moral norms (cf. Jonas 2003). In contrary to social norms they therefore do not have alternatives. So if freedom is a value its not imaginable that bondage can be a value too. The more power these concepts of value have to create meaning, the stronger the collective cohesiveness and, therefore, the more individuals that can be bound to them.

Mankind is spread across almost the entire globe. The resulting geographical distances have led to the development of different communities, which have developed different canons of norms and values on the basis of their specific means of coming to terms with existence in different natural and social environments over long periods of time. On the basis of these fundamental values, they have, in turn, produced specific concepts of value ("Wertideen") in order to create meaning. These concepts enter into competition with one another when multiple communities come into contact. For this reason, weak concepts of value lead either to anarchy through loss of the cohesive force of constitutive norms and values or to subjugation under more stable groups and stronger concepts of value.

The strongly competitive nature of concepts of value is visible above all in religiously motivated wars: concepts of value are a major source of conflict potential between groups (cf. "Clash of Cultures" by Samuel P. Huntington).

5 The Model of Sustainable Development as a Concept of Value

As already stated at the outset, the model of sustainable development is an example of a concept of value ("Wertidee") and therefore culturally determined.

Considered in a global context, this concept of value finds itself in competition with others and, for this reason, with other peoples' and societies' canons of values and norms. To date, the objective fact of cultural diversity (which again may be traced back to differences in the development of values and norms in different environments) has scarcely been reflected upon in the debate surrounding sustainable development.

As a concept of value, "sustainable development" rests on a number of normative settings that are not called into question in most works on sustainability (neither are they defended). "Demand for justice" ("Gerechtigkeitsanspruch") and "the responsibility principle" ("Verantwortungsprinzip") are two of the very basic components of almost all models of sustainable development.

Because of this lack of reflection, I would like to briefly discuss both of these normative elements, which are central to concepts of sustainable development. In the cases of both "justice" and "responsibility", we are dealing with subjective concepts of value, which again as we have already discussed have culturally specifically connotations. The normative constitution of both will now be briefly discussed.

5.1 Justice

What is justice? Different cultures answer this question in different ways. This gives evidence to the fact that justice itself is a morale value. In some cultures, justice means that men and women have different rights and duties. (Woman in muslimic countries are often not allowed to leave their places without permission of their husbands) This notion is indefensible in terms of our Western (or, perhaps, even specifically German) understanding of fundamental values. The definition of the just and unjust is often related to access to rights because the exact definition of what is just is not an arbitrary choice, but rather, is ethically and normatively justified, typically on the basis of legal decisions. Rights are determined by the social structure of a society. The nature of hierarchies, distribution of power, and opportunities for agency are culturally diverse and play an important role in the distribution of rights. The field of law again refers us to normative regulations and value systems, which are themselves culturally specific.

Even the concept of justice, as it exists in Germany today, has its linguistic and semiotic roots in advanced civilizations of the occident that have been of decisive influence to the Western Europe societies: the ancient Greek, Roman-Latin, and the Arabian cultures, the celtic Germanic ("das Germanische") and, of course Christianity, as well.

Because the field of law is distinguished by the normative setting of central values, which are constitutive for the community or group, every community protects this field and its associated values and norms and defends them from foreign influences.

5.2 Responsibility

Essentially, responsibility is like justice itself a moral category. Fundamentally, however, there is a connection between agency and responsibility. It's without question that people can only be held accountable for actions in contexts where they have acted under their own responsibility. The principle that a particular form of agency is necessary for (moral) responsibility can be derived from ancient Greek philosophy. The ability to influence decisions, i.e. participation, characterizes and limits agency: people can only take responsibility for decisions that they were able to influence.

The definitions of agency and participation in collective decisions are, in turn, culturally specific. They are directly tied to the social structure and the dominant hierarchies and/or power structures. In Western Europe, the bourgeois individual has been developing since the Middle Ages: expanding the extent of his agency and demanding participation on the basis of the principle of democracy. The individual's binding influence on collective decisions is guaranteed by the democratic principle, and this – among other factors – makes for a very extensive agency. This extends to the election and recall of governing officials and, in some cases, to direct democracy, as in Switzerland.

In this context, the authors of concepts of sustainable development assume that people always have the ability to participate in political decisions; in reality, this is only true for a small number of the countries or societies that exist at present. Democratic participation is experienced and institutionalized in different ways in different countries. This can be observed even within the context of the countries of the former Eastern bloc, which are still dealing with the legacy of the recent (in terms of contemporary history) dictatorships. The political structures of countries such as Russia function completely differently from those in the West.

The same is true for the countries of South America, such as Chile, although most of them are named "democracies". For this reason, the issue of democracy is particularly emphasized in the debates surrounding sustainability in these countries – at least in those cases where the topic has become a source of discussion. In this way, a political dimension to sustainability has been postulated.

In many other cultures and countries (such as Indonesia or Afghanistan), which have developed through the merging of distinct tribal groups, individuals' political participation only extends to taking part in village councils. This is, then, also the limit of individuals' spheres of influence and responsibility.

As responsibility depends mainly on participation and the agencies of individuals which are directly connected to principles of sharing power, it becomes obvious that different concepts of sharing power lead to different concepts of responsibility. The principle of responsibility must therefore be understood as fundamentally culturally specific and not as a universal.

The examples of "justice" and "responsibility" have shown that different meanings – historically developed and culturally specific – are attached to certain basic concepts of morale value in the axiological context of sustainable development. It becomes clear that, the priorities within a canon of social and moral values vary in reaction to cultural disposition. There may also be values that have not yet played any role in thinking on sustainable development, but which are constitutive for certain societies and groups. Conversely, particular interpretations of presumably universal concepts of value (our understanding of justice or responsibility, for example) may be unacceptable or, because of fundamentally different understandings of these concepts, useless for certain societies.

6 Normative Ethical Settings of the Concept of Integrative Sustainability

Through its entire orientation, its explicit and explicit assumptions, and its normative demands, the "Konzept der integrativen Nachhaltigkeit" ("Concept of Integrative Sustainability") of the Helmholtz-Society ("Helmholtz-Gemeinschaft", cf. Kopfmüller 2006; Kopfmüller et al. 2001; cf. the contribution by Jürgen Kopfmüller in this volume) is a concept of value that is clearly based on a heterogeneous, democratic, detraditionalized, individualized, and pluralistic society. This concept's genesis in terms of the history of ideas and the canon of values upon which it and its normative demands are based have never been adequately and transparently explicated, nor reflected upon in terms of the consequences of its application in Germany or other countries. As a result, the Concept for Integrative Sustainability has remained historical (that is, it is not historically informed).

Conversely, it may be concluded that concepts for sustainable development in other cultural contexts can only become meaningful, inspire identification, and, therefore, can only influence behaviour, if they are compatible with preexistent concepts of value, or, better yet, if they are developed on the basis of these.

Sustainable development can, in the end, only be initiated in other cultures by initiating a process of reflection upon that culture's own concepts of value, from which its own understanding of sustainable development will evolve.

References

Banse, G.; Metzner-Szigeth, A. (2005): Veränderungen im Quadrat. Computervermittelte Kommunikation und moderne Gesellschaft. – Überlegungen zum Design des europäischen Forschungs-Netzwerks "Kulturelle Diversität und neue Medien" –. In: Banse, G. (ed.): Neue Kultur(en) durch Neue Medien (?). Das Beispiel Internet. Berlin, pp. 17–46 (in German)

Geertz, C. (1987): Dichte Beschreibung. Beiträge zum Verstehen kultureller Systeme. 5th ed. Frankfurt/M. (in German)

Gehlen, A. (1956): Urmensch und Spätkultur. Bonn (in German)

Gehlen, A. (1962/1940): Der Mensch. Seine Natur und seine Stellung in der Welt (7th ed.). Frankfurt/M. (in German)

Hansen, K. P. (2003): Kultur und Kulturwissenschaft (3rd ed.). Tübingen, Basel (in German)

Hauser, R. (2010): Technische Kulturen oder kultivierte Technik? Das Internet in Deutschland und Russland. Berlin (in German)

Jonas, H. (2003): Das Prinzip Verantwortung: Versuch einer Ethik für die technologische Zivilisation. Berlin (in German)

Kant, I. (1977/1781): Kritik der reinen Vernunft. In: Kant, I.: Werke in zwölf Bänden. Vol. 3. Frankfurt/M. (in German)

Kopfmüller, J.; Brandl, V.; Jörissen, J.; Paetau, M.; Banse, G.; Coenen, R.; Grunwald, A. (2001): Nachhaltige Entwicklung integrativ betrachtet Konstitutive Elemente, Regeln, Indikatoren. Berlin (in German)

Kopfmüller, J. (ed.) (2006): Ein Konzept auf dem Prüfstand. Das integrative Nachhaltigkeitskonzept in der Forschungspraxis. Berlin (in German)

Weber, M. (1982/1904): Die "Objektivität" sozialwissenschaftlicher und sozialpolitischer Erkenntnis. In: Weber, M.: Gesammelte Aufsätze zur Wissenschaftslehre. Tübingen, pp. 146–214 (in German)

The Role of the Cultural Heritage at the Local Sustainable Development Programs

János Szlávik, Miklós Füle

1 Global and Local Values

The concept of sustainable development is inherently related to the future. Its original definition identifies this idea with the preservation of the living opportunities of future generations. If we take a closer look at the future quality of life, we have to recognise the extraordinary role local cultural values and traditions play in the determination of the identity of a particular generation. Cultural values, therefore, require the analysis of past and present events. The root of all future effects lie firmly in the past and the present.

If we accept this logical sequence to be true, we can deduce that sustainable development – as natural, social, and economic philosophy – does not appear as a radical paradigm replacing the conventional, growth-oriented model of society, but rather as a way of thinking gradually evolving from it. In this change on an historic scale, the preservation of cultural traditions means the numerous threads of ever-latent continuity and stability between the old and the new.

Values – including the cultural values of sustainability – are very difficult to define, because usually they appear as the result of heterogeneous and unique phenomena. If we isolate *global values* and *local values* from these phenomena, we can pose the question as to how much weight these value groups (global and local) will influence the new social philosophy of sustainability from the perspective of future generations? Another question is whether the weights we perceive today will change, and if so, in what way and with what dynamics?

Would it be desirable from the point of sustainability if the *global* economic, natural and social perception – which regards all movements of civilisation as part of a large single system – would dominate the values of micro communities and individuals, or whether survival would rather arise from small social groups adopting a lifestyle which would rely largely on their own resources?

The last half century has undoubtedly brought with it the strengthening of globalising processes. Amidst the current financial and economic crisis one question remains, and that is whether this tendency has gone past its zenith, or whether we are still moving along an upwards-pointing path, fuelling further globalisation? Can we take the spread of local heritage organisations in industrialised countries in recent years as an indicator of the increasing importance of local values? Can we be certain about these statistics reflecting public thinking, or are we merely facing a phenomenon where welfare societies can simply afford financially supporting these organisations and are keen to do so as well?

The results of a recent survey we have conducted in a small town in Hungary are puzzling. This survey was conducted as part of the creation of an LA-21 programme. The population surveyed was asked to rank by importance the development they would like to see in certain areas in their locality. Of their choices (education, agriculture, traditional craftsmanship, home construction, industry development, services, transport, tourism) the least often chosen was traditional craftsmanship. Naturally, it would be a fallacy to generalise from the results of one locality, but this example does raise the question whether the preservation of traditions are a natural and imminent part of public thinking, or whether this perception needs to be strengthened?

If for reasons of manageability we insist on categorising values requiring special support in sustainable development, we ought to be thinking in terms of *historical, aesthetical, moral* and *use values.*

Historical values include legends, stories conveyed by written word or word of mouth, related to the immediate or nearby surroundings. Its force of unity lies in family ties, that is, all events happened to immediate family, to predecessors of relatives. Our ancestors took part in the events, happening locally or in the neighbouring localities. Being part of these concrete – and frequently non-verifiable – accounts of events, in theoretical or indeed, very real form, reaffirms a segment of the ties to the locality, to the geographical region.

The identification and application of *aesthetic values* refers to currently existing identities in taste, which are remnants of the past and which will continue to exist in the future. Particular groups, for example, have a common way of thinking about clothing (hereby we do not only refer to clothing manufactured with traditional folk decorations, but the preference of using certain materials over others, or indeed, the use of a traditional motif in a – perhaps – stylised fashion).

Such a tradition of the aesthetic kind appears in architecture particular to a locality or a micro region, both in terms of style and materials used. For example, in the case the North Balaton Highlands of Hungary, many newly-built summer homes feature thatched roofs, which is based on a locally produced building material. Constructors may have often seen such buildings in their childhood, which have gone to affect their taste in adult life too. Not insignificantly, such a building – with a modern interior design and comfort – protects the uniform image of the village fitting the local taste, affecting the decisions taken by future generations. (Furthermore this offers an environmentally friendly and sustainable solution to the adaptation to climate change.

Moral values incorporate the necessity of coexistence of humans and nature through choices of the "what may be done and what may not" kind, even though the original intention frequently remains unidentifiable. For example, in the Hungarian villages the traditional thinking of not throwing food away or using clothing as long as it was physically still possible arose from the commands of poverty. The concept of poverty meant that one was only able to obtain scarce goods (such as clothing, food, fuel for the fire, etc.) for their family, therefore it was essential that the existing, already owned combinations of materials had to be used for the longest possible length of time with the smallest possible loss. The global interpretation of sustainability works along a similar logical way of thinking. Because of the scarcity of materials, demands must be satisfied in the most economical way.

Use value does not refer to the sometimes irrational affection towards old objects, but it is rather an approach with a very direct economic result, whereby local products manufactured in the traditional way will remain used for a longer time, thus saving the material and energy requirements as well as the cost of labour sacrificed for a replacement product. The technology of producing goods used by past generations can have result in direct benefits too. Adobe, a traditional and typical construction material of straw, clay and water was frequently used 50 to 100 years ago, which is enjoying a renaissance in Hungary. Provided it remains sufficiently protected from humidity, it is a construction material with excellent thermal properties, which is being used again more frequently.

Preserved use value has a certain effect, providing continuity between the generations, which was formulated by a university colleague as follows: "... our father's hammer, worn smooth over the years, can help us with our work, whilst holding our father's own hands..." (Miklós Istvánffy).

2 Relationship of Sustainability and Local Values

A number of questions may be asked about the previous statements:

- Will these differences in values not further fuel segregation, instead of the cooperation desired between humans, areas and countries?
- It may also arise that these values rooted in history (often local history) do simply mean a certain nostalgia, and whether they are in aid of the development of future generations.

The preliminary answer in both cases is that frequently the maintenance of such local and micro-regional traditions of nature, lifestyle and economy do not mean a gaze back into the past, but rather serve as a realistic basis for a sustainable future.

Our claim can be proved by the following. Diversity enriching and strengthening the ecological system is a fundamental principle in natural sciences, and this will hold for future societies as well. A globalised world, provided that local particularities will have disappeared from it, will resemble the grey environment of housing estates.

A famous simile by Konrad Lorenz states that the structure of modern cities resembles cancerous cells, which, when compared to healthy cells appear rather unstructured, and their strongest motivation is unlimited growth (cf. Lorenz 1988).

In terms of sustainability, a well-structured locality or micro region living up to its heritage, rich in information would be desirable. Literature considers the preservation of capital important, regardless of whether we refer to the weak or strong interpretation of sustainability. There is, however a third aspect of sustainability, a further interpretation, which states that besides capital (especially natural capital) the revenues derived from this capital must be preserved too, because the "man of the present" of any age can only live off the revenues, but not the capital itself. Naturally, an existence can be derived from the capital itself – as numerous examples around the globe have indicated – but this way of existence is by no means sustainable.

The sustainable development of the economy and its only means of growth is, for example, sustainable tourism, the development of ecotourism. This sector of services and production refers to the purveyance and use of the natural resources, historical resources, folk traditions, typical foods, local produce and food to and by tourists.

In this manner of generating revenues most of the income is produced by local values and resources (whilst preserving and developing these values and activities). Most of these activities require a lot of human labour, and much of the revenues produced locally may remain there or within the region. These differences in values act against segregation, by making local communities more open in such a way that local customs are not threatened, but encouraged.

When we talk about sustainability, we frequently refer to the importance of preserving natural capital, often forgetting about the built-up environment at the same time. Naturally, we do not mean to talk about the primitively structured and aggressively spreading big city, as described by Konrad Lorenz.

The built up world, including not only buildings but the urban structure that has been in continuous development throughout history, we often consider to be modifiable without any adverse effects. We usually consider construction as development, and we rarely or incorrectly consider the losses of value as a result of demolition.

When we refer to local programmes of sustainability, a built-up environment that is worthy of preservation and is sustainable must also form part of that.

The houses of our grandfathers ought to be preserved with the necessary maintenance and infrastructural development, and the techniques used in their construction, the structures, functions and materials can be used in newly constructed buildings as well. Traditional buildings of thatch and adobe are comfortable during the hottest of the summer days even without air conditioning, which, in combination with the contemporary energy, water and wastewater and urban residue treatment systems is not only sustainable, but also very comfortable.

The concept of sustainable work culture must be also mentioned as part of the cultural values of sustainability. For centuries, much of the Hungarian territory consisted of wetlands (because of its pan-shape), with a rich fish population, rich bird and wildlife. After much of the wetland was drained in the 19th century, the risk of floods and summer drought has gradually increased as a result of climate change, which requires the construction of flood drains. These drains can function as wetlands throughout the year, with a rich fish stock and avian life. A good example of this is Lake Tisza, part of the Hortobágy National Park.

However, when locals were asked about their opinion of this development opportunity, there was a serious resistance, as the working culture of the people – as a result of the past fifty years of intensive agricultural activity – have lost their skills of fishing and fowling.

Heritage and heritability as components of value are very vulnerable. Isolated instances of significant pollution may be overcome by nature over a period of years or decades, as, for example, a river will recuperate. However, if a successive chain of passing on traditions is broken, the tradition may die out completely.

It should be noted that this kind of knowledge has still been on the decrease in recent years, and this effect is only worsened by environmental disasters. A decade ago, a significant cyanide poisoning occurred on the River Tisza, effectively reducing fish stock to a level whereby fishing as a full-time occupation has been reduced to nearly null in most places, and halting completely in some places. As there were no job opportunities for fishers, the intermediate level fisherman training has been cancelled (in 2008).

3 Cultural Values and Traditions of Lake Tisza

Legends, traditions, crafts in the area are mostly related to the dominant agriculture. This, for example, is echoed in the name of the City of Tiszafüred. As legend has it, one of the most popular kings of Hungarian history, the famous King Matthias the Righteous was offered shelter for the night by a fisherman near the River Tisza. The fisherman gathered a big bunch of grass to make a comfortable bed for the King. After a good night's sleep on the fresh grass, the

King bequeathed that the place be known from thereon as Fűrend (fű = grass, rend = bunch [of grass]). This name was modified later to Füred, and then – as the city is on the River Tisza – to its current form of Tiszafüred.

Oral traditions have immortalised the names of two people. One of them, Gyuri Józsa (Gyuri is the nickname of the Hungarian form of George) was a landlord born in1789, who was very generous on the one hand, regularly giving clothes to poor children, paid for medicine during the cholera epidemic for those in need, and he commissioned the first permanent bridge on the River Tisza. On the other hand, he is remembered popularly as a quirky, eccentric man, who has been the perpetrator of countless pranks and practical jokes, ranging from noisy night-outs to abducting women.

The other man was called Pista Pénzásó (roughly translated as Moneydigger Mack), who was believed to be a táltos, a gifted medicine man and clairvoyant of pagan Hungarian beliefs. He was supposed to have been born with a tooth, a tell-tale sign of such a gift. He left his home at the age of six, and dedicated his life to finding treasures. He was a poor man, with a frightful appearance. According to the legend he waited on Saint George's night out in the fields to wait for flames erupting from the Earth, a sign of gold buried in the ground. He explained his poverty by saying that the treasures he found were cursed, so he didn't keep the gold. He was good at handling animals, and his foretellings were received well by his peers. He died around his 80th birthday, and it is said that on that day, a huge storm swept the area.

The more peaceful parts of the 18th century have influenced the production of not everyday use items, those used on special occasions positively. Craftsmen on the banks of the River Tisza have excelled in the manufacture of saddles, especially the so-called oriental saddles, which they have produced at an artistic level. The oriental saddle is special because it distributes the pressure on the horses' back by using fitting wooden saddle ribs, whereas western saddles are supported at four points only. Hungarian horsemen have used these saddles in the wars against the Ottoman invaders, and later Hussars adopted the oriental saddle as standard, and the best and most beautiful of these saddles were crafted in Füred. A written source cites a saddle maker's presence in 1715, and their number increased drastically, so much so that by the War of Liberty of 1848–1849 most of the saddles of the cavalry were made right here. A rich collection of saddles can be found in the Museum of Tiszafüred reflecting craftsmanship throughout the ages, with some of the most beautifully decorated ones being made in the second third of the 19th century.

Pottery has been an important craft in the area, which provided plenty of good quality river clay, and fragments of pots have been found dating back to the Neolithic Age. The lesser known variety of pots, called black pottery, which has gained its name from the soot getting burnt right into the terracotta itself, whereas enamelled ceramics have arrived a lot later in the area. One of the oldest pieces of doubly fired earthenware is a wine jug from 1828. Typical shapes include Miska jugs, in the shape of a shepherd, spice pots and jugs. Predominant colours include red, white, yellow and rarely green. Typical patterns include birds standing on branches with a flower in the beak, pomegranate, waving row of leaves. The fame of the masters of years gone by is carried on by Imre Szűcs, who has opened his workshop in Tiszafüred in 1970.

Painted furniture appeared in the popular heritage after 1830. Blue and red decorations were predominant on beds and chest, where the patterns of the wood were highlighted in black. From the end of the 19th century, the traditional methods of painting furniture have been abandoned, and as furniture has changed its function, its colour has become a uniform brown.

As we can see, the traditional lifestyle, culture and work culture is not something that can be kept under dust in a museum, but at times it can be a sustainable answer to new challenges. If all this is lost, the practical applicability of sustainable development will be endangered.

Villages play an important role in local and micro regional sustainability in Hungary.

4 The Special Role of Villages

Small localities play a special role in keeping the population in the countryside, and this is emphasized in the strategic plans of sustainability of the European Union. An environmentally conform local economy and lifestyle is an important element of a sustainable way of life in harmony with nature, which is more difficult to implement in an urban environment, especially in a big city. However, the services offered by a city, especially that in job opportunities push rural population towards the cities, and as a result the trends of population distribution have shown a decrease in rural population.

Even today, villages remain the most important form of settlement in the Hungarian countryside, therefore it deserves special attention. In reference to villages we mean settlements which both include the features of the natural environment (topography, water, natural and agricultural vegetation); history, memories of local events, as well as the history of the local population, creativity, past and present economy and basis of living.

In other words, *natural environment* is an essential element of a village, as well as the *layout,* which has evolved over the centuries, and finally the *buildings* remaining in the village. These three elements together shape the village.

Figure 1: Sustainability Criteria of Villages

Community
State
Government
Local councils
Local-patriotic initiatives

RESPONSIBILITY
ACTIVITY

Production value and energy	HERITAGE	TRADITION	THREATS	TASKS OF VILLAGE RENEWAL
Environment	Agricultural land Hills, valleys Forests, waters Other environmental elements	Knowledge of basics of living and production Knowledge of the surroundings: stories, superstitions, legends	Investments into energy production and transport, telecommunication, mining, industrialisation	Ecological management of investments. Protection of the natural environment. Maintenance of knowledge of the surroundings, legends
Village, Locality (locality limits)	Historical village centre Old village Village layout	Structural image of the village in foundation and history, usually remaining invisible, also village image	Valuation of the moral aging related to village environment, modernisation at all costs	Protection of village centre in function and size in developments, Local urban protection
Buildings	Village houses Church Curia Shops, etc.	Use, size, structure of buildings	Modernisation False developments Fashion hypes	Modernisation in line with traditional size, mass and structure trends, Protection, maintenance of inherited building stock

Agrarian sciences, Village sciences
Architecture of settlements → Ethnography
Folk architecture, Local history, Protection of Monuments

DISCOUNT
SUPPORT

Source: Szlavik et al. 2002, p. 22

A well preserved and living village image is both intellectual and economic value. Intellectual, because it is the source of identity arising from the community, the person and the culture.

There are no two villages alike, just as there aren't two identical village houses, yet the designs, body shapes and structures revolved around five or six basic schemes in the entire Carpathian Basin. Yet there were some 280 distinct types of houses on the turn of the last century. A value of uniqueness is primarily present in old villages, old village sections, centres and Old Towns. Respect for the village is particularly increased if all this is coupled with the unique and living traditions, customs, clothing, foods and local knowledge of the residents, as well as numerous other human values.

We have introduced and quoted authors about the value of the local level, and that it will grow in importance as a source of value in the future. However, is this true in context of the global informatics network, the Internet?

Kristóf Nyíri, a philosopher dealing with this issue poses just this question: how will a village community change if its residents increasingly become users of the Internet? His answer to his own question is "[...] surprising. Being part of a network outwards increases internal cohesion" (Nyiri 1998, pp. 1286f.).

The explanation to this statement is that in a rural community having become part of the Internet will experience an improvement in training and working conditions, and the attractive forces pulling residents away from villages will weaken. International relations can be managed and shaped without the interaction of a nation-state. A bustling club life can form around the "tele-house", the hub of connections, and the computer network can be used to inform residents of the village itself, to organise programmes, to establish the so-important partnerships for Local Agenda 21.

This can strengthen forms of local and direct democracy, which can become very successful when synchronised with the democratic institutions directly elected locally, the local councils.

These thoughts are in congruence with the principle of subsidiarity, promoted by the European Union and included in its development programmes. Based on these, we could be certain of their realisation.

However, the situation is not this reassuring by far, since short-term producer and consumer interests can ruin such natural and constructed environmental cultural values in a very short period of time, which could otherwise serve as a basis of future sustainability.

References

Fule, M. (2008): A Sustainable Program of a Small Region in Hungary. In: Periodica Oeconomica, Vol. 2008/No. 1, pp. 103–115 (University of Paris, Sorbonne IV; Eszterházy Károly College)

Lorenz, K. (1988): A civilizált emberiség nyolc halálos bűne [Civilized Man's Eight Deadly Sins]. Budapest (in Hungarian)

Marjainé, Szerényi Zs. (ed.) (2005): A természetvédelemben alkalmazható közgazdasági értékelési módszerek [Economic Evaluation Methods Regarding the Natural Environment]. Budapest (Ministry for Environment and Water Management) (in Hungarian)

Nyíri, K. (1988): Globális társadalom és lokális kultúra a hálozottság korában [Global Society and Local Culture in the Age of Networked Society]. In: Magyar Tudomány [Hungarian Science], No. 11, pp. 1286–1297 (in Hungarian)

Szlavik, J. (2005): Fenntartható környezet és erőforrásgazdálkodás [Sustainable Economics of Environment and Resources]. Budapest (in Hungarian)

Szlavik, J. (2007): Environmental Economics. Budapest

Szlavik, J.; Turchanyi, G.; Fule, M. (eds.) (2002): Guideline for Adaptation of Local Agenda 21 Programs. Budapest (Ministry for Home Affairs)

Water Issues and Sustainability

A Cultural Aspect

Virender K. Sharma

1 Population Growth and Water

There is an increasing trend in world population, which is expected to gain 2.7 billion people by 2050, resulting in the total world population exceeding 9.2 billion.[1] Most of the population growth is in developing countries, contributing to more than 2%. In some parts of Africa, Asia and the Middle East, the growth is more than 3%. Comparatively, the population growth in developed countries is below 1%. India, China, Pakistan, Nigeria, Bangladesh, and Indonesia account for half of the annual global growth. The population of sub-Saharan Africa is expected to more than double by 2050, adding more than 800 million people to an estimate made in 2002. Significantly, the amount of water on Earth today is the same as when civilizations first settled thousands of years ago. Yet, the number of people needing water has increased dramatically. On average, 40% of the resident's residence currently lack access to quality water. About one billion people lack access to safe drinking water (cf. WHO/UNICEF 2004).

Only 2.5% of the Earth's water is fresh water. Sixty percent of freshwater is frozen in glaciers, 30% is in groundwater, often deep below the Earth's surface, and 10% is in lakes, streams, and rivers. Farming and ranching account for 70% of the world's freshwater use. Freshwater animal species are disappearing faster than those on land or residing in the sea. Drought further threatens the survival of many endangered species. In the United States of America, large portions of the arid Southwest (defined here as California, Nevada, Arizona, New Mexico, and Utah) have experienced prolonged drought since 2001 (cf. MacDonald 2010). The annual precipitation in 2002, 2003, 2007, and 2009 averaged 22–25% below the 20th-century mean. The climate change makes the availability of water complicated. For example, the wide variation in climate: from cold to mild and humid in Northeast Asia; hot and humid, with or without a dry season in Southeast Asia and South Asia; and semi-arid or arid in West Asia. The differences in climate cause water scarcity throughout the region. A study conducted in Canada explains how climate change may threaten Canadian water supplies

1 The Author wishes to thank *Rachel Gilman* for her comments that improved the text greatly; Center of Ferrate Excellence is also acknowledged.

(cf. Pelley 2004). Interestingly, Canada is the second largest country in the world, but it receives only 7% of the world's water supply in the form of rain and snow each year. Any climate change on the water source will trigger water shortages and changes in the delivery of fresh water to the Arctic Ocean.

There are currently three postulations regarding water's relation to climate change (cf. Schnoor 2010):

(i) water is a static resource,
(ii) water is a renewable resource, and
(iii) water is replaceable by desalinating the ocean for more water.

Generally, humid areas have increasingly retained more water and arid areas have increasingly grown drier over the entire planet for the last 100 years (cf. Milly et al. 2008). Therefore, earth is recognized as a climate-changing environment. Water as a renewable resource requires the continual replacement of damaged or decaying resources. In reality, water will need limitless resources, groundwater and surface water in particular. However, recharge rates of groundwater are not sufficient to replenish aquifers. Furthermore, renewable resources are being depleted by unsustainable practices including contamination of surface waters and sediments, mining of groundwater, clean-cutting of forests, and overfishing of seas. Significantly, more than 1.4 billion people live in river basins where recharge rates are lower than the use of water, leading to the depletion of groundwater and the desiccation of rivers. This will cause a more widespread and desperate shortage of water with increasing population. An approach to obtain more water through the desalination of ocean water is less likely and also very costly. This method will require massive amounts of energy and will generate enormous volumes of brine to desalinate seawater.

2 Water Quality and Diseases

Humans recognize water as the most precious natural resource, but it is regularly disregarded through the pollution of oceans, lakes, and rivers. Water pollution affects the environment, including eco-systems, and ultimately makes water undrinkable. According to the United Nations, approximately 1.5 billion people worldwide lack safe drinking water, and attributes to at least 5 million deaths per year, resulting from waterborne diseases. One cause of water pollution is the infestation of bacteria, viruses, protozoa, and parasitic worms of water resources through sewage systems and untreated waters. Figure 1 represents the deficiency of improved water, regionally, and the deaths of children related to diarrheal symptoms (cf. WHO/UNICEF 2004). More than 40% of the population in Oceania and sub-Saharan Africa do not have access to improved water. Significantly, deaths due to diarrhea-related diseases in sub-Saharan Africa are greater than any other regions.

Figure 1: A Comparison between the Lack of Access to Improved Water and Sanitation, and the Deaths Attributable to Diarrheal Diseases

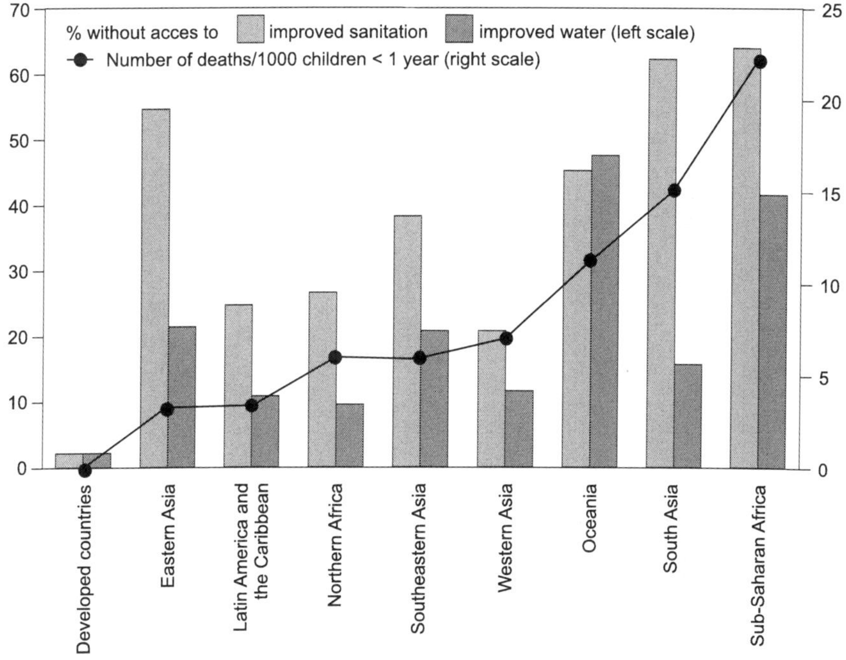

Source: Adapted from WHO/UNICEF 2004

In recent years, the Multiple Exposure-Multiple Effect (MEME) model was used to systematically understand the factors that influence exposure and health outcomes (cf. Briggs 2003; Montgomery/Elimelech 2007). Additionally, it is important to consider the result of proximal causes, such as contaminated drinking water with pathogens and climate change, and the distal causes resulting from social, economic, and demographic trends (shown in Figure 2).

This model can help to examine the ability of water, sanitation, and hygiene interventions to reduce exposure and improve health outcomes. Figure 2 clearly demonstrates the reduction of pathogens in water may be achieved by considering the environmental, cultural, and economic conditions of a particular com-

Figure 2: Exposures and Health Outcomes are Complicated by Interrelated Factors

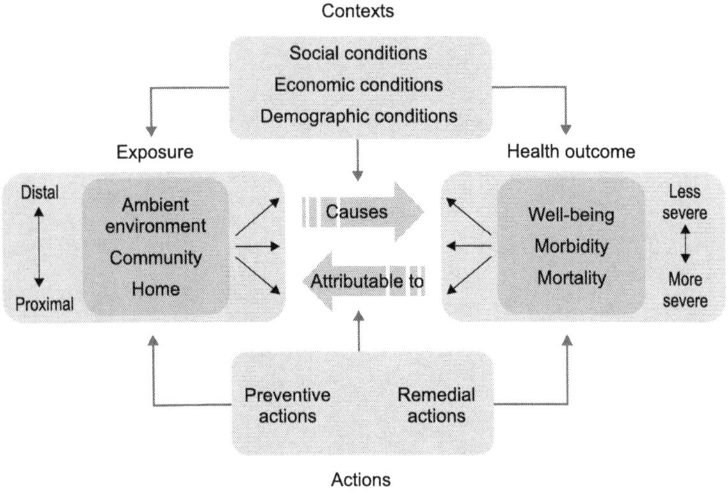

Source: Adapted from Briggs 2003

munity. In the case of pathogens with several routes of transmission and/or vertebrate hosts, there will be an increase in complexity for the risk assessment. *Chlamydia trachomatis* is an example of a pathogen with multiple routes. This bacterium causes the potentially blinding disease trachoma in which droplets containing *C. trachomatis* are spread through contact with contaminated pillows and clothes, the touching of infected eyes, and eye-seeking flies – *Musca sorbens* – that serve as mechanical vectors (cf. Mabey et al. 2003). Significantly, when animal and human hosts coexist, both can serve as reservoirs for pathogen survival and reproduction, compounding the challenge of describing the risk of exposure. Examples include nontyphi *Salmonella, E. coli,* and the bovine species of *Cryptosporidium* (cf. Eisenburg et al. 2001). In summary, the household treatment of water and improved sanitation can significantly reduce the risk of exposure (cf. Sobsey 2006).

3 Strategies for Achieving Water Sustainability

Strategies to achieve water sustainability in the future should include water conservation, influence of climate change on the water cycle, stormwater detention, water transfers, conjunctive use, importation of water supplies to areas of need, and reclamation and reuse of treated wastewater. The experiences in Singapore discovered it was cheaper to reuse wastewater (both domestic and industrial) and to treat water to meet drinking water standards. Preserving the precious water resource for the future will require reclaiming and reusing treated wastewater.

3.1 Reuse of Treated Wastewater

Social attitude towards reusing treated wastewater is critical to meet water demands for the future. It is essential for greater acceptance through politicians and the general public. The variation in social attitude is extreme. Developed countries may directly reject the reuse of potable water regardless of the high standards of treatment. A study conducted by Aquarec estimated only ~2.4% of Europe's total treated effluent is currently being reused (cf. McCann 2005). As shown in Figure 3, the reuse of treated water varies widely in Europe. Most of the European countries use ≤ 1%. Cyprus (100%) and Malta (83%) are using very significant volumes of available output. Spain, Italy, and Greece reuse 5–

Figure 3: Europe's Varied Approach to Reuse

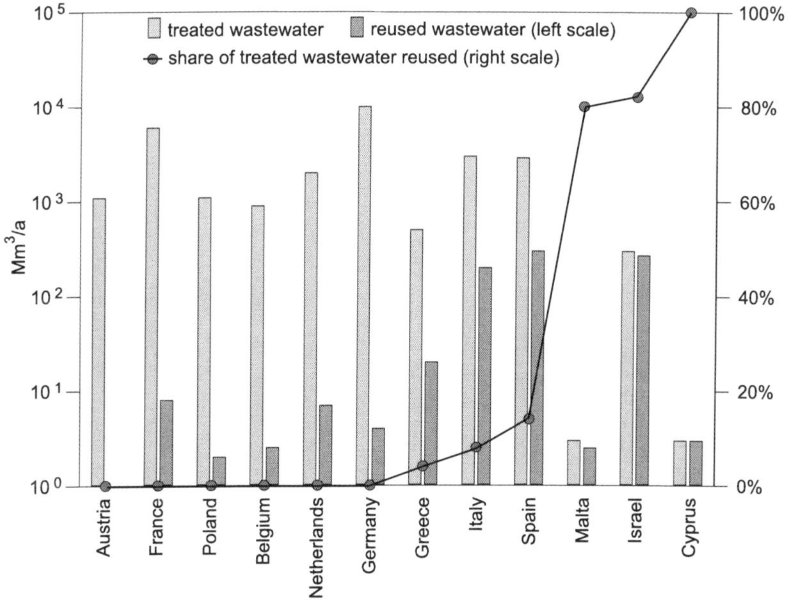

Source: From Eurostat, National Statistics, scientific publications

12% of the national effluent volumes. In comparison, the people of water-poor countries may drink water of any quality as an alternative to dying of thirst.

3.2 Treatment of Water and Wastewater

Iron is an important element involved in the development of advanced material in treating wastewater to reclaim and reuse. The name iron is from the Old English word, aern, which can be traced back to the Celtic word, isarnon. In time, the "s" was dropped from usage. Eight-hundred billion tons of iron ore resources are estimated worldwide, of which more than 230 billion tons is iron. Among the largest iron ore producing nations are Russia, Brazil, China, Australia, India and the USA. Worldwide, 50 countries produce iron ore, but 96% of this ore is produced by only 15 of those countries. The inner core of the Earth is believed to be a solid iron-nickel alloy. Iron-nickel meteorites are believed to represent the earliest material formed at the beginning of the universe. Studies show there is considerable amounts of iron in the stars and terrestrial planets, such as Mars, the "Red Planet", which is red due to the iron oxides in its crust. Iron is the precious element for various treatments of water decontamination for drinking and fresh water usages (cf. Zhao et al. 2010). One of the advanced materials made of iron is an emerging compound that will help to meet the demand of water in the 21st century.

The treatment of contaminated water presents an effective strategy to sustain the global water supply; however, current treatments are not sufficient to control the pollution problems (cf. Schwarzenbach et al. 2010; Shanon et al. 2008). Disinfection of water by the commonly-used chlorine treatment produces potentially carcinogenic byproducts (cf. Richardson 2009). Alternate oxidants such as chloramines generate other halogenated byproducts, which have even higher levels of toxicity (cf. Zhang et al. 2010; Zhou et al. 2009). Ozonation also generates the carcinogenic bromate ion when treating bromide-containing waters (cf. Gunten 2003).

High-valent iron-based compounds (ferrates) are emerging disinfectants and oxidants in water treatment (cf. Sharma 2007, 2010a; Sharma et al. 2005; Sharma et al. 2010). Ferrates are environmentally friendly and can address the concerns associated with the common treatment approaches. For example, ferrate(VI) (FeVIO42-, Fe[VI]) does not produce the bromate ion because of its non-reactivity with the existing bromide ion in waters (cf. Sharma 2010b). Thus, ferrate has become advantageous over other commonly-used chemicals in the wastewater industry. Examples include the oxidative transformation of nitrogen- and sulfur-containing compounds, pharmaceuticals, and estrogens (cf. Sharma 2008, 2011; Sharma et al. 2008a, 2009, 2011). Ferrate can also be used as an oxidant and coagulant in a single chemical. This application has been demonstrated by removal of arsenic and cyanide (cf. Jain et al. 2009; Sharma et al. 2008b; Sharma/Sohn 2009). Ferrate has thus become advantageous over other commonly used chemicals in the wastewater industry. The ferrate compound has also attracted interest for applications in "green chemistry" because the byproducts of its use, iron oxides, are environmentally friendly.

References

Briggs, D. (2003): Making a Difference. Indicators to Improve Children's Environmental Health. Geneva (WHO)

Eisenburg, J. N. S.; Bartram, J.; Hunter, P. R. (2001): A Public Health Perspective for Establishing Water-Related Guidelines and Standards. In: Water Quality Guidelines, Standards, and Health. Assessment of Risk and Risk Management for Water-Related Infectious Disease. Geneva (WHO), pp. 229–256

Gunten, U. von (2003): Ozonation of Drinking Water. Part II: Disinfection and By-product Formation in Presence of Bromide, Iodide or Chlorine. In: Water Research, Vol. 37, pp. 1469–1487

Jain, A.; Sharma, V. K.; Mbuya, O. S. (2009): Removal of Arsenite by Fe(VI), Fe(VI)/Fe(III), and Fe(VI)/Al(III) Salts. Effect of pH and Anions. In: Journal of Hazardous Materials, Vol. 169/No. 1–3, pp. 339–344

Mabey, D. C.; Solomon, A. W.; Foster, A. (2003): Trachoma. In: Lancet, Vol. 362, pp. 223–229

MacDonald, G. M. (2010): Water, Climate Change, and Sustainability in the Southwest. In: PNAS – Proceedings of the National Academy of Sciences, USA, Vol. 107/No. 50, pp. 21256–21262

McCann, B. (2005): Breaking the Reuse Barrier. In: Water 21, Vol. June, Issue 7.3, pp 29–30

Milly, P. C. D.; Betancourt, J.; Falkenmark, M.; Hirsch, R. M.; Kundzewicz, Z. W.; Lettenmaier, D. P.; Stouffer, R. J. (2008): Stationary is Dead: Whither Water Management? In: Science, Vol. 319, pp. 573–574

Montgomery, M. A.; Elimelech, M. (2007): Water and Sanitation in the Developing Countries: Including Health in the Equation. In: Environmental Science & Technology, Vol. 41, pp. 17–24

Pelley, J. (2004): Climate Change Threatens Canadian Water Supply. In: Environmental Science & Technology, Vol. 38/Issue 11, p. 200A

Richardson, S. D. (2009): Water Analysis: Emerging Contaminants and Current Issues. In: Analytical Chemistry, Vol. 81, pp. 4645–4677

Schnoor, J. L. (2010): Three Myths about Water. In: Environmental Science & Technology, Vol. 44, p. 1516–1517

Schwarzenbach, R. P.; Egli, T.; Hofstetter, T. B.; Gunten, U. von; Wehrli, B. (2010): Global Water Pollution and Human Health. In: Annual Review Environmental Resources, Vol. 35, pp. 109–136

Shannon, M. A.; Bohn, P. W.; Elimelech, M.; Georgiadis, J. G.; Marĩas, B. J.; Mayes, A. M. (2008): Science and Technology for Water Purification in the Coming Decades. In: Nature, Vol. 452, pp. 301–310

Sharma, V. K. (2007): Disinfection Performance of Fe(VI) in Water and Wastewater. A Review. In: Water Science and Technology, Vol. 55/No. 1–2, pp. 225–232

Sharma, V. K. (2008): Oxidative Transformations of Environmental Pharmaceuticals by Cl2, ClO2, O3, and Fe(VI): Kinetics Assessment. In: Chemosphere, Vol. 73, pp. 1379–1386

Sharma, V. K. (2010a): Oxidation of Nitrogen Containing Pollutants by Novel Ferrate(VI) Technology. A Review. In: Journal of Environmental Science and Health, Part A: Toxic/Hazardous Substances and Environmental Engineering, Vol. 45, pp. 645–667

Sharma, V. K. (2010b): Oxidation of Inorganic Compounds by Ferrate(VI) and Ferrate(V). One-electron and Two-electron Transfer Steps. In: Environmental Science & Technology, Vol. 45, pp. 5148–5152

Sharma, V. K. (2011): Oxidation of Inorganic Contaminants by Ferrates(VI), (V, and (IV): Kinetics and Mechanisms. A Review. In: Journal of Environmental Managements, Vol. 92, pp. 1051–1073

Sharma, V. K.; Kazama, F.; Jiangyong, H.; Ray, A. K. (2005): Ferrates as Environmentally-friendly Oxidants and Disinfectants. In: Journal of Water and Health, Vol. 3, pp. 45–58

Sharma, V. K.; Li, X. Z.; Graham, N.; Doong, R.-A. (2008a): Ferrate(VI) Oxidation of Endocrine Disruptors and Antimicrobials in Water. In: Journal of Water Supply: Research and Technology – AQUA, Vol. 57/No. 6, pp. 419–426

Sharma, V. K.; Yngard, R. A.; Cabelli, D. E.; Clayton Baum, J. (2008b): Ferrate(VI) and Ferrate(V) Oxidation of Cyanide, Thiocyanate, and Copper(I) Cyanide. In: Radiation Physics and Chemistry, Vol. 77/No. 6, pp. 761–767

Sharma, V. K.; Anquandah, G. A. K.; Yngard, R. A.; Kim, H.; Fekete, J.; Bouzek, K.; Ray, A. K.; Golovko, D. (2009): Nonylphenol, Octylphenol, and Bisphenol-A in the Aquatic Environment. A Review on Occurrence, Fate, and Treatment. In: Journal of Environmental Science and Health, Part A: Toxic/Hazardous Substances and Environmental Engineering, Vol. 44/No. 5, pp. 423–442

Sharma, V. K.; Graham, N. J. D.; Li, X. Z.; Yuan, B. L. (2010): Ferrate(VI) Enhanced Photocatalytic Oxidation of Pollutants in Aqueous TiO2 Suspensions. In: Environmental Science Pollution Research, Vol. 17/No. 2, pp. 453–461

Sharma, V. K.; Luther III, G. W.; Millero, F. J. (2011): Mechanisms of Oxidation of Organosulfur Compounds by Ferrate(VI). In: Chemosphere, Vol. 82, pp. 1083–1089

Sharma, V. K.; Sohn, M. (2009): Aquatic Arsenic: Toxicity, Speciation, Transformations, and Remediation. In: Environment International, Vol. 35/No. 4, pp. 743–759

Sobsey, M. D. (2006): Drinking Water and Health Research. In: Journal of Water Health, Vol. 4, pp. 17–21

WHO – World Health Organization; UNICEF – United Nations International Children's Emergency Fund (2004): Meeting the MDG Drinking Water and Sanitation Target. In: A Mid-Term Assessment of Progress. Geneva (WHO)

Zhang, S. H.; Miao, D. Y.; Liu, A. L.; Zhang, L.; Wei, W.; Xie, H.; Lu, W. Q. (2010): Assessment of the Cytotoxicity and Genotoxicity of Haloacetic Acids Using Microplate-based Cytotoxicity Test and CHO/HGPRT Gene Mutation Assay. In: Mutation Research – Genetic Toxicology and Environmental Mutagenesis, Vol. 703/No. 2, pp 174–179

Zhao, D.; Jaroniec, M.; Hsiao, B. (2010): Editorial for Themed Issue on "Advanced Material in Water Treatments". In: Journal of Material Chemistry, Vol. 20, pp. 4476–4477

Zhou, W.; Boyd, J. M.; Qin, F.; Hrudey, S. E.; Li, X. (2009): Formation of N-nitrosodiphenylamine and Two New N-containing Disinfection Byproducts from Chloramination of Water Containing Diphenylamine. In: Environmental Science & Technology, Vol. 43, pp. 8443–8448

Strong Sustainability across Culture(s)

Barbara Muraca, Lieske Voget-Kleschin

1 Introduction

By addressing the issue of a "sustainability culture", scholars as well as policy makers, stakeholders, educators and the like plead for basic attitudes, more or less institutionalized (i.e. established) values, ethical orientation that contributes to implement sustainable life-styles – i.e. mainly behavioral patterns, which reflexively consider the environmental impact of each action and choice (sustainability culture). However, the cultural dimension of sustainability is crucial not only when it comes to the implementation of a sustainable path beyond and beside technological improvements in terms of efficiency. Culture, considered as an essential dimension of sustainability, includes and addresses the very way we understand education, learning, scholarship, thinking, and acting, both individually and collectively. Accordingly, speaking of a cultural dimension of sustainability implies a radical rethinking of this understanding in the face of the pressing environmental and social challenges connected to the idea of "sustainable development" (cf. Stoltenberg 2010, pp. 300f.; cf. also Ott/Voget 2007) In this latter meaning, the "cultural dimension" of sustainability does not only refer to the implementation side, but radically challenges the basic understanding of human-nature and the humans-other-humans relationship. In more general terms, the very concept of sustainable development is the outcome of a cultural process, in which diversified normative ideals about human development and the growing awareness about the "material conditions" of and the limits for human development across different "cultures" have come together (cultural dimension of sustainability).

In this paper we will first address the ethical background of the idea of sustainability and explain the roots of the contemporary sustainability discourse by drawing on the notion of boundary concepts that help bridging "cultural" differences and serve as a compass within the complex debate. Concluding that sustainability as a boundary concept does not offer sufficient guiding potential and thus necessitates further specification, we will then offer two approaches that allow such a specification while avoiding a too rigid and predetermined grid. We locate ourselves in the wake of the second approach, i.e. the Theory of Strong Sustainability (TSS). Distinguishing a dimension of justice and a dimension of the circumstances of sustainability allows us to locate issues of sustainability culture and the cultural dimension of sustainability in a normative theory of sustainability. Finally we open the TSS to critique against universalism and offer a path that bridges universal normativity and cultural embeddedness.

2 The Ethical Roots of the Sustainability Concept

The complex idea of sustainability is the outcome of different intertwined threads running across history, societal movements, scientific research, and political aim-setting (cf. Grunwald/Kopfmüller 2006; Ott/Döring 2008). After the Rio-summit, which contributed to globally establishing the discourse and communication frame for a "sustainable development", the term "sustainability" has often been used as a catch-phrase without specific meaning.[1] In this regard, the sustainability concept can be considered as a so called "boundary object": boundary objects create a shared vocabulary, even though the precise understanding of various parties may differ significantly. Such boundary objects facilitate communication across disciplinary boarders (cf. Brand/Jax 2007).

Armin Grunwald points out that any discourse requires a pre-deliberative agreement among participants regarding what the discourse is about (cf. Grunwald 2009, p. 47). That is, being able to articulate differences in the precise understanding of sustainability already presupposes some vague shared notion about sustainability. Grunwald considers the historically established background of the sustainability discourse in terms of a "predeliberative consent", i.e. a kind of generally (not by means of reasoning or reflective deliberation) accepted ground, which survives and roots further controversies and conflicts in the specific definition of what sustainability is held to be like (cf. Grunwald 2009, p. 47). According to Grunwald, this predeliberative consent is acknowledged in a rather programmatic way by international political agreements on sustainability (cf. Grunwald/ Kopfmüller 2006). He holds that this political and societal praxis mirrors a basic shared intuition[2] of our life-world ("Lebenswelt"): On the one hand, it roots in a generally shared diagnosis of and uneasiness with respect to our current non-sustainable path of development. On the other hand, it is characterized by an intuitive acceptability (legitimacy) of the idea of sustainability as a collective goal, which so far has not been seriously questioned by any contrary argument from neither science nor ethics. However, the predeliberative consent is firstly provisional and secondly unspecified and therefore in need of clarification.

---

1 Some scholars consider the famous definition of the Brundtland-report a bad compromise between the needs for preservation of natural capital and the aspirations for economic growth.

2 He speaks in terms of a dimension of the "life-world" (Lebenswelt), which refers to not yet reflexively expressed and discursively debated intuitions.

2.1 Two Salient Conceptions of Sustainability within the German Discourse

Grunwald identifies two main pathes – at least within the German discourse – for this clarification: the Integrative Concept of Sustainability of the Helmholtz-Gemeinschaft (ICS) from 2001 and the Theory and Praxis of Strong Sustainability (TSS) from 2004.[3] The ICS defines three constitutive elements of sustainability. In a first step these elements are "translated" into general goals of sustainable development. In a second step these goals are specified in the form of minimum conditions for sustainable development. These conditions are formulated as substantial sustainability rules. The substantial rules are complemented by instrumental sustainability rules entailing necessary framework conditions that allow for the realization of sustainable development (cf. Kopfmüller in this book).

The TSS conceptualizes sustainability as a theory with eight levels (see Table 1). The first level specifies the idea of sustainability in terms of intra- and intergenerational justice. The second level argues in favor of the highly limited or rather non-substitutability of natural capital by man-made capital and thus for a conception of strong sustainability. This yields a Constant Natural Capital Rule and three management-rules on the third as well as three guidelines for sustainable development on the fourth level. Levels five to seven entail operational aspects (cf. Döring 2009; Ott/Döring 2008; Schultz et al. 2008).

According to Grunwald, the ICS basically adopts the predeliberative consent, thereby aiming to develop a theoretically well grounded, consistent and practicable concept both for the operationalization of the sustainability ideal and for various analysis on sustainability (cf. Kopfmüller 2006, p. 25). ICS intends its approach in terms of an operationalization of the Brundlandt definition.

On the other hand, by addressing the question of justification and justifiability of that very predeliberative consent, the TSS searches for a plausible and arguments-based justification for the sustainability discourse on the ground of discourse ethics (cf. Döring et al. 2007) and thus performs a "rational corrective" to clarify the diffuse discourse on sustainable development that takes place in society (cf. Grunwald 2009). According to the TSS, sustainability necessitates a clearer definition that offers non-arbitrary orientation ground for action without becoming too rigid. TSS holds that a vague and nebulous understanding of sustainability works to the advantage of those who have the factual power to

---

3 In the international discourse on sustainability there are but few approaches that aim at a philosophical and normative analysis from the point of view of inter- and intragenerational justice (cf., among others, Dobson 2003; Norton 2005). A thorough presentation of these approaches and a comparison with ICS and TSS would go beyond the scope of this paper.

establish a definition for decision making. In contrast, discursive "work on the concept" based on a rational formulation of moral intuitions in the face of other real or virtual participants to the discourse challenges power-holders to deliver well-founded arguments and to lay down assumptions, personal interests and implications. Intersubjective discourse allows participants to articulate the shared and often implicit ideals and rules that provide the ground for regarding some arguments as better than others (cf. Ott et al. 2011). Therefore, defining sustainability should be based on the results of such intersubjective discourse.

Table 1: Theory of Strong Sustainability – Multi-Level-Concept

Level	Contents
Idea: inter- and intra-generation justice	We do have moral duties towards future humans. Contemporary humans should be able to at least live above a certain minimum standard, future generations should not be worse off than "us". The minimum-standard can be substantialized by drawing on Nussbaum's capability list (cf. Nussbaum 2001).
Conception: strong sustainability	Natural capital cannot be substituted for by man-made capital tout-court: substitution between natural capital and man-made capital is highly limited and depends on the qualitative specificity of natural capital. Main arguments: Multifunctionality of ecological processes; Precautionary principle; More freedom of choice for future humans; Better compatibility with the with basic, shared intuitions concerning duties in terms of nature conservation and environmental protection.
Sustainability Rules	Constant Natural Capital Rule; three management rules: • To confine the rate of use of renewable resources so that it does not exceed their rate of regeneration. • To confine the rate of use of non-renewable resources so as to simultaneously create equivalent alternatives in terms of renewable resources. • To confine emissions so that they do not exceed the absorbing capacity of ecosystems and to minimize emissions of nondegradables.
Guidelines for Sustainable Development	• Efficiency • Sufficiency • Resilience
Dimensions of Policy Making, such as land use, forestry, climate	
Objectives	
Special Concepts and Models, such as differentiated land use, contraction and convergence, etc.	
Implementation, Monitoring	

Source: Drawing on Ott/Döring 2008

More specifically, discourse ethics relies on a transcendental-pragmatic justification of the procedural rules of the discourse (those rules, which any participant has ipso facto accepted by participating in the discourse accept). Accordingly, on the ground of discourse ethics it is not necessary that discourses actually take place among all concretely involved persons. Rather, it is sufficient to construe a virtual discourse in the face of so-called "generalized others" (i.e. potential participants to the discourse, who allegedly accept the discourse rules; cf. Benhabib 2004). In such a virtual discourse, first, all relevant arguments from scientific literature as well as from societal and political debates are reconstructed. Second, these arguments undergo a rational and analytical scrutiny according to criteria such as consistency, plausibility, acceptability of implications for all potential participants. By developing a normative theory of sustainability and thus claiming a clear stance in the scientific debate between weak and strong sustainability, TSS aims at framing the theoretical setting of the sustainability discourse from the perspective of critical practical philosophy. By means of an analytical scrutiny of the widespread agreement entailed in the pre-deliberative consent, TSS critically addresses the very core of the idea of sustainability (inter- and intragenerational justice; diversified concept of natural capital etc.) in order to shape a comprehensive normative theory in terms of a universal claim; this theory can thus offer a well-founded ground for the societal and political process of decision-making (cf. Grunwald 2009; Ott/Döring 2008).

3 Beyond TSS: Capabilities Approach and the Cultural Dimension of Sustainability

3.1 Justice and its Circumstances

In accordance with Konrad Ott and Ralf Döring (cf. Ott/Döring 2008) we draw on the Brundtland-definition that conceives of sustainable development as development "that meets the needs of the present without compromising the ability of future generations to meet their own needs" (WCED 1987, p. 43). We take this definition to capture the essential characteristics of the shared understanding of sustainability as discussed above. These encompass first, that sustainability is about distributive justice towards contemporary and future humans – that is, inter- and intragenerational justice (cf. Norton 2005; Ott/Döring 2008). Second, the definition conceptualizes the claim for sustainable development as a dilemma: the aim to achieve a decent quality of life for contemporary humans threatens the possibilities to achieve a decent quality of life for future humans. That is, claims for sustainable development presuppose certain scarcity in the resources that are necessary to achieve justice, most prominently natural resources. The insight that claims of justice do only occur under certain circumstances, inter alia (moderate) scarcity is not at all new but can be traced back to David Hume (cf. Hume 1998). Accordingly, claims for sustainability are only understandable insofar as we conceive of humanity's (natural) livelihood as (moderately) scarce. That is, claims for intergenerational justice are only comprehensible insofar as we understand that contemporary action has the potential to undermine future generations options to live a good human life (see footnote 4). Again, the awareness of our ability to impact the future and thus future generations is nothing new. Why else would humans have built churches and palaces, found businesses or fought for freedom? However, relatively widespread awareness (in the sense of a predeliberative consent) that our contemporary dealing with nature undermines futurities options to live a good life dates back to the middle of the last century at the earliest. We maintain that a significant part of the different perspectives on sustainability does not result from different ideas about justice but from different perspectives in regard to the circumstances under which these claims ought to be achieved. By way of example, the differences between the conceptions of weak and strong sustainability do not only rest on normative differences but result from different views regarding the question how to delineate natural capital and in how far a so-delineated natural capital, constitutes an indispensable aspect of humanity's livelihood. However, this question can be framed as asking what counts as a resource (i.e. what one understands as natural capital) and in how far these resources are scarce respectively – that is, as a question regarding the circumstances under which justice is to be achieved. Thus, one characteristic about the sustainability discourse is that it problematizes the circumstances under which claims for inter and intragenerational justice are raised. Accordingly, we hold that to satisfy the aim of specifying sustainability in a way that allows for non-arbitrary orientation ground while avoiding unnecessary rigidity necessitates an explication of the circumstances under which claims for intra- and intergenerational justice have to be achieved. Accordingly we follow Marius Christen and Stephan Schmidt in distinguishing two dimensions of a theory of sustainability: justice and the circumstances of sustainability (cf. Christen/Schmidt 2011).

3.2 Justice

Specifying the normative nature of sustainability means specifying what we claim when we ask for justice towards contemporary and future generations. This entails the following questions (cf. Page 2007a, 2007b, 2007c):

(1) *The scope of justice:* This concerns the identification of those beings that qualify as legitimate recipients of benefits and burdens. Sustainability asks for justice towards contemporary and future beings. But which beings are

entailed by claims for justice? Do these claims cover only humans (anthropocentrism)? Or do they entail sentient animals too (pathocentrism)? While Ott and Döring leave this question open and tend to include also sentient animals into the scope of justice, we claim that an anthropocentric position can lead very far in terms of positing limits to the substitutability, insofar as it goes beyond the flat anthropological assumption as in the model of homo oeconomicus. In fact, in our conception human-nature-relations are not only instrumental, but encompass also eudaimonistic,[4] aesthetic, and spiritual relations as well as relations of fundamental dependency (cf. Muraca 2010a, 2011).

(2) *The shape of justice:* This concerns the pattern according to which benefits and burdens should be distributed. Popular answers to this question encompass efficiency, equality, priority and sufficiency. Priority argues that it matters most to benefit those people worst off. Sufficiency claims that as many people as possible should have enough. The question about what is considered to be "enough" refers to the third question: depending on anthropological and ethical assumption, the minimum-socket can be intended in various ways. On the one hand one may hold that a society that meets a sufficientarian standard of justice would still allow for gross distributional inequalities; on the other hand, by claiming that in a world of limited resources inequality beyond a certain threshold entails oppression and injustice, one may also argue in favour of limited inequality. In contrast to an egalitarian standard of justice such an argument does not hold equality as such to be normatively preferable but is based on the reasoning that equality is instrumentally necessary to achieve justice.

(3) *The currency of justice:* The currency or metric specifies in regard to which criterion the pattern of justice should be evaluated. Common notions are welfare, resources and capabilities. In this paper we take side with the capability approach According to the capabilities-approach the currency for distributive justice are "capabilities to function" and the focus lies on people's substantial freedom to achieve the life that they have reason to value. Functionings are defined by Amartya Sen as "the various things a person may value doing or being", such as being healthy and well-nourished, being safe, being educated, having a good job, being able to have intercourse with loved ones and the like (Sen 1999, p. 75). Accordingly, functionings are related to income and goods but only insofar as they factually serve the achievement of functionings: i.e. what counts is what people are actually able to do with them: Capabilities refer to the substantial freedom to enjoy

4 The eudaimonistic refers to the good human life intended as the life worth of a human being and not in terms of mere subjective happiness (cf. Muraca 2010b).

the various combinations of functionings that the person can achieve. Insofar as functionings encompass those things a person values doing or being, the culturally stratified meaning of a good plays a crucial role with regard to its power of enabling the enjoyment of functionings. As Michael Walzer has shown, we cannot distribute goods until we understand what the goods mean and how they are valued. Accordingly, distribution is relative to social meanings (cf. Walzer 1983).

3.3 The Circumstances of Sustainability

In the context of this paper, specifying the circumstances under which claims for justice towards contemporary and future humans are made, means to explicate a description of the nature-society system in which sustainability is to be achieved. By drawing on Georgescu-Roegen's theory of funds, the TSS develops a complex concept of natural capital. Instead of describing natural capital as an aggregative quantum this concept classifies qualitative differences of the various elements of Natural Capital. This allows considering their reciprocal relation as well as their respective relation to human needs and values (cf. Egan-Krieger 2009; Ott/Döring 2008). Accordingly, conceptualizing the circumstances of sustainability with respect to the concept of natural livelihoods necessitates a differentiated analysis. Such an analysis can serve as a background for intersubjective discourses about the axiological status of natural processes and entities (i.e. attribution of value, relevance, and cultural meaning), as well as for a normative consideration about the role natural livelihoods (can) play for "a good human life". Regarding this latter aspect we refer to the capabilities approach and investigate if and in which regard the ideas underlying the capability approach can be employed in a conceptualization of the circumstances of sustainability.

According to the capability approach individuals convert means (goods and services) into functioning. The evaluative currency of the capability approach consists in the freedom to achieve certain functionings. This is described by the capability set. The capability set can be conceived as an opportunity set of achievable functionings. The extent of freedom people have access to can then be described as the extent of the capability set.[5] The extent of the capability set results from concurrence of the availability of certain means (goods and services) and three so called conversion factors, that is, personal heterogeneities, social conditions and environmental conditions. By way of example, the degree

5 The extent of the capability set is not only dependent on the number of options from which an individual may choose. In contrast the quality of the different options is at least as decisive in constituting the extent of the capability set.

to which having access to a bicycle increases the mobility of a woman in sub-Saharan Africa depends – inter alia – on her physical condition and ability to cycle (personal heterogeneities), the social (and legal) acceptance of her wearing clothes that are suitable for cycling as well as being allowed to leave the house (social conditions) and a terrain suitable for cycling (environmental conditions) (cf. Robeyns 2005, p. 99).

The point we would like to stress in this paper is that the capability set is a result of the concurrence of the availability of certain means and certain personal, environmental and social circumstances (see Figure 1). In other words this means that the personal, environmental and social circumstances define how far certain goods and processes can be conceived as means and services respectively.[6] Relating this insight back to what we said in regard to the circumstances of sustainability we point to the influence of the conversion factors on the definition of what aspects of nature are conceived of as constituting the natural base of our livelihood. By way of example, insofar as claims of sustainability are based on the insight that contemporary demand on services from natural capital (sensu TSS)[7] may undermine future generation's ability to live a good human life, it presupposes ideas about which natural processes can count as ecosystem services and in how far these services can be either dispensed with or substituted for. These presuppositions are in turn influenced by the three conversion factors as given above.

In the following, we focus on the social circumstances. Regarding the question of how this concept can be specified, Ingrid Robeyns gives the example of "public policies, social norms, discriminating practices, gender roles, societal hierarchies [and] power relations". In regard to the example of the bicycle given above she points out that "if a government or the dominant societal culture imposes a social or legal norm that women are not allowed to cycle without being accompanied by a male family member, then it becomes much more difficult or even impossible to use the good [in this case the bicycle] to enable the functioning" (Robeyns 2005, p. 99). Habitualized values and norms therefore play a major role in influencing the social conditions.

---

6 An example of how personal heterogeneities affect the conception of a certain good as means, a pair of glasses forms a very valuable if not indispensible means for a strongly short-sighted person while it is near useless for a person who is not ametropic (or far-sighted).

7 The concept of natural capital as used in TSS conceptualizes nature not only in terms of resource but also as a productive factor. Accordingly, we use the term "services" in order to account for the contribution of this productivity to a good human life. However, we reject the reductive understanding of "ecosystem services" in terms of measurable and quantifiable unities.

A thorough research about/on the influence of social conditions from a sustainability perspective, that is, research that asks about the relation between social and environmental conditions and social conditions and goods and services

Figure 1: The Capability Set as Resulting from Concurrence of the Availability of Certain Means and Personal, Social and Environmental Conversion Factors

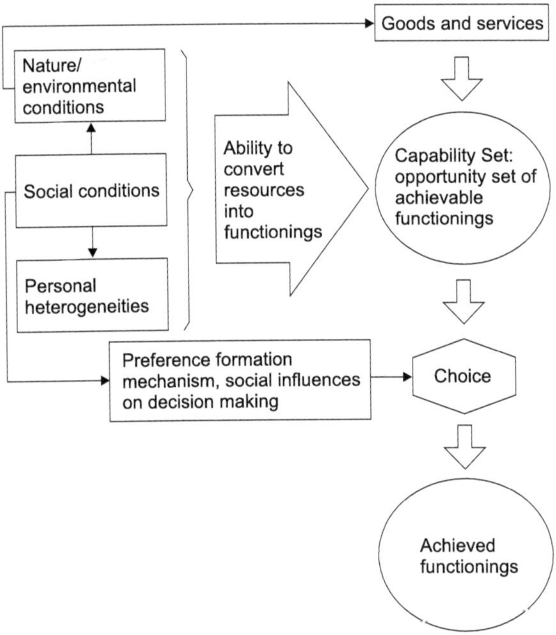

The arrow connecting nature/environmental conditions on the one hand and means (goods and services) on the other hand aims to acknowledge that in some way or other all goods and services stem from natural processes. Furthermore, it depicts that the extraction from nature and the conversion into goods and services that are ready for humans to use does also lead to (positive but most notably) negative feedbacks onto nature. The arrow pointing from social conditions towards personal heterogeneities shows that social decisions can influence personal heterogeneities. An example would be the existence and extend of publicly provided education. Furthermore, social conditions do also influence environmental conditions, as in the case of standards for the approval of cars that can have profound impact on emissions of greenhouse gases, particulate matter and noise.

Source: Based on Robeyns 2005, p. 98

respectively,[8] is still largely missing. Such research is an important challenge regarding the cultural dimension of sustainability. This perspective would also encompass questions about how basic attitudes, values, and ethical orientation conducive to the implementation of sustainable life-styles emerge and can be established. The capability approach focuses on capabilities so as to respect people's different ideals of the good life in enabling them to choose which functionings to achieve. What people choose is

> "profoundly influenced by [...] family, tribal, religious, community or cultural ties and background. [...] One could question, therefore, to what extent this is a choice at all. If we label it as a choice, it would at the very least remain a constrained choice. This does not mean that these constraints always have to be negative or unjust; on the contrary, some people might find them very enabling and supporting." (Robeyns 2005, p. 102)

Questions regarding the character of such constraints, their development and change and the possibilities as well as the acceptability of influencing these constraints are crucial elements in the cultural dimension of sustainability. Against this background for example the claim for "sufficient life-styles" would not only address individual choices but also have to consider the social (as well as the environmental and personal) conditions, in which these choices could occur. Uta von Winterfeld claim for a "right to sufficiency" and for a consideration of sufficiency in terms of a political category beyond individual life-style-issues leads very much in this direction (cf. Winterfeld 2002; cf. also Voget 2009, 2011).

In this paragraph we have shown that in shaping our view regarding the question what aspects of nature can count as resources and ecosystem services, the cultural dimension of sustainability asks for a reconstruction and possibly also a rethinking of our basic understanding of human-nature, and, based on this, humans-other-humans relationships.

4 Conclusive Remarks: Strong Sustainability between Universal Normativity and "Cultural" Embeddedness

One possible objection against the overall normative frame of the TSS comprises the argument that the idea of intergenerational and intragenerational justice is culturally rooted and cannot claim a universal validity beyond its scope or origination. According to this argument, moral principles simply mirror established values, which arise and are valid only within their shareable context. How-

8 In terms of capital this could also be coined as the question of a conception of social capital and the complementarity or substitutability of social and natural capital respectively.

ever, if we want to avoid falling back onto a mere cultural relativism, in which no claim can be made for generally valid normative principles, two paths seem promising: the pragmatist and the hegelian approach. According to the pragmatist approach, the terms of reference are offered by institutionalized values, which are widely accepted, hold a provisional validity due to their acknowledged plausibility, and in spite of their being different in several respects can overlap as to their pragmatic implications and orientation for action. In other words, it is not a matter of conflicting theoretical horizons or worlds views; rather, what is needed is a search for plausibility and pragmatic viability on the ground of accepted common goals (cf. Dewey 1996).

The second approach aims at mediating between a normative ideal, which is held to be independent from the factual historical realizations of values, and the simple observation of this very realization in its multifaceted shape. By drawing on Georg Wilhelm Friedrich Hegel, Axel Honneth proposes the idea of "exceeding validity" of historically and factually institutionalized (habitualized) values and norms as a mediating category. Accordingly, leading normative ideals have been establishing themselves throughout modernity and are being developed, enriched, and extended to the inclusion of more and new facets along a path of "progress" with respect to our moral understanding (cf. Fraser/Honneth 2003; Honneth 2008). Thus, the normative validity claim of an accepted normative ideal exceeds its current historical realization and points towards at future developments (in terms of regulative ideals, orientations, intuitions, and values), which imply a further development of ethics. The consideration of intergenerational justice, i.e. the inclusion of future generations in the scope of distributive justice, could be read in terms of this moral advancement. Similarly, the consideration of the natural livelihoods as a necessary condition not only for human existence but also for our self-understanding as human beings and for a "good human life" could also be interpreted in terms of this moral advance. The concept of sustainability established itself at a peculiar historical moment as an ideal rooted in factual intuitions, but its normative validity transcends its context of emergence. At the same time it challenges the core of our moral development by pushing our moral intuitions further. It is not only a matter of extending the scope of justice, by simply extending the goods to be distributed to include natural resources. Rather, in the light of sustainability as a "culturally" embedded normative ideal the common understanding of human-nature and human-human relationship can be challenged: we can be "seduced" to new patterns, new meanings, and new perspective. According to Honneth, struggles for recognition in terms of the societal acceptability and visibility of diversified patterns of life are a crucial element in this moral advance. Accordingly, issues concerning the idea of a "good life" are no longer confined to private life-style concepts, but may become fundamental claims about the interpretation of the basic value patterns that serve as orientation for society. Thus intended they belong to the core field of justice issues and require negotiation in intersubjective discourses. According to Sen what counts is not what kind of individual preferences people entertain in their private perspectives, but what they "value and have reason to value", i.e. what they claim in the face of others as their idea of what is a good human life (cf. Sen 1999). Furthermore, the capabilities approach shows that claims about the "good life" are influenced by diversified factors and constraints, among which "cultural" assessments and stratified values can play a major role.

In this understanding, the concept of sustainability is the negotiation frame among "culturally" different interpretations of the validity excess of institutionalized values. This negotiation frame can be intended in terms of a more or less structured discourse, whose rules of interaction can be likewise considered as the outcome of stratified processes of negotiations and therefore institutionalized patterns. According to the TSS, the golden path for persuasive discourses is the so-called reflexive equilibrium between one's own basic intuitions and the reasonable and rational arguments (i.e. including common sense as well as rational reflection, which is different from a narrow understanding of rationality in terms of instrumental calculus) that one is expected to deliver in an intersubjective setting. Reflexive equilibrium requires a constant examination of one's one deepest beliefs in the face of others even when the others are not actually present. It enables a participatory process of learning and facilitates the further development and reinforcement of one's own ethical and social values while strengthening one's own sense of "making a difference". Life-styles are also the outcome of habitualization processes, which can lead to a reduction of one's own options for social actions. The reflexive process described here can thus bear an emancipatory power and open up new paths for the shaping of social patterns relevant for a sustainable development (cf. Ott et al. 2011).

References

Benhabib, S. (2004): Situating the Self. Gender, Community and Postmodernism in Contemporary Ethics. Cambridge

Brand, F.; Jax, K. (2007): Focusing the Meaning(s) of Resilience: Resilience as a Descriptive Concept and a Boundary Object. In: Ecology and Society, Vol. 12/No. 1: 23 [online] (URL: http://www.ecologyandsociety.org/vol12/iss1/art23/)

Christen, M.; Schmidt, S. (2011): A Formal Framework for Conceptions of Sustainability. In: Sustainable Development (in print)

Dobson, A. (2003): Citizenship and the Environment. Oxford

Dewey, J. (1996): The Collected Works of John Dewey. Ed. by L. A. Hickman. Charlottesville/VA (The Electronic Edition)

Döring, R. (2009): Einleitung: Theorie und Praxis starker Nachhaltigkeit. In: Egan-Krieger, T. von; Schultz, J.; Thapa, P. T.; Voget, L. (eds.): Die Greifswalder Theorie starker Nachhaltigkeit. Marburg, pp. 25–38 (in German)

Döring, R.; Egan-Krieger, T. von; Muraca, B.; Ott, K. (2007): Die ethische Idee der Nachhaltigkeit und ihre Kommunikation. Zweite aktualisierte und überarbeitete Auflage. In Michelsen, G.; Godemann, J. (eds.): Handbuch Nachhaltigkeitskommunikation. Grundlagen und Praxis. München, pp. 97–110 (in German)

Egan-Krieger, T. von (2009): Naturkapital als Schlüsselkonzept einer Theorie der Nachhaltigkeit. In: Egan-Krieger, T. von; Schultz, J.; Thapa, P. T.; Voget, L. (eds.): Die Greifswalder Theorie starker Nachhaltigkeit. Marburg, pp. 159–168 (in German)

Fraser, N.; Honneth, A. (2003): Umverteilung oder Anerkennung? Frankfurt/M. (in German)

Grunwald, A. (2009): Konzepte nachhaltiger Entwicklung vergleichen – aber wie? Diskursebenen und Vergleichsmaßstäbe. In: Egan-Krieger, T. von; Schultz, J.; Thapa, P. T.; Voget, L. (eds.): Die Greifswalder Theorie starker Nachhaltigkeit. Ausbau, Anwendung und Kritik. Marburg, pp. 41–64 (in German)

Grunwald, A.; Kopfmüller, J. (2006): Nachhaltigkeit. Eine Einführung. Frankfurt/M., New York (in German)

Honneth, A. (2008): Gerechtigkeitstheorie als Gesellschaftsanalyse. Überlegungen im Anschluss an Hegel. In: Menke, C.; Rebentisch, J. (eds.): Axel Honneth: Gerechtigkeit und Gesellschaft. Berlin, pp. 11–29 (in German)

Hume, D. (1998/1748): An Enquiry Concerning the Principles of Morals. Oxford

Kopfmüller, J. (2006): Das integrative Konzept nachhaltiger Entwicklung: Motivation, Architektur, Perspektiven. In: Kopfmüller, J. (ed.): Ein Konzept auf dem Prüfstand. Das integrative Nachhaltigkeitskonzept in der Forschungspraxis. Berlin, pp. 23–37 (in German)

Muraca, B. (2010a): Denken im Grenzgebiet. Prozessphilosophische Grundlagen einer Theorie starker Nachhaltigkeit. Freiburg, München (in German)

Muraca, B. (2010b): Growth, Degrowth, and the Right to a "Good Life": A Scrutiny of the Ethical Assumptions in the Growth-Degrowth Debate with Respect to Distributive Justice. In: Proceedings of the 2nd International Degrowth Conference. Retrieved February 15, 2010 (URL: http://www.degrowth.eu/v1/index.php?id=122)

Muraca, B. (2011): The Map of Moral Significance: A New Matrix for Environmental Ethics. In: Environmental Values (in print)

Norton, B. (2005): Sustainability. A Philosophy of Adaptive Ecosystem Management. Chicago

Nussbaum, M. (2001): Women and Human Development. The Capabilities Approach. Cambridge

Ott, K.; Döring, R. (2008): Theorie und Praxis starker Nachhaltigkeit. Marburg (in German)

Ott, K.; Muraca, B.; Baatz, C. (2011): Strong Sustainability as a Frame for Sustainability Communication. In: Godemann, J.; Michelsen, G. (eds.): Sustainability Communication. Interdisciplinary Perspectives and Theoretical Foundations. Heidelberg a.o. (in print)

Ott, K.; Voget, L. (2007): Ethical Dimension of Education for Sustainable Development. Education for Sustainable Development, 1. Retrieved December 18, 2009 (URL: http://

www.bne-portal.de/coremedia/generator/pm/en/Issue__001/Downloads/01__Contributions/Ott__Voget.pdf)

Page, E. A. (2007a): Climate Change, Justice and Future generations. Cheltenham

Page, E. A. (2007b): Intergenerational Justice of What: Welfare, Resources or Capabilities? In: Environmental Politics, Vol. 16/No. 3, pp. 453–469

Page, E. A. (2007c): Justice Between Generations: Investigating a Sufficientarian Approach. In: Journal of Global Ethics, Vol. 3/No. 1, pp. 3–20

Robeyns, I. (2005): The Capability Approach: A Theoretical Survey. In: Journal of Human Development, Vol. 6/No. 1, pp. 93–114

Schultz, J.; Brand, F.; Kopfmüller, J.; Ott, K. (2008): Building a “Theory of Sustainable Development”: Two Salient Conceptions within the German Discourse. In: International Journal of Environment and Sustainable Development, Vol. 7/No. 4, pp. 465–482

Sen, A. (1999): Development as Freedom. Oxford

Stoltenberg, U. (2010): Kultur als Dimension eines Bildungskonzepts für nachhaltige Entwicklung. In: Parodi, O., Banse, G., Schaffer, A. (2010): Wechselspiele: Kultur und Nachhaltigkeit. Berlin, pp. 293–311 (in German)

Voget, L. (2009): Suffizienz als politische Frage. In: Egan-Krieger, T. von; Schultz, J.; Thapa, P. T.; Voget, L. (eds.): Die Greifswalder Theorie starker Nachhaltigkeit. Marburg, pp. 209–224 (in German)

Voget, L. (2011): Nachhaltige Ernährung. In: Greening the University (ed.): Wissenschaft und Nachhaltigkeit. Marburg (in print) (in German)

Walzer, M. (1983): Spheres of Justice. New York

Winterfeld, U. von (2002): Reflexionen zur Suffizienz als politischer Angelegenheit in sieben Etappen. In: Linz, M.; Bartelmus, P.; Hennicke, P.; Jungkeit R.; Sachs, W.; Scherhorn, G.;Wilke, G.; Winterfeld U. von (eds.): Von nichts zu viel. Suffizienz gehört zur Zukunftsfähigkeit. Wuppertal, pp. 27–37 (Wuppertal Papers, No. 125) (in German)

WCED – World Commission on Environment and Development (1987): Our Common Future. Oxford

3.

Sustainability – Political and Educational Implications

Sustainable Culture

A Contrast to an Efficiency Society?!

Renate Hübner

1 Efficiency Logic as Driver of a Non-Sustainable Culture of Material Values

In my opinion, the impacts of intensive, wasteful resource consumption in the affluent countries are still underestimated. Increasing soil sealing changes the water balance and biodiversity, and ever more emissions pollute the air and soil. The consumption of energy and non-renewable resources is as high as ever and is on the increase still. Many of the changes caused by these developments are already irreversible. Man's relationship to nature, in fact, lacks sustainability. And so does the relationship between man and his fellow man: Prosperity and lifestyle of the dominant well-off 25 percent of mankind are at the expense of the remaining 75 percent of the world's population. Not only does the poverty of the earth keep growing, but, with today's worldwide availability of information, they are increasingly aware of their privation and of the global social imbalance. It may well be expected that the resulting sense of unfairness and injustice, of helplessness and, probably, of having nothing left to lose eventually will contribute to more migration and to terrorism. Developments like these, in turn, will make the rich countries increasingly protect themselves and their prosperity and isolate themselves instead of sharing fairly.

In view of all these impacts, the culture and subsistence strategies of the rich countries can hardly be maintained in the long run. This has actually been known since the end of the 1980s. When Agenda 21 was signed by almost all countries in the world on the occasion of the 1992 UNCED Rio Summit, hopes were raised and a spirit of optimism, of "on to new pastures", was in the air. A myriad of measures were developed and many of them (for example more efficient production methods, ecological product design, and renewable resources strategies) were successfully implemented on a regional or individual level. At the same time, various activities (for example professional training programs, regional Agenda 21 processes, and new forms of development cooperation) were initiated to promote education and the shaping of political ideas. Nevertheless, little has changed so far in the patterns of social and economic behavior. It is far from being fair that resources are distributed according to the geopolitical distribution of power. The injustice of it all is manifest in the alarming figures of worldwide starvation and increasing diseases and in the enlargement of the poverty gap also in the wealthy countries. On top of that, the increasing energy and land consumption, growing quantities of waste, etc., reveal that we have not succeeded in reducing the *absolute* consumption of resources, particularly in the rich countries.

Why have the last two to three decades' numerous efforts to achieve social changes towards sustainable development remained so unsuccessful? Of course, it is not enough to dwell on the mere call for a changed culture and subsistence strategy which sounds as abstract as the call for a sustainable development. Yet, what is it that must change or be changed to resolve the problems threatening the future? And what are the obstacles impeding the required changes? How can they be overcome? The existing national and international sustainability policy papers, mostly classified by fields of practice and scopes of political action, say that change, for example, must come from less traffic, less energy consumption, smaller quantities of waste, increased recycling, green tourism, renewable energy sources, and an increased production of eco-efficient products. However, such phrases, too, remain abstract for being anonymous and do not allow one to derive neither appropriate strategic recommendations nor priorities in the case of conflicts of goals. As for obstacles and their overcoming, there is no easy answer either because the mere asking for such obstacles may be perceived as criticism of most of the circumstances and conditions that exist. For all that, I believe that it is important to find an answer. In the following, I will try to sound out the system logic of the subsistence strategies that currently determine our culture without lapsing into criticism of liberalism or capitalism.

By discussing the example of waste policy as practiced in Austria since 1990, contradictions that may arise from actual waste avoidance are roughly outlined. I will try to shed light on how the dilemmas escalated over several years for the eco-political goal of waste avoidance due to the system logic of social subsystems. This description of the failure of waste policy has nothing to do with pointing fingers. In fact, having been conceived as an instrument of sustainable development, it is waste policy that is particularly suited for analyzing the contradictions that are inherent to the system and that can reveal and identify the great social relevance of the efficiency of systems and facilities as being the phenomenon that may be driver of our non-sustainable use of resources and material goods.

If that is the case, then a policy of "less is more" that is required for sustainable development compromises the efficiency of facilities and, thus, is in contradiction to one of the key indicators of the previous success of our society, to its *efficiency*. This, in turn, causes a political impasse where no one wants to make decisions: Everybody agrees that it is necessary to reduce waste and resource consumption, but doing so successfully in an "efficiency society" would mean to hit the most sensitive nerve of the respective system and its culture. Such fears might explain why our society is immune to resource reduction and waste avoidance. I will conclude with discussing the contributions science could make to resolve the impasse that society has gotten itself into due to the diversity of truths (cf. Abels 2009, p. 49).

2 Austria – An Ambitious Eco-pioneer

From the late seventies through to the early nineties, Austria was considered a pioneer in the development and implementation of environmental technologies. During that time, the quality of most of the country's lakes and rivers was restored to drinking water level, factory fumes were purified by means of high-grade filter systems, and landfill sites were turned into high-tech facilities whose complex subsystems hardly impaired the quality of local soils, air, and groundwater. The development of these innovative technologies had been forced, so to speak, by legal guidelines (prohibitions and dictates, emission and immission limits) that had been relatively strict as compared to international standards. Eventually, however, the initially very controversial regulations yielded superior technologies that are in demand worldwide until the present day and led some Austrian companies to the very top in fields like sewage treatment, waste incineration, landfill construction, and solar panel engineering. As evident from several examples such as particulate matter, traffic development or energy consumption issues, Austria, for all that, did not manage to perpetuate and extend that success to its environmental policy during the last 15 to 20 years. My own 15 years experience made me take a closer look at the field of waste management.

2.1 New Waste Management Approaches: The Polluter-pays Principle

The 1990 amended version of the Waste Management Act was intended as a milestone in the combat against floods of waste and the wasteful use of goods. The new ways of approaching a sustainable use of goods were based on the polluter-pays principle and, along with it, the extended producer responsibility. The polluter-pays principle involves the idea of "homo oeconomicus", hence was conceived to make each waste producer pay the cost of the disposal of his own refuse or garbage and, as a result, avoid waste as much as possible in order to save costs. This legally elusive principle (cf. Fischer 2001, p. 49) may raise many problems when applied to practice in a division-of-labor society.[1] First

1 Cf. http://www.umweltdatenbank.de/lexikon/verursacherprinzip.htm [10.2.2011].

and foremost, it calls for an answer to the question of who is the waste producer or polluter: The consumer, distributor or manufacturer of products? Without clarifying this intricate issue, the polluter-pays principle was enshrined in the Austrian waste legislation in 1990 and the first regulations were adopted to oblige polluters to collect and recycle certain types of salvage: Batteries (1990), used cooking fat (1990), beverage containers, all wrappings and packaging (1992), fluorescent tubes (1992), cooling units and refrigerators (1993), debris (1993), scrap vehicles (2002), and electronic scrap (2005).

Other countries had not gained any practical experience either in applying the polluter-pays principle and the extended producer responsibility. Judging by the legal wordings, the producing and distributing industries, being obliged through waste legislation to take back and recover the (salvage) products produced and marketed by them, were defined as being the polluters. Strictly speaking, industry thus was obliged to ensure the collection and recovery of the goods it had put into circulation but was not bound to perform the respective services itself.

Since it was intended to relieve the responsible municipalities (and ease their waste collection and disposal budgets), this new definition marked a turn in the previous waste policy. Similar efforts to implement the polluter-pays principle both legally and practically were taken in the European neighbour countries (for example in Germany, Switzerland, France, and Denmark) at the same time.

2.2 The Pioneering Character of the Packaging Ordinances

At the beginning of the 1990s, packaging ordinances (consisting of target and measures ordinances) were considered to be pioneering both in view of legal and organizational aspects. There was neither any relevant theoretical expert knowledge nor much comprehensive practical expertise. Neither economy nor politics were experienced in drawing up and establishing area-wide collection and recovery systems, including the associated financing and registration or reporting systems.

Looking for experts able to carry out studies and projects on the planning and implementation of the collection and recovery of waste materials and products, politicians and economists (representing the industry that puts such materials into circulation and is obliged to take them back) found that the subject had not yet been (sufficiently) analyzed or illuminated either by the consulting services (e.g. technical boards), or by the then just emerging environmental consulting companies, or by science. Being forced to resort to the know-how of very few institutions with practical experience in organizing waste material collections, those in charge decided to cooperate with the non-profit association Austria Recycling (organizers and developers of waste glass, waste paper, waste oil, and scrap metal collections), the Austrian Packaging Institute, and the team involving a waste scientist from the Vienna University of Economics and Business. Over many years, part of that team had already been establishing a waste glass and waste paper collection concept together with some interested Austrian municipalities.[2] The (not primarily scientific) practical knowledge gained in the team and the long-standing experience in informing and motivating private households with a view to implementing waste material collection provided the basis for approaching novel studies and projects. The main base data for planning and operating the relevant collection systems consisted of figures on the expected quantities of goods sold (or rather put into circulation) and on estimated quantities of waste products that can be collected and recovered separately. These data are essential for designing and developing area-wide collection and recovery systems and for planning the capacities and infrastructures of collecting systems (waste containers), collecting logistics (routes, rhythms, and vehicles), and sorting and recovery techniques. Moreover, they are a prerequisite for polluter-based financing, reporting, and billing systems.

In 1993, *Altstoff Recycling Austria,* a waste recycling concept referred to as the ARA system, was founded on the basis of the first comprehensive cross-sectoral packaging collection study (cf. Hauer et al. 1992). Being conceived for the collection and recovery of packaging waste, the ARA system was as pioneering as the packaging ordinances it was based on. The almost parallel developments in Germany, the Dual System and the "Green Dot", seemed to corroborate the Austrian approach.

2.3 The Release Option – Should Waste Collection and Recovery be Left to the Companies or to a Higher-level System?

The above concepts fulfilled yet another important function: They were the basis for discussions and decisions made by interest groups, associations, and individual companies on whether (joint) industry solutions would suit the needs of firms putting materials into circulation or whether the extended producer responsibility laid down in the respective ordinances should be assumed individually by the producers or "circulating" companies themselves. It was due to the strong initiative of the Austrian Federal Economic Chamber and the Ministry of the Environment that each waste product ordinance was eventually allotted a system

2 In 1946, shortly after the end of World War II, the Association Austria Recycling (formerly Österreichische Produktionsföderungsgesellschaft – Austrian Production Promotion Association) was founded to collect waste materials for industry because, at that time, the Austrian basic industry could not afford to buy raw materials on the world market. Systemic waste materials collection was started around 1965 (cf. Schelmbauer 2006).

which, throughout Austria and instead of the "circulating" industry, assumed, and still assumes, the obligation of taking back and recovering waste such as packaging (ARA), electronic scrap (UFH), scrap cars (ÖCAR), or debris (BRV). However, since it has never been obligatory to use these systems, some companies chose to prefer a "release" option, i.e., develop their own collection and recovery solutions and submit by themselves the records of proper waste management required by law. Each of the legally accepted collection and recovery systems was required to provide the infrastructure, services, and motivation schemes that are the basis for the collection and recovery of waste products one hopes to be returning to the relevant producers. Although the companies, in fact, were obliged to contribute to reaching the objectives laid down in the ordinances, the given general conditions did not allow holding a single company or system responsible for the extent to which the overall waste management objectives would be achieved.

New experience was gained from that time on both in practice and in politics and legislation. Further knowledge then was created by continuously analyzing and evaluating the new findings with a view to optimizing the existing systems and establishing new regulations. While industry used these results to develop own solutions with the option to make money out of the new possibilities, politics used them to draw up future basic conditions, and the systems used them to get concepts optimized. The experience and findings were eventually increasingly adopted in different fields of science (for example in waste science, redistribution logistics, packaging research, and materials research).

Although, as mentioned above, the polluter-pays principle and extended producer responsibility were applied to further product groups in accordance with the packaging ordinances, it often took many years until after seemingly endless debates between politicians, business people, consumers, and ecologists the final regulations could be passed. While increasingly considering scientific lines of arguments, these discussions interestingly enough revealed the diverseness and complexity of the many product groups, their sectoral structures, and structures of use. This diverseness and complexity were posing great challenges regarding the conception of billing systems in accordance with the requirements of collection and the demands of polluters. As a matter of fact, refrigerators, TV sets, batteries, or, let's say, cooking fats cannot be collected in the same way as plastic bottles or old newspapers. However, the knowledge about waste goods and products was hardly utilized for studying, e.g. patterns of use or issues of obsolescence or wear research to develop new and, above all, more sustainable solutions for using goods.

3 Critical Reflection (I): Achievement of Objectives and Manner of Approaching the Targets of the Regulations

Now that some years have passed, the question arises whether the strategies and concepts tried out in the past have been efficient: Have the targets been achieved as desired by ecology and waste policy? Given the increasing quantities of goods and products, this must be answered in the negative and the following questions have to be studied to get to know the reasons:

1. Were (or are) the legal basic conditions and formulations suited to achieve the waste and resource reduction objectives of the waste legislation?
2. Which inspection and quality management measures were applied in the case that targets were not met?
3. Are the systems suited to contribute to achieving the targets of the waste legislation?

Giving a comprehensive answer to these questions would probably require assistance from legal experts. For all that, my experience and observations suggest posing yet another more important and more fundamental question:

> *Is it possible and are we allowed to seriously pursuing waste avoidance in our economy and culture without endangering the system?*

I will approach this issue in two steps: First of all, and again by referring to the example of the Austrian packaging ordinances, I will discuss the measures taken when targets were missed. Secondly, among other things on the basis of simple system-theory findings, I will expound why a reduction of all of the wastes produced would indeed endanger our present subsistence strategy.

Let me start by saying that "waste" cannot be put on a level with "residual waste". Legal laypersons in particular should know that wastes are understood as being all of the residues our society gets rid of and that either cannot be recycled or used again or can be re-used only after having been dismantled or singled out and/or recycled. Recoverable products or materials or potential recyclables are clearly classified as waste throughout the OECD countries and the EU. An increase in the amount of collected and recycled recoverable materials thus reduces the amount of waste (residual waste) that would have to be incinerated or deposited but does not contribute to reducing the overall quantity of wastes.

In spite of the large number of waste management measures implemented (collection ordinances, recovery ordinances, and recovery systems), the objectives of "sustainable waste avoidance" (§9 AWG)[3] have not been achieved and

3 BMfLFUW (Federal Ministry of Agriculture, Forestry, Environment and Water Management) Waste Management Act (Abfallwirtschaftsgesetz – AWG) 2002, 2009.

the quantities of waste have been increasing constantly by 1–3 percent each year on the average, which, by the way, runs more or less parallel to the economic growth. This did not even change when the quantity of separately collected and recycled recoverable materials increased and when that increase was acclaimed in the media every five minutes ("again a new record in waste collection"). The share of recyclable materials, particularly that of returnable containers and reusable packagings, decreased as drastically (cf. Pladerer et al. 2002, p. 8) as did the availability of repairable and long-lived products. As is evident from the example discussed below, the legislator, however, did not use his options to impose one or several of the waste circulation or disposal restrictions laid down in the waste legislation.

(1) Missing the Remaining-quantities Objectives Laid Down in the Packaging Target Ordinance VerpZVO 1999–2001

It was easy to predict that the remaining-quantities objectives laid down in Section 3 of the 1992 Packaging Target Ordinance VerpZVO would not be achieved for 2001. Many of the politicians still considered Austria to be an ecological model country. Hence, it can be assumed that the persons in charge did not want to admit defeat publicly. The remaining-quantities objectives thus were adapted to the status quo – and to the convenience of the industry. This, however, was not done by clearly changing the objectives but, instead, by modifying the basis of calculation (cf. Pladerer et al. 2002, p. 15).

Which alternative solutions could the legislator have chosen? In the Packaging Target Ordinance, it had clearly been laid down that, depending on the causes for missing a target, different restrictions of circulation could be stipulated (see Figure 1).[4]

Why had none of the measures defined by the legislator himself for ensuring target achievement, waste reduction, and environmental protection been implemented? Since restrictions of circulation and disposal were not and are still not in the interest of the bigger part of the producing and distributing industry, it must be assumed that the protection of industry was preferred to the protection of the environment. In spite of several attempts to elucidate that situation to the public, the above development was irreversible and, eventually, the funding of the further promotion of the reusable-packaging initiative "Mehrweg.at" was the only measure taken.

4 BMfLFUW – Federal Ministry of Agriculture, Forestry, Environment and Water Management, 1992.

Figure 1: Extract from the Packaging Target Ordinance (VerpZVO)

§ 5

(1) Werden die Quoten gemäß § 2 unterschritten oder die Restmengen gemäß § 3 überschritten, wird der Bundesminister für Umwelt im Einvernehmen mit dem Bundesminister für wirtschaftliche Angelegenheiten auf der Grundlage des Abfallwirtschaftsgesetzes unverzüglich die zur Verringerung des Abfallaufkommens erforderlichen Verkehrs- und Abgabebeschränkungen erlassen.

(2) Als Verkehrs- und Abgabebeschränkung gemäß Abs. 1 kommt insbesondere in Betracht die Anordnung der Pflicht zur

1. Einhebung eines Pfandbeitrages durch den Abgeber,
2. Abgabe von Waren sowie Gebinden und Verpackungen nur in einer die Abfallsammlung und -behandlung wesentlich entlastenden Form und Beschaffenheit,
3. Überlassung bzw. Sammlung von Verpackungsabfällen, insbesondere getrennt von anderen Abfällen, mit dem Ziel, ihre Behandlung in einer möglichst umweltverträglichen Weise zu ermöglichen oder zu erleichtern,
4. Unterlassung des Inverkehrsetzens von Waren, wenn diese Waren nach ihrem Gebrauch oder Verbrauch bei der Entsorgung geeignet sind, gefährliche Stoffe freizusetzen, und dies nicht oder nur mit unverhältnismäßigem Aufwand verhindert werden kann und
5. Einhebung eines Verwertungs- und Entsorgungsbeitrages.

(3) Bei der Erlassung der erforderlichen Verkehrs- und Abgabebeschränkungen ist auf die Ursachen der Zielverfehlung sowie die spezifischen Produktanforderungen und die damit verbundenen Anforderungen an Verpackungen Bedacht zu nehmen.

Source: Federal Law Gazette, No. 646/1992

Since then, there have been only ordinances stipulating relative collection and recycling rates but refraining from fixing absolute remaining-quantities objectives. In 2005, VerpZVO was repealed in addition and parts of it were transferred to the packaging ordinance (note that the latter meanwhile only stipulates remaining-quantities objectives for glass and metal but not for other packaging materials!). The power to issue statutory instruments for enacting circulation and disposal restrictions in the case of waste-related targets missed was transferred to the Waste Management Act where it was extended from five (see Figure 1) to ten points (Section 14, Paragraph 2, No. 1–10, Waste Management Act AWG 2002/Federal Law Gazette BGBl. 102, 2009). Paragraph (1) gives the following introductory statement:

> „§ 14 (1) As far as it is necessary for achieving the objectives and principles of waste management, particularly the objectives according to Section 9 on the reduction of waste quantities and pollutant contents and the promotion of closed-loop recycling management, the Federal Minister for Agriculture, Forestry, Environment and Water Management is empowered to fix measures in accordance with Paragraph 2 for ensuring [...] per ordinance while fulfilling the requirements of goods distribution and considering the technical and economic options."

The last sentence drastically tones down the entire power to issue statutory instruments, above all in view of the dramatically increasing quantities of waste: As a matter of fact, there was as much as a ten percent increase in the quantities of household refuse and a 15 percent increase in the quantities of separately collected household refuse during the years from 1999 to 2004 (cf. BMfLFUW 2006, p. 24). It seems that out of the sheer concern for considering the technical and economic possibilities, no measures could be taken so far to still achieve the objectives of waste management.

(2) No Eco-oriented Control of Consumption

It has been, and still is, up to trade and business to add license fees to the market prices of entirely different products (e.g. higher-priced products) or, evenly, to the prices of all products of the complete range of goods according to the respective packaging recycling costs or sales strategy. Since, moreover, there is no obligation to show the packaging disposal fees, the buying decision does not get influenced by ecological criteria. As a matter of fact, this reveals that the consumer or user is not regarded as the polluter and that, hence, one does not (as had been intended) make use of the opportunity of controlling the buying behavior with a view to sustainable consumption.

(3) No Hundred Percent Collection

The actually collected quantities have always been, and always are, below the actually circulated and licensed quantities (note that according to Section 11 (7) No. 1 of the Packaging Ordinance, only 60 percent of the licensed quantities must be collected!). It was owing to this fact, at least in the beginning, that the collection and recycling costs were distinctly below the originally assumed values and, thus, far below the revenues. The surplus was used to reduce the license fees (keep in mind the dependence on the quite volatile proceeds of sale) and accrue reserves for delayed recycle flows and future investments. After all, it is laid down in the Austrian waste legislation that the collection and recycling systems must furnish proof of measures taken to promote waste avoidance (Section 29 (2) No. 11). Accordingly, the ARA system invests part of its license revenues in supporting an endowed chair for resource management at the Vienna Technical University. With that money, different measures for "optimization" and "management" of the accumulating waste flows were developed with the objective of increasing the usability and recovery of recoverable materials (material flow analyses and technology development, dismantling and disassembly systems, etc.). These measures are important and very welcome because they contribute to identifying risk potentials of materials and substances and help to avoid such risks through design recommendations or prohibitions.

Nevertheless, they do not serve to avoid or reduce the total waste volume or change the consumption behavior.

In view of these contradictions, not typically Austrian but known throughout the EU (just think of the continuing discussions about deposits on non-refillable beverage containers in Germany), there is every reason to doubt the seriousness of waste avoidance. New hope seems to arise from the waste hierarchy established in 2008 in the amended EU waste framework directive. That hierarchy puts waste avoidance in the first and re-use in the second place, hence prefers these two options over recycling, other recovery methods (e.g. energetic recovery), and waste disposal (cf. EC 2008, article 4).

However, when during the last financial and economic crisis in 2009 and 2010 there was a slight decrease in the amounts of waste (and, according to Statistik Austria, also in energy consumption) as well as a small increase in the demand for repair services, politicians pulled out all the stops to crank up consumption (e.g. scrapping bonuses for cars, refrigerators, washing machines, or tax reductions for private households).

Both industry and politics have seemed or seem to be afraid of noticeable changes in consumption behavior and of reduced consumption in case that the restrictions on circulation and disposal would be implemented. Different groups of society, mainly NGOs from the fields of consumer and environment protection, have been passing criticism on these developments and on the acting persons or political parties. The role of science during the respective years has remained unclear and it is difficult to determine the possible scientific "discipline" of such critical debate and all its basic legal, political and practical conditions.

4 Critical Reflection (II): Efficiency Dilemma and Systems' Self-interests

4.1 Recycling Society and Slavery of Technology

Progress in sorting and in waste recovery has brought about lots of achievements and has raised the hopes placed in the principle of closed-loop recycling management maintaining that wastes are just resources in the wrong place and that, according to the ideal of nature, any type of waste is usable. Intelligent resource management, thus, would simply have to ensure that waste, just like in nature, occurs in such a way that it can be used or utilized by other organisms. The "biological analogy" approaches of industrial ecology (cf. Isenmann/Hauff 2007, p. 5) and material flow analysis (cf. Baccini/Brunner 1991) provide the scientific fundamentals. Based on these, the EU waste management strategy meanwhile stipulates that the European Union shall develop into what Germans call a “Gesellschaft mit Kreislaufwirtschaft” (a “society with closed-loop recycling management“) or what is referred to more clearly as “recycling society” in English or as “économie du recyclage” in French (KOM(2011) 13). Considering, among other things, the intrinsic logic of waste collection systems, how can a strategy aiming for “more and better recycling” (EC 2011, p. 7) contribute to achieving the primary goal of avoiding waste? And how can it be ensured that recoverable goods and materials are actually recovered?

4.2 The Efficiency Dilemma

The developed rather intricate collection and recovery systems had been conceived as non-profit associations without self-interests. However, just like any other system, these systems had and still have their own best interest and basic right to preserve themselves, to be efficient (!), and, if possible, to grow. It stood to reason that waste avoidance, for example through repair and return systems, of course would not contribute to the efficiency of waste collection and recovery facilities and would also endanger the efficiency of production plants, storage and transport capacities. According to Susanne Hartard, the constraint to be efficient is a “technosphere symptom” (Hartard 2010, p. 180). This term describes the society’s dependence on existing technologies on account of the financing models by which these technologies are actually rendered possible and explains why highest planning reliability is required and why, consequently, changes of expected behaviors are neither reasonable nor desired.

The vision of the European Commission to turn the European society into a “recycling society” gives reason to fear that the efforts outlined will at most contribute to qualitative but hardly quantitative waste avoidance and that, hence, the EU Commission will not get out of the double dilemma posed by efficiency. Both, the industrial large-scale production plants and the sorting and recycling facilities want to and are forced to operate at full capacity and, considering the existing growth-oriented general conditions, must, in addition, permanently inrease their capacities.

5 Contradictions are not Surprising! Cultural Change and the Role of Science

The above discussion reveals the contradictions and conflicts of objectives that, of course, are triggered by waste avoidance measures and shows that these contradictions are probably caused and determined by the efficiency dilemma that inevitably arises from a subsistence strategy following the *economy-of-scale* principle:

- Systems living on the collection, recovery, and disposal of waste cannot be interested in waste avoidance.
- Lifestyles and forms of consumption that would really lead to waste avoidance would endanger industry and trade, hence job security. The great significance of jobs in our society makes politics that risk more unemployment prone to being blackmailed. (It can be assumed that new business models and a resource tax would only shift the growing loss of jobs in the industry.)
- Given the existing general conditions, also the government probably has no genuine interest in waste avoidance: Tax cannot be raised on unsold products.

This raises the question how a culture that is trapped in the constraints of efficiency can get rid of its self-inflicted dependence. Efficiency constraints do neither stop at individuals nor at the social services (consider the development of the health and education system or of the "prestige" of a busy schedule in good social positions) and may be assumed to be the "secret" hidden values that shape our social development more than we are conscious of.

So far, science does not really raise hopes of a change. According to Heinz Abels, the ever greater differentiation and more profound specialization has been resulting in an unmanageable pluralization of rationalities, i.e. in a multiplication of truths. This increasing predominance of rational aspects rather leads to a paradoxical (non)-effectiveness of science, i.e. to a situation where "the paradoxical case becomes normal in the sense that, given the rationalization of all social conditions, one ends up with conditions that no one desires, that is with undesired conditions" (Abels 2009, p. 12). The rationalities that, in sum, contradict one another are the result of the diverging logics of the different sub-systems of the society. Even though each of these logics is true in itself, the bulk of them increasingly paralyze the decision-making ability and decision-makers of our society due to the concurrence of the partly contradictory truths. The citizens and consumers are irritated and confused, and politicians are reserved and hesitant instead of creating clear rules (new working groups are established, and maybe further studies are commissioned, compare e.g. the debate about refillable/non-refillable beverage containers, health hazards of mobile phone radiation, etc.). In view of that political impasse, the industry and the consumers keep on making their decisions as before. With the existing patterns persisting, a change of "old habits" is not "rewarded", thus is not reasonable according to the respective system logic, and sustainable behavior is of no appreciable benefit. In view of this, the industry offers solutions/products that promise the greatest economic success under the given general conditions. The consumers prefer the "more comfortable" and most convenient solutions as long as there are no clear, serious and credible political signals.

What could be done on the part of science to help our society out of the impasse it has been contributing to? In my opinion, the emerging disputes and initiatives criticizing growth reflect the other side of the efficiency dilemma. Given that only constant growth ensures efficiency in saturated markets, growth is the result, not the cause of our subsistence strategies. So far, however, disputes have remained rather theoretical, and precise policy recommendations are not in sight.

In my opinion, it would make sense to look for the "drivers" and interdependencies of the dominant systems and develop scenarios for escaping the efficiency dilemma. In addition, it is important to learn how to handle the many factually justifiable contradictions that of course arise when it comes to changing existing patterns. Surely, the predominant subsistence strategy is driven, among other things, by the widely ruling and promoted technological innovation competition on the part of the industry and the behavior of consumers that is probably rather determined by the buying than the use of the respective goods. It remains to be found out which disciplines are suited to critically deal with these issues.

In the medium to long term, a well-founded investigation of the first complex of topics should succeed in freeing the social and cultural trajectories from the dependence on large-scale, cost-intensive investments. It may well be that such issues are beyond the present possibilities of access of the individual segments of economic science. But joint approaches and a critical reflection of one's own branch as regards the contribution of economy to the public weal of a society are toeholds for new ways. The second complex of topics is an at least as great challenge to science and demands cooperation, among others, with non-economic disciplines.

Why do consumers – meanwhile against better knowledge – succumb to and let themselves get stressed by the obligation to buy? What is the magic about material goods (cf. Hübner 2010a)? Can it be that it is the buying process itself that is so exciting and satisfying? Has the need the consumer wants to satisfy still anything at all to do with the respective goods? And what is behind slogans such as "if economy prospers, we all prosper" (Austrian Federal Economic Chamber WKO)? They seem to be right to everyone at first sight. But at second sight, they evidently reverse facts: Economy is there for man, not vice versa! Quite obviously, the reasons why we prefer buying goods to caring for their reasonable needs-based use have not yet been sufficiently investigated and things are being turned into their opposites instead: While marketing and market, PR and consumption research chairs are mushrooming (with the objective of developing still better methods for stimulating buying behavior), commodity sciences chairs, once at the core of any economic university, continuously decrease, at least in German-speaking countries.

Although it may be that commodity sciences have concentrated (too) long on the knowledge of materials, production methods, sales, etc.; they would be suited for becoming the nucleus of a new type of interdisciplinary commodities research. Within the framework of the latter, both socio-psychological phenomena that, regardless of marketing strategies, are related to the symbolic and functional significance of goods, and the phenomenon of shaping one's identity by "must haves" (cf. Fromm 1976; Ullrich 2006) instead of by borrowing or sharing goods could be investigated. Besides, together with legal experts, one could try to get to the bottom of what, in the face of the ruthless waste of resources, is conceived by the term "property" and by the polluter-pays principle. Finally, it would make sense to develop methods that, based on an economy with principles of good supply instead of maximum sales, would be able to ensure a slow change of the existing structures towards a new subsistence strategy and a culture that increasingly relies on values other than the economic ones. The assumption that cultures succeeding in the above can escape the pressure to grow is presently discussed by many elite economists but is rather the result than the cause of our industrially oriented subsistence strategy.

The insights provided in the course of the collection and recycling of recoverable products and the analysis of return, reprocessing and sharing systems (cf. Hübner et al. 2005; Stahel 2010) permit and demand that the treatment of goods is viewed altogether differently than is presently done within the economics canon emphasizing as efficient as possible production and sales methods and maximum profits through maximum quantities of products sold. The EU efforts to implement an integrated product policy as a contribution to sustainable consumption (cf. Hübner 2010b, p. 62) reveal, among other things, the importance of considering the stage of use, the application and utilization of goods, and the questions as to which and why things happen to the products while they are not used (anymore). Already in 2001, these different aspects were outlined in "Güter im Haushalt: Gut genutzt oder gut getrennt" ("Goods in private households: Optimal use or optimal separation") (Hübner 2001), thus providing a basis for new and innovative approaches to the three-stage chain of consumer activities.

The above two groups of topics

- the efficiency dilemma as a consequence of an efficiency-fixed economy of scale and a global because globalizable (!) subsistence strategy that is based on size effects, and
- the role of material goods as material and immaterial phenomena in our society between *practical value and exchange value* (that is assumed to go back to Aristotle)

may offer great scientific challenges. But besides that, I would like to express the hope that while discussing the unsolved questions, possibilities will open up of coping with a phenomenon that meanwhile may be considered the greatest obstacle on the way to sustainable development: The *rebound effect*. According to that effect, "economy or savings achieved by more efficient technologies are always overcompensated by increased use and consumption" (Aachener Stiftung 2011). This means that a more efficient manufacturing of products and a more efficient provision of services can create lower prices due to which more is consumed in spite of constant income restrictions. Since this, in turn, reinforces the consumption spiral, a real escape from this vicious cycle or "boomerang effect" is not achieved through the efficiency principle but rather through frugality alone. However, frugality in the sense of a content life without consumption stress, does not fit into the maximum efficiency and growth-oriented subsistence strategy that dominates the values of our western cultures.

References

Aachener Stiftung (ed.) (2011): Lexikon der Nachhaltigkeit. Aachen (URL: http://www.nachhaltigkeit.info/index.php; 15.2.2011) (in German)

Abels, H. (2009): Wirklichkeit. Über Wissen und andere Definitionen der Wirklichkeit, über uns und Andere, Fremde und Vorurteile. Wiesbaden (in German)

AWG – Abfallwirtschaftsgesetz 2002 (i.d.F. 2009). Wien (in German)

Baccini, P.; Brunner, P. H. (1991): Metabolism of the Anthroposphere. Berlin a.o.

BMfLFUW – Bundesministerium für Land- und Forstwirtschaft, Umwelt und Wasserwirtschaft (2006): Bundes-Abfallwirtschaftsplan 2006. Wien (in German)

EC – European Commission (2008): EU Waste Framework Directive, 2008/98/EG C.F.R. Brussels

Fischer, K. (2001): Strategien im Kreislaufwirtschafts- und Abfallrecht unter besonderer Berücksichtigung der Produktverantwortung der Wirtschaft. Heidelberg a.o. (in German)

Fromm, E. (1976): Haben oder Sein. Die seelischen Grundlagen einer neuen Gesellschaft. München (in German)

Hartard, S. (2010): Technikkultur in der Industriellen Ökologie. In: Parodi, O.; Banse, G.; Schaffer, A. (eds.): Wechselspiele: Kultur und Nachhaltigkeit. Annäherungen an ein Spannungsfeld. Berlin, pp. 175–187 (in German)

Hauer, W.; Hübner, R.; Mayr, H.; Rieder, T.; Scharff, C.; Schelmbauer, H.; Vogel, G. (1992): Aufbau eines Systems zur Sammlung und Verwertung von Verpackungsabfällen in Österreich. Feasibility Studie (Grundlagen des österreichischen ARA-Systems). Wien (in German)

Hübner, R. (2001): Güter im Haushalt: Gut getrennt oder Gut genutzt? Redistributionslogistik und neue Chancen im Bereich des Facility Management. Frankfurt/M. (in German)

Hübner, R. (2010a): Die Magie der Dinge. Materielle Güter, Identität und Metaphysische Lücke. In: Parodi, O.; Banse, G.; Schaffer, A. (eds.): Wechselspiele: Kultur und Nachhaltigkeit. Annäherungen an ein Spannungsfeld. Berlin, pp. 119–150 (in German)

Hübner, R. (2010b): Sustainable Consumption in the Integrated Product Policy. In: Krnacová, P. (ed.): Produktová politika a jej sociálno-ekonomické aspekty [Product Policy and its Socio-Economic Aspects]. Bratislava (University of Economics, Faculty of Commerce), pp. 52–65 (in English)

Hübner, R.; Himpelmann, M.; Melnitzky, S.; Stahel, W. R.; Hübner, H. (2005): Reprocessing gebrauchter Güter – eine Strategie der Nachhaltigkeit und ihre Auswirkungen auf die Lieferketten in einer Fabrik der Zukunft (Endbericht im Rahmen des Impulsprogrammes „nachhaltig wirtschaften" des BMWF). Wien (Austria Recycling) (in German)

Isenmann, R.; Hauff, M. von (eds.) (2007): Industrial Ecology: Mit Ökologie zukunftsorientiert wirtschaften. Heidelberg (in German)

Pladerer, C.; Kloud, V.; Gupfinger, H. (2002): Auswirkungen der Novelle der Verpackungszielverordnung 2000 auf das Wiener Abfallaufkommen. Endbericht. Wien (in German)

Schelmbauer, H. (2006): 60 Jahre Austria Recycling. Wien (in German)

Stahel, W. R. (2010): The Performance-Economy (2nd ed.). Hampshire/NY

Thematische Strategie für Abfallvermeidung und -recycling, KOM(2011) 13 endg. C.F.R. (2011) (in German)

Ullrich, W. (2006): Haben wollen. Wie funktioniert die Konsumkultur? Frankfurt/M. (in German)

VerpackVO – Verpackungsverordnung (1992). Wien (in German)

VerpZielVO – Verpackungszielverordnung (1992). Wien (in German)

Personal Sustainability – Including Body and Soul

The Karlsruhe School of Sustainability

Oliver Parodi

0 Introduction

Kindly allow me to make a first personal remark. When it was high time to prepare this article, I fell ill. Upcoming work piled up, deadlines were approaching. I even considered cancelling my contribution due to heavy workload. As you can read, fortunately – or anyway: I managed it. You are probably asking yourselves: What does this boring story have to do with this article, and with sustainability? This or a similar story has already happened to every one of us. And I say, this is exactly what it is about.

I do not only have in mind that stress, subtle self-exploitation, and pressure to perform are omnipresent in our working environment (this also has to do with sustainability). I rather refer to the fact that such everyday situations and occasions, personal acting, and corporal feeling are not related to the leitmotif of sustainability. Sustainability and our own personal existence appear to be completely independent of each other, at least most of the time. In my opinion, however, this is a problem, a major obstacle to the implementation of sustainable development. Hence, we are already right in the middle of our subject.

This shall be outlined now by giving some insights into the School of Sustainability, founded at the Karlsruhe Institute of Technology (KIT)[1]. And especially mention the theoretical background with the link to "culture", respectively to a "culture of sustainability".

1 The School of Sustainability – Framework Conditions

The School of Sustainability[2] is a project initiative of the Institute of Technology Assessment and Systems Analysis (ITAS)[3] and the House of Competence (HoC)[4] at KIT. The school presently is in its starting phase and is supposed to provide interdisciplinary training and education for sustainable development to KIT stu-

1 Cf. www.kit.edu.
2 Cf. www.hoc.kit.edu/schule-der-nachhaltigkeit.
3 Cf. www.itas.fzk.de.
4 Cf. www.hoc.kit.edu.

dents and later to employees and external clients. Interdisciplinary teaching offers are made, offers for compulsory general education apart from the disciplinary studies. In the long term, a separate (masters) study course on "personal sustainability" is considered.

The idea for this school occurred about two years ago. Since then, a concept of such a school has been developed with few funds and high personal commitment, and first events and teaching courses were performed. The core team consists of five persons of varying disciplines. It is dedicated to the growth of the school, organizes events, performs teaching, and accomplishes conceptual work. About ten professors at KIT support this initiative as "mentors and promoters".

2 Objectives of the School of Sustainability

Let us now address the objectives of the School of Sustainability to obtain an impression of its purpose (see Figure 1). The paramount long-term objective is to enhance a "culture of sustainability" (cf. Parodi 2010).

A much more concrete objective is to convey and train for "personal sustainability". Request for a personal sustainability is to overcome the gap between the abstract idea and complex concept of sustainable development – which is acting on a societal level – and the very concrete and tangible individual Doing and Being. The school aims to implement and concretize sustainability in persons (cf. Parodi 2009). I will get back to this soon.

Figure 1: Objectives of the School of Sustainability

Objectives

- ▶ providing a culture of sustainability
- ▶ convey and train *personal sustainability*
  - ▶ conveying knowledge about (theories of) sustainability
  - ▶ teaching (specific) knowledge *for* a sustainable development
  - ▶ training perceptions and attitudes as well as postures
  - ▶ personally experiencing sustainability (or non-sustainability)

Author's archive

3 Culture and Sustainability

Much could be said about the long-term objective of a culture of sustainability. Let me only mention a few major aspects to illustrate the approach pursued by the School of Sustainability. But first let me deal briefly with the term of "culture" used here.

3.1 Culture

"Culture" here shall not be understood to be "high arts" or "other, foreign cultures", but something much more basic: Culture as a basic constitution of human communities. Culture is something normal, it is the glue that keeps communities together (e.g. by common traditions, such as shaking hands, joint parties, a joint legal canon). The term "culture" used here is based on the theory of culture by Klaus P. Hansen (cf. Hansen 2000). Culture is that which appears to be matter of fact to all members.

And this is what is planned to happen to the idea of sustainability. Sustainability shall be internalized, enter the cultural background of the matter of fact, and become just something normal. In the end, sustainability shall be lived.

Culture always encompasses both the collective and the individual. To be more exact, culture is the interaction of collective and individual. These are the poles between which culture happens. And that's important for the approach of the School of Sustainability, where the collective and the individual side of sustainable development are regarded and supported (see Figure 2).

Apart from tangible materiality and institutions, spirituality/mentality is also covered by culture. Moreover, thinking, perceiving, feeling, and emotions are parts of culture (for instance, culture-specific feelings in Japan in contrast to Germany or America).

Figure 2: Important Elements of Culture (Extract)

Culture ...

- ▶ as a basic constitution of human communities
- ▶ is the glue that keeps communities together
- ▶ is something normal; normality
- ▶ as the interaction of collective and individual
- ▶ covers thinking, perceiving, feeling

Objects of culture

- ▶ tangible things, institutions and mentality/spirituality

Source: Following Hansen 2000

3.2 Non-culture

Let me now point out a basic and delicate detail that relates culture to sustainability, or, separates our modern culture from sustainability: Within the framework of a functional theory of culture, culture may generally be referred to as a program for the permanent existence of a collective (cf. Böhme 2001). Hartmut Böhme stated that

> "'Culture' is a communal and community-creating order mechanism [...] established to ensure spatial permanence and temporal continuity. It is both the productive and conservative moment of 'culture'." (Böhme 2001, ch. 3; transl. by the author)

Culture is aimed at conserving a collective (during continuing change). Essentially, culture deals with nothing else than permanence or, to be more exact, with a permanent, continuous development of collectives.

Klaus Töpfer, former executive director of UNEP and protagonist of international sustainable development, said on the basis of his experience gained:

> "We are basing our entire Western way of life on three grand delusions: By ignoring that we are living at the expense of our environment, the developing countries and the following generations." (Töpfer 2006, transl. by the author)

This is neither permanent nor viable nor sustainable.

It is agreed that 'today's Western culture' so far has been a non-sustainable culture. According to the statement of Böhme above and a functional understanding of culture, this means that our culture is (functionally) perverted. It does not meet its purpose proper. Its existence is under threat. Or, to bring it to a point, our sometimes highly praised modern culture probably is no culture at all, but a non-culture (in German "Unkultur").

This clearly shows that the conception of sustainability is associated with fundamental social and cultural criticism! No wonder that wide implementation meets with resistance (of the existing cultural institutions). This inherent (non-explicit) cultural criticism of the sustainability leitmotif always has to be kept in mind. Sustainable Development does not focus on cosmetics (environmental compatibility, changed production methods, process conducts), but, if you take it seriously, eventually on a fundamental change in the history of mankind.

3.3 Culture of Sustainability

As already stated, culture of sustainability basically means: living of sustainability. In more detail, this could mean: Implementation and translation of the basic values and ideas of the sustainability debate into a lived culture. Sustainability would be entrenched in the community and in the individual. Sustainability would become a convention, a tradition, something usual, and matter of fact.

A culture of sustainability would be the implementation of sustainable development. Then sustainability is reflected in the human and embodied by humans. And, let me add this, when taking the claim of scientific/ethic concepts of sustainability seriously, implementation of this claim or of these concepts in a culture of sustainability would have far-reaching consequences and an enormous importance. As we know from the concepts of sustainability (cf., e.g., Kopfmüller et al. 2001: Schultz et al. 2008) sustainability claims to be anthropocentric, generation-overlapping, and global. In terms of culture, this means nothing else than talking about mankind (see Figure 3).[5]

Figure 3: Some Corner Marks of a Culture of Sustainability

Culture of Sustainability

- basically means: living of sustainability
- implementation and translation of the basic values and ideas of the sustainability debate into a lived and living culture
- sustainability would become a convention, a tradition, normality
- sustainability is reflected in the human and embodied by humans
- claims: global, anthropozentric, generation-overlapping
    - that means: Mankind!
- a gigantic task, of historic dimension, a shift in history of humanity

Author's archive

This creates an enormous claim and a gigantic task which reflects the large gap between the idea of sustainability and its implementation, in spite of all political efforts on the UN or national level. Establishing a culture of sustainability eventually is a task of mankind and would be a result of historic dimension. For the time being, we can summarize that it is a remote target and a far way to go.

4 Initial Situation

Nevertheless, some steps on this way have already been made, many successes have been achieved, but many things are not yet settled or still unclear. Let me mention some aspects serving as a basis for the work of the School of Sustainability.

On the national and international level, some elaborated and detailed scientific concepts and political strategies (or better: strategy papers) for sustainable development are available. Examples in Germany are the Sustainability Strategy

5 We are living in a global *society* for decades or even centuries. There is a global division of labour, movement of goods, political interaction, knowledge transfer, etc., but there's still no global culture, no global collective with the identity of human (or humanity). Mankind is still a vision but not a lived culture.

of the Federal Government from the year 2002 (cf. Bundesregierung 2002) and the Sustainability Strategy of the State of Baden-Württemberg (cf. Landesregierung Baden-Württemberg 2007). However, these concepts and strategies in general are contrasted by an entirely non-sustainable reality. Instead of a culture of sustainability, these widely spread non-culture of sustainability prevails. And here, you will certainly agree: The gap between knowledge and acting, between the idea and implementation of a sustainable development still is very large.

Despite large efforts and many initiatives, education for a sustainable development still is a sub-culture in the education sector, in Germany at least. There is neither a subject of sustainability nor does this topic play a major role in primary and continuing education planning. It still is a marginal phenomenon in university education – with notable exceptions (e.g. Leuphana University of Lüneburg, Hochschule für nachhaltige Entwicklung Eberswalde (FH), Alanus University of Arts and Social Sciences (Alfter bei Bonn) and it does not play any role at all in the excellence sector of universities (cf. Schneidewind 2009).

It also has to be said that the current zeitgeist in the German/European education sector (keyword "Bologna") rather is opposed to education for sustainable development. Acceleration of teaching, compaction of contents, equalization of topics, and orientation to the labor market, (or to the needs of industry), make this topic go to the dogs in education and as a lived principle. Education continues to be subject to efficiency, to the trend of rationalization and economization. I'd nearly like to say: No free people are educated (like Wilhelm von Humboldt's principle of education), but useful people. Instrumentalization and the "Verzwecktheit" of man and his life are still enhancing, also in the education sector.

One last remark about education and with it, let me come to the next point, the approach pursued by the School of Sustainability: (Not only) in Germany, education is accomplished mainly by conveying knowledge via the head or, which sounds even more horrible, via the brain.

5 Approach and Major Elements

Let me state what you might have noticed already: The School of Sustainability is no purely scientific venture. It is an education effort strongly based on scientific, ethical, and philosophical findings. These findings are conveyed in their entirety. The School thus claims to offer education even beyond pure science. (Still, it is intended to conduct one's own research at the School of Sustainability.)

It is aimed at reaching what we called "personal sustainability", at concretizing sustainability in every individual. For this purpose, it is required to establish the connection between the collective dimension, the abstract, complex idea and theory of sustainable development, and the individual life, everyday living, thinking, feeling, perceiving and acting.

Two Pillars

Consequently, the School of Sustainability is based on two pillars: In its scientific and ethics foundation the School of Sustainability refers to "The Integrative Sustainability Concept" mainly developed by ITAS (cf. Kopfmüller et al. 2001). It is conveyed and practiced in exemplary cases (cf., e.g., Kopfmüller 2006). Beside this theoretical and conceptual knowledge of sustainability there is a lot of complementary knowledge for sustainable development available at KIT and (partly) integrated into the School of Sustainability. This pillar of knowledge transfer of the school is established, is solid education for sustainable development.

Apart from the classic purpose of knowledge transfer and enlightenment, by teaching the theories and applications of sustainability for the education of discerning cosmopolitans, who see and gage their own actions and that of others and other communities in the light of the idea of sustainable development, there is a second pillar for the school which – one could argue – is going further, deeper and is more personal in terms of pedagogy (see Figure 4).

Figure 4: The Conceptual and Institutional Architecture of the School of Sustainability

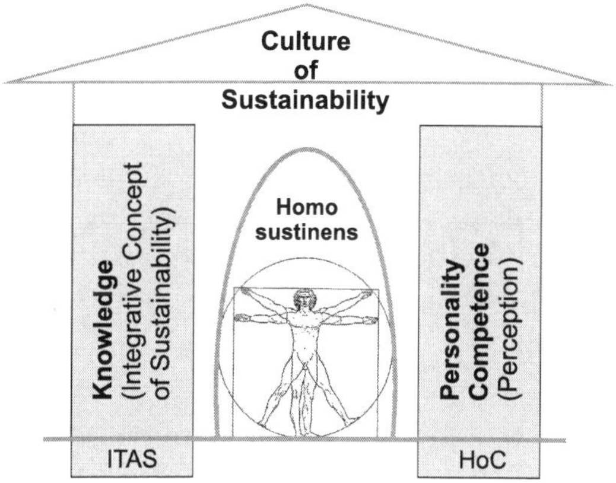

Author's Archive

The second pillar of the school of sustainability is based on an aesthetic and perception training, personal experiencing and exercising. Training for sensuality including physical exercises enabling the student to experience himself and his body in the environment, experiencing himself and his body in a living relationship to the world which surrounds him is an important building block. Positions and postures are being tried, rehearsed here, awareness and self-awareness is being practiced. The world shall be perceived with different eyes and ears than with the distanced view of a scientist looking at an object and with different hands than the possessive hands of the homo faber and oeconomicus, who aim to own and control everything touched. Here the focus is on subjectivity. People are allowed to be touched and moved by things.

One can categorize this pillar with the keyword "personal acquisition of skills (personality competence)" and "experiential education". Perhaps it stretches a bit further, and it is about more than just personal ability: about being and about identity.

6 Ethics and Aesthetics of Sustainability

This second pillar of the School of Sustainability may look unfamiliar and it needs explanation – due to the fact that it is uncommon and unconventional. Why do we need this second pillar? What is the theory behind it? At the bottom lies an extended understanding of sustainability. Or perhaps the explicit mentioning of the other face of the same coin on sustainability, which is implicit in the academic discourse, but not explicitly named or analysed there.

Sustainability as a scientific-ethical concept is common in scientific and academic communities. And the prevalent political strategies are based on these concepts. In these concepts one can characterize sustainability as a global scientifically-based ethical theory of a not-so-bad life. It is about the diagnosis of deficits (overuse of resources, damage caused to the environment, social inequality) and rules and instruments for their balance. Sustainability is not, like in the ancient philosophy and ethics, a theory of the good and successful life, a life plan, but – phrased in postmodern terms and added by a few degrees of freedom – it shows the guidelines for a not-bad life (see Figure 5).

Our School now aims to add an "aesthetics of sustainability" to this present and sophisticated ethics of sustainability. In this context aesthetics has two meanings: First, in the ancient meaning of Aesthesis (= perception) and second, the modern meaning: beauty; a self-worthy purposeless beauty. But why do we need aesthetics of sustainability in addition? Two hypotheses can be formulated here, both derive from the background of a permanent gap between knowledge about and acting for sustainability, between theory and practice.

(1) *Aesthesis Thesis:* It is not enough to know the concept how to change the world sustainably. To effectively change it, one must perceive this world, find a sensual approach and finally put yourself in relation to the world around you, the world you are living in (and the world that comes after your existence). And – due to the fact that it is perceived now in the view of a non-sustainable development – it must be perceived differently.

(2) *Beauty Thesis:* It is insufficient to aim only for a useful, an ethical correct world for the human being in the framework of sustainability (catchwords "resources" and "justice"). It must be a beautiful world too that is worth preserving, living in and passing on to generations or to reconstruct.

The following will provide evidences for both theses – not for their proof but to make them plausible.

Figure 5: Sustainability as a Matter of Ethics and Aesthetics

Sustainability as Ethics
- sustainability as a global scientific-ethical concept
- as an ethical theory of a not-so-bad life
    - diagnosis of deficits (environmental damage, social inequality, etc.)
    - and rules and instruments for their balance

and:

Sustainability as Aesthetics
- sustainability as a matter of perception
    - Aesthesis Thesis
- sustainability as a matter of beauty
    - Beauty Thesis

Author's archive

6.1 Evidences for the Beauty Thesis

Let us start with the Beauty Thesis: The world of sustainability is reasonable, precious, useful, etc. The one thing she is not: beautiful! One fundamental term in sustainability thinking and acting is scarcity. (The idea of sustainability has evolved from the awareness of shortage. Our resources will come to an end and some are scarce. This existed in forestry in the 16th and 18th century (cf. Grober 2010) as well as in the report of the Club of Rome 1972 (cf. Meadows 1972). Care/Worry, in German "Sorge", is another fundamental building block for sustainability: The worry about the existence of mankind, the fear of environmental or social catastrophes and, as an answer to this, the Precautionary Principle and the ethical impetus of the "unconditional obligation/duty of mankind to exist" (cf. Jonas 1986).

In the context of sustainability some (by all means plausible) horror scenarios are described, dreads and worries are nourished and being answered by a sour ethics of "you must" (duty) and "you should not/ you should" (rules) to prevent the apocalypse. This may be justified as long as sustainability is being used as a mere steering instrument for the use of resources. By now the present concepts and strategies of sustainability encompass more. With its global and holistic demand to look at all people and all the dimensions of human actions, with its rules reaching into every area of cultural issues, the idea of sustainability has risen to a design for society (or a life design) – without claiming it most times.

"Scarcity", "necessity to safe", "worry", "fear", "duty" might picture a lot, but it does not draw a picture of a desirable development or future, nor a picture of sustainability, that is truly desirable. Excluding every beauty from a future sustainable world leaves her crippled, deprived of human feature, in the end monstrous (catchword "eco dictatorship"). Such a vision is far from being desirable. A world is required too that is worth aiming for out of yourself, out of one's own aesthetic feelings. And it requires a world that is aimless and purposeless, simply existing in its beauty.

Even bèautiful things have a value that is worth keeping. In contrast to other discussions about sustainability this value has its roots away from a means-end relation, in which everything (every forest, every lake, every social relationship and every culture) is useful and purposeful. A not-bad-life is not only what it is all about. Obviously that is not enough. It is rather important that life and a sustainable development are beautiful and worth living.

With the help of the School of Sustainability we want to convey a sustainable future and development, that one should not be driven by moral or by duty only but which one can recognized and felt as being desirable also. To do this the (sour) ethical sustainable universe needs widening. We want to side:

the worries – with joy;
the scarcity – with plentifulness (away from material wealth);
the material having – with the personal being;
the duty – with the desire;
the shall – with the will and want.

6.2 Evidences for the Perception Thesis

Now to the Evidences for the Perception Thesis: Psychology, Pedagogy, Perception Theory, Culture Theory, (biological) System Theory and many others we know about it: Perception opens and forms our access to the world and with that – and that is crucial – the way in which we are dealing with the world around us.

Perception plays a central role in the way we are handling the world around us.[6] Here is a contemporary statement from the "Handbuch der Sinneswahrnehmung":

> "Before man starts thinking in words and categories he perceives his environment with his senses. He 'grasps' and 'collects' his world in the very sense of the words and acquires it in this way. The senses are the interface between humans and the environment, sensual perception is the prerequisite for the communication with the environment. Sensual perception gives people a vision of the world, lets them discover relationships and gives them insights. However senses need stimulation and practice to prevent them from wasting away. They have to be developed so that processes in the brain can be trained. Therefore a sensual aesthetic education is necessary. Perception is a holistic and active process; senses and reasoning are non-detachable and are one element." (Zimmer 2000, pp. 19f.; transl. by the author)

In antiquity the idea prevailed that ethical education should be sided by aesthetics, a training for the sensual perception. Without aesthetics ethics would become stunted. For a successful life in community one does not only need the "shall", the ethics, but essentially the aesthetics. The significance of aesthetics becomes vivid in Aristotle's' works about politics and state governance. Even here, in this concrete subject, Aristotle's emphasizes the importance of aesthetics and the aesthetical education of citizens (cf. Aristoteles 2005). For example he is pointing out that musical education (in the wider sense: for harmony, rhythm of life) is a precondition for a successful (good) life in the community (Polis). Another hint may give the modern idiom of Politics as "Art of the Possible" (originally "Politik ist die Kunst des Möglichen", Otto von Bismarck). This Art can not be professional managed without the sensuality for the moment and sensibility for the possible and necessary.

Furthermore, perception can be allowed to have a far more basic and essential role for "human abilities": e.g. perception as the basis for reasoning powers or as the fundament for cognitive abilities or the presently propagated openness or creativity. And even rationality (in German "Vernunft") is not unaffected by perception: According to Friedrich Schiller there is "no other way to turn the sensual human into a rational, right-minded human, than to make him aesthetic beforehand" (Schiller 1795; transl. by the author). One does not have to follow this statement through, but you surely cannot deny it completely. Assuming that

6 The use of the word "wahrnehmen" (perceive) in the German language shows that perception has both a receptive as well as an active side. "Wahrnehmen" in German is not only a passive act of receiving, of sensual perception, but an active act of doing something, like for example somebody fulfilling his duties or keeping to his date. Then he is doing this, turning the perception into a fact, a thing of reality.

sustainability is a rational thing, respectively a question of rationality – and I think only a few will deny this – then Schiller's quote will gain a wide scope.

Today, like 2000 years ago, perception is done by the body, the senses – this cannot be denied. So you have to imply (or incorporate) the body, the senses in the curriculum of sustainability too.

A training of perception is essential – this is, e.g., being recognized and put to practice in reformed pedagogic concepts and the education in early childhood. Still common is to simply raise the stimulus for the senses (catchwords: "multi-media") instead of refining the senses, to train them and to practice them. By the time for pupils and students in continuing and higher education is not much room for physicalness and sensuality; the brain is being fed with information, the perception is wasted. The knowledge, the concepts of the world which are conveyed in school and university are getting more and more complex year by year, but perception and perception training are becoming less important the older the pupils are getting.

A conclusion of the hypotheses on aesthetics as perception and beauty could be the following: It takes the openness and sensibility for the present, for the here and now (for the beauty and the ugly, the just and the unjust) to be able to create a tomorrow that is worth living in. It needs a vivid relationship to your environment as a motivation for its preservation, or change. Therefore you must include the body, the senses and the soul.

And, from the perspective of a culture of sustainability one could say: A culture without beauty would (at least) be poor and sad. But a culture without an adequate perception would be dull, literally blind and deaf and not in the situation to last.

7 About the School

A few more words about the naming of the venture "School of Sustainability" and some teaching examples may be helpful to bring the school to life.

7.1 The Naming

Why "School"? We would like to carry over what school meant in the original sense: from Latin "schola", it once meant "leisure", "pausing for a moment", "Muße", "Innehalten" in German, and more: "Innehalten" means to be quiet and listen inside you.

We want to take our school seriously in this sense; contrasting it with the concentration of time – as a societal and personal phenomenon – and giving it space, where quietness and pausing for a moment are common elements of the running of the school. Next to brainstorming even brain-silencing finds its place in the School of Sustainability.

Personal Sustainability, the training of the perception, the insight into the wider context of sustainability, the correlation to your own life are not things that can be conveyed in a hurry; they need time, free-time, must mature and be practiced. (Perhaps the school can contribute to protect the endangered species "time", which is – as an element of personal freedom – threatened with extinction by mechanization, rationalisation and economising of our every-day life.)

7.2 Teaching Examples

It is planned that courses are run for each pillar "Sustainability Knowledge" and "Personal Competence/Perception Training" and – these might be the most interesting – some courses combine the two pillars. Here are some examples already realized:

"Sustainability at the KIT – Vision and Reality": Starting from the scientific discourse about sustainable development the existing teaching environment of the student, the KIT, is perceived and analysed in terms of sustainability. After consulting the students certain aspects like energy- and water supply, food, equal opportunities, rooms for social meetings at the KIT are looked at. The task is to work out the subject, to present it to the other students and to discuss it with the group. At the end of the course students should be in a position to differentiate between sustainable alternatives of actions and less sustainable alternatives for actions in the private sector and at the university and be able to pursue these.

Other running events are for example:

- Sustainability, ideas of man and personal skills;
- Basics of personal sustainability I;
- Sustainable companies need staff trained in personal sustainability;
- Solar energy facility for a charitable organization (a service learning unit – projected);
- Reading, listening and active non-doing (projected);
- Series of lectures "Sustainability – very close" (e.g. "Post carbon future" in 2010);
- Mobility, infrastructure, urban development for a sustainable society (summer school 2011).

"Refreshingly Sustainable – Experience Water": This summer school in 2010 took place for three days in a seminar house up in the Black Forest. Subject: The question of the "culture of sustainability", which is even an academic challenge at the university can be existentially experienced in the handling of water. Water as the basic element of life, as global challenge for the supply and as a symbol of the history of culture is being analysed in talks and discussions and is being experienced in sensual orchestrations in- and outdoor this summer school.[7]

The event consisted of pure elements to transfer knowledge, like for example the teaching of basics of sustainability as well as exercises in perception. A main part of the event was outside at waters. At first some students were confused by the sometimes unusual (open and sensual) form of the event – at which at one time a glass of 12,000 year old water was degustated and enjoyed, accompanied by stories from 12,000 years of cultural history of water. At the end of the summer school all students came and voiced a positive feedback about the unusual format. Asked, whether an "inner order" had resulted from the seminar, many answered (independently of each other) "Be more watchful with water" and "To spread the idea of sustainability".

8 Critique

Despite the enthusiasm for the School of Sustainability and despite all beliefs, that such ventures make sense and are important, I would like to mention at this point one can have a critical view on the School of Sustainability – and, in my view, sometimes should.

Firstly, the School of Sustainability's approach is unusual. What is more, social criticism (or criticism of culture) is being passed on through it and in it. This is suspicious and not well-received in some places. Additionally it is not a totally academic, and a value-laden venture on a university, the social stronghold of science (and its assumed neutrality). This too causes friction. And: Mentioning body and soul is disturbing university as a knowledge factory. So much for the criticism from outside, this must be taken seriously and where appropriate agreed to live with it.

But criticism should come from the inside too; one should be and stay watchful and discerning. The following applies from Friedrich Hölderlin's extension "Where danger is growing, the saving is growing too": in the view of a non-sustainable development, education for sustainable development is growing. But and also the opposite has proven to be historically true: Where the saving is growing, danger is growing too. (And be it that the saving becomes a dogma and the intended saving is turning into a nightmare.)

7 Up to three credits are given for taking part in the event and for the corresponding elaboration. The elaboration was supposed to be a personal reflective account. The form of the product is deliberately left open for the student to decide; it is possible to deliver it in form of a sound document, photos, texts, poems, video clips – and they should have been reflected in their meaning.

The approach of the School of Sustainability is – following Hölderlin's extension: delicate, dodgy if you take it seriously. One must be aware at all times that one operates in the field of personal and cultural foundations by dealing with "personal sustainability". One does not only get knowledge across but it is all about personality and influencing the students – by for example the training of perception or by conveying values. That is dodgy. But, one must add, that this is otherwise left for the cultural uncontrolled growth, respectively is being done elsewhere in a culturally 'natural way' just without criticism and self reflexion. Looking at it this way, the School of Sustainability is still fine.

The only thing that worries me is that such a School of Sustainability will expedite a professionalization of man, trim the human being, constrain his freedom by educating him so deeply. The question is: What is left from the human existence beyond his profession "human"? All I can do is to have trust in the anarchic, creative side of man; to enter a new world beyond sustainability and the professional human.

But, I would know – at least today – how to decide between an advancing, disastrous and non-sustainable development cutting human freedom – and the professional sustainable human.

References

Aristoteles (2005): Buch 7–8: Über die beste Verfassung (Übers. u. erl. von E. Schütrumpf). Darmstadt (Aristoteles. Werke in deutscher Übersetzung, Bd. 9: Politik) (in German)

Böhme, H. (2001): Was ist Kulturwissenschaft? (URL: http://www3.culture.hu-berlin.de/hb/static/archiv/volltexte/texte/kuwilex.html; 25.08.2011) (in German)

Bundesregierung (2002): Perspektiven für Deutschland. Unsere Strategie für eine nachhaltige Entwicklung. Berlin (URL: http://www.bundesregierung.de/nsc_true/Content/DE/__Anlagen/2006-2007/perspektiven-fuer-deutschland-langfassung,templateId=raw,property=publicationFile.pdf/perspektiven-fuer-deutschland-langfassung; 25.08.2011) (in German)

Grober, U. (2010): Die Entdeckung der Nachhaltigkeit. Kulturgeschichte eines Begriffs. München (in German)

Hansen, K. P. (2000): Kultur und Kulturwissenschaft (2nd ext. ed.). Tübingen (in German)

Jonas, H. (1986): Das Prinzip Verantwortung. Versuch einer Ethik für die technologische Zivilisation. Nördlingen (in German)

Kopfmüller, J. (ed.) (2006): Ein Konzept auf dem Prüfstand. Das integrative Nachhaltigkeitskonzept in der Forschungspraxis. Berlin (in German)

Kopfmüller, J.; Brandl, V.; Jörissen, J.; Paetau, M.; Banse, G.; Coenen, R.; Grunwald, A. (2001): Nachhaltige Entwicklung integrativ betrachtet. Konstitutive Elemente, Regeln, Indikatoren. Berlin (in German)

Landesregierung Baden-Württemberg (2007): Nachhaltigkeitsstrategie Baden-Württemberg – Jetzt das Morgen gestalten (URL: http://www.nachhaltigkeitsstrategie.de; 25.08.2011)

Meadows, D. H. (1972): The Limits to Growth. A Report for the Club of Rome's Project on the Predicament of Mankind. New York

Ott, K.; Döring, R. (2004): Theorie und Praxis starker Nachhaltigkeit. Marburg (in German)

Parodi, O. (2009): Die Schule der Nachhaltigkeit – ein Anfang. Karlsruhe (working paper) (in German)

Parodi, O. (2010): Drei Schritte in Richtung einer Kultur der Nachhaltigkeit. In: Parodi, O.; Banse, G.; Schaffer, A. (eds.): Wechselspiele: Kultur und Nachhaltigkeit. Annäherungen an ein Spannungsfeld. Berlin, pp. 97–115 (in German)

Schiller, F. (1795): Über die ästhetische Erziehung des Menschen, in einer Reihe von Briefen. 23. Brief. Quoted after Rittelmeyer, C.: Über die ästhetische Erziehung des Menschen. Eine Einführung in Friedrich Schillers pädagogische Anthropologie. München 2005, p. 104 (in German)

Schneidewind, U. (2009): Nachhaltige Wissenschaft. Plädoyer für einen Klimawandel im deutschen Wissenschafts- und Hochschulsystem. Marburg (in German)

Schultz, J.; Brand, F.; Kopfmüller, J.; Ott, K. (2008): Building a "Theory of Sustainable Development": Two Salient Conceptions within the German Discourse. In: International Journal of Environment and Sustainable Development, Vol. 7/No. 4, pp. 465–482

Töpfer, K. (2006): Globale Umweltveränderungen. Konsequenzen für Technikentwicklung und Technikfolgenabschätzung. Speech on the Conference "Technology Assessment in der Weltgesellschaft" (NTA2), Berlin, 22.11.2006 (in German)

Zimmer, R. (2000): Handbuch der Sinneswahrnehmung. Grundlagen einer ganzheitlichen Erziehung (8th ed.). Freiburg im Breisgau (in German)

Integrating Art and Education for Sustainable Development

A Transdisciplinary Working Process in the Context of Culture and Sustainability

Verena Holz

1 Introduction

The paper outlines an exemplary art and cooperation project with the aim to show innovative strategies in terms of specific challenges to the concept of Education for Sustainable Development (ESD).

The challenges concern the (1) sensitivity of people in terms of global change and (2) the implementation of future-oriented ways of life including participation competences to shape a sustainable society. A case study of the German Federal Office for Environment shows: most Germans know the current major problems of global change but this knowledge has no consequences for their daily life (cf. UBA 2008, pp. 37ff.). It seems that knowledge about future scenarios is not necessarily transferred rational behaviour and courses of action – an issue that has to be considered also by education concepts. Ute Stoltenberg and Gerhard de Haan emphasize: ESD has to break new ground to meet challenges of future life (cf. Haan 2002; Stoltenberg 2001).

Against the background of the implementation process of ESD the particular research interest of this paper consists in using art as a supporting element in the learning process and aesthetic approaches as involvement for further occupation with the subject of sustainability. The object of investigation is a transdisciplinary cooperation project that connects artists, teachers, university staff, children, students, parents and other involved persons.

The cooperation project and theoretical concerns both focus on what constitute an adequate learning environment for ESD in a primary school. Who is participating in what kind of matter in this process? The paper describes key factors and milestones concerning the cooperation project as an approach to new, transdisciplinary education paradigms. In my methodological approach I will discuss the concept of transdisciplinary research and its function regarding sustainable development. The paper closes with the outline of further research interests based on the first results of the transdisciplinary research project.

2 Sustainable Development

Global change is the origin and inducement for sustainable development, conjoining our presence with our future. It challenges all people as stakeholders with different functions on various social layers: e.g. consumers, teachers, entrepreneurs, politicians but also persons whose existence is threatened immediately by the impact of global change. Issues of equitable allocation of resources to contemporary and future generations as well as strategies of implementation of sustainable lifestyles are debated in the context of sustainable development. The development process is sufficiently complex – it connects different cycles concerning human and non-human life of different dimensions (e.g. economic, social, ecological, cultural, political, technical) within ethical parameters and fault-tolerant visions of our future (cf. UNO 1992).

In contrast to the "daily-life perception" of many people, sustainable development isn't another wording for a concept to cope with environmental challenges. It rather centralizes anthropogenic global problems that have ecologic, economic, social, cultural and political consequences. The international discourse on sustainable development points out the significance of cultural questions and phenomena within the process: The first principle of the "Action Plan on Cultural Policies for Development" adopted by the UNESCO in 1998 says that: "Sustainable development and the flourishing of culture are interdependent" (UNESCO 1998).

The German government specifies this statement:

> "Sustainable development is not only the technocratic way of an efficient economy, eco-friendly production and healthy life. Technical innovations are essential, but not sufficient as moving power for sustainable development. Sustainable development is concerned with a vision of how we want to live in the future – with imagination and creativity. In this spirit it is a task of shaping and creating, based on values, social models and our cultural tradition challenging creative potentials of society. [...] It requests to change trails." (Bundesregierung 2002, p. 21)

This citation displays that typical single approaches to global change represented by genuine professional areas (e.g. environmental engineering) have become obsolete in support of integrative approaches. What kind of function takes education as constructive authority in the context of those transdisciplinary paradigms of development?

3 Education and Aesthetic Approaches – The Project "Growing sculpture. *Heiligengeistschule Lüneburg*"

It seems essential to point out that ESD differs from sustainable development as political process in its self-conception.[1] ESD can be understood as a cross-social learning-, alteration- and negotiation-process (cf. Stoltenberg 2006). That implies controversial discussion and the act of formulating different positions within a normative framework as basic principles. Hence ESD should not be interpreted as a system of rules with concrete targets (e.g. "waste separation in schools") but rather as space of options and experiment. Thereby it seems important to connect the ecological sphere with others to clarify the holistic extension of sustainable development. The objectives of ESD concentrate on: Empowerment to participation, envisioning future, systemic thinking, reflection and cooperation (cf. Tilbury et al. 2002). As to its practical application – particularly in the German non-formal education sector the idea behind ESD is analogous to the perception of sustainable development often mixed up with former concepts of Environmental Education (cf. Rode/Wendler 2009). How to deal with this problem? Stoltenberg suggests a four-dimensional analytical framework to deconstruct current arrangements and comprehend interferences as well as the integration of cultural, economic, ecologic and societal processes. Beside specific learning and working methods, factual and procedural knowledge facilitate people to participate in the application process of sustainable development (cf. Stoltenberg 2009). It corresponds to the goals of the United Nations Decade of ESD. The concept emphasizes potentials of shaping society and participation encouraging new approaches, methods and forms of knowledge. A strategy that characterizes the cooperation project which is the objective below.

The postulation of the UNESCO and German government to integrate culture and establish new forms of access to global change, was strengthened by the "Tutzinger Manifest" 2002. It claimed explicitly to integrate persons engaged in the cultural sector like artists or cultural managers due to their ability to bring the vision of sustainability to life – via ideas, visions and existential experience. As they have the idiosyncratic knowledge about symbols, rituals und practices that can be imparted to a multitude of people. Also Hans Dieleman indicated the significance of artists as key change agents and Hildegard Kurt and George Steinmann outlined the specific forms of questions that art formulates with regarding society (cf. Dieleman 2008; Kurt/Steinmann 2002). These debates contextualize the initiative of the cooperation project "Growing Sculpture. Heiligengeistschule Lüneburg".

1 *Heiligengeistschule* is the name of the cooperating primary school in the German city of *Lüneburg*.

Against the background of the image that primary schools can be seen as greenhouses for our future, discrepancies of quality enhancement with ailing school buildings, the lack of financing, social and cross-cultural conflicts and political demands are revealed. These problems affect likewise the daily school life at *Heiligengeist* School *Lüneburg*.

The Swiss artist Steinmann traditionally dedicates his work to questions of sustainability, ecology and future orientation. His comprehension of art and the spirit of his work are influenced by a specific bond to nature and its aesthetics – spiritually charged, partial by residencies with people living closed to nature, like Native Americans or the Komi. With his work he doesn't only pick out sustainable development as a central theme, his projects also contribute to sustainable development. E.g. with the installation of a bridge and a refuge[2] in a very poor region in Bernese Oberland (Switzerland) he sensitized local people to revalue the natural, cultural and social richness of their landscape. Simultaneously he opened the region to eco-tourism (hiking only), which enhanced the economical status of the community of *Saxeten* (cf. Steinmann 2006).

Considering the precarious situation in primary schools as well as the sustainability initiative at Leuphana University of Lüneburg[3], Steinman instigated a cooperation process with the Institute for Integrative Studies[4] and the und.Institute Berlin. The project started in February 2009.[5] It was guided by the following questions:

- What kind of education and working contexts qualify our children and us as teachers, artists and academic staff for future living?
- How can sustainable development be experienced and how do we define its role in school education?
- What are the basic principles regarding the implementation of ESD?
- What are the results of the aesthetic analysis regarding the school building, learning environment and socio-cultural processes? What impact has the

2 Both the bridge and the refuge are made from ecological materials and stand out due to specific aesthetics in terms of the contemplative ambience of the locality; cf. http://www.george-steinmann.ch/15saxeten.html (April 18, 2010).

3 Leuphana University of Lüneburg, represented by Gerd Michelsen and the Institute of Environmental & Sustainability Communication, is housing the UNESCO Chair of Higher Education.

4 The Institute for Integrative Studies at Leuphana University of Lüneburg dedicates its research to ESD in elementary school, kindergartens, secondary school systems and further education with regional cooperation partners.

5 The first period of the project (February 2009–February 2010) was funded by Altner-Combecher foundation for ecology and peace. A second period is being launched at the moment.

environment on learning processes? How can they be replenished through other perspectives?
- How can people be sensitized to their school environment?

How can different groups of people get involved in this learning-, alteration- and negotiation process?

- From the visual/public arts perspective: Creation and construction of new rooms at *Heiligengeist* School under sustainable und aesthetic aspects and methods (architectural intervention).
- From the social perspective: Creation of social innovations. That means to redefine social structures, relationships and fields of responsibility – perceiving school as social organism.
- From the scientific perspective: Implementation of ESD by a parallel education program for teachers, students and pupils and lead back process experiences to scientific conceptions regarding the implementation of ESD.
- From a general point of view: Conceived as an art project, the cooperation is supposed to attract people like teachers, parents, children, politicians and local stakeholders. Secondly, the instigation of a public dialogue about innovative forms of education and the role of aesthetic and sensual issues concerning approaches and the learning environment should be activated.

4 Methodological Challenges: Transdisciplinarity and Social Innovation Research

The theoretical and methodological objective from a scientific perspective lies in the advancement of future-oriented education concepts. Results of the exchange run in the enhancement of settings, methods and content of education in the context of sustainable development. Methods of developing theory can be characterized in cyclical processes, which on the one hand generate practice-changing theory and on the other hand feed back theory-changing practical experience. Anselm Strauss describes the procedure primarily as exploring and designing rather than examining and approving (cf. Strauss 1996; cf. also Kehrbaum 2009).

In inter- and transdisciplinary organized education process, experts are respected as partners within a common project and adequately perceived. Transdisciplinarity thereby aims to create new structures of knowledge and methods (cf. Brand 2000). The question of perspective takes an active place in this process. An artist or social scientist for instance identifies different coherencies than a medical scientist, economist or biologist. By this means different forms of experience, cognitive structures and knowledge exist – each of them relevant in terms of global change. Jasmin Godemann differentiates disciplinary perspectives in opinions, attitudes and values that are based on particular assets of knowledge and empirical experience – a complexity, which has to be taken into account in communication processes. She also points out the asymmetry of knowledge and power divide in those situations.

Next to the integration of knowledge the following aspects play a decisive role in transdiscplinary projects (cf. Godemann 2007):

- Communication;
- Coordination of tasks and processes;
- Creation of a common base of knowledge;
- Disciplinary self-reflexion.

It seems evident that transdisciplinary learning processes in the context of ESD have little in common with teacher-centred models of instruction. Following a constructivist interpretation of the learning process and focussing on key questions of society like the phenomena of global change as inducement, it appears important to allocate sufficient materials and possibilities for further learning.[6]

Transdisciplinary research processes can be contextualized theoretically and methodologically in contemporary paradigms of social sciences. Stoltenberg points out, that "the self-perception of education in contexts of sustainable development involves consequences on contents, methods and organisation processes" (Stoltenberg 2006, p. 81) and suggests to include approaches of innovation research in social sciences, inasmuch sustainability can be perceived as concept of social innovation (cf. Stoltenberg 2006). In this context research e.g. asks for conditions regarding the alteration of learning processes and educational institutions as well as other societal stakeholders. It concentrates on a complex social reality that has to deal with linguistically imparted cohesions of action and meaning as well as conceptions of reality (cf. Leggewie 1996).

As for the methodology of the evaluation process in transdisciplinary research Grounded Theory can be considered as adequate approach as it is located traditionally in principles of pragmatism philosophy. Its procedural research logic is based on the complementing antagonism of theory and practice, which generates forms of contingent knowledge (cf. Jonas 1992; Kehrbaum 2009).

Single social sub-processes (workshops) have been described and analyzed methodologically by Participant Observation (cf. Friedrichs/Lüdtke 1973).

6 "Education", understood under a critical constructivist perspective, means especially the individual and little influenceable process of acquiring knowledge and developing specific skills in a well-prepared learning setting; cf. also Klafki 1976.

5 Art as Impetus for Creativity, Process Orientation and Social Change

As this transdisciplinary, process-oriented research project implies a complex output; I will outline major milestones, key factors and observation results of the implementation in the primary school.

It was already mentioned the project distinguished itself from others by an exceptional cooperation of the following Partners: George Steinmann (artist), Hildegard Kurt (curator, artist, cultural scientist), the Institute for Integrative Studies (represented by Ute Stoltenberg and Verena Holz) and the Teaching staff at *Heiligengeistschule Lüneburg.*

According to the open conception of sustainable development a strategic and aesthetic approach consisted in the indeterminacy of the process. Against the advice of transdisciplinary research, working fields were appointed but no concrete vision concerning results and further development existed. This principle was explicitly intended by the artist in order reduce a dominant impact from one perspective. It also determined the working process in the student seminars.

Likewise the name "Growing Sculpture" suggests an adequate form of development and growth of all constitutive elements as alternative draft to economical growth. The idea and conception of the "Growing Sculpture" traces back to Joseph Beuys concept of "Social Sculpture". It implies a political dimension to art as impetus for social change.

Moreover participation was an essential working principle. The artists were involving teachers in their findings about ecological, social and aesthetic problems and potentials in *Heiligengeist* School at nearly any time. They asked pupils, parents and teachers for their perception of problems.

It was astonishing to observe, that the primary school teachers who – following Pierre Bourdieu's theory and results of our Participant Observation – have at least in a cross sectional view different perceptions and comprehension of art and its functions from the artist, were highly motivated by his vision and project presentation. The engagement and identification with the project of the teaching staff retained during the whole period, even if the planned architectural intervention was financially not ensured. Teachers report that via the art process they feel 'perceived and appreciated' in their function and situation.

Taking into account the complexity of the project, it is evident, that pupils don't have a concrete idea of the alteration process in their school. Nevertheless they were involved indirectly in the ESD projects created by the students. For instance, the children copied working methods of Steinmann by producing watercolours from fruits and vegetables to paint with. In another activity they picked out classroom atmosphere as a central theme and combined it with global learning contents like "how do children learn at school from other parts in the world".

The external communication of the project and its idea turned out to be complex and difficult due to the lack of a concrete prediction of results in the first months after project launch. Moreover it was not always easy for people who had no experience with art projects to retrace the principle of process orientation.

The graphic chart below gives an overview of the cooperation process and further prospects (see Figure 1).

In the following I will sketch the measures and achievements during the first period (February 2009–February 2010) of the project:

- Lectures and vocational trainings on ESD its implementation in school curricula and classes were held for teaching staff at *Heiligengeist* School Lüneburg.
- Furthermore four student seminars were given in context of the project with the objective to develop and realize ESD projects in the primary school. As a result two ESD projects at *Heiligengeist* School were realized with students and a 2nd and two 3rd classes.
- The curator Hildegard Kurt organized Workshops for teachers and parents of *Heiligengeist* School *Lüneburg*.
- The social, cultural and territorial environment of the school was examined and re-valued by all participants. The artist George Steinmann created a conceptual design of the architectural intervention visualised with scale models. Furthermore a transdisciplinary exchange of all cooperation partners within regular meetings was inaugurated. The local press, local and federal state politicians as well as municipality and parents were involved in those processes.

This was the beginning of a comprehensive networking activity: The artist was invited to conferences in order to point out the meaning of art and sustainable development in regional contexts. Moreover the project was awarded as "UNESCO Decade Project 2009/2010".

6 Conclusion

From a methodological point of view the observation, participation and documentation of such a process contains a range of challenges. E.g. the artist's vocabulary of describing processes differs from the scientific terminology of humanities and its cognitive structures, which may result in methodological problems. Therefore it could be of a further interest to examine the role of language in the transdiciplinary research process.

Figure 1: A Transdisciplinary Art Project Cooperation as Innovative Ground for an Implementation of ESD

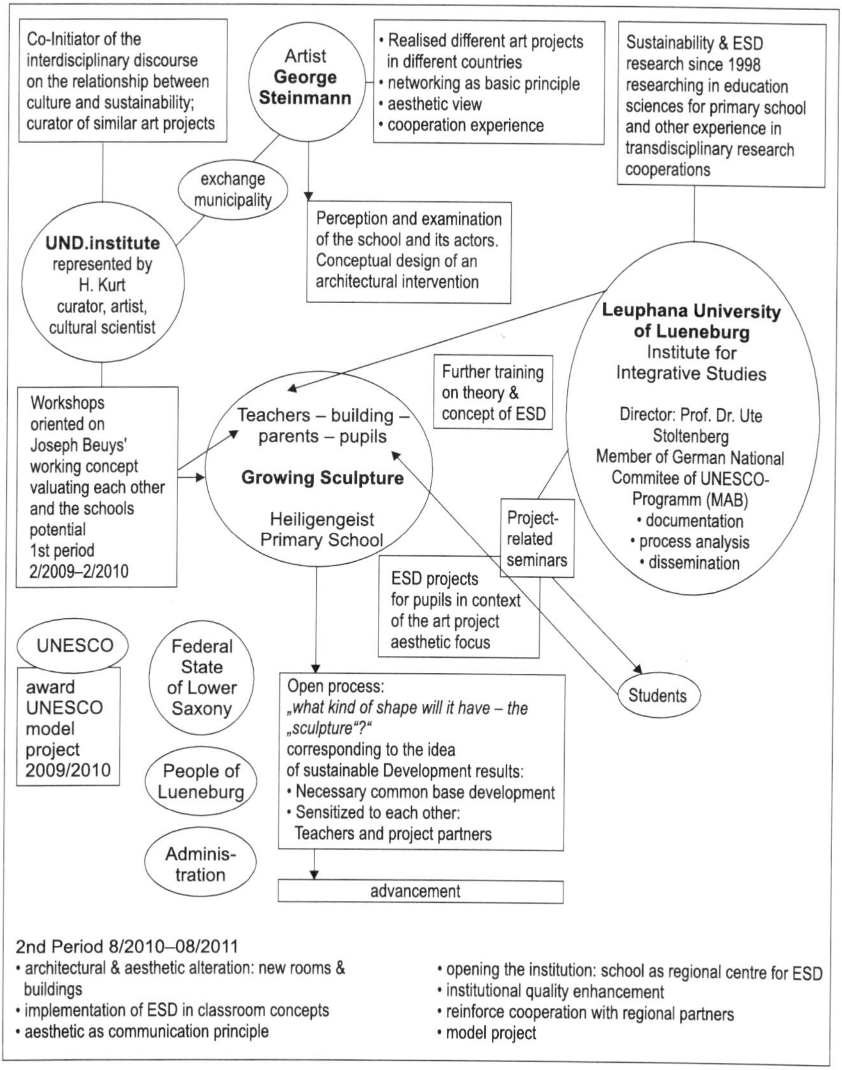

Author's archives

Considering the implementation of ESD in an environment, where there seemed to be no capacity for conceptual reflexion, such aesthetic and transdisciplinary forms of access with detailed, close perception of social processes turned out to be a qualified approach. Taking into account that mind-changing procedures require a particular duration, such methods of revaluating and respecting an adequate growth of social processes seem to have a high impact. At the end of period I the project found a footing to further common work with concrete prospects like the architectural intervention and the creation of a locality to enhance regional learning processes in the context of ESD and establish forms of innovative and future-oriented learning. The next step of research could consist in a qualitative interviewing process of all cooperation partners and participating students to investigate the impact of this particular approach to the perception and willingness to deal with sustainable development.

References

Bundesregierung (2002): Perspektiven für Deutschland. Unsere Strategie für eine nachhaltige Entwicklung. Berlin (in German)

Brand, K.-W. (ed.) (2000): Nachhaltige Entwicklung und Transdisziplinarität. Besonderheiten, Probleme und Erfordernisse der Nachhaltigkeitsforschung. Berlin (in German)

Dieleman, H. (2008): Sustainability, Art and Reflexivity: Why Artists and Designers May Become Key Change Agents in Sustainability. In: Kagan, S.; Kirchberg, V. (eds.): Sustainability: A New Frontier for the Arts and Cultures. Frankfurt/M., pp. 108–146

Friedrichs, J.; Lüdtke, H. (1973): Teilnehmende Beobachtung. Einführung in die sozialwissenschaftliche Feldforschung. Weinheim, Basel (in German)

Godemann, J. (2007): Verständigung als Basis inter- und transdisziplinärer Zusammenarbeit. In: Michelsen, G.; Godemann, J. (eds.): Handbuch Nachhaltigkeitskommunikation. München, pp. 86–96 (in German)

Haan, G. de (2002): Die Kernthemen der Bildung für eine nachhaltige Entwicklung. In: ZEP – Zeitschrift für internationale Bildungsforschung und Entwicklungspädagogik, Vol. 25/ No. 1, pp. 13–20 (in German)

Jonas, H. (1992): Pragmatismus und Gesellschaftstheorie. Frankfurt/M. (in German)

Kehrbaum, T. (2009): Innovation als sozialer Prozess. Die Grounded Theory als Methodologie und Praxis der Innovationsforschung. Wiesbaden (in German)

Klafki, W. (1976): Aspekte kritisch-konstruktiver Erziehungswissenschaft. Weinheim a.o. (in German)

Kurt, H.; Steinmann, G.: Interview mit George Steinmann. In: Kurt, H.; Wagner, B. (eds.) (2002): Kultur – Kunst – Nachhaltigkeit. Die Bedeutung von Kultur für das Leitbild nachhaltige Entwicklung. Bonn a.o., pp. 239–246 (in German)

Leggewie, H. (1996): Preface. In: Strauss, A.; Corbin, J. (eds.): Grounded Theory. Grundlagen qualitativer Sozialforschung. Weinheim, pp. v–ix (in German)

Rode, H.; Wendler, M. (2009): "Früher nannten wir es Umwelterziehung". Kommentierte Grundauszählung zur quantitativen Befragung zur außerschulischen BNE – ausgewählte Ergebnisse (unpublished) (in German)

Steinmann, G. (ed.) (2006): Das Werk Saxeten. Eine wachsende Skulptur von George Steinmann; 2002–2006 [ein Kunst- und Bauprojekt des Kantons Bern]. Bern (Bahnhöheweg 92: G. Steinmann) (in German)

Stoltenberg, U. (2001): Diskurs über Nachhaltigkeit als Herausforderung für Disziplinen zur ethischen Vergewisserung – konkretisiert am Bereich der Erziehungswissenschaften. In: Altner, G.: Michelsen, G. (eds.): Ethik und Nachhaltigkeit. Frankfurt/M., pp 222–238 (in German)

Stoltenberg, U. (2006): Innovationsforschung. In: Rieß, W.; Apel, H. (eds.): Bildung für eine nachhaltige Entwicklung. Aktuelle Forschungsfelder und -ansätze. Wiesbaden, pp. 81–86 (in German)

Stoltenberg, U. (2009): Mensch und Wald. Theorie und Praxis einer Bildung für nachhaltige Entwicklung am Beispiel des Themenfeldes Wald. München (in German)

Strauss, A.; Corbin, J. (eds.) (1996): Grounded Theory. Grundlagen qualitativer Sozialforschung. Weinheim (in German)

Tilbury, D.; Stevenson, R. B.; Fien, J.; Schreuder, D. (eds.) (2002): Education and Sustainability. Responding to the Global Challenge. Cambridge a.o. (IUCN Commission on Education and Communication)

UBA – Umweltbundesamt (2008): Umweltbewusstsein und Umweltverhalten der sozialen Milieus in Deutschland. Dessau-Roßlau (URL: http://www.umweltdaten.de/publikationen/fpdf-l/3871.pdf) (in German)

UNESCO – United Nations Educational, Scientific and Cultural Organization (1998): The Stockholm Conference 30 March–2 April 1998. Action Plan on Cultural Policies for Development (URL: portal.unesco.org/culture/.../12290888881stockholm.../stockholm_actionplan_rec_en.pdf; April 18, 2010)

UNO – United Nations Organization (1992): Konferenz der Vereinten Nationen für Umwelt und Entwicklung. Agenda 21. Rio de Janeiro (in German)

Standing on Mount Lu

How Economics Has Come to Dominate Our View of Culture and Sustainability – and Why It Shouldn't

Silja Graupe

1 Introduction

The study of economics has changed in the era since the Berlin Wall fell and a triumphal neo-liberalism, summed up by Francis Fukuyama in 1992 as "the end of history", dominated the political discourse.[1] In 1992, the „end of history" named the global tendency to free market policies, the shrinking of government economic intervention, and Western style democracy. Things have not, however, gone as planned. 2008–2009, for instance, witnessed the most massive state intervention in the economy since the Depression, as governments around the world massively backed up a collapsing global financial system. Meanwhile, the incipient transformation in the way the study of economics is conceived has evolved in tandem with the global system. Traditionally, economics systematically reflected in various methodological ways upon a specific sphere of our lives: the world of trade and markets. The unity of economics was thus secured by means of a common object of research, which could sustain a plurality of explanatory approaches. But contemporary mainstream economics has come to be monopolized by a certain subjective mode of looking upon the *entire* world. In this single conceptual framework, it proposes to give us a certain and permanent control over every aspect of our lives as long as we accept the precepts of "rationality". What clearly distinguishes economics as a discipline, thus, is not its subject matter any longer but its approach (cf. Becker 1976, p. 5). By means of a disciplinary "mission creep" the methodological tools of a certain kind of economics, such as "rational choice," "utility" or "profit maximization", are presented as tools to analyze

> "all human behavior, be it behavior involving money prices or imputed shadow prices, repeated or infrequent decisions, large or minor decisions, emotional or mechanical ends, rich or poor persons, men or women, adults or children, brilliant

1 Part of this paper was presented on the occasion of the "Global Dialogue Conference" at Aarhus University in Denmark on November 5, 2009, and might also be published in the proceedings of this conference.

> or stupid persons, patients or therapists, businessmen or politicians, teachers or students." (Becker 1976, p. 8)

In short, economics has become imperialistic (cf. Lazear 1999). And as this imperialism continually expands so as to include "fertility, education, the uses of crime, marriage, social interactions, and other 'sociological', 'legal', and 'political problems'" (Becker 1976, pp. 8f.), it seems only natural to incorporate both culture and sustainability also. Because of the power of the economic model, the latter two invasions of an intellectual territory that was previously deemed to be outside the realm of economics are well worth examining.

In the definition of economics that served as the standard model up until the 1970s, economic objects and processes were seen as embedded within culture, with the latter term denoting the sphere of those practices involving affects, beliefs and institutions that evolve according to norms that are independent of, and ethically superior to, those of economic activity. As such, culture was considered a prerequisite of the economy, but not as an object that could be reduced to the utilitarian paradigm of economic reflection. The classic sociologists, in fact, conceptualized culture specifically to distinguish our non-economic activities from our economic ones.

> "On the one hand 'cultural parameters' are brought in – especially in the case of international comparative studies – whenever functional or otherwise 'rational' explanations do not suffice to explain certain phenomena. On the other hand, the cultural sphere is hypothesized as the social locus eluding the rational constraints of both economy and public authorities." (Werner/Lackner, p. 41)

Today, mainstream economists are intent on weakening this sharp demarcation line by applying to culture the same tools of subjective preference (with the assumption that preferences are invariant over time, ordinal and transitive), and the same utility maximizing calculations, as are used when applied to rational choice in the marketplace. In this way, creative and performing arts, our world's cultural heritage, ethical norms, family life and friendships, are all subsumed under the models of economics (cf. Towse 2005). Though a lot of questions have arisen from the mismatch between the predictions of rational choice theory and psychological experiments on choice making behavior even within the economic sphere itself (cf. Tversky/Kahneman 1981), the economic model that reduces the study of culture to another set of utility maximizing behaviors has been extremely successful in penetrating all spheres of cultural study and policy-making. How are we to define and measure the utility of cultural phenomena? How are creative and performing artists really motivated? On what scale do we measure the value, not to speak of the "efficiency", of customs and traditions? Economics, especially its sub-discipline cultural economics, does not simply answer these kinds of questions, but it generates the paradigm in which asking these questions come naturally. At the same time, cultural economics' idea of cultural management goes a long way: it has made us perceive culture, or any part of it, as a predictable and orderly resource that should be planned, budgeted, and controlled (cf. Klein 2008).

In certain ways, the concept of sustainability, especially in its ecological dimension has met a very similar fate. This was not a topic that, for many reasons, swam into the ken of the economist as a reasonable object of research until recently. If anything, nature was considered a container from which we could draw resources without any limit, and dispose of our waste without any social cost (cf. Daly 1999). As such, the ecosystem was at best considered a mere adjunct to the economy. This adjunct did not constitute an object of economic investigation in itself, however, as the latter only dealt with marketable goods and resources that could be priced. And as long as nature's elements remained unpriced, that is, outside of any market, they were not considered part of the economic sphere. Coined in modern terms, they were treated as positive and negative externalities, conditioning economic activity in as much as it took place within the living environment but forming by itself no object for economic analysis. Like culture, it was logically outside of that analysis, just as economic activity was embedded within it. This mindset, however, has considerably changed as the economic approach is now being applied to any kind of object no matter if it involves money prices or just *imputed* prices. While formerly nature's parts needed to be actually traded on real markets prior to becoming an object of economic analysis proper, now they are a priori treated *as if* they had a price and *as if* they were marketable.

> "Prices, be they the money prices of the market sector or the 'shadow' imputed prices of the nonmarket sector, measure the opportunity cost of using scarce resources, and the economic approach predicts the same kind of response to shadow prices as to market prices." (Becker 1976, p. 6)

Nature is thus embedded within economics. As such, it is turned into a totality of *ecosystem services* that are calculated and predicted by an economic analysis that begins by assigning them current and future prices, and thus incorporates them into the system of costs and benefits. The reduction to pure quantitative units of utility makes everything from the weather system to the migration of butterflies subject to their assigned utility or wealth functions, which are then used to design policy. Given the dominance of economic thinking over any other value system, the issue of environmental sustainability now becomes a simple object of investigation, like the inflation rate, which is first to be measured by means of indicators, benchmarks, audits, and other reporting systems, and then to be efficiently managed and controlled. Ultimately it is thus tantamount to *sustainable exploitation:* getting the most out of natural assets for the sake of those who can, and in fact, do make the calculations.

It might be objected that economics has done nothing here to change the goals of either sustainable development or cultural formation, but simply crystallized both into quantitative units amenable to calculation as a means to instrumentalized social policy concerning the underlying reality of the environment. On a more general plane, mainstream economics places emphasis on the fact that it "does not deal with ends as such" (Robbins 1935, p. 24).

> "The ends and purposes themselves lie beyond the action and the reason; they are for our theory [...] merely data, which we cannot further analyze by means of our science. [...] They themselves stand outside our explanation." (Mises 2007, p. 15)

However, we contend that this mindset amounts to a deep seated problem rather than its solution, for if culture and sustainability are subordinated to the instrumental logic of economics, their true meanings become inevitably blurred by a contradiction: economists are treating them both as instruments and as ends in themselves while simultaneously claiming that there exists no kind of reasonable language by which to express the value of the latter. Thus, culture and sustainability are likely to be reinterpreted as mere means towards an ultimately unjustifiable end. In addition, all of human activity gets invariably preconceived not only as maximizing behavior but also as being coordinated through the market (cf. Becker 1976, p. 5). All people are thought of as unconsciously acting under the order of prices telling them what to do and what to leave undone (cf. Hayek 1996). Thus, what at first appears as a mere change of heuristic in actuality points to a shift in the value accorded to extra-economic value: culture and sustainability have been processed so as to seamlessly correspond to the spirit of anonymous market transactions. The market, then, penetrates into the realm of every social activity, and essentially replaces the human and the natural as the highest term of reference.

What becomes visible here is an isomorphism between culture on the one hand and sustainability on the other. Metaphorically speaking, their identity stems from the credo that all aspects of our lives need to be looked through the same colored glasses, or in other words, that everything is susceptible to being analyzed in terms of rational choices once we make everything a market. But this identity is simply due to a certain fixed mindset, to the rigidity of a pre-given epistemology. This important insight, however, mostly remains hidden from view in that it is presupposed. For the more the economic approach is taken to be universally valid, the less we dare to question its premises. Eventually, we even come to consider such questioning as both trivial and ultimately unfeasible. As a consequence, we begin to uncritically conflate its way at looking at the world – the color of its lenses – with the colorfulness of reality itself. In order to overcome this epistemological and conceptual bottleneck, I consider it necessary to carefully reconsider the relationship between economics, culture and sustainability.

Let us first attend to the relationship between the former two. As we have seen, mainstream economists consider their own discipline – at least implicitly – as being analytically prior to and, thus, ultimately independent of culture. As such, they favor a universalistic approach: the methodological procedures underlying their research projects are not considered to derive from a given culture's way of life, but are elaborated a priori. They excuse an empirical lack of acquaintance with a particular culture, since what is important is that one can quantify over any behaviors within it and find maximizing strategies and indifference curves. In this way, however, economists turn a blind eye to one of the most important insights of the cultural turn in the humanities and social sciences: today, we cannot consider cultures a mere object of research. For the researcher herself is always going to be entangled in deep cultural assumptions that tacitly inform as well as shape underlying research strategies prior to any particular act of observation or theory formation (cf. Lackner/Werner 1999). Said differently, cultures inform the presuppositions researchers have implicitly inherited not only from their disciplinary traditions but, as well, from the pool of assumptions sedimented over generations into the language, customs, and the life forms of the society they live in. Bringing "culture" back into economics thus cannot amount to studying the former by means of a set of analytical tools preset by the latter. It means first and foremost uncovering the hidden background assumptions of economic analysis itself. This in turn requires that economists heighten or actually develop the faculty of self-reflexivity. "The cultural turn is invariably associated with a critical revision of what has been formerly considered as self-evident truth" (Werner/Lackner 1999, p. 44). Living in a globalized world as we do today, this is not idle criticism, nor the expression of some fashion for postmodernism. Rather, we have become aware that the simplifying procedures by which Western social scientists have operated for centuries in order to reduce cultures to intellectually manipulable unities have resulted in an overemphasis on the homogeneity of cultures, as though marginal groups, the oppressed and poor, and the structures of privilege that advantage certain classes, ethnicities, and genders were minor cultural features. Since the movements of the sixties and their reflection in the social sciences, it is generally granted that the existence of a single organizing framework cannot be taken for granted even within a given culture. Even in Western cultures, the assumptions about the structure of preferences made by mainstream economists like Becker have failed, along with the idea that the price system reveals something "deep" about some universal tendency to maximize. But when we move these assumptions across even more diverse cultural context, rather spectacular misunderstandings arise. Here, *a tertium comparationis,* from which to bring important differences and commonalities into perspective, has first of all to be generated (cf. Yousefi/Mall 2005). It cannot be determined by the methodological procedures of any scientific approach a priori. To the contrary, these methods need to be turned into an object of reflection in the light of the world's different epistemologies and ontologies instead (cf. Graupe 2007). Revising, in this way, the relationship between culture and economics also opens up possibilities to critically rethink the relationship between economics and sustainability. More concretely speaking, it allows us to first rediscover the unspoken background assumptions and implicit presuppositions hidden in economics' dealing with nature and even the world in general, and then to critically question and even transcend them by means of intercultural dialogue. Thus it becomes possible to systematically free sustainability from its status as another object of economic analysis and to fathom the rich scope of its possible meanings by means of a multi-perspective approach.

In what follows, I will attempt to sketch out an example of the explanatory power that can be drawn from this latter possibility. In doing so, I begin by focusing on one of the most powerful pre-analytic visions in mainstream economics, namely, its game metaphor. Then we will further immerse ourselves in this metaphor in order to demystify the pre-analytic vision of mainstream environmental economics vis-à-vis the central role played by competition, nature, and responsibility. Here, my approach will be implicitly informed by Chinese and Japanese intellectual traditions. In the second part, I shift to making explicit my reliance on East Asian philosophical sources in order to point to another ludic tradition, which, contrasted with the European one, can give us another understanding of competition, nature and responsibility. In this part of my paper, my goal is not to prove that the Japanese and Chinese conception of play is unique or superior; rather, my detour through Asian intellectual traditions should be construed, as Francois Jullien once put it, as "an attempt to deepen our own comprehension of the state of things, to renew the impulse to question, to rediscover the joys of inquiry" (Jullien 1992, p. 18). In Chinese there is an expression, "We cannot see the true face of Mount Lu because we are standing on top of it" (Sun Tzu 1993, p. 45). My paper is, so to speak, designed to attain an external perspective so as to see with greater clarity at least some aspects of the "true face of Mount Lu", upon which economists all too naively stand. In my concluding section, then, I am going to summarize our findings in an attempt to systematically rethink the core idea of sustainability.

2 Uncovering Economics' Preanalytic Vision

Ever since Adam Smith, economists have likened free market competition to a game played for the purpose of winning, in which the responsibility of the players is limited to obeying the rules of fair play.

> "In the *race* for wealth, and honours, and preferments, he may run as hard as he can, and strain every nerve and every muscle, in order to outstrip all his competitors. But if he should justle, or throw down any of them, the indulgence of the spectators is entirely at an end. It is a violation of *fair play,* which they cannot admit of." (Smith 1790, part II.II.11; emphasis by me, S.G.)

This is not only an explicit statement of the case as in Smith but also, and even more importantly so, an implicit assumption of economic models. The game metaphor has become so deeply embedded in economic theory and model building that it constitutes the common basis of understanding in the field; a basis that is all the more solid since, being so integral, it often seems unnecessary to comment on it. If you take away the game metaphor, economics as a discipline would almost collapse. It is on this ground that I am justified in seeing this metaphor as the determinant of what economists consider relevant in understanding and addressing the environmental problem or any other aspect of sustainable development. Moreover, it has a prescriptive aspect, meaning that any policy to overcome environmental problems cannot violate the game metaphor. We must have competition, there must be "players", there must be "prizes", or "incentives", and the "rules" must be limited to allowing the players to fairly compete. So when economists speak of the "tragedy of the commons" or the "prisoner's dilemma" or, on a more practical plane, try to weigh the costs and benefits of alternative environmental policies to deal with air pollution, water quality, toxic substances, solid waste, and global warming, they concern themselves largely with devising changes to the rules of the international economic game, while uncritically assuming the game structure itself as pre-given and unalterable. In doing so, they derive their arguments from a pre-analytic vision that serves as the basis of reflection but is never turned into an object of attention. It is precisely this latter gap that this subsection is designed to fill in by presenting five propositions that implicitly govern the vision of environmental economics.

According to mainstream economics, competitors exist prior to the process of competition. We can take this as a sort of economic axiom. Uncritically affirming this pre-analytic vision, the *first proposition* we find is *that environmental economics considers economic agents as logically prior to their market environments and as ultimately independent from them. More generally, this reflects a culturally biased ontological assumption of context independent agency.*

The methodological fiction of an entirely isolated person has a long history in political economic analysis. It was under the sign of this fiction that relations between persons and property were loosened from all social entanglements in the bourgeois revolutions of the 18th and 19th century, when classical economics, in coordination with the lineaments of the capitalist order, came of age. The privileged metaphor for the isolated person in economics is Defoe's Robinson Crusoe: a man systematically cut off from the rest of humanity, whose individual desires and experiences are expressed in primitive accumulation, the production of tools for home use, and the systematic exploitation of the resources of his island for his pleasure and utility (cf. Defoe 1938). Friedrich Hayek, Nobel Laureate in economics in 1974, was right to claim that economic theory has advanced from the classical economists' use of such extreme forms of methodological individualism, with their stagnant consideration of isolated and self-contained individuals (cf. Hayek 1980, p. 6). Yet, if each man is not an island in neo-classical economics, each man is a player. My point is not that economics mistakenly supposes a world of single-player games, but that it analyzes competition as if it consisted "of a number of independent households, a number of Robinson Crusoes, as it were" (Friedman 1982, p. 13). Most games we cannot play alone, and economists have rarely interested themselves in solitaire. But by supposing only competitive play, economics presupposes other competitors who, somehow, in the same mold as their opponent, are only located on an opposite side at the same time. Strangely, however, competition neither defines nor shapes the competitors' identities according to the economic tradition.[2] While the players make decisions in social situations, those decisions are made on the ground of preferences and intentions that are defined exclusively by reference to themselves. Each is thought to define the content and borders of her social bonds herself (cf. Nawroth 1961, p. 55). More specifically, we are thought to compete neither because we enjoy playing with others nor because we wish to mold ourselves in the process of competition but only because we seek to achieve a certain preset goal. Repeating Smith vision of play, we run as hard as we can, and strain every nerve and every muscle in order to outstrip all our competitors. In this pursuit of ours, we depend on fellow men only as means to our pre-determined ends. Thus, "the first principle of economics is that every agent is actuated only by self-interest" (Edgeworth 1881, p. 16): Each player is an independent entity whose interactions with others are determined by given motives, goals, and intentions (cf. Becker 1976, pp. 5–13). The "unconditioned striving for personal advancement – even at the cost of the ruin of one's competitor" (Homann/Blome-Drees 1992, p. 26) becomes the great and singular cause of social interaction while cooperation, altruism, love, and the mere enjoyment of playing are all excluded by economic models.

Mainstream economics preconceives this cause not only as independent from any alteration by the players, but also from the process of competition as such. We are not socialized into being competitive; rather, individuals' goals, intentions and strategies logically precede their social interaction. Self-interest, defined solely in terms of winning and gain, is unalterable among human beings by any conceivable course of events. Within game theory, for instance, econo-

2 I have shown this in more detail in Graupe 2007, pp. 146-150.

mists conceive games as given matrices of payoffs by means of which actors rank the desirability of expected outcomes – measured in terms of profits, quantities, or utilities – prior to entering the game as such. From the standpoint of the logic of competition, market environments thus must be premised as a kind of pre-existing stage upon which all economic games are performed. This means, among others, that the commons, or the environmental assets that nobody owns, can never serve as objects of intentional strategies, but instead only function as the pregiven, unquestioned background against which these strategies play out. Simply put, competitors do not do battle upon the battlefield to conserve or preserve it, but instead, adapt their tactics to its pre-conceived contours in order to pursue their individual goals; The battlefield – in this context, the environment – serves as the premise but not the result of self-interested intentional action.

As game theory tellingly demonstrates, such cognitive blindness even persists if environments happen to be damaged in the process of competition in such a way that they cannot be renewed. Only if we invent a new game in which the overhaul of these damages could be turned into a goal benefiting some player do we approach any rational for sustainability. But any game targeting the environment would depend upon not changing the rational of players as such – as the possibility of changing the rationale of players would, by a chain reaction, put into question the whole of the game metaphor. This is, at least, the lesson we are supposed to draw from the tragedy of commons and other game theoretical images of social interaction. Here, players pursue their individual self-interest even as they diminish the capacity of the commons to renew themselves, thus damaging it to the ultimate cost of all (cf. Hardin 1968). The dynamics of deterioration is taken as an accident that affects neither the pre-given preference structure of the players nor their frenetic will to win. This is because the latter two are considered essential properties of the agents in the process, irrespective of the specific situation in which the activity of competing goes on (cf. Becker 1978).[3] This fundamental idea also determines the logic of rational choice theory, the standard economic framework for understanding and formally modeling social and economic interaction. Here individuals are always weighing the costs and benefits of outcomes (with an eye to their own profit) prior to taking action. As Philip Mirowski has remarked, this makes preferences independent of both space and time: outcomes of interaction are not allowed to depend on how agents go about consuming or producing in the here and now of social interaction (cf. Mirowski 1989). The very activity of trading, for instance, is believed not to socialize either consumers or producers. As John Maynard Keynes critically remarked, "it does not count the cost of the struggle but looks only to the benefits of the final result

3 This is because, as Becker states, economics must proceed upon the presupposition of *stable preferences,* which do not change in time.

which are assumed to be permanent" (Keynes 1926, part III). Taken to the extreme, economic agents are thought to remain wholly unaffected by nature's destruction. For them, environments, as the etymology of the word suggests, are taken for granted as the circumstances within which they live. Even in the face of severe environmental crises they think of themselves as maintaining their integrity as unviolated wholes. Their identity corresponds with the fixed boundaries of the ego or I, which is considered "the unity of the acting person. It is given without question and cannot be dissolved through any thought" (Mises 1940, p. 34).

After mainstream economics has established the irreducibility of the individual to its own satisfaction, it next establishes the irreducibility of the market. Our *second proposition* is: *the relationships between players are externally defined by the pre-existing rules of the Smithian game. Thus, there exists a given, omnipotent framework that determines the range of possibilities for the outcome of competition, but is itself unaffected by any competitive game in particular. Fundamentally, this further reflects a cultural bias towards a metaphysics of atomism.*

Even though mainstream economics preconceives agents as entities pregiven to the process of competition, it does not think of them as being entirely socially independent. As noted before, its object of study is not Robinson Crusoe, but the interplay of many Robinson Crusoes. It remains, then, to say what connects them all. Figure 1 illustrates the fundamental economic situation, in which a series of external relations (R_1, R_2) connects the discrete individuals *A* with other individuals *B*, and *C*.

Figure 1: Agents as Externally Related

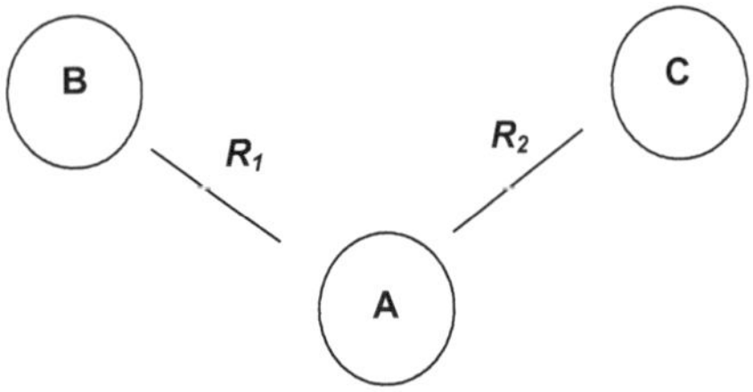

Source: From Kasulis 2002

Here, the relations are not themselves *A* but instead something that associates *A's* entity with *B's* and *C's* entity. A enters into her relationships in such a way that it remains essentially unchanged: if the connections were broken or dissolved, *A* would still be *A*. This does not mean, of course, that the relationships have nothing at all to do with *A's* character. If *A* chooses to be in the relation R_1 and R_2 with *B* and *C* respectively, this indeed reflects something about *A's* own nature. That is: *A* has made the positional choice to get connected to the other entities *B* and *C* by means of external relationships. But the latter are not considered part of what *A* is; rather, all retain their autonomy in their independent choices to be connected. In short, an atomistic metaphysics obtains where primary existents bond together externally to form the parts of a larger whole.

Implicitly grounding itself in such metaphysics, mainstream economics understands the economy to be constructed from entities in external relations with each other. Put in the words of Smith, social cooperation in free market economies is thought to arise purely "from a sense of utility, without any mutual love or affection" (Smith 1790, part II.II.16). Economic man is believed to voluntarily agree to the social relationships upon which he depends, which are in turn independent of his agreement. Mainstream economics, however, does not grant individuals the freedom to creatively devise other social relationships. The latter are, rather, conceived as the preset menu of choices, which individuals may either fully accept or reject. Their freedom consists in entering the game and accepting its rules – or not entering the game at all. And just as a menu is unchanged by those who select items from it, the rules of the game, which define the relationships between self-interested players, are unchanged by anything that happens in the course of the play: once one chooses to compete, one must invariably follow them. This is to say that there is no freedom to alter the form of one's relationship whilst playing. One might try to choose where to position oneself on the playing field, but the positions are already given in the same way that the squares of the chessboard are already given.[4] Even upon defeat, the player cannot alter the rules of the games – else a different game would be played. In short, economics invokes the metaphor of games "as a form or spell of play or sport, especially a competitive one played according to rules and decided by skill, strength, or luck" in order to model and analyze free market competition (Hayek 1996, p. 184). More specifically, it seeks to distinguish

> "the day-to-day activities of people from the general and customary framework within which these take place. The day-to-day activities are like the actions of the participants in a game when they are playing it; the framework, like the rules of the game they play." (Friedman 1982, p. 25)

> "In discussing ordinary games, we have little or no difficulty in distinguishing between the *rules* of the game as such and *plays* of the game within these rules [...] Rules provide the framework of the playing of the game, and many different patterns of play may take place within given rules [...] In a socio-political context, the same distinction apply between rules of social interaction and the patterns of behavior that take place within these rules. The distinction here is often more dif-

4 Adam Smith mentions the metaphor of the chess game explicitly in Smith 1790, part VI.II.42.

ficult to make than in ordinary games, and the discussion of the latter is helpful precisely in this respect. The validity of the distinction between rules and behavior within rules is general, however, over all interaction settings." (Brennan/Buchanan 1985, pp. 5f.)

One of the most crucial characteristics of economic analysis here becomes the necessity "to separate the process through which rules are determined from the process through which particular actions within those rules are chosen" (Brennan/Buchanan 1985, p. 6). Individual self-interest expresses itself in tactics that play out solely in the context of a nexus of pre-established, external and independent relationships. Coining another important metaphor of economics, Smith expresses this insight most famously by likening the economy to a machine:

> "The wheels of the watch are all admirably adjusted to the end for which it was made, the pointing of the hour. All their various motions conspire in the nicest manner to produce this effect. If they were endowed with a desire and intention to produce it, they could not do it better. Yet we never ascribe any such desire or intention to them, but to the watch-maker, and we know that they are put into motion by a spring, which intends the effect it produces as little as they do." (Smith 1790, part II.II.19)

The mechanical image encoded in the pre-analytic vision of economics is that of agents who must bow to forces and obey principles the they cannot hope to understand, on the one side; and on the other stand forces and principles such that they are shaped by a transcendent creative power standing sovereign, and even absolute over both economic agents and their activity. In as much as the mechanism of the machine is ultimately designed by an engineer standing outside and over above the machine and its parts, the rules of competition are thought to be designed by an outside force working behind the back of individuals. From any perspective within the game, this process of creation and construction remains utterly inexplicable. Rules are, so to speak, created ex nihilo: neither the players nor their playing do share in their making.[5] "Play takes place within the rule, but play does not constitute part of the rules" (Brennan/Buchanan 1985, pp. 5f.). Thus the Smithian metaphor postulates that "a good game requires acceptance by the players both of the rules and of the umpire to interpret and enforce them" (Friedman 1982, p. 25). For the players, the dynamics of relating freely are systematically excluded by the rules of the game (cf. Hershock 2006, p. 27).

Our third *economic proposition* is as follows: *mainstream economics implicitly preconceives the competitive struggle of the few to take place within certain spatial and temporal boundaries. Competition is thought to take place inside some 'playing-field' so that the competitors tacitly position themselves*

5 For the concept of *creatio ex nihilo,* its strong influence on Western tradition and its marked absence in Chinese thought compare (cf. Ames/Hall 2003, pp. 16f).

against everything outside that playing field – culture, nature, and all agents not playing on the field. Given these framework externalities, the key concept of environmental economics, must arise not only regularly but also systematically. On a foundational plane, this reflects a cultural bias toward dualistic thinking expressed in terms of inner and outer.

Once the economy is considered as a form or a spell of competitive play played according to rules, it follows that these rules are tacitly assumed to delimit a playing space. We can see this with Smith's metaphor of the race, for instance, which premises a pre-assigned racing track of definite length, a definite starting signal, and a destination. Additionally, it filters the number of competitors, creating another boundary between the outside non-competitor and the inside competitor. More generally speaking, competitive games need to be thought of as spatially and temporally constrained, with a limited population of players, because one can only seek to outrun certain competitors on a given playing field in this moment. This is the meaning of the economist's phrase, bar to entry. What takes place at another setting, or at the same setting at another time, is without avail. Inevitably, it remains external to the race for wealth, honors and preferments. Competitive games designed for winning are thus implicitly exclusive. Only the foot racers race against the foot racers. The various forms of game theory, for example, take competitors to be competing only against their own kind, thus presupposing certain limits to the population of competitors. Also they assume that competitors must interact within certain known spatial and temporal boundaries because otherwise the possible payoffs could not be known a priori. The prisoner's dilemma for instance only conceives of two players entering the game, which automatically ends upon conviction. Also, the game is thought to remain confined to the spatial boundaries of two isolated prison cells. These temporal and spatial limitations of play and limitations of the population of competitors are not the objects of strategic reflections, but rather are unquestioningly accepted at the competition's start.

We can reframe this issue in this way: mainstream economics simplifies competition into a series of discrete finite games whose boundaries remain, from the perspective of the competitors, both inexplicable and not negotiable.[6] This is the only way it can model these games. This strategy hides the problems inherent in the very conception of such boundaries, which is closely connected to environmental economics' notion of externalities. This problem arises because in finite games, there exist no meaningful ways for agents to relate to the natural and cultural environments placed outside competition's boundaries. Standard economic theory emphasizes the fact that there is a bound on the number of possible voluntary participants in a competition. This however only serves as one

---

6 I borrow the notion of finite games from James P. Carse (cf. Carse 1986).

face of the fact that any finite game must necessarily exclude some agents who could potentially play, and that their exclusion is not voluntary. This does not mean that the excluded are thus not affected by the game's process. However, their concerns don't count for those playing within the defined boundaries, as indeed all players are concerned with their own self-interest. In their will to win, competitors concentrate on those who are defined as opponents within the game, but remain entirely indifferent to the needs and aspirations of the bystanders. The well-being of non-players invariably remains external to inner logic of the game. It so happens that these games do affect the non-players, however. For instance, the competition among steel makers uses energy from coal and materials from iron mines and disposes of wastes so that it leaves a large environmental footprint – but the steel makers themselves are only concerned with their own profits. The external effects of commerce – from sicknesses born of polluted rivers to global warming – do not only occur regularly, they are built into the system. For it lies in the very nature of finite games to exclude not only bystanders, but also entire geographical regions as well as future generations. The very logic of finite games keeps outsider's needs below the radar of those who are happy enough to be in the game at present. Put into economic terms, Pareto efficient situations usually only hold for a given set of individuals, the selected players, so as to cast into the dark the fate of those "third parties" unhappy enough not to have been included in that set right from the start.

It is worth noting here that the possession of money either explicitly or implicitly provides the ticket to entry for economists. "The market process includes and excludes. The boundary is demarcated by money. If one has money, one has the ticket to the play of the market" (Brodbeck 1996, p. 229). This is to say that "solely the binary code of paying or not paying counts: whoever pays, receives, what he wants; whoever fails to pay, because he can't or won't, becomes a bystander" (Schramm 1997, p. 150).

> "Any persons who are not acquainted at every moment with the prevailing ratio of exchange, or whose stocks are no available for the want of communication, must not be considered part of the market." (Jevons 1970, p.133)

Because they can get no access to the market game, their powers are reduced to zero, and in a competitive society they cease to exist (cf. MacPherson 1962, p. 56). Men who have no possessions to which others can ascribe a positive value find their existences within the boundaries of economic competition annihilated and, consequently, are pushed to its margin. This, of course, also holds true for all cultural and social phenomena that elude monetary expression. In as much as competitors turn a blind eye against the possible degeneration of their playing field, i.e., their immediate competitive environments, the conditions of their wider cultural and natural environments also remain below their radar.

My *fourth proposition* concerns the regulatory premises derived from our above-analyzed notion of externalities. *While mainstream economics has traditionally neglected the subject of externalities altogether, due to its insistence on analyzing competition in terms of finite games, environmental economics seeks to internalize external effects into the market framework. To do this, it tries to devise ways in which the rules of the game can be manipulated from the outside while preserving competitive behavior within game. Fundamentally, what is at stake here is the belief in a transcendent creative power standing sovereign and even absolute over both agents and their activity.*

Consider, for instance, global warming. Over the last several decades as temperatures have trended upwards, an increasing number of environmental economists have agreed that it can be considered an external effect of competition, whose elimination systematically eludes the inner logic of the game. The question, then, is not if the field of economics is aware of the problem at all, but rather how it poses a solution to the problem. Oversimplifying complicated matters somewhat here, the allocation of carbon emission certificates appears a good example of how the system of exchange, or market, must be preserved at all costs. Some central authority, deployed by nations or the entire international community, first sets a specific goal, say reducing carbon dioxide by an amount said to be sufficient to limit global warming to 2°C by 2050. Subsequently, the central authority caps the amount of carbon dioxide every economic agent is allowed to emit, limiting total emission to a certain level. Companies or other groups pay for emission permits and are required to hold an equivalent number of allowances representing the right to emit a specific amount. Because I assume my audience is well aware of the emission trading scenarios currently in circulation, let me skip the details and get straight to the underlying structure of argument here, which has a long tradition both in economic and political theory. Modern environmental economics confidently turns to the unquestioned presupposition that some external agency can design, alter and enforce the rules of the game independent of the inner logic that prevails within the competitive framework, so as not to impinge upon the principle of competition. More concretely speaking, the state here assumes its customary role

> "to provide a means whereby we can modify the rules, to mediate differences among us on the meaning of rules, and to enforce compliance with the rules on the part of those few who would otherwise not play the game." (Friedman 1982, p. 25)

Here, the state is considered a transcendent agency standing sovereign, and even absolute over the interplay of self-interested individuals:

> "What the state does [...] is to alter some of the terms of the equations each man makes when he is calculating his most profitable course of action. But this need

> not affect the mainspring of the system, which is that men do calculate their most profitable course and do employ their labour, skill, and resources as that calculation dictates. [...] The state may, so to speak, move the hurdles in advantage of some kinds of competitors, or may change the handicaps, without discouraging racing." (MacPherson 1962, p. 58)

Bluntly put: due to their pre-analytic vision, mainstream economics, including the sub-genre of environmental economics, models the world, literally, on a board game where the players compete with each other under rules set by a higher power until they achieve optimum performance. Put in the words of Hayek, "as individuals we must bow to forces and obey principles that we cannot hope to understand, while still progress and even the survival of civilizations depends on them" (Hayek 1959, p. 127). In the liberal traditions of the 18th and 19th century, the supreme force was ascribed to God – now it is ascribed to the market mechanism (cf. Büscher 1991).

> "Although the old God dies, an old sin lives: God's erstwhile children often try to take his place. The independent existence (the aseity) traditionally ascribed to an omnipotent personal being called God can be vainly arrogated by human beings themselves." (Stenson 1989, pp. 122f.)

One might consider, at this point, where the economist herself fits in all this. Is the economist in the market? On the side of the umpire? According to their own theory, (monetary) incentives chiefly motivate the players in the game to obey the game's pregiven rules; but somehow the economic scientist has the power to step outside the game so as to design the rules. For "it is the economists who design the rules of the game" (Kyrer 2001, p. 7). Economists, in their theory, are proxies for the God's eye perspective that sees the totality of the games and the externals of the games. They not only contemplate the spectacle, but also have a divine-like power to predict and control the performance of the economy. They only need to find the switches, apparently, for the mechanism. Thus, they think of themselves, or at least the body of knowledge they possess, as allowing them to transcend the self-interested behavior and rationality of *homo oeconomicus,* albeit not – as we have seen with their little examined pre-suppositions – self-reflectingly so. This has led to the economic triumphalism which we saw all too much of in the so called "Great Moderation" of the past two decades – although less so since the beginning of the slump. Interestingly, economists seemingly don't notice the performative contradiction in saying that the players can only attend to their strategies for maximizing their self interest in competitive games, but that they, the economists, can possess both knowledge of these strategies and yet transcend them in their models, which are not self-interested. Therefore, the logic according to which they have the possibility to devise and enforce the rules of the game remains altogether inscrutable from their own premises. The ultimate question of who is to design the rule of the game, and how he is to accomplish this task, remains unaccounted for.

Another point worth mentioning here refers to the role of nature within competitive markets. As Herman Daly and others have pointed out, economics has traditionally referred to ecosystems not as the site within which the economy operates, i.e., what surrounds it, but as a subsystem of the economy that includes extractive sectors as well as dumps (cf. Daly 1999). This inverses the real relationship between nature and the economy. In conformity with the pre-analytic vision of mainstream economics, nature is defined for all intents and purposes as an aggregation of resources subordinated to economic agents. Mainstream economics considers nature's ecological web only as discrete objects or elements upon which economic man directs the force of his rational calculations and behavior. The river that passes by a power plant, for instance, is just an immediate resource for disposing of waste, and not a flow operating within the total global water economy. As such, these elements are not taken as the essential environs of competitive games – literally the physical material of the playing field and the players – but only as elements to be calculated upon within the game's pregiven matrices of possible in- and outputs. Contemporary environmental economics, inasmuch as it sticks to the mainstream paradigm, is prone to adopt this understanding of nature insofar that it seeks to internalize economy's externalities by making them, too, subject to a market game. This field of economics thus reframes strictly environmental issues in the language of rules and incentives that will be accepted by economic agents as mere obstacles or handicaps in their unimpeded race for wealth, or as incentives to be used by these players to best each other in their competitions and as bars to entry. Said differently, environmental economics does its best to reframe environmental issues in a language of abdication, restraint and obstruction that, if viewed from the viewpoint of the competitors, holds no positive meaning. Economic man may be coerced to irrevocably bow to the rules of the game designed to protect the environment, but only due to an elaborate scheme of incentives and punishments, not to deeper insight into the planetary community of man and nature on the part of the individual.

The *fifth economic proposition* deals with the theme of responsibility: *Both for mainstream economics in general and environmental economics as a subgenre posits responsibility against all forms of creative and spontaneous responsiveness. Thus, responsibility is confined to a negative notion, namely, that of strictly obeying pre-given rules within certain temporal, spatial and population boundaries. As such, it reflects a cultural bias towards an ethics that is primarily a morality of principles.*

"There is", Nobel Laureate Milton Friedman famously wrote, "only one social responsibility of business – to use its resources and engage in activities designed to increase its profits so long as it stays within the rules of the game".[7] Here we can see, from what we said above about finite games, that Friedman's statement is in full conformity with the pre-analytic vision of mainstream economics. The systematic locality of moral responsibility, following a long-standing tradition in the history of economic thought, is disconnected from the whole of the economic and ecological system. This locality does not lie within the process of competition but is pushed to the latter's margin. "The systematic location of morality for a free market economy consists in its framework of regulations" (Homann/Blome-Drees 1992, p. 35). Moral responsibility is thought to be fully embodied by the rules of the game, which then permits each move within the game to follow the logic of profit seeking. Morality, then, becomes a question of fairness of the competition – as in our original quote from Smith. As the rules of the game are thought to be exhaustively determined by an outer force, moral duty within the competitive process becomes wholly identified with the profit motive, and is adjusted only with that goal in mind. Economic agents are obliged to strive for their own personal advantage; their unconditional will to win is turned into a moral imperative itself. Each competitor needs to outrun the others without fail, because otherwise the social benefit accruing from the 'invisible hand', which from an absolute standpoint is believed to guide competition as a whole, will not be optimized. What I would like to point out here specifically is the fact that such a vision of responsibility runs the risk not only of downplaying our spontaneously responses to the immediate needs of our fellow human beings and our natural environs – it even precludes it. Because unstinting obedience to rules governing competition combined with the profit seeking goal are considered necessary preconditions of competitive play, they can never be abrogated, not even on behalf of compassion in the face of emergencies, such as famine, or ocean acidification. As the German ethicist Karl Homann unapologetically states, spontaneous help must be considered a "mortal help" and spontaneous sympathy for one's neighbor as unethical.

> "We must not yield to the intention, in the face of hungry children of the poorest of the poor, to give unedited 'spontaneous' help, because such conduct not only doesn't solve the problem but makes it worse. [...] The conduct of a Saint Martin will only sharpen the poverty problem in developing countries and would be in that respect unethical, perhaps even a crime." (Homann 2003, pp. 20f.)

The other is best helped, then, by strictly adhering "with the most obstinate stedfastness to the general rules" (Smith 1790, part III.I.122). As the Japanese ethicist Watsuji critically remarks: "every form of solidarity here can only finds its expression in a law, and responsibility and duty can only be enacted through coercion" (Watsuji 1996, p. 25).

---

7 Milton Friedman in: New York Times Magazine, September 13, 1970.

The five propositions common to mainstream economics and mainstream environmental economics come down to this: interhuman relationships are seen as subordinate to a universal framework of laws and regulations, elaborately enforced by incentives and punishments, with the result that equality (before the law) and freedom (to strive for one's own personal advantage) are thought to complement each other and form the complete principle of civility upon which the social whole depends (cf. Gallu 1989, p. 91). More bluntly put, it is believed that the negative impacts of competition, inflicting immeasurable suffering upon millions, can be thrust aside by appeal to some outside force, be it an "invisible" or "visible hand".[8] The problem to be solved remains merely to decide on the best possible framework, be it "natural", "public" or "divine". But what if the process of competition as such happens to determine, in our complex societies, what the rules of the game are supposed to mean? What if the paradigmatic distinction between the rules of the game and playing the game is an illusion? As long as economists, bounded by the pre-analytic vision of finite games, paradigmatically presuppose this separation, such questions do not even swim to their view. They will, in as much as politicians, not only in the face of climate change and environmental degradation, but also in relation to continuing financial and economic crises, continue their knee-jerk call for "new rules of the game". It is precisely this conceptual deadlock that, to my opinion, we need to overcome by engaging in intercultural dialogue with those Asian traditions that expressly do not share the pre-analytic universal vision that is capable of dictating rigid rules of the game, but instead urge us to explore an entirely different vision of play.

3 An Alternate Vision

As early as 1705 Gottfried Wilhelm Leibniz wrote in regard to the Chinese:

> "Their language, their character, their way of life, their craftsmanship, *and even their games* are so different from ours as if they were people from another globe; it seems possible that even a very simple, but precise account of what they practice could give as a more useful opening than to study the rites and motives of the Greek and the Romans to which so many scholars attach." (Quoted in Jullien 2005, p. 16)

While I am far from advocating Leibniz' insight in its entirety here, I do share its basic vision that the Chinese and Japanese visions of games can in fact give us an opening to think beyond the pre-analytic vision and the privileged game

8 The Japanese philosopher Keiji Nishitani, for example, strongly opposes this belief (cf. Nishitani 1990).

metaphor we have been discussing. Again, my argument here is far from universalizing some best game metaphor. I am not saying, for instance, that the contemporary Chinese and Japanese are all in disagreement with the foundational premises of mainstream economics if the latter is explicitly uncovered. However, clearly the other extreme, taking all cultural differences to be minor variants on the same premises, is ethnographically suspect, and tends to hide the acculturation processes by which the global market system came about. Cultures do disagree, most often below the radar of awareness, about their foundational premises. This is actually a creative affordance given to us by the plurality of cultures. Thus, in this section of my paper, I want to touch briefly on the very possibility of an alternative view of games, rules, environments and players. In doing so, I think I am contributing in my own way to the development of both critical and creative tools to expand the range of common solutions – and possible frameworks in which these problems and solutions can be articulated – to the environmental crises that all cultures today jointly face.

Summarizing the problem discussed in the preceding sections, we could say that environmental economics' concept of responsibility hinges on the presupposition of an external power or agency, standing sovereign, and even absolute over competing, autonomous individuals. As the risk of oversimplifying matters here, it seems to me that East Asian philosophy would regard the failure to examine this presupposition as more than the bad luck that we don't have more curious economists – it amounts, instead, to a systematic failure. This is because for them "there is no view from nowhere, no external perspective, no decontextualized vantage point. We are all in the soup" (Ames/Hall 2003, p. 18). Overcoming environmental crises cannot be a question of discovering another or better idea of an absolute ruler, designing independently an ever more efficient framework of continued competition. Rather, the hope of limiting the struggle of egoists through an exterior force, a prime mover, becomes regarded in itself as illusionary. This is to say that the infinite terror of egotistic action – which, in the West, finds form in the Hobbesian image of the primitive jungle – cannot simply be thrust aside by "the renunciation of the opposing sides being imposed by something from the outside" (Nishitani 1990, p. 259) – that is, the Hobbesian solution. Every effort aiming at releasing the suffering of people, which lies in the reality of their absolute opposition as competitors, through reference to a pre-given universal "seems like trying to scratch your feet through the soles of your shoes" (Nishitani 1990, p. 260).

More concretely speaking, in the Chinese and Japanese traditions we find a pre-analytic vision that does not hinge on the notion of some originative and independent source of order or, expressed differently, on a "two-world" theory that categorically separates some independent source of order from what is orders (cf. Sun Tzu 1993, pp. 46–50). Speaking in terms of our game metaphor, this vision supposes something radical: that instead of redefining the role of the umpire vis-à-vis the constitution of the rules, we simply abandon the notion of an independent umpire. Said differently, we do not seek to externally change or redefine some of the individual rules of the present game but to undertake an entirely different kind of play; a play, in which playing and ordering are so enmeshed that any rules are continually and attentively shaped and redefined in the very process of play itself. However, abandoning the notion of the umpire is only the first step – or rather, is dependent upon other steps. Most notably, the core assumptions of economics' methodological individualism must be re-analyzed. In his fascinating book on philosophy and cultural difference, Thomas Kasulis argues that the basic cultural orientation for the Japanese is not one of context independent agency but the intimacy of "belonging-with" (cf. Kasulis 2002). As stated earlier, the pre-analytic vision of economics makes us think that economic actors exist autonomously, and so independently from one another. Their relationships, defined by the rules of the game, are additive, not integral, to their individuality (refer back to Figure 1). If the basic cultural orientation is one of intimacy, however, then agents are thought to be internally connected: "It is part of the essential nature of the relatents that they are connected as they are; they are interdependent, not independent, entities" (Kasulis 2002, p. 36). In game terms, relations are now seen as integral to the players: how they interact with others defines their very identity as players. In a strong sense, they only exist in the "inbetweeness" of playing with others.[9] What A is depends, in a fundamental way, on the relations he maintains with B and C. To dissolve its internal relationships with others would not merely disconnect him from the other two; it would actually transform an aspect of himself (see Figure 2).

Such vision of agency surely

> "amounts to an ontological gestalt shift from taking independent and dependent actors to be first order realities and relations among them as second order, to seeing relationality as first order (or ultimate) reality and all individual actors as (conventionally) abstracted or derived from them." (Hershock 2006, p. 147)

Such shift does not only turn the assumption of context independent agency upside down; it simultaneously alters the notion both of competitors and competition. On the surface, this means that we have to abandon Robinson Crusoe to his place in our childhood – as an economic idol, he is misleading at best. Players don't choose to connect to others according to their pre-determined preferences.

---

9 Cf. for example the work of the Japanese scholar KIMURA Bin, who states: "The 'betweenness of person and person' *(hito to hito to no aida)* and 'betweenness' *(aida)* do not signify merely a relationship between two individuals. The 'betweenness of person and person is the 'locus' *(basho)* functioning as the source from out of which both I and others arise" (quoted in Odin 1996, p. 70).

On a deeper level, we should no longer conceive of the game as a pre-given matrix of payoffs determined by external rules, but rather see the very dynamics of the process of playing as primary, shaping both players and play in an on-going, evolving and ever changing process. Playing, here, becomes a subjectless, processual event, a "determination without a determining agent who could govern events from a superordinated level" (Nishida 1999, p. 166). Accordingly, setting its rules from any position outside the play would not only be a useless attempt but also an ultimately distractive and destructive one (cf. Hershock 2006, p. 138).

Figure 2: Agents as Internally Connected

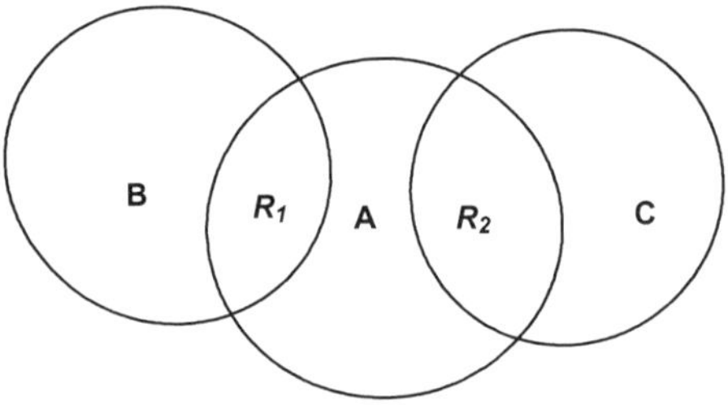

Source: from Kasulis 2002

4 Rethinking the Core Idea of Sustainability

Unfortunately, I don't have the space to discuss in detail the rich meaning of this alternate vision here. But in this last section of my paper I would like to suggest that it might offer us a suitable starting point for carefully rethinking sustainability. Summarizing our findings, we might say that our vision has broadened from one that can only countenance finite games to one that intuits infinite plays, which, as they have no predetermined form or content, do not exhibit any fixed entanglements (cf. Shimomura 1990).[10] As we have tried to show above, the pre-analytic vision of games behind mainstream economics makes players prone to consider their environments as simply pre-given settings, upon which they can play out their individual interests. Consequently, the latter attempt to follow a menu of set strategies derived from previously modeled situations (cf. Jullien 2005). As such, they remain incapable of reacting within the game to the concrete and site-specific circumstances of the game, even in the face of irreparable damage. According to the East-Asian pre-analytic vision as I sketched out

10 Shimomura uses the Japanese term *kukan*.

above, however, economic activity comes to be considered an *infinite game,* in which skillfulness depends on adequately responding to the potentiality of situations, adapting oneself skillfully to the changing events while shaping these events in turn. One acts relationally, not by distancing oneself theoretically from the situation, but by means of active improvisation (cf. Hershock 2006, p. 150). Such improvisation includes not only the fact that in some games the common rules of the game are altered even as the plays are being made, but, as importantly, the potential of the player being changed in the midst of play, as part of the game: protest against the economic conditions of our days becomes ultimately self-referential – "a criticism of an order in which one's self is a constitutive factor" (Sun Tzu 1993, p. 69).

But does this really encourage us to understand the concept of sustainability in radically different ways? I would suggest here that our two pre-analytic visions might possibly agree upon a very broad definition of sustainability as the *capacity to endure;* yet they will differ in fact upon *what* can, and in fact should endure. Let us have a look again at the imperialistic efforts to redefine sustainability in truly economic terms. If we were to truly take seriously its pre-analytic visions, then we would need to attribute the capacity to endure first and foremost to economic agents. This is because their pre-given motives, goals, and intentions are presupposed to outlast the course of events. More specifically, their self-interest is thought to persist both in time and space, including their irrevocable will to win. Yet, we don't mean that true human beings outlast the Smithian race for wealth, honors, and preferments. For any specific person always runs the risk of being barred from playing. The Smithian race unfolds within a border, and only those who are inside this border can be meaningfully defined. Moving outside the competitive sphere, thus, is tantamount to ceasing one's economic existence. As William S. Jevons, one of the founding fathers of the modern economic approach, formulates it:

> "Any persons who are not acquainted at every moment with the prevailing ratio of exchange, or whose stocks are no available for the want of communication, must not be considered part of the market." (Jevons 1970, p. 133)

"If he can get no access [to the market – S.G.], his powers are reduced to zero, and in a competitive society he ceases to exist" (MacPherson 1962, p. 56). Thus, "paying or not paying – that is, literally, the ontological question in commerce" (Luhmann 1990, p. 104). Said differently, it is only a general trait of human behavior – the will to win according to one's own self-interest – that can always prevail according to the pre-analytic vision of mainstream economics. This in turn means that whatever is not done in the interest of winning is not part of the game – and therefore does not have the capacity to endure, neither within nor without the competitive sphere. It is liquidated as inefficiency, sooner or later.

If we consider competition to exist solely for the purpose of winning like Smith does, then we must presuppose its definite ending. Otherwise we could choose no winner. Though we might consider free market competition as a series of games, it is nevertheless true that none of these games are designed to subsist. Instead they have fixed temporal, spatial, and numerical boundaries: a finite game has a definite ending, a circumscribed playing field as well as a selection process for continually expelling players, although, exogenously, new ones continually appear and enter the game. And as we have seen, nothing within these boundaries works to prevent the players from inflicting damage and suffering on the social and ecological environs outside these boundaries, even if, in the long term, such damage and suffering might eventually come to threaten their very own existence. Taking account of that long term while competing in the short term is hazardous, allowing other players in the game a competitive advantage. Thus, the pre-analytic vision of mainstream economics makes it for instance almost impossible to understand sustainable development as "the development that meets the needs of the present without compromising the ability of future generations to meet their own needs" (cf. the Brundland definition of sustainability). In the Smithian game the umpire can at best punish violations of fair play among a given number of competitors. But he systematically remains incapable of attending to the needs of, say, the next generations of players or spectators. The needs of the social, ecological and temporal environs could thus only be factored in by bringing the specific game to an end, changing both its rules and matrix of its payoffs and then starting off a new round of games. As we have seen, this is precisely the logic underlying current political endeavors of combating climate change. As we have also seen, however, the difficult task of amending rules is nothing to be possibly mastered by anyone competing within the boundaries of free market competition. It rather needs to be imposed by some outside force. Mainstream economists, however, still owe us an explanation to how this force itself could potentially outlive the economic struggle of all against all itself, especially considering its 'neutrality; is, itself, caught up in the web of maximizing behaviors. Neither does it tell us how to change ourselves so as to become a source of paradigmatic innovations from within the field of economic interaction.

I would argue here that we do not only need to continue altering some of the individual rules of economic competition despite economics distorted view of sustainability but to start undertaking a very different *kind* of play. We need to change the economic understanding of sustainability as such. It seems that cross-cultural comparison along the line that I have been sketching out above can set us on the right track here. For what in fact endures in an indefinite game is the very process of playing as such. And this process in turn depends on adequately responding to the potentiality of situations, adapting oneself skillfully to the changing events while shaping these events in turn. One acts relationally, not by distancing oneself theoretically from the situation, but by means of active improvisation (cf. Hershock 2006, p. 150). Here I think it might be important, however briefly, to ask about the self – the implication that self-interest implies self-identity, under the aegis of individualism. If the self really doesn't identify with itself, but with its family, its institution, its nation, its environment, whatever, perhaps this is because the self can't identify with self, as it is vacuous as an identifying term. Thus, the whole idea that we are ultimately basing our economics on individualism faces the problem that the self is anything but an individual-identifier. In this sense, the play could make the player. To adequately respond to the tragedy of the commons, for instance, one does not passively await the removal of obstacles to the game by an external agency but begins to act so as to change one's own character. One needs to grow responsive to the present situation – beyond both the morality of fixed principle and economics' deeply ingrained presupposition that we can and should not to alter our egotistic natures, but rather hedge it about with rules so as to mitigate its most disastrous effects by taming it from the outside. While *homo oeconomicus* thus becomes unmasked as truly unlivable figure, sustainability becomes a function of enriching relationships that are, necessarily, irreducibly shared; relationships that are not only expressed by contracts and communicated through price signals within the market sphere but also by other forms of communication (cf. Ostrom 1990, pp. 1–28).

As such, sustainability comes to be linked to the quality of a suite of variations in which the theme can change, not with gaining a definite victory (cf. Sun Tzu 1993, p. 62). My hope is that upon this alternate vision of sustainability adumbrated here we might eventually grow capable of conceiving our growing interrelatedness not as a threat to our individuality but as a heightened potential for developing and nourishing our personalities in a net of relationships expanding beyond any spatial, temporal or numerical boundaries. My more humble hope, however, is that the ambulant, existential dissatisfaction we feel with economics hidden pretense to define any aspect of our life according to its pregiven set of analytical tools crystallizes in a program of rigorous intercultural critique – including, but not limited to, culture and sustainability – so as to make the Mount Lu upon which economists uncritically stand a continuous part of our field of attention

References

Ames, R. T.; Hall, D. L. (2003): Dao de Jing. A Philosophical Translation. New York

Becker, G. (1976): The Economic Approach to Human Behavior. Chicago

Brennan, G. F.; Buchanan, J. (1985): The Reason of Rules. Cambridge

Brodbeck, K.-H. (1996): Erfolgsfaktor Kreativität. Die Zukunft unserer Marktwirtschaft. Darmstadt (in German)

Büscher, M. (1991): Gott und Markt – religionsgeschichtliche Wurzeln Adam Smiths und die "Invisible Hand" in der säkularisierten Industriegesellschaft. In: Meyer-Faje, A.; Ulrich, P (eds.): Der andere Adam Smith. Beiträge zur Neubestimmung von Ökonomie als politischer Ökonomie. Bern, Stuttgart, pp. 123–144 (in German)

Carse, J. P. (1986): Finite and Infinite Games. A Vision of Life as Play and Possibility. New York

Daly, H. (1999): Uneconomic Growth in Theory and in Fact. In: Feasta Review, No. 1 (April), pp 1–15 (URL: http://www.feasta.org/documents/feastareview/daly1.pdf)

Defoe, D. (1938): The Life and Adventures of Robinson Crusoe. A York "Mariner". Edinburgh

Edgeworth, F. Y. (1881): Mathematical Psychics. An Essay on the Application of Mathematics to the Moral Sciences. London

Friedman, M. (1982): Capitalism and Freedom. London, Chicago

Gallu, E. (1989): Sunyata, Ethics and Authentic Interconnectedness. In: Unno, T. (ed.): The Religious Philosophy of Nishitani Keiji. Encounter with Emptiness. Berkeley, pp. 188–200

Graupe, S. (2007): The Basho of Economics. An Intercultural Analysis of the Process of Economics. Heusenstamm

Hardin, G. (1968): The Tragedy of the Commons. In: Science, Vol. 162/No. 3859, December 13, pp. 1243–1248

Hayek, F. A. (1959): Missbrauch und Verfall der Vernunft, Ein Fragment. Frankfurt/M. (in German)

Hayek, F. A. (1996): Die Anmaßung von Wissen. Tübingen (in German)

Hayek, F. A. (1980): Individualism and Economic Order. London, Chicago

Hershock, P. (2006): Buddhism in the Public Sphere. Reorienting Global Interdependence. New York

Homann, K. (2003): Anreize und Moral, Gesellschaftstheorie – Ethik – Anwendungen. Münster (in German)

Homann, K.; Blome-Drees, F. (1992): Wirtschafts- und Unternehmensethik. Göttingen (in German)

Jevons, W. S. (1970): The Theory of Political Economy. Harmondsworth

Jullien, F. (1992): The Propensity of Things. Toward a History of Efficacy in China. Cambridge/MA

Jullien, F. (2005): Vortrag vor Managern über Wirksamkeit und Effizienz in China und im Westen. Berlin (in German)

Kasulis, T. P. (2002): Intimacy and Integrity. Philosophy and Cultural Difference. Honolulu

Keynes, J. M. (1926): The End of Laissez-Faire. London (URL: http://www.panarchy.org/keynes/laissezfaire.1926)

Klein, A. (ed.) (2008): Kompendium Kulturmanagement. München (in German)

Kyrer, A. (2001): Neue politische Ökonomie. München, Wien (in German)

Lackner, M.; Werner, M. (1999): Der Cultural Turn in den Humanwissenschaften. Area Studies im Auf- und Abwind des Kulturalismus? Bad Homburg (Schriftenreihe Suchprozesse für innovative Fragestellungen in der Wissenschaft, Nr. 2) (in German)

Lazear, E. P. (1999): Economic Imperialism. Stanford

Luhmann, N. (1990): Ökologische Kommunikation, Kann die moderne Gesellschaft sich auf ökologische Gefährdungen einstellen? Opladen (in German)

MacPherson, C. B. (1962): The Political Theory of Possessive Individualism. From Hobbes to Locke. Oxford

Mirowski, P. (1989): More Heat than Light. Economics as Social Physics, Physics as Nature's Economics. Cambridge

Mises, L. von (1940): Nationalökonomie. Theorie des Handelns und des Wirtschaftens. Geneva (in German)

Mises, L. von (2007): The Ultimate Foundation of Economic Science. Indianapolis

Nawroth, E. E. (1961): Die Sozial- und Wirtschaftsphilosophie des Neoliberalismus. Heidelberg (in German)

Nishitani, K. (1990): Vom Wesen der Begegnung. In: Ohashi, R. (ed.): Die Philosophie der Kyōto Schule. Texte und Einführungen. Freiburg im Breisgau, pp. 253–274 (in German)

Nishida, K. (1999): Logik des Ortes. Darmstadt (in German)

Odin, S. (1996): The Social Self in Zen and American Pragmatism. New York

Ostrom, E. (1990): Governing the Commons. The Evolution of Institutions for Collective Action. Cambridge/MA

Robbins, L. (1935): An Essay on the Nature and Significance of Economic Science. London

Schramm, M. (1997): Spielregeln gestalten sich nicht von selbst, Institutionenethik und Individualethos in Wettbewerbssystemen. In: Aufderheide, D.; Homann, K. (eds.): Wirtschaftsethik und Moralökonomik. Normen, soziale Ordnung und der Beitrag der Ökonomie. Berlin, pp. 147–176 (in German)

Shimomura, T. (1990): Mentalität und Logik der Japaner. In: Ohashi, R. (ed.): Die Philosophie der Kyōto Schule. Texte und Einführungen. Freiburg im Breisgau, pp. 380–384 (in German)

Smith, A. (1790): Theory of Moral Sentiments (6th ed.). London (URL: http://www.econlib.org/library/ Smith/smMS.html)

Stenson, S. H. (1989): Beyond Science and Technology to Absolute Emptiness. In: Unno, T. (ed.): The Religious Philosophy of Nishitani Keiji. Encounter with Emptiness. Berkeley, pp. 114–142

Sun Tzu (1993): The Art of Warfare. New York

Towse, R. (2005): A Handbook of Cultural Economics. Cheltenham, Northampton/MA

Tversky, A.; Kahneman, D. (1981): The Framing of Decisions and the Psychology of Choice. In: Science, Vol. 211/No. 4481, pp. 453–458

Watsuji, T. (1996): Watsuji Tetsuro's Rinrigaku. Ethics in Japan. New York

Yousefi, H. R.; Mall, R. A. (2005): Grundpositionen der interkulturellen Philosophie. Nordhausen (in German)

Sustainable Development

An Issue of the Office of Technology Assessment at the German Bundestag

Armin Grunwald

1 Introduction

Sustainability as a societal vision is – at least on the political-programmatic level – not only potentially acceptable, but does, in fact, meet with correspondingly broad approval across all societal groups and political positions, nationally and internationally. The number of nations which have signed and ratified the documents of Rio 1992 and the corresponding follow-up papers and the numerous local or regional activities are impressive.

In monitoring and assessing developments and trends relevant to sustainability as well as in designing political instruments, measures and strategies for sustainability governance (cf. Voss et al. 2006) scientific analysis and advice is required to a high degree, in particular for developing adequate strategies to deal constructively with the enormous uncertainties involved (cf. Grunwald 2007). Therefore, sustainability has become a major issue also in Technology Assessment (TA) giving scientific advice to political bodies.

In this paper I will briefly describe the work in this field which has been done by the Office of Technology Assessment at the German Bundestag (TAB, see Sec. 2) at the occasion of TAB reports on different issues such as energy, tourism, and access to information (see Sec. 3). As a more cross-cutting issue a new TAB project on "Parliaments and Sustainability" will be introduced briefly (see Sec. 4). In most of the TAB studies on sustainability issues the cultural dimension is present but more or less as a background dimension. In the last-mentioned cross-cutting project, however, this will be different because there is a need to develop and implement a new "culture" of dealing with sustainability at the level of parliaments which is a challenge to political culture and to accordingly shaping political institutions.

2 The Office of Technology Assessment at the German Bundestag

The Office of Technology Assessment at the German *Bundestag* (Büro für Technikfolgen-Abschätzung beim Deutschen Bundestag, TAB) was founded in 1990, and has become a permanent institution of the German legislature.[1] The purpose of the TAB is to provide contributions to the improvement of the legislature's information basis, in particular, of research- and technology-related processes of parliamentary discussion. Among its responsibilities are, above all, drawing up and carrying out TA-projects, and – in order to prepare and to supplement them – observing and analyzing important scientific and technical trends, as well as societal developments associated with them (Monitoring). Since 1990, TAB has been staffed by the Institute for Technology Assessment and Systems Analysis (ITAS) of the Research Center Karlsruhe. The 20th anniversary of TAB was celebrated in 2010 in a ceremony conducted by the President of the *Bundestag.*

TAB is oriented strictly on the German *Bundestag's* and its committees' information requirements. TAB's principal is the Committee for Education, Research, and Technology Assessment. The choice of subjects for TA-projects as well as their delimitation and specification is the *Bundestag's* responsibility. Decisions on the urgency of problems and the scientific advice desired belong on the political agenda. The choice of topics and of problems to be treated is primarily a political responsibility.

The decisions made in the preliminary stages of a TA-project have decisive influence on the results obtained and on determining which questions can be answered. With the design of a TA-project, it is also determined which aspects of the investigation, which interactions, or which segments of a subject area are relevant for the desired analysis or problem solution, and which are not. Preliminary decisions about the scientific disciplines which are to participate in providing information and on the experts to be consulted also belong in this category. These preliminary decisions are frequently made by TAB, in a close dialogue with the legislature, in particular with the group of rapporteurs which is in charge of taking care about the many interfaces of the Committee and TAB. In order to support this process TA-investigations are often carried out as so-called "pre-studies", the purpose of which – besides an initial appraisal of the state of research – consists in a transparent, comprehensible, and purposeful inquiry into the possible research designs, the formulation of questions, goal directions, etc. The legislature then has the opportunity to decide on a reflective clarification of the subject matter and the design of the respective TA-project. Treatment of the topics set in this manner by the legislature is carried out by TAB in scientific independence and neutrality (Grunwald 2006).

TAB is a small unit (at present, ten scientists). The various requests and topics are treated by obtaining a number of expert opinions on the respective

---

1 This Section is a modified version of the corresponding Section in Grunwald 2003, where TAB's work was analysed with respect to expectations concerning "democratizing expertise".

subject from scientific institutions. The results of this groundwork are evaluated by the TAB-team, are concentrated on the legislature's advisory requirements, and are summarized in the form of a report to the legislature. By means of this networked method of operation, the pertinent competence and knowledge of the science system can be mobilized, case- and subject-specific, for the legislature's purposes in decision-making. The results of TAB studies sometimes lead to *Bundestag* resolutions, sometimes they have indirect influence on processes of opinion formation and decision-making in the legislature.

The subjects of the TAB's studies stem from all fields of technology. The "classical" TA-subjects, such as technology and the environment, energy, and bio- and genetic engineering, predominate. There are also studies on selected fields of science and technology (e.g., on new materials) and on new and emerging technologies such as nanotechnology or synthetic biology. An increasing share of studies on medical technology (Health Care Technology Assessment) and on Information Society issues can be observed in recent years.

3 Sustainability Issues at TAB – Some Examples

The "leitmotif" of Sustainable Development leads to challenges for nearly all fields of policy-making, far beyond being merely a new phrase for environmental protection (cf. Grunwald/Kopfmüller 2006). The following selection of finished or ongoing TAB projects might be a bit arbitrary because sustainability is an issue in most of the TAB studies. The main criterion of selection was to show the thematic diversity of sustainability research at TAB.[2]

(1) Electric Mobility Concepts and Their Significance for the Economy, Society and the Environment (ongoing)

Over the last few years, electric mobility has once again been the subject of lively discussions due to new, more powerful rechargeable batteries and the high volatility on the oil markets. Political objectives such as reducing the dependency on oil, more efficient energy transformation, significant CO_2 reductions and lowering local emissions from transport are important drivers of electric mobility. Electric mobility is therefore a prominent topic in sustainability discussions on the future of mobility and of the energy infrastructure.

---

2 For more information see the homepage of TAB (www.tab.beim-bundestag.de) which includes English versions of the Work Programme and of the summaries of finished projects. The descriptions given at the following pages are short versions of the information which can be found there. Also contact persons can be identified and approached via TAB's homepage. The full text of finished reports is available for download (German language).

A series of challenges still have to be solved. The lithium-ion battery which is deemed to be the key technology today still has to be substantially improved with regard to costs, energy density, weight, cycle and calendar life, and speed of charging. A charging infrastructure has to be implemented and business models have to be developed. For electric mobility services to be successfully diffused and used, it is imperative that these are aligned to their users and take their needs and preferences into account. Actually, there is high uncertainty concerning most of these challenges.

Policy support can make a decisive contribution to solving these challenges. Electric mobility is already being promoted by the German government in numerous research programmes and pilot projects. However, there has been no comprehensive compilation of the currently available results up to now. The main task of this TAB project will be providing such an overall picture which is essential for a wide-ranging discussion and evaluation of electric mobility and for any decision about political objectives and measures in this context. Conclusions and recommendations will be derived for the further development and promotion of electric mobility in Germany. The following steps are planned:

(1.) Establish the foundations for a comprehensive evaluation of electric mobility. This starts with an extensive description and analysis of the technologies and applications regarded. The focus here will be on vehicles with traction batteries (plug-in hybrids and battery electric vehicles). Hydrogen-powered fuel cell vehicles are included for comparison. Promising market penetration scenarios and transport concepts for integrating electric mobility into today's transport systems are described and analyzed. The impacts of electric mobility on local authorities and cities are considered as is their role in introducing electric mobility. Finally, energy scenarios for the improved integration of fluctuating renewable energy sources due to the use of electric mobility are described and analyzed.

(2.) Evaluate comprehensively technologies, applications and development scenarios with regard to sustainability aspects such as greenhouse gases, air pollutants and noise over the life-cycle of batteries and vehicles, critical raw materials, opportunities and risks of shifts in the automotive value added chains and their impacts on Germany as an automobile producing country, effects of electric mobility on employment, road users' acceptance of electric mobility as well as expected impacts on their mobility behaviour.

(3.) Provide an overall assessment of electric mobility and its potentials and draw conclusions. Different support strategies and measures are described and critically assessed. Finally, conclusions and recommendations are derived for the further development and support of electric mobility in Germany.

(2) Ecological Farming and Biomass Production (ongoing)

The national sustainability strategy of the German government includes the aim of increasing the proportion of ecological farming in the next few years to 20% of productive agricultural land (from 5.4% in 2008). At the same time, the share of renewable energy in primary energy consumption shall be increased to 10% and in gross electricity consumption to at least 30% by the year 2020. Biomass represents the most important renewable energy source, accounting for around two-thirds of the whole.

Provision of bio-energy depends increasingly on the agricultural cultivation of energy crops. This cultivation also covers areas which were previously used for food production or were part of set-aside schemes. At the same time, ecological food production requires a larger land area per unit produced compared to conventional production. These developments indicate increasing competition concerning land-use. Analyses carried out by TAB in the context of the most recently concluded project "Opportunities and Challenges Facing New Energy Crops" have shown that the future development of competition for acreage is dependent on a multitude of factors.

The aim of the TAB project is to examine whether ecological farming and biomass production for energy and material purposes can be interconnected more closely in order to satisfy a growing demand simultaneously in both areas or not. If the latter is true, a priority would have to be set either on ecological farming or on biomass production. There will be the following focus points of investigation:

- Competition between the two sustainability aims of ecological farming and energy crop use as part of renewable energy production (in particularly acreage requirements under different conditions).
- Determining reasons and impediments to changing over to ecological farming in the past few years (for instance, influence of the spread of energy crop cultivation)
- Opportunities for integrating bio-energy production and energy crop use in ecological farming and their effect on acreage requirements and ecological system benefits.

(3) Reduction of Land Use Rate. Objectives, Measures, Impacts (finished in 2005)

The high consumption of land for settlement and transportation is a significant problem on the route to sustainable development. Soil as an environmental medium is a non-reproducible resource which is one of humanity's finite natural assets fulfilling many essential functions. Land cannot however actually be "consumed" in the proper sense of the word; but it can be used in such a way, that the spectrum of future opportunities for use are significantly restricted. As the supply of land is limited and non-reproducible, the various types of utilisation are in competition with each other. As the ecological value of the soil is not generally reflected in the real estate price, land is frequently consumed in the "ecologically wrong place". A regionally differentiated approach is required, which takes the different quality, carrying capacity and susceptibility of soils into account. The overarching goals of sustainable development have to be the maintenance of the multifunctionality of soils, the protection of open spaces and the pursuit of a land reserves policy, which also opens up the broadest possible range of possibilities for use to future generations.

The final report on the TAB project "Reduction of Land Use Rate – Objectives, Measures, Impacts" is not concerned with an analysis of the usefulness of the "Target-30-ha" of the German sustainability strategy or with alternative types of land use. The report is more concerned with a critical discussion of instruments and measures with regard to their contributions to the achievement of objectives.

(4) *Internet and Democracy. Analysis of Network-based Communication from Cultural Aspects (finished in 2005)*

This TAB study addresses the impacts of Internet communication on democracy and its cultural foundations (cf. as former study Paschen et al. 2002). The approach to this diverse topic is shaped by the following questions:

- How is the Internet changing the technological possibilities for political information, communication and participation?
- What cultural changes induced by the Internet are evident with consequences for political communication?
- What visions and potential of the Internet for democracy and what related concerns have been and are being discussed in the academic literature, and how should these be evaluated today?
- How are institutions of the executive and parliament viewing and using Internet communication? How far is this contributing to achieving the democratic potential of the Internet?
- How are civil society actors using the Internet for political communication and what change is this leading to in the political public? How true is the idea of the Internet as a new form of political public (public on the net)?
- Where is there political need and opportunity for shaping this, specifically at the German Bundestag?

The "leitmotif" of sustainability is touched by these questions mainly by equity issues concerning the access to information and communication technologies (the digital divide issue) as well as via the exploration of the potential of the Internet for approaching some of the social dimensions of sustainable development such as enabling far-reaching participation. In this project, there is a direct link to culture, in particular to cultures of political communication and its changes in the Internet age.

The Internet is accordingly investigated as a possible medium for supporting and strengthening democracy. In dealing with sceptical assessments and concerns on the one hand and high-flying visions and expectations on the other hand, the report (cf. Grunwald et al. 2006) seeks realistic answers to the question of the Internet's impact on political communication and democratic culture. The line of argument in the report is:

- start from the normative paradigm of a deliberative democracy which is solidly justified by democratic theory and rooted in political discourse and culture;
- look at the Internet's possible contributions for achieving these normative concepts;
- review the reality of political Internet communication and study if and how far this potential is already realised;
- identify promotional factors and also obstacles which have so far prevented implementation;
- use this as a basis for identifying political opportunities for action. In particular proposals were made toward the implementation of petitions to the *Bundestag* via the Internet which had remarkable influence in the last years. E-petitions were established at the *Bundestag* and opened up a new window for political communication between members of parliament and citizens.

(5) Internet Communication in and with Developing Countries. The Example of Africa and Opportunities for Development Co-operation (finished in 2008)

Since the 1990s Africa has moved back up the political agenda – above all as a result of the United Nations Millennium Declaration and African reform and unification aspirations. On the other hand the use of information and communications technologies to promote social development continues to remain marginalised in the discussion on international development policy. In this field primarily the sustainability dimension of intra-generational justice is addressed by looking at development challenges, opportunities and strategies.

The topicality of the issue is demonstrated by looking at the current programmes and strategies pursued by African states and regional organisations, at the practice and statements made by the institutions of African civil society, as well as at the local, in part extremely rapid development of the Internet and mobile telephony. German development policy and cooperation will have to continue to occupy itself with this issue and to clarify its own strategy simply because of the interest in Africa itself in the implementation of information and communications technologies for the promotion of development.

The TAB report (cf. Coenen/Riehm 2008) addresses the reality and potential of Internet use in sub-Saharan Africa giving emphasis to the issues of democratic development, government action and civil society; economic development and trade as well as to education, research and technological development. The focus of the investigation is on Internet use which is not viewed as detached from other conventional (e.g. radio and television) and modern (e.g. mobile telephony) information and communications technologies. The analysis is thus also a contribution to the overall discussion on the use of information and communications technologies for development (ICT4D).

(6) Future Trends in Tourism (finished in 2006)

Demographic, socio-structural and socio-cultural developments have always led to changes in tourist demand and faced service providers in tourism with substantial need to adjust. These constant challenges have expanded and intensified considerably in the first few years of the new millennium. War and tourism, extreme weather, the ongoing internationalisation of tourism and the ageing of society (increasingly prominent in public awareness) have emphatically demonstrated the latent vulnerability of tourism as a boom industry. The survival of the tourist industry depends, on the one hand, decisively on recognising relevant trends and allowing for them in good time. On the other, tourism is related with many sustainability issues and goal conflicts which make this field to a prominent area of study also with regard to sustainable development (cf. Klein-Vielhauer 2009; cf. also Petermann 1998, 1999).

The focus of the TAB project "Future trends in tourism" was addressing the themes "demographic change", "EU expansion" and "security, crises and dangers". The report

- identifies the relevant trends and their implications for tourism in Germany and by Germans, on the basis of a review and an analysis of current socio-demographic data;
- looks at the impacts of the eastward expansion of the EU and considers what trends in vacation traffic can be expected in and from the new EU nations and to and from Germany;
- describes current and future potential dangers to tourism and discusses possibilities for improving information, prevention and crisis management.

These three themes raise numerous important research issues. For example, interdisciplinary approaches could monitor and analyse the demographic shift periodically, taking into account tourist aspects such as the development of travel motivation and behaviour in different age groups. In expectation of growth in tourism from the EU expansion, the consequences of this could be explored in dialogue between politics and science, for example if and how framework conditions could be created which increase travel to Germany. Research into risk and consequences should analyse and evaluate future tourism in the shadow of possible structural global peacelessness, the consequences of climatic change and growth in epidemics. Finally, all these trends and challenges should and could be assessed with respect to sustainable development in order to allow designing pathways to establishing a more sustainable culture of tourism.

These examples show the rich diversity of sustainability issues dealt with at the German Bundestag and its Office of Technology Assessment. More or less, the cultural dimension of sustainability is present in most of these studies. However, mostly this is only the case in form of a cultural "background" of sustainability while other sustainability aspects such as environmental issues, challenges of future responsibility or equity are in the foreground.

4 Sustainable Development at Parliaments – a New TAB Project

In this cross-cutting project addressing the question in what way and by what means parliaments (better) tackle challenges of sustainable development. More emphasis will be given to the relations between sustainability and culture, in particular with respect to political and democratic culture.

Following the UN Earth Summit in Rio in 1992, a great variety of activities were initiated in politics and society all over the world. Quickly it became clear that the political perception and realisation of the goal of sustainability pose far-ranging challenges to governments and parliaments, specifically to their established procedures and to their organisation based on a division of labour. The long-term trends of social development and the effects of political measures must be identified and taken into account. Political actions must be coordinated among numerous affected departments. A high degree of coordination with special interest groups in society is necessary if long-term goals affecting more than one area of policy are to be achieved. To this end, procedures as well as forms of institutionalisation (e.g., interdepartmental programs, creation of specialised scientific institutes, boards of inquiry, expert committees, communication fora between politics and society) have been established by parliaments and governments in many European countries.[3]

3 The European Parliamentary Technology Assessment institutions constitute the EPTA network; cf. www.eptanetwork.org for information about the European landscape of parliamentary TA.

The politics of sustainability has provided new momentum for the long-term orientation of politics and the formulation of corresponding goals in all countries. Awareness of long-term and interdepartmental policy formulation has been sharpened and has led to new forms of "governance". A TAB report (TAB working report no. 86 published in 2003) confirmed that both the initiative and the further development of sustainability policy are essentially carried by the executive. At the governmental level, sustainability policy has led to new administrative structures (specific supervisory responsibilities in the Department of the Environment) and to the installation of new institutions (e.g. sustainability councils and task forces in the ministries such as "Green Cabinets"). The role of parliament, in contrast, seems to lie merely in accompanying and supporting the policy of sustainability. Its role as a forum for public consultation and as a body supervising the executive probably, however, does not exhaust the potential of parliament, according to the results of the TAB study mentioned above.

On the other side, the German *Bundestag* has, compared with many parliaments in other countries, made a considerable contribution to national sustainability policy, in particular by creating the Commission of Enquiry on "Protecting People and the Environment" as well as appointing the parliamentary advisory body on sustainable development (see Ulla Burchardt in this volume). A range of measures can, however, further strengthen its role in German sustainability policy, ranging, for example, from exercising its budgetary powers more strongly to control governmental programmes and draft legislation with regard to their contribution to promoting sustainable development, to regular plenary debates on the status of German sustainability policy and finally to intensive use of the options for monitoring the sustainability of laws and programmes (cf. Grunwald/Kopfmüller 2007).

In this new TAB report an overall review and some country studies are planned, the latter as examples that analyse in depth how the parliaments in other countries have initiated institutional innovation and learning processes. These should then be examined with regard to whether they can be transferred to the structures and procedures of the German Bundestag. Against this background some institutional and procedural options to strenghten the role of the German Bundestag will be identified. Three basic focal points of parliamentary work are of particular interest in this context:

- accompanying the work of the government on the topic of sustainability, and supervising the work of the government from the perspective of its contribution to sustainable social development;
- participating in a substantive sense in the further development and implementation of sustainability strategies (definition of sustainability goals and

measures, proposals for legislation with particular relevance for sustainability policy;
- stimulating and supporting social discussion about sustainable development by handling sustainability issues in a prominent and public manner and by establishing the principles of sustainability, such as by means of participation and communication in the work of parliamentary agencies and committees (councils, hearings, and commissions of enquiry).

In doing this a considerable contribution to a "culture of sustainability" shall be made at the level of parliaments.

References

Coenen, Ch.; Riehm, U. (2008): Entwicklung durch Vernetzung. Informations- und Kommunikationstechnologien in Afrika. Berlin (in German) (engl. version available: http://www.tab-beim-bundestag.de/en/publications/books/cori-2009-118.html)

Grunwald, A. (2003): Technology Assessment at the German Bundestag: "Expertising" Democracy for "Democratising" Expertise. In: Science and Public Policy, Vol. 30/No. 3, pp. 193–198

Grunwald, A. (2006): Scientific Independence as a Constitutive Part of Parliamentary Technology Assessment. In: Science and Public Policy, Vol. 33/No. 2, pp. 103–113

Grunwald, A. (2007): Working Towards Sustainable Development in the Face of Uncertainty and Incomplete Knowledge. In: Journal of Environmental Policy & Planning, Vol. 9/No. 3, pp. 245–262

Grunwald, A.; Banse, G.; Coenen, Ch.; Hennen, L. (2006): Netzöffentlichkeit und digitale Demokratie. Tendenzen politischer Kommunikation im Internet. Berlin (in German)

Grunwald, A.; Kopfmüller, J. (2006): Nachhaltigkeit. Eine Einführung. Frankfurt/M., New York (in German)

Grunwald, A.; Kopfmüller, J. (2007): Die Nachhaltigkeitsprüfung: Kernelement einer angemessenen Umsetzung des Nachhaltigkeitsleitbilds in Politik und Recht. Karlsruhe (Forschungszentrum, FZKA No. 7349) (in German)

Klein-Vielhauer, S (2009): Framework Model to Assess Leisure and Tourism Sustainability. In: Journal of Cleaner Production, Vol. 17/No. 4, pp. 447–454

Paschen, H.; Wingert, B.; Coenen, Ch.; Banse, G. (2002): Kultur – Medien – Märkte. Medienentwicklung und kultureller Wandel. Berlin (in German)

Petermann, Th. [assisted by Hutter, Ch., and Wennrich, Ch.] (1998): Folgen des Tourismus. Vol. 1: Gesellschaftliche, ökologische und technische Dimensionen. Berlin (in German)

Petermann, Th. [assisted by Wennrich, Ch.] (1999): Folgen des Tourismus. Vol. 2: Tourismuspolitik im Zeitalter der Globalisierung. Berlin (in German)

Voss, J.-P.; Bauknecht, D.; Kemp, R. (eds.) (2006): Reflexive Governance for Sustainable Development. Cheltenham

4.

Case Studies: Sustainability – Is it worth it?

Scientific Utilization of Energy and Sustainable Economy Development in China

Ge Yang

Since the economic reform which occurred at the end of 1970's, the Chinese economy has achieved significant success. Currently China is the second largest economy in the world from the view point of GDP, just after the United States. After 30 years of economic development, the economic development of China has experienced change from an "extensive, low efficient" mode to a sustainable growing mode. The "extensive low efficient" economy growing or development mode essentially consumes large volumes of resources, including energy, to achieve rapid growth of GDP, which causes havoc to the ecological environment. At the beginning of the 21st century, the Chinese government introduced the concept of scientific development based on the experience and lessons of economic reform and development. Under the theory of scientific development, emphasis is on solving problems of urban-rural development, regional development, social economy development, the harmonious development between humans and nature from the view point of sustainable economy development, while continuing to take advantage of the essential role of the market in the allocation of resources.

The sustainable economy growth in China is a great subject, which includes problems from various aspects. In this paper, the scientific utilization of energy in China will be discussed as an example of the approaches to sustainable economic development in China.

1 Choices between Energy Utilization and Economy Growth Modes

How to utilize energy is closely related to the economy growth and development modes. Under the extensive and low efficient growth or development mode, it definitely will cause abusive usage or waste of energy, which is a harsh reality in China. It can be demonstrated by the energy consumption in western China. Because the extensive linear economic development mode has been applied for a long time in western China, the economy growth in that area got stuck in the circle of more products to be created, more resources consumed, and more wastes generated. In order to achieve 10,000 RMB (~$1,500) increase in industrial value, it requires more than 6,000 kilowatts/hour electricity consumption in Qinghai, Guizhou, Shanxi, Inner Mongolia, Gansu and Guangxi provinces, especially for Qinghai and Guizhou which requires more than 13,000. To compare the energy consumption all over China in terms of standard coal consumption, in order to obtain 10,000 RMB (~$1,500) GDP, the provinces of Shanxi, Guizhou, Qinghai, Inner Mongolia, Gansu and Xinjiang need to consume above 2.0 tons of standard coal, while 1.5 to 2.0 tons of standard coal are required for Liaoning, Jilin, Hebei, Shanxi, Yunnan, Chongqing, Heilongjiang and Sichuan, and less than 1.0 ton of standard coal will be consumed in Guangdong, Zhejiang, Jiangshu and Fujian. The average energy consumption to gain 10,000 RMB (~$1,500) output value is 0.947 ton of standard coal in western China, which is 1.63 times Shanghai, at 0.583 ton. In general, the energy utilization efficiency in western China is much lower than in the east, which causes severe consumption and waste of natural resources and serious damage to natural ecological environment in the west (cf. Zhang 2007, pp. 120–126).

It is obvious that economic growth based on high investment, high cost and high emission is low efficient growth. It is to be noted that the labor efficiency of manufacturing in China is only equivalent to 1/30 of the United States, 1/18 of Japan, 1/16 of France and 1/12 of Germany. The energy utilization efficiency by energy consumption per unit of GDP in China is much lower than the international advanced level. If one treats the number for Japan as 1, then the consumption for Italy is 1.33, France and Germany is 1.5, UK is 2.17, US is 2.67, while it is as high as 11.5 for China. As for the output efficiency per ton of standard coal, China is about 28.6% of US, 16.8% of the European Union, and 10.3% of Japan (cf. Wang 2001, pp 231–236).

The root cause of the high investment, high cost and high emission economic growth is non-recyclable utilization of resources. From the resource process and their environmental impacts standpoint, economic development undergoes three different modes. The first is the traditional economy mode, which is a unidirectional linear process of

"resources → products → emission".

This economy mode causes serious environmental issues and resource crises. The second is a "first pollution, last treatment" mode. Under this mode, one has started to have concern about environmental issues, with emphasis on control and treatment of pollution at the end of the production process. The last one is called circular economy mode, which is a closed loop feedback process as

"resources → products → wastes → renewable resources".

Currently, 1/3 of world steel production is from recycling. Furthermore, zero even negative resource consumption economic growth has already been achieved in some industries among the developed countries. However, the recovery rate and overall utilization efficiency of resources in China are still low, causing many of the recyclable and reusable resources to become wastes.

The Chinese government takes "building a conservation-minded and eco friendly society" as basic national policy, which can only be achieved by changing the economic growth mode from "extensive, low efficient" growth to circular economic growth and development. Under this policy, encouraging low energy consuming and recyclable industries is the key point to accomplish effective protection and sustainable utilization of resources (cf. Chen 2005).

2 Strategy of Scientific Energy Utilization in China: Development and Utilization of Renewable Energy

In order to achieve sustainable economic development, China is to bring "development and utilization of renewable resources" into the state strategy for economy development, to treat the development and utilization of renewable resources from a strategic perspective (cf. Zhao 2001, pp. 24f.).

First, energy safety and climate change is the driving force for the development of renewable energy technologies and industries in China. The energy industry is the basic industry for national economic and social development, and is the important material base for human society. In human history, every major advance in human civilization was accompanied by the change and improvement of energy sources, especially the presence of the steam engine with coal as the energy source, which greatly pushed forward the world economy and societal development. Energy has been one of the core concerns of all the countries in the world since the 1970's, including China. With the depletion of fossil oil and the concern of green gas emissions, energy conservation, energy efficiency and exploitation of renewable energy sources have become the main theme of the energy development in the world, which is also the international background for China to develop and utilize renewable resources.

Secondly, the renewable energy industries in China have entered a fast development stage. Renewable energy is a key energy source in China that plays an important roles to meet energy needs, prevent and control environmental pollution and improve environmental quality (cf. Han 2009).

The Chinese government has valued renewable resources for a long time. China has launched multiple large-scale water conservancy projects since 1950's, and a series of mid to large scale hydropower plants were built. Small scale hydropower stations were simultaneously developed all over the countryside of China. Since the 1980's, new technology development, utilization and industrialization of wind power, solar energy and biomass energy, have made steady progress with government support. For example, biogas has been applied and promoted in the rural areas of China since the early 1970's. The household biogas pools solved both energy and hygiene issues by utilizing household waste as the source. According to statistics of the Ministry of Agriculture, the production of biogas in rural areas will reach 13 billion m^3 annual capacities, which will reduce the emission of carbon dioxide by over 50 million tons and produce about 400 million tons of biogas manure. Altogether the biogas output value in China is over 40 billion RMB (6.57 billion USD). More than 40 million households in rural areas will use biogas by the end of 2010, which is about 33% of all rural residents in China. As for solar energy applications, China currently is the No. 1 country in utilizing solar thermal energy. On the roof of many residential buildings, solar water heaters are set up to replace fuel as the main source for hot water and other thermal needs. Since the beginning of the 1980's, a large number of small scale wind power plants have been built up in western China, including Xinjiang and Qinghai provinces, to supply electricity to discrete rural areas that have not been covered by power grids.

In the 21st century, energy in China enters a fast development period. The exploration of hydropower has been accelerated by simultaneous development of hydropower plants at different scales. In 2009, the newly added installed capacity of hydroelectric power from small scale hydropower plants is higher than that from large scale ones. The large scale development of winder power industries was promoted by franchise bidding and other means. In the year 2010, the newly installed wind power generating capacity in China is about 16 million kilowatts, and the total wind power generating capacity reached 42 million kilowatts, which is No. 1 in the world.

By the end of the year 2009, the total renewable energy utilization in China is equivalent to about 200 million tons of standard coal, which accounted for 8% of the total primary energy consumption, in which the hydropower generation capacity reached 117 millions kW including 38 millions from small scale hydroelectric stations. The newly installed in-grid wind power generation capacity is about 26 million kW, and the total wind generation capacity reached 50 million kW by the end of 2010. In the meanwhile, more than 30,000 small scale off-grid wind power generators with 30 kW annual generation capacity, are manufactured each year. The power generating capacity from biomass is about 2 million kW. Over 1,500 large scale biogas pools are built in China that can generate more than 1 billion cubic meters of biogas annually, which offers clean energy source for households in rural areas. The photovoltaic industries in China have grown rapidly in the past few years, and the total capacity reached 2,000 MW while 400 MW was added in 2010 alone. A number of private photovoltaic companies are listed on NYSE and NASDQ in the past two years, and formed a Chinese PV industry sector in the international stock markets. The annual production capacity of solar thermal water heaters reached 1,800,000 m^2 in 2010, and the total installed solar thermal water heater is about 90 Mm^2. The geothermal utilization is about 445 Mm^3 annually. Moreover, the ground source heat pump technology (GSHP) was introduced to China in recent years, which is a great energy saving technology.

Third, the strategy and direction of renewable energy development and application in China: renewable energy plays a very important role in the current and future efforts of building a sustainable economy with reducing greenhouse gas emissions by conserving energy. China issued mid to long-term development plan of renewable resources in China in 2007. According to that plan, the renewable resource will account for 15% of total energy consumption by 2020, in which: the hydroelectric installation capacity will reach 300 MkW including 75 M from small scale hydropower plants; the installed wind power generation capacity will reach 30 MkW, which has already been achieve by the end of 2010 (42 M); the installed biomass power generation capacity will reach 30 MkW and ethanol and bio-diesel yearly production will be 12 Mtons; the photovoltaic installation capacity will be 1.8 MkW and solar thermal water heater will be about 300 Mm^2. Together with ocean energy and geothermal energy, the total utilization of renewable resources will account to 600 Mtons of standard coal by 2020. With the increasing demands of energy in the next 30 to 50 years, the strategic stand of wind power utilization will become more and more important in China, which is projected to have the capacity of 300 M to 500 MkW by mid-century, which is 1/3 of the total wind power capacity in China. With the advance in technology and reduction in cost, the solar energy generation will be extensively developed after 2020, and it is expected that 10% of the total power generation capacity will come from solar energy by 2050, about 200–300 MkW. The total renewable resources will account to 30% or more at 2050, which will contribute to the sustainable growth in both China and the world.

Last, to take effective measures to promote the development and utilization of renewable resources, and the following measures are essential for China (cf. Congress 2006):

(1) Using renewable resources development as the assessment index of building a resource thrifty and eco-friendly society; enhancing the public education program to prompt the enthusiasm of the public to utilize renewable resources.
(2) Applying preferential price policy and mandatory quota policy, as well as government procurement, to increase government investment and financing from capital market.
(3) Making it mandatory for state owned power grid operation enterprises and petroleum enterprises to purchase electricity from renewable resources and bio liquid fuels. The appropriate state departments will make laws or regu-

lations on the technical standards, engineering specifications and building management codes for using renewable resources.

(4) Perfecting the cost sharing policy on electricity bills. The state departments will perfect the power tariff based on the technology difference when utilizing different types of renewable energy and regional differences. For instance, the cost of electricity from PV power generation is relatively high, about $3 per grid unit. However, with technology advance, the cost will be greatly reduced in the future.

(5) Providing more financial investment and tax preference towards renewable resources.

(6) Increasing investment on new technologies to expedite scientific and technological progress and innovation. According to the "mid to long term technology developing plan from 2006 to 2020" issued by the State Council of China, energy is in the first priority. With the development of the Chinese economy, the state department, as well as local governments, will significantly increase investments on science and technology development. This will provide critical financial support for the development and utilization of renewable energy. Only by promoting technology innovation can we solve the problems of high cost and low efficiency, which in turn will ensure the success of renewable energy on the energy market in a larger scale.

(7) Enhancing international communication and cooperation. Developing renewable energy is the fundamental means to protect energy safety and deal with global climate change, which requires the collaborative work from countries all over the world. China has already collaborated with lots of countries to develop and utilize renewable energy. The experience, developing thoughts, and policies of other countries were used as references to promote and perfect the laws and policies for scientifically utilizing energy. Moreover, the Chinese economy is also moving forward by a series of large scale international collaboration projects. Recently, clean energy became the hot spot for investment companies in international capital markets, which includes green manufacturing and biotechnology enterprises. Seeing the great potential of the Chinese economy, a lot of countries have turned their investment focus on China in the past few years. The Chinese government has already made an international technology plan for renewable resources and new energy, for guiding the technological cooperation between government and non-governmental organizations to promote the further development of renewable resources.

By the way, the problem between bio ethanol and food safety will also need to be resolved. Bio ethanol has been utilized in large scale all over the world, especially in North America, which cost significant amount of corn as the raw material and had major impacts on the food prices in the international market. In European countries, producing bio fuel from vegetable oil caused a similar effect. From the food safety in China and global food supply security standpoints, a food crop is not suitable as the direct source for biomass, which has become the common understanding by more and more countries these days. From the sustainable growth standpoint, crops other than food crops, including wastes from food crops such as straw, should be used as the source of bio ethanol. To do so requires major R&D advances in technologies. There are a number of enterprises and research institutes that are focusing the development of such technology in China, and certain achievements have been made in these fields. This problem will be finally resolved with the further investment on technological innovation. On the other hand, bio ethanol can also be produced by crops other than for food, such as sugar cane and cassava that can produce both sugar and alcohol. Thus, the basic principle to use biomass as the renewable resource is made by Chinese government, which is the development of biomass can not affect food safety, as well as the diversity of species and water resources.

3 Case Studies of Scientific Application of Energy in China

The scientific utilization of energy to promote the sustainable economic growth in China is illustrated by the following case studies:

(1) Sustainable Developing Plan of Photovoltaic Industry: Suntech

Suntech Power Inc. was founded in 2001 by leading solar scientist Dr. Zhengrong Shi, and is the world's largest producer of silicon solar modules. It offers clean power for every application and market, from off-grid systems, to homes, to the world's largest solar power plants. Their solar modules are installed in over 80 countries. Suntech has offices in 13 countries, including regional headquarters in San Francisco, California; Schaffhausen, Switzerland; and Wuxi, China. It is listed on the New York Stock Exchange (NYSE: STP). Suntech is a proactive policy advocate and a supporter of numerous environmental awareness initiatives, and works with numerous organizations to advance environmental stewardship across the world, and is committed to the highest occupational health and safety management standards.

The promise of solar power is critically important to solving today's energy demands in an environmentally sensitive way (cf. Wang 2009). Solar energy offers unparalleled potential for developing nations, where a lack of reliable electricity has stunted education, research and economic development efforts. Suntech has worked with partners in several developing countries to harness sunlight for transformative projects that power schools, NGOs and non-profit institutions. Suntech Power Holdings Co., Ltd. (NYSE: STP), the world's largest producer of solar panels, was recently honored with the "Global Leader Award 2011" from Murphy&Spitz, designed to recognize sustainable companies for exceptional environmental, health and safety (EH&S) practices. The recognition coincides with Suntech becoming one of the first global solar companies to achieve both OHSAS18001 and SA8000 certifications, two respected occupational health and social accountability standards. Suntech also implements an Environmental Management System, which was certified according to the ISO14001 standard in April 2006.

(2) *Energy Development Strategy and Measures of Nanjing, China (cf. NSED 2006, pp. 31–45)*

(a) Strategy of Clean Energy Development

The energy utilization structure in Nanjing city is different than the cities that use coal as the primary energy source, since the majority of the fossil oil and coal are imported. Therefore, the energy development strategy in Nanjing emphasizes increasing the ratio of oil and natural gas in the primary energy structure, while promoting clean coal processing technologies. Clean coal processing technology development will focus on the processing, combustion, transformation and pollution control techniques to reduce emission and improve utilization rates. The key point for optimizing energy structure is: gradually decrease the ratio of coal in the primary energy structure by substituting coal with gas and electricity. This will increase the ratio of high quality and efficiency clean energy source in the energy structure. Electricity is a high quality energy that has very important impacts on the energy structure and ecosystem in future energy development. Electricity has the advantage of high efficiency and is clean, which will hold a dominant position in the future global energy structure. The electricity consumption consists of 13.3% of the total energy consumption in Nanjing in 2004. 76% of the total consumed electricity was from the power plants located in Nanjing, while the rest was from outside. Nanjing will promote electrical generation from coal, natural gas and green resources to gradually reduce the direct consumption of coal by residential end users. By doing this, the goals of improving environmental quality, increasing energy utilization efficiency, reducing the dependence of external energy will be fulfilled, which will accomplish the electrification of the economy and residential life in Nanjing.

(b) Strategy for Improving Energy Efficiency

To improve energy efficiency and reduce the energy consumption by per product is the fundamental energy development strategy in countries all over the world, including China. In order to achieve that, the Nanjing government will

(b1) rationally adjust the economic structure to reduce high energy consuming industries and products, and encourage the development of low energy consuming industries, business, products and technology; build up standards for improving energy efficiency to start up energy conservation projects; perfect the energy policy by using energy efficiency improvement as the basic principle, to guide the energy market. In order to do that, low energy consuming industries such as service, software industries, information technology, business and commerce, tourism exhibition, finance and insurance, modern logistics, real estate, information consultation will be encouraged in Nanjing.
(b2) upgrade old infrastructures with new and high technology. Two types of upgrading will be involved: functionality replacement and automatic controlling system add-ons to the existing infrastructures. For example, the replacement of manual operated lathes with CNC lathes, can significantly improve the accuracy of products while reducing energy and materials costs, and increase the labor efficiency. For other examples, the equipment operating rate can improve from 70% to 90% when an automation system is added to the cement production line. The railroad transportation capacity can improve by more than 20% when using computer systems, and the energy consumption can be reduced by 50% per ton of synthetic ammonium in chemical industries when an automatic controlling system is applied.
(b3) manage and upgrade energy infrastructures by utilizing information technology. In order to scientifically manage energy, using information technology to manage and transform manufacturing infrastructures has become the common understanding all over the world. In addition, the energy security issue including coal, fossil oil and nature gas has already become a global issue. Protecting the safe production and supply of energy is a major factor affecting the operation of society. Nanjing will reference the foreign advanced experiences, to ensure the energy safety with modern technologies.

(c) Strategy of Energy Conservation

An energy conservative, circular economy with energy conservative manufacturing and consuming modes will be built in Nanjing by the following means:

(c1) Building a comprehensive circular economy evaluation system, and perfecting the spatial arrangement of industries. Upon the perfecting of the scientific data collecting systems, a comprehensive evaluation system includes economic growth, resource consumption, environmental quality as well as welfare will be built up to reflect the building progress of a well-off society.

(c2) Promoting the construction of eco-industrial parks and eco-enterprises, to truly put into effect energy recycling and reuse. There are 4 national-level, 5 province-level and a number of city-level industrial parks in Nanjing. However, uneven development, insufficient utilization and recycling of energy has occurred in these industrial parks, which has led to less efficiency of these parks. Thus, the construction or reform the eco-industrial parks will greatly be benefited by the city's circular economic policy. To integrate the materials, water and energy circulation among the enterprises in the parks by rationally encouraging the coupling relationships between different industries, maximize utilization of energy and minimize emission of wastes will be accomplished within these eco-industrial parks. Applying new technologies in traditional manufacturing process and developing new products are highly encouraged, which will improve the energy efficiency and ecological benefit.

(c3) Building a highly integrated energy system to improve the efficiency of energy utilization, as well as recycle and reuse. Improving the energy efficiency in the eco-industrial park by applying new technology and new infrastructures to reduce the overall energy consumption in the parks. To step utilize energy by using a district heat supply system, ordering heat by power and promoting heat and power cogeneration. Finally, optimizing the energy structure in the parks by selecting low cost clean energy sources.

(3) Energy Development and Utilization in Northwestern China and the Choices of Chinese Energy Strategy

The strategic energy resources in northwestern China are very rich, and are the fundamental bases of the economic development of China. The development and utilization of the strategic energy resources in the northwest will benefit not only the Chinese economy, but also greatly the local economies. The special natural condition in the northwest has made it the richest in natural resources while the weakest from an ecological standpoint. The large scale long term exploitation of natural resources in this area has already caused serious ecological problems. Therefore, accurate evaluation of the sustainable energy utilization in the northwest area is critical for making regional macroscopic policy to implement the strategy for the development of the western regions by the State Council of China (cf. MRI 2003).

(a) The status of strategic energy resources and sustainable utilization in northwestern China

Strategic energy resources usually refer to coal, fossil oil, and natural gas. The northwest regions have 40% of coal, 31% of fossil oil and 60% of natural gas in the whole country, while Xinjiang and Shanxi provinces have the most strategic resources within the northwest area. Xinjiang has rich fossil oil, natural gas and coal, and the expected crude oil and natural gases storage is 30 billion tons, about 25% of the whole country. Shanxi province has 1/3 of the natural gas storage in the northwest area, and about 270 billion tons of coal. Other provinces in northwest China also have significant amount of energy resources.

All the newly discovered oil and gas field in China are located in the northwest area, as well as the entrance of oil and gas resource from Central Asia. The energy development in the northwest region has played an irreplaceable role in the sustainable growth of the Chinese economy.

(b) The relationship between the energy development in northwest area and the sustainable growth of Chinese economy

The status of energy production and consumption in northwestern China and the whole country can be studied by the energy production elasticity index and energy consumption elasticity index, as illustrated in Table 1. According to Table 1, the total energy production is more than consumption in northwest region of China, which is the contribution of northwest region to the sustainable economic growth of the whole country.

The energy production index and consumption index are compared between northwest regions of China with the whole country. As can be seen, the energy production indices of northwestern China are much higher than the average level of the whole country, while the energy consumption indices are only slightly higher than the average, which indicates that the energy production ability in this area is higher than other regions in the country. Therefore, the northwest regions significantly contribute to the sustainable economic growth of the country from the energy standpoint.

Table 1 also illustrates the energy contribution indices of the northwest region and their relationship with the national energy production and consumption indices. Furthermore, both energy production index and consumption index increased each year, while the consumption rates are lower than the production rates in these regions.

Table 1: Comparison on the Energy Production Index and Energy Consumption Index in Northwestern China and the Whole Country

Year	Energy production index in northwest (1)	Energy production index in whole country (2)	Difference in energy production index (3)	Energy consumption index in northwest (4)	Energy consumption index in whole country (5)	Difference in energy consumption index (6)	Energy contribution index of northwest (7) = (3)–(6)
1991	–0.18	0.10	–0.28	0.09	0.55	–0.46	0.18
1992	–0.04	0.16	0.20	0.37	0.37	0	0.20
1993	0.92	0.26	0.70	0.68	0.45	0.23	0.47
1994	0.98	0.53	0.45	0.62	0.44	0.18	0.27
1995	0.61	0.80	–0.19	0.55	0.63	–0.08	–0.08
1996	0.55	0.28	0.27	0.39	0.59	–0.20	0.47
1997	0.89	–0.02	0.91	0.32	–0.09	0.41	0.50
1998	0.29	–0.79	1.08	0.11	–0.53	0.64	0.44
1999	0.47	0.18	0.29	0.87	0.16	0.71	–0.42
2000	0.36	0.29	0.07	0.31	0.42	–0.11	0.18
2001	1.20	0.80	0.41	0.77	0.41	0.36	0.05
2002	1.99	0.51	1.48	0.92	0.66	0.26	1.18
2003	1.52	1.39	0.13	1.30	1.53	–0.23	0.36
2004	1.53	1.42	0.11	1.54	1.59	–0.05	0.16
average	0.79	0.42	0.37	0.62	0.51	0.12	0.25

Source: After State Statistical Bureau 2006

(c) Choices of energy strategies of China in the current stage

With the rapid growth of the Chinese economy, there are increasing demands in energy. Shortage in energy supply has already become the bottle neck for further economic development in China. Although the energy resources in northwest regions can temporarily solve the energy requirements of the Chinese economy, a long term energy development plan is critical for healthy sustainable growth of the Chinese economy (cf. Nie/Zhang 2006).

(c1) Energy Conservation Strategy: Energy conservation is closely related with the sustainable growth of the economy. The Chinese government pays close attention to the conservation of energy resources, with emphasis on both energy development and energy conservation, which put energy conservation in the first priority in the energy strategy. The Chinese government launched "Law of the People's Republic of China on Conserving Energy" on November 1, 1997, and

put it into full effect on January 1, 1998. The law consists of various energy efficiency standards that emphasize the importance of conserving energy.

The State Council of China passed the "comprehensive energy reduction program of work" that was made by the Development and Reform Commission and related departments on June 3, 2007. According to the "Twelfth National Economic and Social Development Five-Year Plan", it required to reduce energy consumption by 20%, waste emissions by 10% of per unit GDP during the five year plan period. By the end of 2010, the energy consumption to achieve 10,000 RMB GDP is reduced from 1.22 tons of standard coal to lower than 1 ton level in China.

(c2) Energy Development Strategy: The lack of high quality energy source is the root cause for a series of problems in China including environmental pollution and low energy efficiency. Therefore, adjusting and optimizing energy structure is the key line of energy development in China. By reducing the ratio of coal and increasing ratio of oil and gas in the primary energy structure, promoting the development and utilization of new energy and renewable energy, accelerating the energy development in northwest, the energy safety in China will be well protected (cf. CAS 2000).

(c3) Energy Safety Strategy: According to "China Energy Statistical Yearbook 2004"and the total consumption and import volume of crude oil and oil related products, the dependency of domestic petroleum consumption on import in 2004 was as high as 40%, which was reduced by 2% in 2005. It is expected that the dependency of domestic petroleum consumption on imports will reach at least 55% in China by 2020. This will cause increasing risk in security of oil supply in China. Thus, the discovery and exploitation of oil and gas resources in western China will play a critical role in solving the strategic problem of energy safety. Furthermore, the price fluctuation of the international oil markets is influenced by a number of factors including shortage on energy supply and higher demands, which also create great a challenge in energy safety protection.

In addition, China is promoting "Energy Diplomacy" with Russia and other Middle Asian countries, which is closely related to the sustainable economic growth and energy safety.

(c4) Energy and Environment: There are some degrees of inevitable side effects on the environment during the process of energy production and consumption. The fossil oil supply is limited, which also caused the run out of natural resources and damage to ecological systems. The current air pollution issue in China is mainly caused by energy consumption, especially direct burning of coal in residential life. Environmental protection becomes extremely important in the economic development process in China these days. In northwest regions, the ecological environment deterioration occurred mainly in the energy exploitation

process. Therefore, protecting the local ecological environment is the key point for sustainable growth in these areas during the energy developing process. Development and utilization of new energy and clean energy sources have practical importance for sustainable society development, and the energy strategy of China must include environmental requirements.

4 Conclusion and the Future

Scientifically utilizing energy is the objective requirement of sustainable economic development in China. On the other hand, sustainable economic development is the basis for developing a sustainable society including culture and civilization. In the following 50 years, China will concentrate on the goal of modernization, which includes a steady growing economy, fair society, improved democracy, diversified culture, better ecological environment and high quality life styles (cf. Hu 2007). In order to do that, scientific development and utilization of energy will play the key role in sustainable development of China.

In the 21st century, the issue of over spending energy and nature resources is one of the fundamental issues that China must address for further development. Scientifically utilizing energy is the urgent need of today's China economic development, and must be practiced immediately under the scientific developing concept of "comprehensive, balanced and sustainable development".

References

CAS – Chinese Academy of Sciences, Information Center for Resources and Environment (2000): Strategic Choice for National Adjustment of Energy Structure. In: Advances in Earth Sciences, Vol. 15/No. 2, pp 64–73

Chen, L. P. (2005): Research Review of the Sustainable Energy Development. In: Land Resources Information and Resources Information, Vol. 11, pp. 34–41

Congress (2006): 10th National People's Congress of China. China Renewable Energy Law. Beijing (in Chinese)

Han, W. K. (2009): Development of Renewable Energy Issues. In: The 11th National People's Congress of Article Seminar Lecture Notes, No. 2, pp 1–10 (in Chinese)

Hu, J. T. (2007): Hold High the Great Banner of Socialism with Chinese Characteristics in Order to Win New Victories in Building a Moderately Prosperous Society and Strive. In: The Chinese Communist Party National Congress in the Seventeenth. Report. Beijing (in Chinese)

MRI – Macroeconomic Research Institute of the NDRC Energy Research Institute Research Group (2003): Energy Strategies for Sustainable Development in Western. In: Macro Economic Research, No. 11, pp 1–14

Nie, R.; Zhang, Y. Z. (2006): The Strategy Selection of Energy Development in China in the 21st Century. In: Natural Resource Economics of China, Vol. 19/No. 5, pp. 43–51 (in Chinese)

NSED – Nanjing Sustainable Economic Development Strategy and the Total Energy Research Group (2006): Nanjing Economic Strategy of Sustainable Development and Energy Research. Provided by Nanjing Statistic. Nanjing (in Chinese)

State Statistical Bureau (2006): China Statistical Yearbook 2006. Beijing (in Chinese)

Wang, L. (2009): Status and expectation of PV industry in China. In: Chinese Journal of Power Sources, Vol. 33/No. 8, pp737–739

Wang, W. Z. (2001): Comparative Study of International Sustainable Development Strategy. Beijing (in Chinese)

Zhang, L. (2007): Energy Eco System. Strategic Study on the Energy Development in Northwestern China. Beijing (in Chinese)

Zhao, Y. (2001): Sustainable Energy Development Strategy. Beijing (in Chinese)

Risks of Unsustainable Technologies

János Szlávik, Miklós Füle

1 Circumstances

One of the fundamental stereotypes of post-World War Two (WW2) Hungarian primary education was that Hungary was a country poor in natural resources, a fundamental weak point of the national economy. A sole exception to this was bauxite mining and related aluminium industries, whereby Hungary has managed to stay in the forefront of global aluminium production, a merit based on mostly quantitative figures.

Bauxite mining north of Lake Balaton has commenced in 1928 by a German-owned firm. (the shortage of working capital is apparently not a new problem in Hungary). As part of the compensations after the defeat in WW2, the company became Soviet property, and was taken over by the Hungarian State in 1954. The group of companies in the Bakony Mountains with the largest output was privatized in 1996.

The storage tank that burst and caused the 2010 Red Sludge Disaster belongs to the Hungarian Aluminium Producing and Trading Ltd. (in short: MAL). After privatization, the company has acquired companies closely related to the aluminium industry (such as the bauxite-mine in the Bakony Mountains, the aluminium furnace in Inota, etc.). The company produces hydrate and alumina products, as well as alloys for aluminium casting. The company exports some 70–75% of its products to Western European countries.

Production peaked in 1980 when with a production of 2.950.000 tonnes Hungary was the 8th largest producer of bauxite in the world. This number decreased rapidly, falling to only 515.061 tonnes by 2007, a mere 19th place globally. This sharp drop could be traced back to unfavourable production conditions, as the more prevalent deep mining is much more costly than the less frequently feasible surface extraction. The quality of the ores is mediocre.

During the production of alumina, a large quantity of red sludge is produced, about 1,5 to 2 tonnes of sludge per each tonne of alumina. During this process, a strong lye is added to the bauxite, and alumina is extracted. The remaining waste material is the red sludge. In most parts of the world, the valuable lye is recovered from the sludge and used again in the process. The name of this substance comes from the discolouration caused by iron-oxide (ferri-oxide) contained in the sludge. Red sludge is strongly alkali, typically around pH 11–12, but at the time of the Red Sludge Disaster, the alkalinity of the storage ditches was measured to be pH 13. As a result of the technology used, the substance is at a wetness of 40–45%, which means that it can be pumped, and this is how it is deposited in the storage ditches lined by dykes. Besides containing ferrous compounds, it is rich in other metal oxides, whilst its radioactivity is minimal.

In storing red sludge, a so-called method of "Dry Storage" can be used, whereby the moisture content of the sludge is reduced by drying to under 25%. After the disaster American and Australian experts could not comprehend why the sludge was so corrosive, as after five to seven washing routines the alkalinity of the substance should have been minimal. The means of storage becomes critical in legislation when we consider that under EU regulations dry-stored red sludge is not considered to be hazardous waste. After Hungary's EU accession, red sludge was removed from the list of hazardous waste materials. According to the January 2011 resolution of the EU the Hungarian authorities unduly changed the classification, as the method applied for storing red sludge in Hungary is high-moisture wet storage, rather than dry storage.

The ten storage ditches constructed over a period of 70 years contain some 30 million cubic metres (1.06 billion cubic feet) of sludge. The walls of the last storage facility, Ditch 10, are some 60 metres (197 feet) wide at the base, and are 25–30 metres (82–98 feet) tall. It was permitted to store 4.2 million cubic metres (148 million cubic feet) of sludge. It was being filled at a rate of 1000 cubic metres (35.300 cubic feet) per day from the alumina factory in Ajka.

2 What Happened?

On the 4th of October, 2010, at 12.28 on a Monday noon, the officer on duty at the Ajka Police alerted the local fire brigade with the news that a patrol officer has reported that "something's awfully draining from the dykes". This dyke was the wall of Ditch 10, the storage facility near the village of Kolontár.

The civil association cooperating with the Regional Directorate General for Disaster Management was informed of the dyke bursting at 12.38. The association was lead by one of the most experienced Hungarian rescue professional. The first news bulletins reported a rusty-coloured liquid billowing down towards Kolontár village from the dykes. The emergency services intended to get information about the composition of the substance to get the appropriate hazmat suits, only to be informed by MAL on telephone that there was no problem, "it's just a red-coloured liquid".

Instead of giving a chronological account of events, we would like to quote from a news report, as this excerpt strikingly condenses the events.

> "The red sludge was coming down from the crop lands with a terrible noise. The house of the Juhász family was on the other side of the creek, at the part of the village closest to the ditch. There were four people at home. Zoltán Juhász, his wife Erzsébet, their three-year-old daughter Dóri and their youngest, Angyalka of just 14 months. They heard a noise as if a train had just rushed past their house. The next moment, the deluge smashed against their front door and ripped it open. They couldn't make their escape in that direction.
>
> Erzsébet grabbed Angyalka, but she got such a blow from the masses of mud that she dropped her baby. The little girl sank in the red sludge, her mother had no chance of finding her. The tide was rising so quickly, and their instincts of survival drove them to try to find an elevated location. First they attempted to get up to the attic, but their deepfreeze was flipped by the sludge and blocked the stairs. Zoltán immediately smashed the window and grabbed the gutter. He was standing in the red sludge up to his waist, but at least he could stop himself from being washed away. Erzsébet also climbed up to the window, but she stayed inside to try to keep holding on to her daughter Dóra with one hand. She lay the daughter on the bed, which was by now drifting atop 1.5 metres (5 feet) of thick, red sludge.
>
> 'Don't move, try to keep still' – said the mother to her daughter, and the little girl lay on the bed like a piece of wood." (Simon 2010)

Altogether ten people died in this disaster, including Angyalka. Injuries are estimated at about 140. Some of the victims drowned in the deluge, whilst others died as a result of their extensive and severe skin injuries. Even though considering the circumstances the rescue work was carried out quickly and professionally, a profound emotional shock could be felt at every level. When the representative of MAL declared two days later that even though red sludge is alkali but is basically not harmful to humans, the obviously irritated Minister of the Interior coordinating the rescue efforts responded by saying that perhaps the management of the company should take a dip in it.

The main conclusions of the reports relying on investigations and analyses about the metallic contents of the red sludge, about the radioactive conditions, about the air quality and about drinking water supply were the following:

- Experts of the National Environmental Health Institute and the Hungarian Academy of Sciences have conducted independent investigations and have found no significant metallic pollution in the sludge, and the concentration of toxic metals does not exceed the limits in the soil. However, the solution extracted from the industrial waste was at pH 11.8, indicating a very highly corrosive effect.
- Arsenic was also found to be under the limits permitted for wastewater sludge. Heavy metals contained in the sludge did not penetrate the soil deeper than a depth of 10 centimetres (4 inches), and they do not exceed the

limits even at those depths. It is therefore reasonable to deduce that deep-lying soil layers and the first aquifer layer are not directly threatened. However, the soil cannot be used for the production of previously grown agricultural products (such as wheat, maize and vegetables).
- After conducting laboratory analyses, the State Medical Centre has resolved that red sludge is dangerous to human health, to living organisms and the environment due to its high corrosiveness. This damages skin surfaces and may intensify the adverse effects of other pollutants.

The matter of liability, the identification of the exact causes of the dyke bursting is likely to be determined in a lengthy legal procedure. Additionally we would like to mention that one of our geologist colleagues from the Budapest University of Technology had written a report in the beginning of the 1980s about the environmental risks in relation to the soil composition in this area. He reported that the area under Ditch 10 consists mostly of marshy, lea soil, except for the north wall of the ditch, which is mostly clay. These soils behave differently under wet conditions, and this poses a risk in the statics of any artifacts built on them. He even mentioned Ditch 10 as a bad example in his university lectures after the storage facility was built. It is unclear to this day whether the current management of MAL Ltd. was aware of this report, which was sent to the legal predecessor of MAL years ago. The management says that they were not, adding that had they been aware of it, they would have built the facility elsewhere.

The level of corporate social responsibility was relatively small compared to the associated true risks. MAL Ltd. has obtained this plant cheap, but it hasn't carried out the damage recovery work it has promised. Furthermore, after the disaster occurred, the company has communicated in such a way which reflected not only their corporate social insensitivity, but it has also communicated with local residents in an explicitly hurtful manner, whilst initially denying any liability.

3 Damages

3.1 Health and Environmental Damages

The most significant and irreversible damage caused by the red sludge disaster is the loss of ten lives. This catastrophe has been a tragedy for more than just the immediate families, and it has greatly reduced the sense of security of the remaining local residents. After this disaster the risks of old and environmentally dangerous technologies and their remains surfaced in several post-communist states.

The damages incurred by nearly 150 people can only be partially reversed and compensated. Their economic and human effects will be felt for a long time yet.

The cited report compiled by the Hungarian Academy of Sciences may give the illusion that fundamentally apart from human damages no significant environmental damage has been incurred. These reports do not mention a crucial aspect of the nature of these processes, namely the extraordinary complexity of the ecosystem. If we consider the reports of the individual effects and regard them from the aspect of the entire ecosystem and their mutual interactions, the picture we get is very different indeed. The near instantaneous appearance of several thousand cubic metres of red sludge in the local ecosystem may have currently unforeseeable effects.

Thus besides human tragedies and the perishing of these localities, life has all but vanished in the River Marcal and the Torna Creek. Both were teeming with a rich aquatic wildlife and fish in particular, even as recently as the summer of 2010. Both riverbanks were popular recreation locations of the area. According to expert evaluations, treatments with acids, gypsum and nitrates have saved life in the Rába and Danube rivers, but long-term effects remain unknown as yet, because if toxic metals are present in the sludge, for example, the acidic treatment may dissolve them and they may be released in the Rába and the Danube, causing immense pollution. Besides the devastation of natural wildlife (including plants and animals), few mentions were of the death of domestic animals, which are not merely economic damage.

3.2 Socio-economic Damages

One of the most spectacular effects of the red sludge disaster is the widespread destruction of dwellings and other buildings.

Besides the environmental and health damages, a number of not apparent but very direct and painful problems have plagued the residents. Several evacuees who have lost their homes and had been offered temporary shelters in gym halls have complained that their bank has threatened them with cancelling their mortgages. The banks argued that because their house was destroyed entirely, therefore there was no real estate property to guarantee payment, so the banks claimed that the remaining mortgage debts were to be paid in a single payment transaction. Another local resident reported that since he was unable to go to work, he was fired.

Perhaps the most significant social, cultural and emotional blow to the people losing their houses, their personal memories and valuables is the long-term loss of a sense of community a sense of local safety, the feeling of “being at home”, which offered safety for their everyday lives.

A personal statement offers a good description of the situation. This statement was made by Brigitta Érseklakiné Markos at the Capital City Court at the filing of the compensation claim against MAL Ltd. She said:

> "Most of our friends have moved, the area has been shattered. We would go too, but we can't sell our home, house prices dropped to a half. The two children go to school in Ajka, at least they get some clean air there. I need to go to a psychiatrist; they said I have post traumatic stress. State compensation is only given to primary victims." (HVG 2011)

4 Externalities: An Environmental Economic Evaluation of the Disaster

If we are talking about externalities, immediately a question arises: this disaster was the negative consequence of which process? The aluminium industrial activities and bauxite mining of MAL Ltd. has a long history. Therefore it seems that this kind of industrial activity has proved to be profitable, at least for MAL Ltd., since it has been constantly buying out smaller companies within the industry, and amongst the proprietors of this company are some of the particularly wealthy citizens of Hungary. Besides all this success, the risk was always present, but the determination and management of the true extent of the risks either could not, or was willingly not carried out.

Foregone preventative technological developments have unequivocally shown everybody the true weight of the negative externalities arising from industrial activities with serious environmental risks. Such an interference has been caused in the ecosystems (and in social and economic wealth too) that its knock-on effects can hardly be predicted at all.

In the environmental economic background of the red sludge disaster lies the serious underestimation of negative external risks and environmental damage costs. (This is shown by the rather gently sloping Marginal Damage Curve – MDC_1 – and the fitted Marginal Abatement Curve – MAC_1 – in Figure 1.)

The decision makers of MAL Ltd. have chosen a pollution-reduction technology using these false predictions. This is not surprising in itself, because corporations typically underestimate their environmental damages and risks. It is up to the environmental protection authority and green civil organizations to ensure that the estimation of environmental damages is realistic and that the aversion technologies ensure environmental security.

In this situation events took a very particular path. As we have mentioned previously, under the 40 years of communist rule, aluminium production was one of the flagships of the Hungarian industry, and it held not only a strong economic position, but a political one as well. Such a position enlarges the possibility of the softening of environmental legislation.

Ever since the mid 1980s, green organizations have been rather strong in Hungary, but for example, the internationally renowned Danube Society (Duna Kör) has focused on the dams on the River Danube. The question of environmental risks posed by industrial activity, and the case of MAL in particular, has been out of the reaches of green movements. Even though local residents were aware of the danger, their weight was negligible against the large corporation.

Figure 1: Falsely Perceived Marginal Abatement and Damage Costs

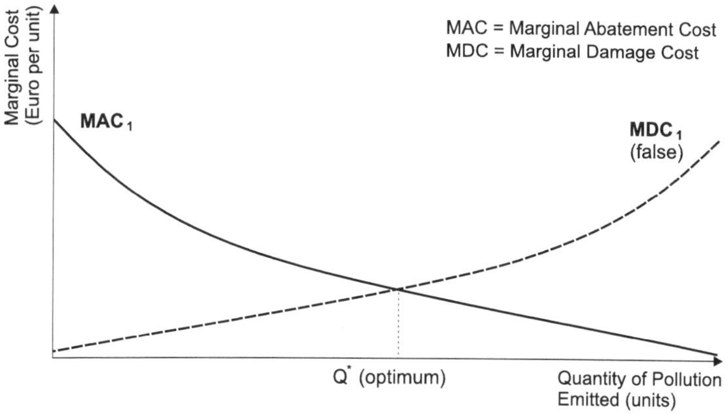

Authors' archive

As the previously cited example from our university shows, even experts were aware of the risks associated with the storage facility, but their warnings were left unnoticed.

As we have previously mentioned, risks didn't just arise from the red sludge itself, but rather from the method of storage which meant deposition with a strongly alkali liquid (reaching pH 13 at times).

The fate of red sludge as a residue is an interesting affair after the 2004 accession of Hungary to the EU. Until the accession, red sludge was considered hazardous waste in Hungary, but EU legislation says that it is not. Through legal harmonization based on incorrect information, red sludge was removed from the Hungarian list of toxic substances. (As legal harmonization was a condition of EU accession, this was a particular problem encountered during the process.)

The misunderstanding may have arisen from the EU practice of drying red sludge and taking its alkalinity down to below pH 10, which is a preventative measure fitting the MDC_2 curve. The Marginal Damage and Abatement Costs are illustrated by MDC_2 and MAC_2.

We will attempt to illustrate the situation after the dyke burst and the red sludge inundated the area through the MDC_3 and MAC_3 curves.

As indicated, due to the significant underestimation a latent risk was present, which led to the catastrophe.

Figure 2: Falsely Perceived and Real Marginal Abatement and Damage Costs with Risk Evident

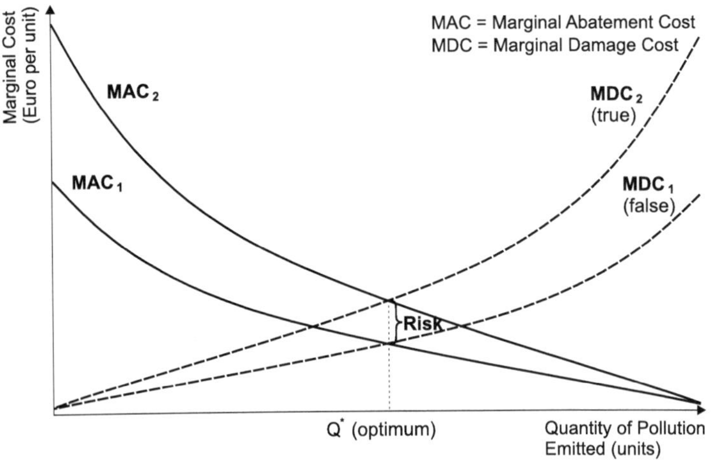

Authors' archive

Figure 3: When Disaster Occurs, a Gap Remains between the Marginal Abatement and Damage Costs

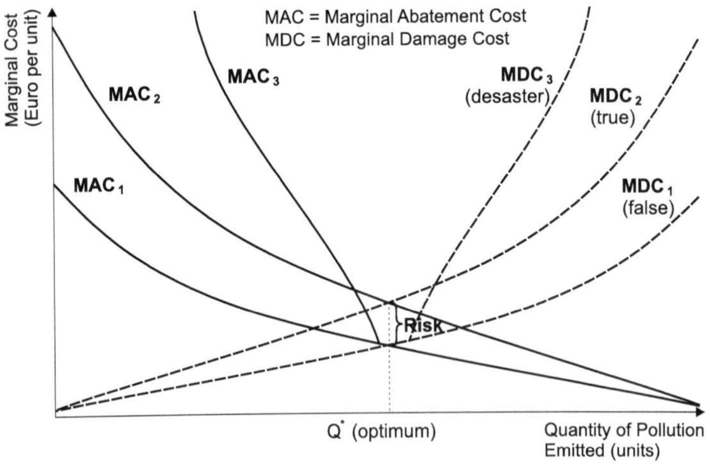

Authors' archive

As a consequence of the catastrophe, the environmental damage costs skyrocketed, and even their partial abatement will require immense expenditures.

Furthermore, previously damages would remain in the rationally abatable economic category, where an economic optimum could be defined and interpreted, which is indicated by Q* on the diagram.

The catastrophe has caused a number of irreversible damages. Before all, such is the loss of ten human lives, the large number of domestic animals lost, and the innumerable loss of wildlife, the destruction of ecosystem in the soil and water, and the disintegration of previously habitable settlements. After the catastrophe, we simply cannot talk about an economic optimum. In a graphical representation of the situation, the two curves have no intersection. The costs and the damages are split by an unbridgeable gap. A part of the damages cannot be treated optimally. Those are final and irreparable.

5 Recovery

The reconstruction of houses, public buildings, roads and other infrastructure is one of the costly but relatively simple tasks of recovery.

It is a seemingly simple matter that energy crops must be planted because of the soil pollution. But this is only seemingly simple. This change requires an alteration in the monoculture as well. Whether the soil will yield an income comparable to previous incomes remains a question. How will the demand for human labour and other investments change? Will the population formerly making a livelihood from agriculture be able to work? Furthermore, how can a family alter its finances if the annual yield of wheat, corn and vegetables is replaced by a perhaps four-five year first yield of an energy crop plantation?

These are questions to which there are no answers yet.

A risk management scenario prepared by the Department of Applied Biotechnology and Food Sciences of the Budapest University of Technology and Economics has concluded that the absolute priority of recovery must be the guarantee of the safety of the local residents. According to this report, the primary pollutant is the red sludge storage facility, but even red sludge collecting in low-lying areas and riverbeds must be taken into account. Considering these, further spreads in the pollutant and damages are to be foreseen, so these ought to be regarded as secondary sources of pollution. The removal of these substances is undoubtedly desirable in order to further reduce the risks posed on residents and the environment. The isolation of the primary source of pollution (the storage facility) has been completed, as a new dyke has been constructed between the ditch and the village of Kolontár.

Sulfates and acids were added to water bodies to reduce the alkalinity of surface waters.

Secondary pollutants – i.e. red sludge deposited during the inundation – have been collected and deposited in Ditch 10A, a storage facility previously not used by MAL. The substance is mixed with soil, and is stored in prisms. This will probably be a temporary solution only.

Sludge deposited in inhabited areas and gardens was removed partly by washing and partly by the removal of the top soil. The remaining ground was dyed red, which was then sprinkled by gypsum. To prevent the dust being carried by the wind, rotation of the remaining soil will be necessary, which hasn't been carried out everywhere.

The recultivation of some 10,000 hectares of damaged agricultural territory remains a significant problem. Wet red sludge has covered this area in a thickness varying between two and 31 centimetres (one and 12½ inches). Two problems have to be solved here. Firstly, the layer on top of the soil surface inhibits the air flow, and secondly, after drying, the dust threatens the living environment. As measurements indicate that the toxic metal content of the sludge does not exceed safe limits, and no significant damage is caused to the soil if the sludge is only mixed in to a ratio not exceeding 10% of soil mass, so a solution could be the plowing of the thinner layers. Thicker layers have to be stripped back first and the remaining layers may be treated by plowing. In any case, it must be ensured that by spring vegetation covers the affected critical areas to minimize the risk of dusting. A feasible solution would be the plantation of the previously mentioned early-sprouting energy crops.

6 Questions of Financing

The disaster has triggered an unprecedented sense of help both in Hungary and abroad. Some two billion forints (about 10 million dollars) were collected as domestic donations only, and the Maltese Relief Organization has agreed with the government to rent apartments for those who have lost their home for a six month period. During this time they can decide if they want to move back to newly constructed dwellings in the affected localities, or if they want to move out, which will be similarly subsidied. Austrian collection drives, protective suits, cleaning equipment and financial donations, as well as the arrival of Slovakian special machinery reflected the cross border help.

Day-to-day relief efforts were funded by the government from the reserve fund of the central budget. A Superfund which exists in the USA and in numerous OECD states is non-existent in Hungary. Similarly, it is not a customary procedure to contract liability risk insurance either. Cost of the disaster to the Hungarian state was nearly 120 million Euro by July, 2011.

The European Union does, however, recommend a liability insurance, but most new member states – most of which come from a communist background – have remained unaffected by this.

Establishing a regime of compulsory insurance for dangerous technologies is an important step when considering the future. Companies with liability decided through court rulings and their owners must also take part in the final financing of the recovery efforts. Criminal prosecution due to the deaths that occurred and the significant damages that were done may also be necessary.

References

HAS – Hungarian Academy of Sciences Research Centre, Institute of Material and Environmental Chemistry (2010): An Interim Summary of Findings of the Investigation until 12 October 2010 into the Red Sludge Disaster at Ajka. Budapest (URL: http://mta.hu/mta_hirei/osszefoglalo-a-vorosiszap-katasztrofa-elharitasrol-a-karmentesitesrol-es-a-hosszu-tavu-teendokrol-125859/)

Galamus (2010): Iszapömlés [Red Sludge Onrush]. In: Népszava, October 4 (in Hungarian)

Gruiz, K. (2011): Vörösiszap-katasztrófa környezeti kockázatmenedzsmentje [Risk Management of the Red Sludge Disaster] (URL: http://enfo.hu/drupal/en/node/7417) (in Hungarian)

HVG – Heti Világgazdaság [Weekly World Economy] (2011), Budapest, February 19, p. 60 (in Hungarian)

Ijjas, F. (2010): Kifakadó sebek – avagy esettanulmány az októberi vörösiszap katasztrófáról [Breaking Wounds – Case Study of the Red Sludge Disaster at October). Professional analysis. Budapest (Budapest University of Technology and Economics, Faculty of Economic and Social Sciences, Doctoral School of Management and Economic Sciences) (in Hungarian)

Romhanyi, T.; Cseri, P.; Boda A. (2011): Iszap [Sludge]. In: Mediprint, Budapest (in Hungarian)

Simon, G. (2010): Vörösiszap katasztrófa: a vadkeleti privatizáció hozadéka? [Red Sludge Disaster: Proceeds of the Wild-east Privatisation?] (URL: http://magardiplo.hu/kezdlap/255-voeroesiszap-katasztrofa-a-vadkeleti-privatizacio-hozadeka) (in Hungarian)

Szlávik, J. (2005): Fenntartható környezet- és erőforrás-gazdálkodás [Sustainable Environment- and Resource Economy). Budapest (in Hungarian)

Tietenberg, T. (1992): Environmental and Natural Resource Economics. New York

Tietenberg, T. (2003): Environmental and Natural Resource Economics (6th ed.). New York

Winkler, G. (2010): Winkler Gusztáv jelentése [Report of Gusztáv Winkler] (URL: http://galamus.hu/index.php?option=com_content&view=article&id=32546&Itemid=115) (in Hungarian)

Tsunami in India's Shorelands

Policy Implications of Learning Sustainability from the Victims

Appukuttan N. Damodaran

1 Background

The Tsunami sea waves that struck India, Indonesia and Sri Lanka in December 2004 were an unforeseen calamity that could not be explained in terms of standard paradigms. This paper looks at the major lessons that arise for policy makers from the Tsunami disaster that impacted South Indian shores during December 2004.

The *Natural Environment Research Council* (NERC) defines in 2000 Tsunami "as waves that travel across the ocean at very high velocities, often in excess of 450km/hr, and possess very long wavelengths and periods".[1] According to NERC, the impacts of Tsunami on shore lands is partly a function of the dimensions of the propagated waves and partly a function of the topography and bathymetry of the coastal zone.

Scholars characterize post Tsunami economic impacts as getting manifested in the following manner: In the first place destroyed vocations take time to recover their activity to pre-disaster levels. The time needed for recuperation varies from vocation to vocation depending on degree and level of preparedness, supply of inputs, availability of transport networks and requirements of the market place, variation in price for products. It is noted that some vocations bounce back while others see decline. Where businesses are destroyed, there are unemployment effects. Indeed it is even noted that there could be shifts in vocations and jobs in the post Tsunami phase.

The Tsunami sea waves that struck India, Indonesia and Sri Lanka in December 2004 were an unforeseen calamity that could not be explained in terms of standard paradigms (cf. Damodaran 2010). Rather in the aftermath of the disaster, the entire discourse on Tsunami in India focused on how the severity of the disaster was exacerbated by faulty land use changes on shore lands, inadequate protection to the poor people staying on the shores, unimaginative coastal zone regulations and inadequate preparations for disaster management in developing countries (cf. Damodaran 2010). In other words, though seen as an abso-

1 http://www.nerc-bas.ac.uk/tsunami-risks/html/TIntro1.htm.

lutely unforeseen natural calamity, the tragedy was analyzed in terms of inadequacy of rehabilitation measures and the inadequacy of poverty alleviation measures among coastal communities.

India's Tsunami tragedy holds many lessons. A case in point is the zone of Nagapattinam in Tamil Nadu one of the worst affected by the Tsunami calamity of 2004. Nagapattnam, the prime victim of the 2004 Tsunami is a delta District of Tamil Nadu in India's east coast facing the Bay of Bengal (see Figure 1). Nagapattnam has a coastal line that is 165 kilometers long with 60 coastal villages, with a cluster of eleven minor ports huddled along the narrow strip.

Figure 1: Geographical Location of Nagapattinam

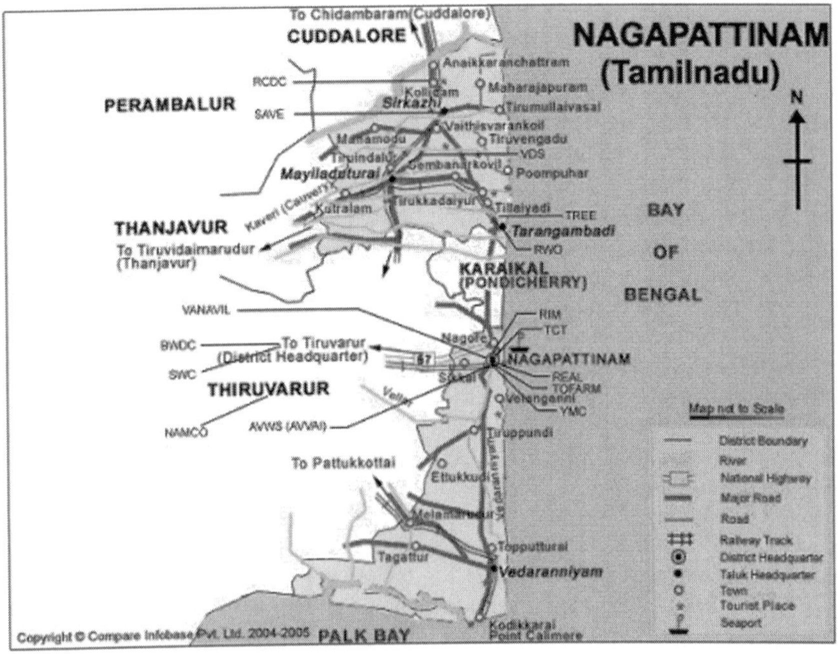

Source: Source:http://www.google.co.in/images?hl=en&source=hp&btnG=Google+Search&aq=f&aqi=&oq=&oi=image_result_group&sa=X&q=Nagapattnam%20Map&tbm=isch

The flat shore and the shallowness of the continental shelf, coupled with absence of sand dunes acted against the town when the Tsunami struck. The Tsunami wiped out buildings, washed away some villages and fishermen inhabiting zones, smashed fishing vessels, killed or marooned local communities.

Table 1 summarizes the impact of the Tsunami on local lives, while Table 2 sums up the loss of assets of households.

Table 1: Impact of the Tsunami in Nagapattinam District

No. villages affected	Population affected	Population evacuated	Human lives lost	Persons injured	Orphaned children	Women widowed
38	196,184	196,184	60,065	2,375	179	294

Source: http://www.tn.gov.in/tsunami/,2006

Table 2: Loss of Assets Due to Tsunami

Cattle	Houses damaged	Agricultural Land in ha	Horticultural Land in ha	Boats damaged	Fishing Nets
12,821	19,630	4,657	457	8,774	7,604

Source: http://www.tn.gov.in/tsunami/,2006

2 The Field Survey of 2007

A field survey was conducted in 2007 to assess the long term incidence of the Tsunami on the affected population of Nagapattnam. 120 households drawn from eight villages of the District were selected for study. The population was chosen on the basis of stratified random sampling. The surveyed population included 60 fishermen from four villages namely Arcottuthurai, Pushpavanam, Vanagiri and Karaikalmedu.

Questions posed to local communities in Nagapattnam sought their account of how Tsunami waves hit them and the nature and character of the risks that it entailed.

The survey yielded the finding that that local communities were badly hit by the loss of assets (boats, agricultural implements and land). Local communities had a better understanding of what their losses were as compared to the official machinery that organized their rehabilitation and recovery. In the post calamity phase, maximum suffering was on account of the delay in asset reconstruction. As a result 90% of the fishermen had to take loans from private lenders and NGOs.

Thus the suggestions of the victims on how to design rehabilitation packages are important for sustainable rehabilitation plans to be formulated. For the victims the best way to accelerate asset reconstruction was to streamline flow of finances and technical help by organizing a steady stream of finance than the "once for all" assistance packages envisaged by State machinery.

3 Shifting Diagnosis and Altering Solutions: From Sea Walls to Green Walls

The initial diagnosis of the Tsunami crisis in India, focused on the seismic roots of the problem, though the solutions proposed were interestingly of a different nature.

In the wake of the Tsunami disaster and its glaring aftermath, response strategies advanced by different stakeholders varied from extreme measures to more realistic and ecological measures of protection. Sections of stakeholders including sections of prominent officials of the government of the affected states argued for construction of seawalls to prevent Tsunami like disasters.

However, there was a substantial section of stakeholders including civil society groups and scientists who opposed the concept of seawalls and argued that it would only create more problems than solving them. As time elapsed, more rational solutions, which advocated ecological steps for preventing Tsunami like disasters surfaced. This included the famous idea of creating and installing a set of green walls in the shape of forestry plantations, including mangroves and other tree species. Indeed the discourse then changed to the wonderful effects green walls could have on mitigating calamities in coastal areas like the Tsunami. Since then there has been a fair amount of emphasis on the part of the state governments affected, to initiate not only immediate rehabilitation measures but also schemes for greater provisioning of resources for constructing green seawalls.

Thus the more important fact is that the Tsunami that hit India in 2004 was a call of awakening for the Government to change their set tack of engineering solutions and see virtues in ecological approaches towards solving natural disasters (cf. Damodaran 2010).

4 Policy Lessons

The main policy lesson that comes out of India's Tsunami story is about the importance of ensuring that perceptions of local communities are mapped and the risk factor assessed based on local perceptions of risk. This is to ensure that the problem of optimism bias is avoided (cf. Flyvbjerg 2006). Local communities who are victims of events are more often than not, pessimistic about the future and are keen to have solutions that work on the ground. An aggregated approach to mapping is called for at the local self Government levels to ensure that a decision that is sensitive to the location of the project is adopted. This serves to facilitate regional and national level decision making involving action to manage calamities and societal risks. The offshoot of such as an approach would be the evolution of a risk communication system that would move away from vertical processes based on top down approaches, to one that is horizontal (cf. Putnam 1993). Horizontal communication systems in turn taps communication patterns that exist amongst a network of organizations (cf. Carrel 2005). Translated to the situation analyzed in this paper, this means local mapping of risks and risk management perceptions that emanate from local networks. Such a corpus of knowledge on risk management will be independent of "top down approaches" that communicate social risks arising from natural calamities in a top down or instrumentalist manner. More importantly as the Tsunami story in India shows, they convert the latter to a more inclusive "democratic" course of action.

References

Carrel, A. (2005): Horizontal Communication: Thought and Afterthought (URL: cityofdawson.com/download/HorizontalCommunication.pdf)

Damodaran, A. (2010): Encircling the Seamless: India, Climate Change and Global Commons. Delhi

Damodaran, A. (2008): Policy for Managing Environmental Risks in India. Report submitted to Ministry of Environment and Forests. New Delhi (Government of India)

Flyvbjerg, B. (2006): From Nobel Prize to Project Management: Getting Risks Right. In: Project Management Journal, Vol. 37/No. 3 (August), pp. 5–15

Putnam, R. (1993): Making Democracy Work: Civic Traditions in Modern Italy. Princeton/NJ

Internet Sources

http://www.nerc-bas.ac.uk/tsunami-risks/html/TIntro1.htm

http://www.epondicherry.com/ngo_web/english/tn-pondy/district-snapshots/nagapatinum-district-snapshot.php

http://www.tn.gov.in/tsunami/,2006

http://www.gandeepam.org/ggf.htm

Sustainability of Marine Fisheries

Marine Reserves, Habitat Restoration, Aquaculture and Stock Enhancement in Florida

Jonathan M. Shenker

1 Introduction

Recreational and commercial fishery species have long been under severe stress across the world. Commercial fishery landings of around 15 x 10^6 metric tonnes in the 1950's increased rapidly to 60–70 x 10^6 tonnes by the 1980s then remained roughly stable at that level through 2008 (see Figure 1; cf. FAO 2008).

Figure 1: Fishery Landings, Aquaculture Production and Human Population Size from 1950 to 2008

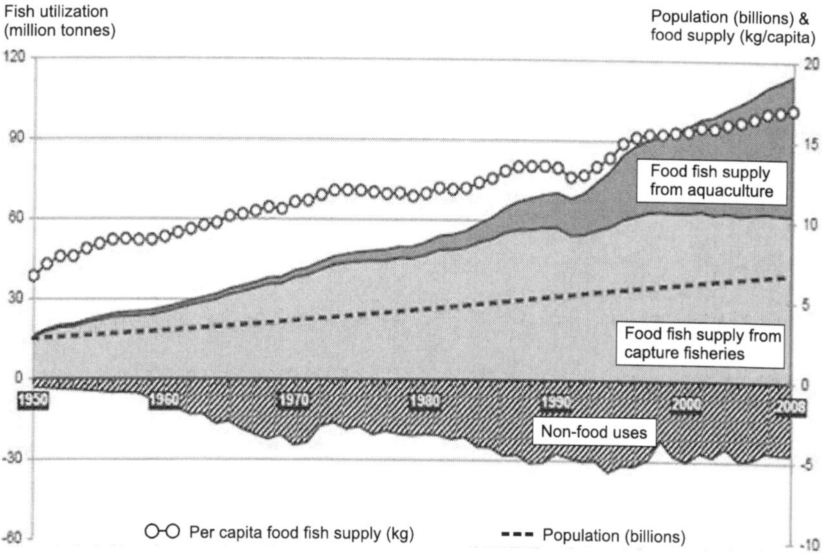

Source: FAO 2008

This consistent level of harvest was achieved through significant increases in fishing technology and development of fisheries for many previously unharvested species. As individual fisheries decline due to intense overfishing, habitat destruction, alteration of freshwater hydrological regimes, pollution and other anthropogenic stresses, their losses can trigger significant alterations in the community structures and trophodynamic interactions within marine and freshwater habitats (cf. Bascompte et al 2005; Coleman et al. 2004; Jackson et al. 2001; Pauly et al. 2003; Pauly/Palomares 2005).

The economic and social implications of fisheries depletion on human societies are enormous. In Florida alone, the marine recreational and commercial fisheries have an annual value exceeding \$5.4 billion and \$1 billion, respectively, and provide over 50,000 jobs to the state. Freshwater fisheries have an annual value of \$2 billion, and provide an additional 24,000 jobs (cf. FFWCC 2011b). The fisheries are clearly a vital economic engine for Florida.

Fisheries management and restoration efforts worldwide include a wide array of strategies, including implementation and (often minimal) enforcement of limits on fishery landings, creation of Marine Protected Areas that serve as refuges and sources of repopulation of surrounding areas, the use of aquaculture to rebuild fishery populations and ecosystem restoration efforts in critical habitats. This chapter utilizes Florida fish species and ecosystems to define some of the potential mechanisms to mitigate losses or restore populations of vital coastal fishery species. A multifaceted, albeit uncoordinated, series of approaches is being implemented by numerous federal, state and local governmental agencies, academic and private organizations. Increasing coordination of efforts is underway to further enhance the effectiveness of the restoration and enhancement efforts. These efforts include creation of extensive protected areas, habitat restoration, enhancement of stocks through aquaculture and release, and management of wild stocks and fishery techniques. All of these efforts can be highly controversial, particularly efforts to restrict catches of wild fishes. Nevertheless, such fisheries management efforts can provide critical tools in restoration of vital fishery populations.

2 Marine Reserves

Florida has the longest coastline of any state in the continental United States (1,217 miles), and contains a greater variety of habitats than any other region in the country. Estuarine and coastal habitats in the northern region of the state are dominated by soft and hard bottom substrates with fringing salt marsh vegetation. Sea grasses and mangroves dominate the vegetation below the middle portion of the peninsula, with coral reefs extending from Miami-Dade County through the Keys to the Dry Tortugas and beyond. Portions of all of these habitats have been incorporated into a variety of Marine Protected Areas (MPAs). Extensive literature is available on each of the numerous MPAs, so only an overview is provided here.

The earliest habitats that function as MPAs were created in the state for reasons other than conservation of fishery resources. President Theodore Roosevelt established the Pelican Island National Wildlife Refuge in 1903. This portion of the Indian River Lagoon, on the eastern shore of the Indian River Lagoon was the first such refuge ever created in the United States. Intended to preserve populations of water birds from hunters seeking plumes and feathers for hats, Pelican Island remains off-limits for fishing and thus provides a local refuge for fishery populations as well.

The establishment of NASA activities at Cape Canaveral provided further protection of habitats. President John F. Kennedy created a series of National Wildlife Refuges around the perimeter of Cape Canaveral to serve as a buffer for space launch activities. For security reasons, much of the region is completely closed to visitors, and the area thus serves as a *de facto* MPA. Fisheries studies have determined that fish populations in and around the protected area are very high, relative to more heavily populated areas elsewhere in the Indian River Lagoon (cf. Johnson et al. 1999; Roberts et al. 2001), although spawning activity within the reserve is not as productive as in adjacent waters (cf. Reyier/Shenker 2008; Reyier et al. 2008).

Since the creation of these earliest MPAs, numerous other habitats along Florida's coast have received varying degrees of protection. In many cases, at least recreational fishing is allowed within a protected area, which focuses more on preserving the habitat structure itself (e.g. many parts of the Everglades National Park and other components of the National Park System).

At least portions of other protected areas have been established as fishery reserves. The 2,800 square mile Florida Keys National Marine Sanctuary, established in 1990, has been zoned into regions designated as Wildlife Management Areas, Ecological Reserves, Sanctuary Preservation Areas, and Special-use Areas that have different management goals and provide differing levels of protection for fishery resources (see Figure 2).

Not all of Florida's MPAs are in coastal or shallow reef habitats. The Oculina Bank is a deepwater coral habitat along the edge of the continental shelf around the 80 m contour (see Figure 3). Heavily fished and damaged during preceding decades, the South Atlantic Fisheries Management Council established a 300 square mile portion of the coral bank as a Habitat Area of Particular Concern in 1984. The HAPC was closed to trawling, dredging, longlining and trapping activities. Further regulations developed in 1994 closed bottom fishing for grouper, snapper and other demersal species. Research in the region is seeking to determine if those fishery closures are saving both the coral habitat itself and exporting fish into surrounding habitats.

Figure 2: The Mosaic of Babitat and Fishery Protection Areas within the Florida Keys National Marine Sanctuary

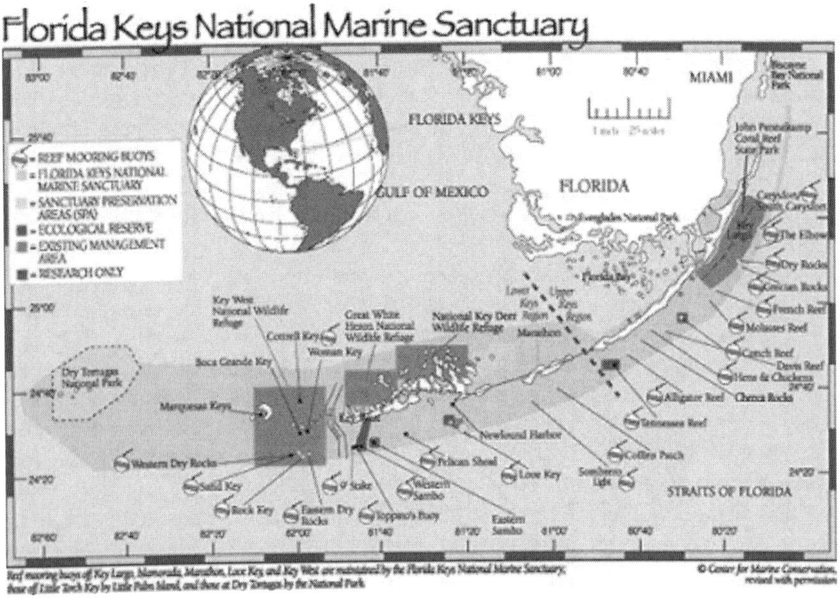

Source: http://www.flmnh.ufl.edu/fish/southflorida/coral/conservation.html

3 Habitat Restoration, Aquaculture and Stock Enhancement in Florida

Establishment of protected areas is a major component of fishery management plans. Other activities in habitat restoration, aquaculture, and stock enhancement have been used in many regions, but the State of Florida recently created a program to combine these various activities within a coordinated framework. The Florida Marine Fisheries Enhancement Initiative,[1] established in 2008, is a network of major fisheries research and aquaculture centers in the state that will pool resources and capabilities in concerted efforts to restore recreational fishery stocks in coastal waters.

1 Cf. www.fmfei.org.

Figure 3: Protected Areas within the Oculina Habitat Area of Particular Concern along the East Coast of Florida

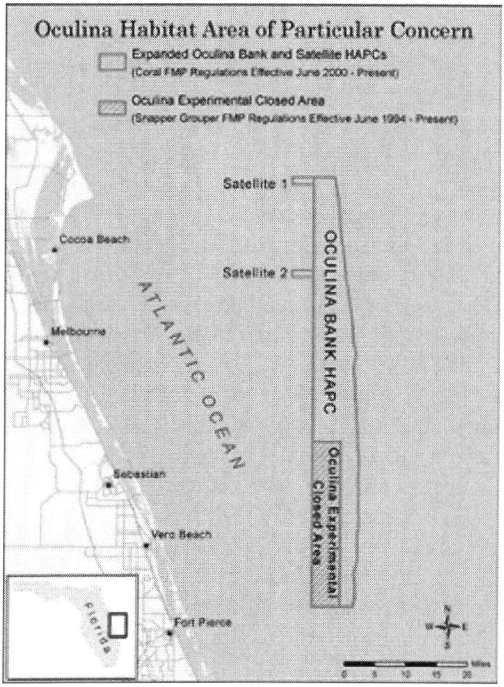

Source: http://www.safmc.net/HabitatManagement/DeepwaterCorals/OculinaBank/Tabid/246/default.aspx

The network builds upon early efforts conducted by the Sportfish Enhancement Research Facility (SERF), operated by the Florida Fish and Wildlife Conservation Commission, and the Mote Marine Laboratory (MML). SERF and MML initiated Project Tampa Bay in 1999 as a large-scale stock enhancement program for red drum *(Sciaenops ocellatus)* in Tampa Bay. The goals of Project Tampa Bay were to develop and test ecologically sound and cost-effective aquaculture methods to produce and release large numbers of juvenile red drum to enhance the abundance of this valuable fishery species.

Adult red drum were collected from Tampa Bay and established as broodstock at the SERF facility located near Port Manatee on the southeast shore of the bay. Over four million juvenile redfish were released into Tampa Bay during the five-year project. Their survival and contribution to the wild population was assessed through intense field sampling, genetic assessment and fisheries monitoring projects. The results of Project Tampa Bay helped determine some of the optimal procedures for conducting large scale enhancement efforts in Tampa Bay and elsewhere in Florida in the future.

An unanticipated benefit of SERF operations are direct habitat restoration efforts. When the facility was initially opened in 1988, an artificial wetland was created to filter nutrients from water being released from the aquaculture operations. This *Spartina* marsh grew rapidly in the water flow. Over 1,000,000 plugs of *Spartina* have since been harvested from the wetland and then transplanted around the shoreline of Tampa Bay to rebuild marsh habitat.

A critical component of Project Tampa Bay is that it followed strict criteria to ensure that all efforts were conducted in an ecologically appropriate manner that sought to minimize the negative effects that have been attributed to stock enhancement efforts in other areas (cf. Bell et al. 2006; Cooney/Brodeur 1998; Perez-Enriquez et al. 1999; Reisenbichler/Rubin 1999). H. Lee Blankenship and Kenneth M. Leber developed a series of recommendations used in Project Tampa Bay to maintain the genetic diversity of released fishes, make sure that released juveniles do not have any nutritional or pathogen health problems, and minimize deleterious ecological interactions with wild fishes and habitats after releases (cf. Blankenship/Leber 1995).

Project Tampa Bay formed the model for the current Florida Marine Fisheries Enhancement Initiative (FMFEI). The FMFEI is composed of a number of existing and planned facilities arrayed around the coast of Florida that will support fisheries enhancement activities in different habitats (see Figure 4). The network of facilities is expandable to permit new facilities to be developed in response to different needs at different locations.

Each component of the network is designed to complement the efforts at adjacent network nodes. At present, the organization focuses on three main regions of Florida: East Coast, West Coast and Panhandle. Each site will support research and implementation of efforts for habitat restoration, aquaculture production and education.

Habitat restoration projects in Florida have been underway for decades, and the FMFEI adds new impetus for additional projects targeted toward fishery production. Projects currently underway include restoration of oyster beds, *Spartina* and mangrove marshes, and reconnection of isolated habitats with existing waterways.

Initial aquaculture efforts at most sites will focus on red drum. The aquaculture technology for this species is more highly refined than for other species, making the red drum an ideal species to start the project (cf. FFWCC 2011a). Subsequent efforts will include developing aquaculture methods for large-scale culture and production of other estuarine and coastal species, such as snook

(Centropomus undecimalis), sea trout *(Cynoscion nebulosus)* and red snapper *(Lutjanus campechanus)*.

Figure 4: Aquaculture and Habitat Restoration Facilities within the Florida Marine Fisheries Enhancement Initiative

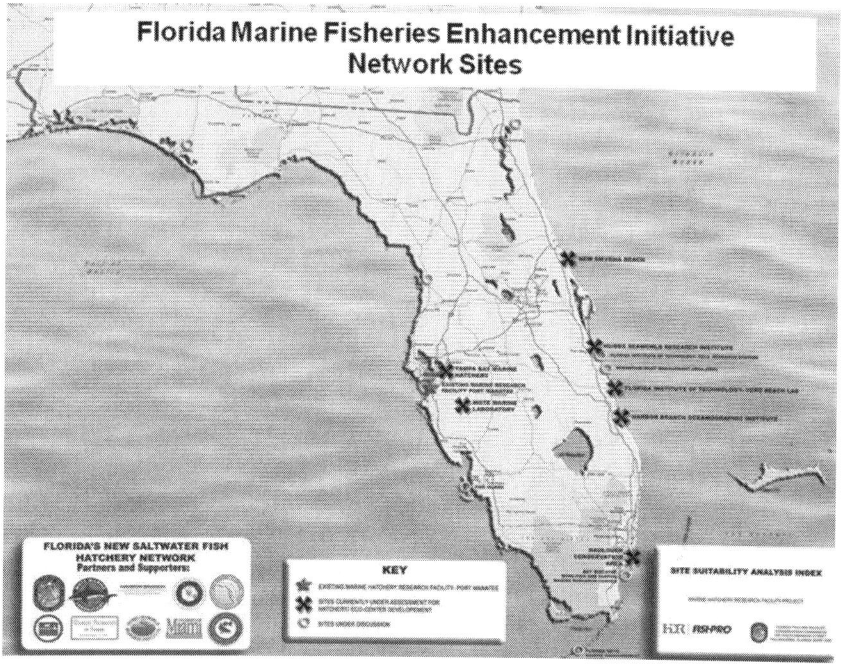

Source: http://www.fmfei.org

The Fisheries Genetics Laboratory of the Florida Fish and Wildlife Commission has developed a series of red drum microsatellite markers that can now be used for parentage analysis, enabling the genetic marking and tracking of all fishes released from aquaculture operations (cf. Tringali et al. 2008). To ensure the genetic integrity of all restoration efforts, broodstock for East Coast efforts will be collected only from east coast habitats, West Coast broodstock will be collected from the Tampa Bay region, and Panhandle broodstock will be collected from north Florida. Similar restrictions will govern the production and release of all other species.

Full details and updates of the FMFEI are available on the organization web site.[2] At present, the existing SERF facility will continue to produce red drum for west coast projects. Releases of east coast juveniles from east coast facilities is first planned for 2012.

The 2011 array of FMFEI facilities are (arranged clockwise around the coast, starting in the northeast portion of the state; see Figure 4):

- Mosquito Lagoon Marine Enhancement Center: Built on a renovated school site within the Spartina marsh habitat in northeast Florida, this site is being developed as a primary site for marsh habitat restoration, the production, growth and release of red drum and spotted sea trout, outreach and education, and as a base of operations for the Florida Marine Patrol that has marine safety and fisheries enforcement mandates.
- Hubbs Sea World Research Institute: A long-time leader in fisheries enhancement efforts in California, the HSWRI is planning a large facility on the Indian River Lagoon in Brevard County. This site will be devoted primarily to large-scale production and release of juvenile red drum and other estuarine species.
- Florida Institute of Technology's Vero Beach Marine Laboratory: The Florida Tech facility is located on four acres of ocean-front habitat in Indian River County. The seawater system provides large quantities of highly filtered seawater, making this a superb site for broodstock maintenance, larval production, and research on new species. Pelagic species such as cobia *(Rachycentron canadum),* mahi mahi *(Coryphaena hippurus),* tripletail *(Lobotes surinamensis)* have been routinely spawned at the laboratory; FMFEI efforts will focus on red drum, red snapper and other species. Additional work at the laboratory will include analysis of optimal "life-skills" training for cultured fish to enable them to adapt to wild conditions. Further studies will center on culture and restoration of sea grass and dune vegetation.
- Florida Atlantic University/Harbor Branch Oceanographic Institution: Situated on the Indian River Lagoon in Fort Pierce, HBOI is one of the premier aquaculture research centers in the world. Researchers are optimizing techniques for growing larval red drum and other species to the appropriate sizes for release into the wild.
- Haulover Park Conservation Enhancement Center: Located on Biscayne Bay, the Haulover Park Center will focus on public education efforts and research on coastal and coral reef fish enhancement.
- Pine Island Marine Enhancement Center: This large site is being planned for construction on donated land on the coastline of southwest Florida. In

2 Cf. www.fmfei.org.

addition to being a center for public education, the site will ultimately be involved in production of red drum and other estuarine/coastal species.

- Mote Marine Laboratory Enhancement Center: The Mote Marine Laboratory has played a major role in decades of fishery enhancement research and programs in Florida. Their Aquaculture Park is the site of ongoing culture research and release efforts with red drum, snook and other species, and they have played a major role in defining the genetic, health and ecological parameters that govern all release activities.
- Port Manatee Stock Enhancement Research Facility: This site is the primary research and production facility for the Florida Fish and Wildlife Conservation Center. Researchers at SERF led Project Tampa Bay, which was the initial enhancement effort that showed properly designed projects can indeed enhance wild populations. SERF will continue to develop culture technologies for new species and will continue to produce juvenile fishes for release.

The Panhandle region of northwest Florida is not yet the site of a Marine Enhancement Center. The Deepwater Horizon oil spill in summer 2010 caused significant damage to portions of the northern Gulf of Mexico, and dramatically illustrated the vulnerability of coastal spawning and nursery sites to human activities. As a result of this oil spill, an announcement of the selection of a site for a Marine Enhancement Center is expected to occur in late 2011 or early 2012. This site will focus on culture and production of red drum and other northern Gulf of Mexico species.

4 Summary and Recommendations

Intense commercial and recreational fisheries are exerting unsustainable impacts on the populations of wild fishery stocks. Aquaculture productivity is rising rapidly, generating annual yields that are similar to that of the total world fisheries. Foodfish aquaculture can have serious environmental effects, and generally does not ease fishing pressure on wild stocks.

Establishment of Marine Protected Areas is one of the most common approaches for trying to restore or enhance wild fishery stocks. MPAs have varying designs for differing objectives, but can serve to rebuild populations in surrounding areas.

Habitat restoration and the use of aquaculture to produce juvenile fishes for stocking are two other vital components of fishery enhancement. The State of Florida is coordinating a new state-wide effort that creates a network of laboratories and hatcheries around the coastline with the goals of a collaborative effort to restore some of the state's recreational fishery stocks. These facilities will seek to maximize their effectiveness by providing their specific areas of expertise to the overall project as well as providing geographic coverage around the state. All aquaculture and restocking efforts will be conducted in accordance with established criteria to maintain the genetic and health integrity of wild stocks, and minimize ecological impacts in the release habitats. This type of state-wide approach that coordinates the skills and expertise available at diverse facilities can serve as a model for fishery restoration efforts in other locations.

References

Bascompte, J.; Melián, C. J.; Sala, E. (2005): Interaction Strength Combinations and the Overfishing of a Marine Food Web. In: Proceedings of the National Academy of Sciences, Vol. 102, pp. 5443–5447

Bell, J. D.; Bartley, D. M.; Lorenzen, K.; Loneragan, N. R. (2006): Restocking and Stock Enhancement of Coastal Fisheries: Potential, Problems and Progress. In: Fisheries Research, Vol. 80, pp. 1–8

Blankenship, H. L.; Leber, K. M. (1995): A Responsible Approach to Marine Stock Enhancement. In: Schramm Jr., H. L.; Piper, R. G. (eds.): Uses and Effects of Cultured Fishes in Aquatic Ecosystems. American Fisheries Society, Symposium 15, Bethesda, MD. pp. 67–175

Coleman, F. C.; Figueira, W. F.; Ueland, J. S.; Crowder, L. B. (2004): The Impact of United States Recreational Fisheries on Marine Fish Populations. In: Science, Vol. 305, pp. 1958–1960

Cooney, R. T.; Brodeur, R. D. (1998): Carrying Capacity and North Pacific Salmon Production: Stock-enhancement Implications. In: Bulletin of Marine Science, Vol. 62, pp. 443–464

FAO – Food and Agriculture Organization of the United Nations (2008): Overview: Major Trends and Issues (URL: ftp://ftp.fao.org/FI/STAT/summary/YB_Overview.pdf)

FFWCC – Florida Fish and Wildlife Conservation Commission (2011a): Raising Red Drum at SERF (URL: http://myfwc.com/research/saltwater/stock-enhancement/general-information/raising-red-drum)

FFWCC – Florida Fish and Wildlife Conservation Commission (2011b): The Economic Impact of Saltwater Fishing in Florida (URL: http://myfwc.com/conservation/value/saltwater-fishing/)

Jackson, J. B. C.; Kirby, M. X.; Berger, W. H.; Bjorndal, K. A.; Botsford, L. W.; Bourque, B. J.; Bradbury, R. H.; Cooke, R.; Erlandson, J.; Estes, J. A.; Hughes, T. P.; Kidwell, S.; Lange, C. B.; Lenihan, H. S.; Pandolfi, J. M.; Peterson, C. H.; Steneck, R. S.; Tegner, M. J.; Warner, R. W. (2001): Historical Overfishing and the Recent Collapse of Coastal Ecosystems. In: Science, Vol. 293, pp. 629–638

Johnson, D. R.; Funicelli, N. A.; Bohnsack, J. A. (1999): Effectiveness of an Existing Estuarine No-take Fish Sanctuary within the Kennedy Space Center, Florida. In: North American Journal of Fisheries Management, Vol. 19, pp. 436–453

Pauley, D.; Alder, J.; Bennett, E.; Christensen, V.; Tydemers, P.; Watson, R. (2003): The Future for Fisheries. In: Science, Vol. 302, pp. 1359–1361

Pauly, D.; Palomares, M. L. (2005): Fishing Down Marine Food Web: It is Far More Pervasive than We Thought. In: Bulletin of Marine Science, Vol. 76, pp. 197–211

Perez-Enriquez, R.; Takagi, M.; Taniguchi, N. (1999): Genetic Variability and Pedigree Tracing of a Hatchery-reared Stock of Red Sea Bream (Pagrus major) Used for Stock Enhancement, Based on Microsatellite DNA Markers. In: Aquaculture, Vol. 173, pp. 413–423

Reisenbichler, R. R.; Rubin, S. P. (1999): Genetic Changes from Artificial Propagation of Pacific Salmon Affect the Productivity and Viability of Supplemented Populations. In: ICES Journal of Marine Science, Vol. 56, pp. 459–466

Reyier, E. A.; Shenker, J. M. (2008): Ichthyoplankton Community Structure in a Shallow Subtropical Estuary of the Florida Atlantic Coast. In: Bulletin of Marine Science, Vol. 80, pp. 267–293

Reyier, E. A.; Shenker, J. M.; Christian, D. (2008): Role of an Estuarine Fisheries Reserve in the Production and Export of Ichthyoplankton. In: Marine Ecology Progress Series, Vol. 359, pp. 249–260

Roberts, C. M.; Bohnsack, J. A.; Gell, F.; Hawkins, J. P.; Goodbridge, R. (2001): Effects of Marine Reserves on Adjacent Fisheries. In: Science, Vol. 294, pp. 1920–1923

Tringali, M. D; Leber, K. M.; Halstead, W. G.; McMichael, R.; O'Hop, J.; Winner, B.; Cody, R.; Young, C.; Neidig, C.; Wolfe, H.; Forstchen, A.; Barbieri, L. (2008): Marine Stock Enhancement in Florida: A Multi-disciplinary, Stakeholder-supported, Accountability-based Approach. In: Reviews in Fisheries Sciences, Vol. 16, pp. 51–57

Climate Change in Several Central and South American Ecosystems

Challenges and Needs for Effective Management

Eduard Müller, Kenyon C. Lindeman

Mounting evidence suggests that we are approaching a threshold period, a time when stocks of natural, social and economic capital are nearing multiple biophysical tipping points with negative impact cascades underway in many regions (cf. IPCC 2007; Rockstrom et al. 2009). The complexity of the interconnections among such internally complex systems makes simple temporal or spatial impact predictions difficult for many cascades, adding to a belief among many decision-makers that there is no real problem or that there is time to deal with the issues later. This approach reflects an understandable lack of familiarity with complex system behaviors and the speed of multiplicative cascades (you don't see it coming) generated by reinforcing feedback loops operating over multiple generations (cf. Meadows 2008). In addition, despite hundreds of real-time news and other media outlets, there is still no real public or political recognition of the fact that many temporarily successful past societies have triggered abrupt internal declines by overshooting tipping points involving natural, social and economic capital (cf. Diamond 2005; Sachs 2008).

Climate change is considered by many diverse analysts and institutions to be the most pressing challenge to biodiversity conservation and, potentially, human societies in terms of quality of life metrics. Increasing climatic variation is affecting ecosystems at all latitudes and beginning to generate impact cascades among linked social and economic systems (cf. Stern 2009). Scientific consensus on the fundamental causes and impacts of climate change has been present for years on the scale of the American Association for the Advancement of Science, American Geophysical Union and many other organizations (cf. Oreskes 2004) yet robust political action remains markedly absent in both developed and developing countries. The public at large and many decision-makers still do not recognize the magnitude or cross-cutting significance of climate change. Relatively few decision-makers acknowledge the potential for interlinked impacts, particularly in terms of the short time scales involved. For many, it is still something that may happen at the poles and towards the end of this century.

Some ecosystems, including mountains and coastal marine areas, are known to be especially vulnerable to changes in climate and impacts are being documented. To illustrate some of the above issues, we summarize several on-the-ground examples from terrestrial systems of the New World tropics and sub-tropics. We conclude by examining the ongoing paralysis in management actions that could otherwise reduce long-term impacts to these ecosystems and their co-dependent social and economic capital.

1 Climate Change and Mountain Systems of Central and South America

Over the last decades, unsustainable development and climate change have significantly reduced biodiversity in many ecosystems. The most recent Global Biodiversity Outlook 3 (2010) states that "the principal pressures leading to biodiversity loss are not just constant but are, in some cases, intensifying". Much research on the impacts of global warming comes from northern latitude ecosystems which, in spite of their complexity, can be comparatively simpler to those found in tropical regions. Considerable research focus has been placed on the measurement and modeling of climate-induced habitat shifts, which can include range extensions up mountains as well as toward the poles (cf. Loarie et al. 2009; Parmesan/Yohe 1993). In tropical mountain areas, these trends are not necessarily gradual or systematic. Changes are often complex and relatively abrupt. Species extinctions in these and other ecosystems have been observed and shifts in remaining populations can show alarming trends (cf. Novacek/Cleland 2001).

Examples of the above patterns can be observed at Monteverde, Costa Rica, a world renowned cloud forest which is also a birthplace of modern ecotourism. Besides its fame for being home to a highly diverse cloud forest and a habitat of the iconic resplendent quetzal *(Pharomachrus moccino)*, it is also known for being the former home of one of the first known victims of climate change, the endemic golden toad *(Bufo periglenes)*. Twenty of fifty species of anurans (frogs and toads) disappeared in a 30 km^2 study area following synchronous population crashes in 1987 (cf. Pounds et al. 1999). Significantly, information from non-scientist, local forest users proved telling. For example:

> "Numerous anecdotal stories of declining amphibian populations convinced scientists that this phenomenon was real [...] Experimental investigations have served to convince the scientific establishment that amphibian decline is indeed a global phenomenon." (Lips et al. 2005)

Today, 32.3% of all amphibians in Costa Rica are endangered or extinct.[1] Population declines have also observed in other Central American countries, such as Panama, in both river and terrestrial amphibians (cf. Lips 1999).

1 Personal communication by Federico Bolaños 2009.

Currently, the resplendent quetzals which symbolize Middle American cloud forests are being threatened to the point where tour guides, in the forest daily (and whose income depends in part on quetzal sightings), are increasingly worried about the reduction of sightings.[2] Keel-billed toucans *(Ramphastos sulfuratus)*, that previously bred only in lowlands and foothills, have moved up to higher altitudes and nested alongside quetzals since 1995 (cf. Pounds et al. 1999). The toucans feed on the quetzal chicks but are not recognized by the parents as a threat; this has not yet been imprinted as may happen over an extended co-evolutionary association. Additionally, there is abundant information from local forest users that toucans are also feeding on woodpecker chicks. Several species of woodpeckers are responsible for building the nests that are later used by quetzals.

These two examples are only indicators of even bigger changes that are occurring. The cloud forests, as the name indicates, are essentially receiving constant humidity from the mist of clouds that condense as warm air rises along the mountain slopes resulting in one of the most complex ecosystems on Earth. Due to increased temperatures, cloud formation is now frequently happening at higher altitudes with increased rainfall. This means that the clouds are now above the cloud forest and are, increasingly, within it. This brings rapid and major changes in temperature and humidity that are affecting the entire ecosystem. Observations for 35 years starting in 1970 in La Selva Biological Station at the foothills of the Central Mountain Range in Costa Rica indicate that climate is getting warmer (approximately 1C) and more consistently wet with a decrease of dry days to about half (cf. Whitfield et al. 2007). Only time will fully reveal the true impacts of these trends.

Changes are also happening in other tropical New World mountain ecosystems. In the Andes, data show that the lower mountain forests have a history of profound but not rapid climate change, suggesting that temperature change in these systems was gradual, perhaps averaging less than one degree Celsius per 1,000 years. The minimum rate of predicted change would be ten times greater than the most rapid temperature change that took place in the past 48,000 years (cf. Bush et al. 2004). The consequences of these changes are already being observed throughout the region, though scientists are still very cautious to state the direct relationship with climate change. One example of this is in Colombia, where the Paramo ecosystem in Chingaza National Park, which supplies about eight million people with water in the greater Bogota area, is being severely affected by a complex association of "invasive" insects and fungi, which have moved up from lower altitudes and are destroying large areas of vegetation. By mid-March 2009, about 38 hectares had been affected, increasing to about 250

2 Personal communications from tour guides and operators between 2008 and 2010.

hectares by early November of the same year. In spite of a 500% increase in six months and substantial impacts on several scales, instead of immediate action, researchers recommended further research in regards to these changes (cf. Medina 2009).

In terms of agricultural systems such as coffee farming on the slopes of mountains from southern Mexico to the northern Andes, there is also evidence of impacts associated with changing thermal and moisture clines on steep slopes. Coffee quality and production volume are highly dependent on climate: better coffee comes from the highlands. Records show significant declines in production which have been attributed to climate change (cf. ICO 2009). Farmers are looking for greater support to be able to adapt while many are still careful to invoke climate change. The lack of absolute proof limits the way this problem is addressed. Losses of production in recent years due to increased rains, drought, frost or coffee borer beetles are often treated as isolated occurrences and not as a part of a larger pattern. Here, as elsewhere, cautiousness from specialists can feed doubt among politicians, though there is increased recognition of the probable connections:

> "Climate change already seems to be affecting coffee production. It is difficult to attribute direct causality, but the changes we are seeing are entirely consistent with climate modelers' predictions." (Baker 2009)

Many other examples of complex changes in these systems are present. Passion fruit growers in northern Costa Rica have pollinated by hand since at least 2008.[3] This can be attributed to the indiscriminate use of highly toxic pesticides used to produce pineapples for northern markets, but shifts in insect populations in neighbouring natural ecosystems suggest that increasing temperatures and changing rainfall patterns also have a role in these complex processes.

2 Traditional Knowledge and Forest Systems

Increasing use of traditional knowledge is being reported in the research literature (cf. Grant/Berkes 2007; Levy-Tacher/Duncan-Glicher 2004), yet, researchers still routinely discount the information provided by local resource users with decades of on-the-ground observations. The use of phases of the moon or other "natural signals" to guide agricultural practices is just "belief". During many years of working with rural communities, many Latin American researchers in varied specialties are slowly beginning to respect the logic of popular knowledge, especially indigenous knowledge. Local communities grow-up living within

3 Personal communications from farmers 2009.

the ecosystems. They often can understand their functioning better than someone from outside the system. This is especially true for the complex interrelationships that occur within the system as a whole. Farming systems are not looked on as only plant-soil-pest associations. They are looked upon as dynamic processes that are influenced by many different factors, including seasonal climatic changes. This has led some farmers to use selected plant associations for pest control, crop rotation associated with forest regeneration and other practices for many centuries.

One example is how Lacandon Indians from Chiapas, Mexico, use ancestral knowledge to restore the forest in degraded ecosystems (cf. Diemont 2006). By mimicking naturally occurring processes to assist the recovery of forest biodiversity through successional stages (cf. Diemont et al. 2006a) they have managed to recover degraded land and turn it into forest habitat in a little over a decade (cf. Douterlungne et al. 2010). Techniques include the use of rapidly-growing balsa trees to limit the sunshine that gets to the ground, eliminating invasive plants such as ferns. These and other practices have potential use to mitigate climate change by fixing carbon, not only in the canopy but also in the soil, and demonstrate the value of indigenous agroforestry and local knowledge in efforts to conserve and restore forests (cf. Dietmont et al. 2006b).

3 The Significance and Management Complexity of the Issues

Regional ecosystems and the economic and social capital they support are now facing an unprecedented combination of tipping points including explosive population growth (from three to seven billion people in the last three human generations). The situation is amplified by highly heterogeneous distributions of resources superimposed upon completely new Industrial and Digital societies that are dependent on the fossil fuels that are accelerating climate variability (cf. Friedman 2009; Satterthwaite 2009; Stern 2009).

It will always be difficult to dissect and assign exact causation among dozens of complex environmental, social and economic drivers, but by many measures, such connectivity among population, climate, energy and social capital exists (cf. Earth Charter 2000). Climate change impacts are particularly hard to establish with clarity due to these same complexities. Also, deforestation, conversion of land for resource intensive monocultures, construction of infrastructure such as dams and urban sprawl, and many other factors, play roles in changes to local climate, making it more difficult to directly correlate these to global changes.

Christopher Field, convening lead author of the Intergovernmental Panel on Climate Change Assessment Report 4 (2007) states: "We are basically looking now at a future climate that's beyond anything we've considered seriously in climate model simulations" (Washington Post, February 15, 2009). Many researchers are documenting unprecedented temperatures, for example: "Record high global 12 month running mean temperature for the period with instrumental data was reached in 2010" (Hansen et al. 2010). In addition, current models are tenuous and can potentially underestimate the probability of abrupt climate change (cf. NRC 2002; Valdes 2011).

In May 2009, CNN England referred to a "silent crisis that is killing 300,000 people each year" based on diverse studies that continue to appear. Today, the crisis is not silent. According to the Consultative Group on International Agricultural Research, 265.7 million people are in areas with high exposure, high sensitivity and low coping capacity, being highly vulnerable to climate change (cf. Ericksen et al. 2011), often in less developed countries. In August 2011 a report by *Oxfam* on the Horn of Africa drought stated:

> "12 million people are in dire need of food, clean water, and basic sanitation. Loss of life on a massive scale is a very real risk, and the crisis is set to worsen over the coming months." (Oxfam 2011)

As this prediction has become increasingly accurate, the headline in the U.S. was pushed to the side by the wedding of a reality TV star and other more marketable fare. Meanwhile, robust intergovernmental political actions are largely absent and moderately ambitious efforts to promote coordinated action on climate change such as the Kyoto Protocol are widely considered to be failures (cf. Dresner 2009).

4 How Well can Traditional Science Address New, Unusually Complex Challenges?

Why is there such apathy or outright resistance in the face of so much scientific evidence? There are many reasons, including an understandable desire for simplistic and upbeat messaging by elected officials who must concentrate on election cycles of only 2–6 years. These major political constraints have been expertly managed over decades by well-documented, doubt-messaging by lobbyists specializing in perception management for corporate clients on scientific issues from health effects of tobacco to ozone to greenhouse gases (cf. Oreskes/Conway 2010).

In addition, paradigms that traditionally constrain scientific participation in political debates can pose major professional challenges to applied scientists. Many scientists are hesitant to speak with authority if there is the slightest degree of uncertainty, even when the odds are high and the consequences of inaction are catastrophic. Since most of the systems in question are highly multivariate and driven by non-linear functions, complexity in both hindcasting and forecasting is guaranteed. Taking positions is therefore a difficult needle to thread for publishing scientists, especially when political decision may be involved. Significantly, however, due to the growing body of evidence and the consequences of inaction, more scientists are taking positions, with concomitant pushback (cf. AAAS 2011).

The importance of consistent qualification of any potentially controversial scientific issue is evident in the wording of IPCC AR 4:

> "Average Northern Hemisphere temperatures during the second half of the 20th century were *very likely* higher than during any other 50-year period in the last 500 years and *likely* the highest in at least the past 1300 years. [...] It is *very likely* that the observed increase in CH_4 concentration is predominantly due to agriculture and fossil fuel use. [...] Most of the observed increase in global average temperatures since the mid-20th century is *very likely* due to the observed increase in anthropogenic GHG concentrations [...] It is *likely* that there has been significant anthropogenic warming over the past 50 years." (IPCC 2007, p. 39)

The justifiably cautious wording of scientists leaves policy space for inaction by politicians and decision-makers, and allows lobbyists, unbound by the standards of peer-review science, to freely manufacture additional doubt.

In addition, the traditional educational focus on thematic specialization for scientists does not fully develop interdisciplinary skill sets needed to examine new and complex issues such as system sustainability in the face of converging issues such as population growth, major extinction events, fossil-fuel dependence, economic models that depend on continuous growth, and climate change. If a scientist wants to have a successful academic career, traditionally he/she must be a specialist, the narrower the field of study, the more focused and deep the potential publication trajectory. Under "normal" circumstances, because of the communication constraints on scientists, technical information takes years or decades to result in governance actions. Highly complex issues are even harder to bring to broad understanding, especially if communication is: (a) centered on process complexity and not clear process trends, and (b) not focused on the simple direct impacts on day-to-day life of an average citizen.

5 Potential Steps Forward

Measurable progress will require paradigm shifts in how we:

(a) do interdisciplinary research,
(b) communicate scientific findings, and
(c) channel knowledge into intelligent (= far-sighted) political decisions.

We must keep science as rigorous as possible but not bury the major findings in process details. Communicating applied science should not always end simply with a publication: when appropriate, scientists should potentially help penetrate essential information into management sectors. Most senior managers and politicians (and their staff) don't have the time or training to read the latest scientific literature. The precautionary principle should be logically applied when data is incomplete. Information must be made even more available. For people in developing countries, access to articles is not possible with the fees of US $20–40 that most scientific journals charge for internet access. Arguably, scientists or those attempting to apply legitimate, spin-less science, should learn and deploy messaging tools from other sectors, including social media, to improve the penetration of key messages. These must explain complex processes in simple ways while giving clear guidance on how to act or react. These are difficult challenges even with non-politicized issues.

Paradigm shifts are difficult to initiate in simple systems, and even more difficult in complex systems, yet they do occur with surprising frequency (cf. Kuhn 1970). Modern society has been structured under paradigms that typically ignore unsustainable human activities, making change seem like an impossible or absurd task (cf. Stern 2009). Governments have failed to acknowledge the early warnings that current governance models require modification to take us successfully into the future. Each IPCC report has been followed by increased empirical evidence of climate related impacts, now reported almost on a daily basis throughout the globe. Meanwhile, increasingly clever attacks on the science, often vested upon unmitigated fossil fuel use (cf. UCS 2007) have manipulated the political windows needed for proactive climate action. The economic meltdown that explicitly surfaced in 2008, with its extreme local through global impacts, is a prominent result of ignoring complex system interactions with rapid negative tipping-points that were not imagined until after the fact. This example reflects a complex system behavior that could similarly occur within the fundamental bio-physical systems that support our social and economic capital (cf. Meadows 2008; Rockstrom et al. 2009). If humans are not able to induce key operational paradigm shifts, global change and other 21st century drivers will force us to. Meanwhile, traditional approaches to doing and applying science are not gaining traction as the windows of opportunity close.

References

AAAS – American Association for the Advancement of Science (2011): Statement of the Board of Directors of the AAAS Regarding Personal Attacks on Climate Scientists. Washington/D.C.

Baker, P. (2009): Climate Change Brews up Trouble for Coffee Growers. In: Science and Development Network, August 5

Bush, M. B; Silman, M. R.; Urrego, D. (2004): 48,000 Years of Climate and Forest Change in a Biodiversity Hotspot. In: Science, No. 303, pp. 827–829

Diamond, J. (2005): Collapse: How Societies Choose to Fail or Succeed. New York

Diemont, St. A. W. (2006): Ecosystem Management and Restoration as Practiced by the Indigenous Lacandon Maya of Chiapas, Mexico. Ohio State University: PhD Dissertation

Diemont, St. A. W; Martin, J. F.; Levy-Tacher, S. I. (2006a): Energy Evaluation of Lacandon Maya Indigenous Swidden Agroforestry in Chiapas, Mexico. In: Agroforestry Systems, Vol. 66/No. 1, pp. 23–42

Diemont, St. A. W.; Martin, J. F.; Levy-Tacher, S. I.; Nigh, R. B.; Lopez, P. R.; Golicher, J. D. (2006b): Lacandon Maya Forest Management: Restoration of Soil Fertility Using Native Tree Species. In: Ecological Engineering, Vol. 28, pp. 205–212

Douterlungne, D.; Levy-Tacher, S. I.; Golicher, D. J.; Dañobeytia, F. R. (2010): Applying Indigenous Knowledge to the Restoration of Degraded Tropical Rain Forest Clearings Dominated by Bracken Fern. In: Restoration Ecology, Vol. 18/No. 3, pp. 322–329

Dresner, S. (2002): The Principles of Sustainability. London

Earth Charter (2000): URL: www.earthcharter.org

Ericksen, P.; Thornton, P.; Notenbaert, A.; Cramer, L; Jones, P.; Herrero, M. (2011): Mapping Hotspots of Climate Change and Food Insecurity in the Global Tropics. CCAFS Report No. 5. CGIAR Research Program on Climate Change, Agriculture and Food Security (CCAFS). Copenhagen, Denmark (URL: www.ccafs.cgiar.org)

Friedman, T. L. (2009): Hot, Flat, and Crowded 2.0. London

Grant, S.; Berkes, F. (2007): Fisher Knowledge as Expert System: A Case from the Longline Fishery of Grenada, the Eastern Caribbean. In: Fisheries Research, Vol. 84, pp. 162–170

Hansen, J.; Ruedy, R.; Sato, M.; Lo, K. (2010): Global Surface Temperature Change. In: Reviews of Geophysics, Vol. 48, RG4004, doi:10.1029/2010RG000345

ICO – International Coffee Organization (2009): Climate Change and Coffee. Current Perspectives. London (ICC 103-6 Rev. 1)

IPCC – Intergovernmental Panel on Climate Change (2007): Climate Change 2007. Synthesis Report. Contribution of Working Groups I, II and III to the Fourth Assessment Report of the Intergovernmental Panel on Climate Change. Geneva (IPCC)

Kuhn, Th. S. (1970): The Structure of Scientific Revolutions. Chicago

Levy-Tacher, S. I.; Duncan-Glicher, J. (2004): How Predictive is Traditional Ecological Knowledge? The Case of the Lacandon Maya Fallow Enrichment System. In: Interciencia, Vol. 29/No. 9, pp. 496–503

Lips, K. (1999): Mass Mortality and Population Declines of Anurans at an Upland Site in Western Panama. In: Conservation Biology, Vol. 13/No. 1, pp.117–125

Lips, L. R.; Burrowes, P. A.; Mendelson III, J. R.; Parra-Olea, G. (2005): Amphibian Declines in Latin America: Widespread Population Declines, Extinctions, and Impacts. In: Biotropica, Vol. 72/No. 2, p. 163

Loarie, S. R.; Duffy, P. B.; Hamilton, H.; Asnerl, G. P.; Field, C.; Ackerly, D. D. (2009): The Velocity of Climate Change. In: Nature, Vol. 462, pp. 1052–1055

Lüthi, D.; Le Floch, M.; Bereiter, B.; Blunier, Th.; Barnola, J. M.; Siegenthaler, U.; Raynaud, D.; Jouzel, J.; Fischer, H.; Kawamura, K.; Stocker, T. F. (2008): High-resolution Carbon Dioxide Concentration Record 650,000–800,000 Years Before Present. In: Nature, Vol. 453, pp. 379–382

Meadows, D. H. (2008): Thinking in Systems. White River Junction/VT

Medina, M. M. (2009): Estado de avance en la investigación de las comunidades de frailejón que están siendo afectadas por insectos plaga y hongos fitopatógenos en el PNN Chingaza [Advances in Research of the Frailejón Communities Affected by Insects and Fungi in the Chingaza National Park Bogota]. Colombia

NRC – National Research Council (2002): Abrupt Climate Change: Inevitable Surprises. Washington/D.C.

Novacek, M. J.; Cleland, E. E. (2001): The Current Biodiversity Extinction Event: Scenarios for Mitigation and Recovery. In: Proceedings of the National Academy of Sciences, Vol. 98/ No. 10, pp. 5466–5470

Oreskes, N. (2004): The Scientific Consensus on Climate Change. In: Science, Vol. 306/No. 5702, p. 1686

Oreskes, N.; Conway, E. M. (2010.): Merchants of Doubt: How a Handful of Scientists Obscured the Truth on Issues from Tobacco Smoke to Global Warming. New York/NY

Oxfam (ed.) (2011): Briefing on the Horn of Africa Drought: Climate Change and Future Impacts on Food Security (URL: http://www.oxfam.org/sites/www.oxfam.org/files/briefing-hornofafrica-drought-climatechange-foodsecurity-020811.pdf; September 2, 2011)

Parmesan, C.; Yohe, G. (2003): A Globally Coherent Fingerprint of Climate Change Impacts across Natural Systems. In: Nature, Vol. 421, pp. 37–42

Pounds, J. A.; Fogden, M. P. L.; Campbell, J. H. (1999): Biological Response to Climate Change on a Tropical Mountain. In: Nature, Vol. 398, pp. 611–615

Rockstrom, J., and 28 others (2009): A Safe Operating Space for Humanity. In: Nature, Vol. 461, pp. 472–475

Sachs, J. (2008): Common Wealth: Economics for a Crowded Planet. New York

Satterthwaite, D. (2009): The Implications of Population Growth and Urbanization for Climate Change. In: Environment & Urbanization, Vol. 21/No. 2, pp. 545–567

Stern, N. (2009): A Blueprint for a Safer Planet: How to Manage Climate Change and Create a New Era of Progress and Prosperity. London

UCS – Union of Concerned Scientists (ed.) (2007): Smoke Mirrors and Hot Air: How ExxonMobil Uses Big Tobacco's Tactics to Manufacture Uncertainty on Climate Science. Cambridge/MA

Valdes, P. (2011): Built for Stability. In: Nature Geoscience, No. 4, pp. 414–416

Whitfield, S. M.; Bell, K. E.; Philippi, T.; Sasa, M.; Bolanos, F.; Chaves, G.; Savage, J. M.; Donnelly, M. A. (2007): Amphibian and Reptile Declines over 35 Years at La Selva, Costa Rica. In: Proceedings of the National Academy of Science, doi:10.1073/pnas.0611256104

Cultural Sustainability and Sustainable Communities Initiative in Developing Countries

Evidence from Vietnam and Indonesia*

Kien To

1 Introduction

1.1 Cultural Sustainability and Sustainable Community

The term sustainable development (SD) was used by the Brundtland Commission which coined what has become the most often quoted definition of SD as development that "meets the needs of the present without compromising the ability of future generations to meet their own needs" (WCED 1987, p. 16). In 2005, the United Nations World Summit confirmed its view on the key pillars of SD by reaffirming to "promote the integration of the three components of sustainable development – economic development, social development and environmental protection – as interdependent and mutually reinforcing pillars" (UN 2005, pp. 11f.). This conventional concept of sustainable development has commonly been illustrated by using three overlapping ellipses like in Figure 1.

However, there has been an emerging opinion that culture is integral to sustainability, particularly with respect to community development. In other words, culture can be framed as the fourth key pillar of sustainability, and cultural sustainability should be considered. As early as 1995, UNESCO published the book "The Cultural Dimension of Development. Towards a Practical Approach", in which it is stated that culture is gradually emerging out of the realm of social sustainability and being recognized as having a separate, distinct, and integral role in sustainable development" (UNESCO 1995, p. 22). Jonathan Hawkes states that culture and cultural heritage must be recognized as parallel to the respect for environment, social inclusiveness, and economic equity (Hawkes 2001, p. vii). The United Nations also emphasizes on the essence of cultural diversity to SD:

---

* This research was conducted when the author was affiliated as a Postdoctoral Researcher (a Fellow of Japan Society for the Promotion of Science) at the Department of Architecture and Urban Design, Faculty of Human-Environment Studies, Kyushu University, Fukuoka, Japan.

> "Peace, security, stability and respect for human rights and fundamental freedoms, including the right to development, as well as respect for cultural diversity, are essential for achieving sustainable development and ensuring that sustainable development benefits all." (UN 2002, p. 9)

Figure 1: The Conventional Three-pillar Scheme of SD

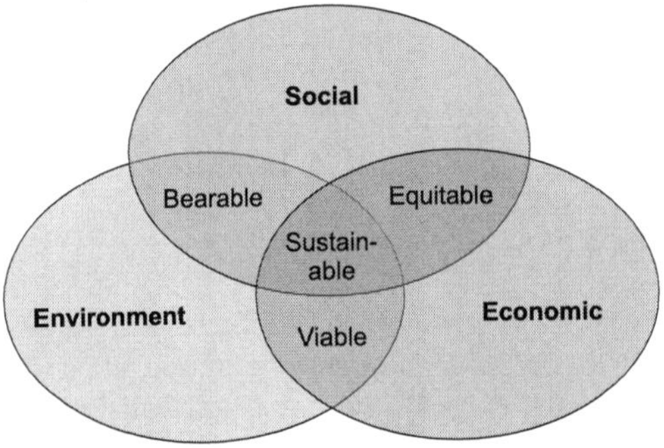

Source: Dréo 2007

In their paper "Culture as a Key Dimension of Sustainability: Exploring Concepts, Themes, and Models", Nancy Duxbury and Eileen Gillette state that "there has been a greater appreciation for culture as a significant component of sustainability" and "this idea is thinly distributed but pervasive in the literature" (Duxbury/Gillette 2007, p. 2).

Figure 2 presents a graphical model of the new and complete four-pillar scheme of SD as a four-set Venn diagram, along with a description of each regime of intersection.

The new scheme retains the three intersections of social, economic, and environmental sustainability, described as being *equitable, bearable* and *viable* respectively. Newly emerged intersections are:

- Zone 7 (Socio-Cultural): Should be *compatible,* as there have been many bad cases around the world where exotic culture conflicted with the local society.
- Zone 9 (Culturo-Economic): Should be *compromisable,* as economic development is often more prioritized than cultural development and preservation, and it also often spoils local traditional cultural values (see the paradox in Figure 9).
- Zone 10 (Culturo-Environmental): Should be *durable,* as the two elements nurture each other along with the evolution of the society.

- Zone 11 to 14 (intersections of three out of four dimensions): Should be *harmonizable,* as these dimensions often conflict with one another and any extreme development of one dimension without balancing with the other two can cause an unbalanced state for all.
- Zone 15 (The ultimate intersection of all the four dimensions): Should be *sustainable* to achieve sustainability (see more in the case study section).

Figure 2: The New and Complete Four Pillar Scheme of SD Illustrated by Four-Set Venn Diagram

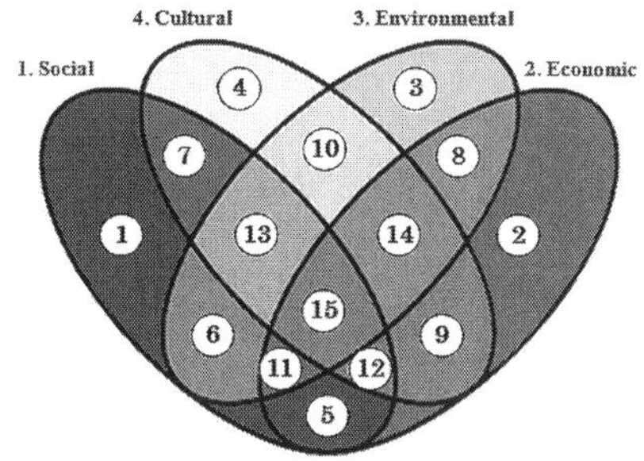

Set / Zone: 1.Social 2. Economic 3.Environmental

Zone	Intersections	Intersections (verbal)	Vision
5	1∩2	Socio-Economic	Equitable
6	1∩3	Socio-Environmental	Bearable
7	1∩4	Socio-Cultural	Compatible
8	2∩3	Econo-Environmental	Viable
9	2∩4	Culturo-Economic	Compromisable
10	3∩4	Culturo-Environmental	Durable
11	1∩2∩3	Socio-Econo-Environmental	Harmonizable
12	1∩2∩4	Socio-Culturo-Economic	Harmonizable
13	1∩3∩4	Socio-Culturo-Environmental	Harmonizable
14	2∩3∩4	Culturo-Econo-Environmental	Harmonizable
15	1∩2∩3∩4	Socio-Culturo-Econo-Environmental	Sustainable

Author's archive

With regard to the cultural pillar specifically, cultural sustainability can be defined as "the ability to retain cultural identity and to allow change to be guided in ways that are consistent with the cultural values of a people" (SDRI 1998, p. 1). Cultural sustainability relates to a number of elements such as tangible elements (heritages, public places, public art, etc.) and intangible elements (local lifestyle, indigenous living culture, traditional identity, etc.). The case study sections will present more about these two elements.

Sustainable community (SC) is a component of sustainable habitat and SD in general. SC relates closely to cultural sustainability, because communities cradle, nurture, inhabit and retain cultures. Like SD, the need to incorporate culture (the fourth pillar) and creativity in SC planning to build sustainable cities and communities should be recognized. One of the important matters of SC is to retain a vital community life. Regarding this issue, Michael Brills interestingly discusses about the problems of mistaking community life (within a neighborhood) for public life (in a public space like a square or a mall), which he believes are "fundamentally different" (Brills 2001, p. 48). He argues that "many people see social relationships as either Private or Public. They don't distinguish an important third form, Community life", and then clarifies that "Public life is sociability with a diversity of strangers; Community life is sociability with people you know somewhat". Finally, Brills emphasizes:

> "Some of our nostalgia and mourning is not for public life at all, not for the world of strangers; it is for something quite different, real and precious: local neighborhood life, community, a world of neighbors and friends, the parochial realm." (Brills 2001, p. 53)

In the case study part, we will see that the citizens at the case sites still retain tight social connection and vital community life, and they value them.

Nowadays, "for the first time in history, more than half the world's population lives in urban areas. Over 90% of urbanization is taking place in the developing world" (World Bank 2011a). Therefore, the way our urban communities (particularly those in developing countries) currently develop will largely determine our success or failure in achieving SC as well as SD goals in the future.

1.2 Community Participation and SC with Focus on Developing Countries

Looking back on the history of community participation,

> "although the idea of participation in building and planning can be traced to preliterate societies, community participation is of more recent origin. It is commonly associated with the idea of involving local people in social development. The most important influences derive from the third world community development movement of the 1950s and 1960s, Western social work, and community radicalism." (Midgley 1986, p. 1)

> "In 1994, a new planning paradigm was declared by the United Nations Centre for Human Settlements in Nairobi, Kenya, stating that new development planning should consider community participation, involvement of all interest groups, horizontal and vertical coordination, sustainability, financial feasibility, and interaction of physical and economic planning. The declaration concluded that community becomes the main agent of development because it is the community, which is directly impacted upon by development planning. The new terminology of anti-centralistic planning such as bottom-up planning, participatory planning, grass roots planning, public involvement, collaborative planning, etc., show that new development planning paradigms should open more space for the public to participate in decision making processes that affected their own lives and future." (Widianingsih 2006, pp. 72f.)

Community participation can be enabled through promoting decentralization. G. Shabbir Cheema and Dennis A. Rondinelli propose 14 specific benefits that may accrue from decentralization (Cheema/Rondinelli 1983, pp. 15f.), such as:

- Decentralization can be a means of overcoming the severe limitations of centrally controlled national planning.

- Officials' knowledge of and sensitivity to local problems and needs can be increased.
- Decentralization can lead to more flexible, innovative, and creative administration.
- Decentralization allows local leaders to locate services and facilities more effectively within communities.
- Decentralization can increase political stability and national unity by giving groups the ability to participate more directly in development decision-making.

Community participation is commonly reflected in community-based planning (CBP), a pattern of participatory planning which focuses on community actions and promotes community involvement in the planning process. CBP comes in many forms, from participation in local organizations to the preparation of a community-based plan for official adoption. CBP may seek to address a variety of issues including preserving neighborhood identities, promoting affordable housing and facilitating new development. It establishes a participatory process for mobilizing communities and planning around grassroots issues and how the issues can relate to the broader municipal planning perspective (compilation from "Community Based Planning Background"[1]).

In developing countries, CBP is rather new and SC seems to be a distant target. These countries are facing many socio-economic and political challenges on the way toward sustainability. Many people are living in the way that they can get quick benefits in the short run, no matter how badly it affects their living environment in the long run, especially with the vision to their future generations. Thus, the environment is getting worse. This is a challenge of balancing developmental and environment priorities that most countries are facing. Moreover, developing countries lack not only financial capacity, but also technology, knowledge, expertise and experience in promoting CBP and SC. Therefore, the role of international collaboration and technology and experience transfer from the foregoers (mainly developed countries) are very essential. For instance, in the case study sections, we can see the important role of *Japan International Cooperation Agency* (JICA), *Deutsche Gesellschaft für Technische Zusammenarbeit* (GTZ) or *US Aid* (USAID) in transferring know-hows, knowledge and experience to Vietnam and/or Indonesia in many collaborative development projects in the two countries. Another big issue for developing countries is the weak urban governance.

1 Community Based Planning Background. eThekwini Online publication (URL: http://www.durban.gov.za/durban/government/abms/index_html/conference/ntsiki/).

> "Regulation of economic activities requires state capacity and commitments that are all too rare in developing countries. Market mechanisms also hold promise to motivate more environmentally sound actions. However, few developing countries have the institutional conditions necessary to advance market-based strategies for environmental protection." (O'Rourke 2003, pp. 1f.)

Therefore, good SC initiatives in developing countries are valuable and encouraging, and should be explored and expanded to more communities.

1.3 From Theory and Concept to Practice and Initiative

In practice, urban planning is very much case-based, in contrast to the general theories introduced above. Urban areas differ with respect to a number of factors such as locality, socio-cultural context, economic development level, local living culture, etc.

To reflect some of the aspects of the theoretical discussion above, such as the intersection among "social", "economic" and "cultural" pillars (see Figure 2, zone 12) in the four-pillar sustainability concept and the community participation movement, the following interesting showcases in two developing countries, i.e. Vietnam and Indonesia, are introduced based on field surveys in recent years.

2 Case Study in Vietnam

2.1 Overview of CBP Issues in Vietnam

Urban planning in Vietnam has been very much top-down oriented. There have been a limited number of bottom-up approaches from the community. According to the World Bank, one of the biggest sponsors for participatory planning projects in the country:

> "In early 2000-s, the government started a new pilot policy to decentralize the decision-making from central to provincial level. The new approach invited local beneficiaries to participate in the decision-making process and the implementation of local development projects. They neither knew how to participate nor had adequate capacity and experience. At the same time, the mechanism for people's participation was weak, and guidance and information to help them take part in the decision-making process were not available." (World Bank 2011b)

Nevertheless, along with the course of international integration, the situation gradually changed.

> "In Vietnam, over two million people have escaped poverty thanks to a bottom-up, participatory planning approach that provided small-scale infrastructure for poor, vulnerable communes and income for local people through employment in its construction." (World Bank 2011b)

There are still big challenges for CBP in Vietnam.

> "For a long time, top-down planning was seen as the way to implement political choices in efforts to improve living standards in Vietnam. However, this led to the development of infrastructure that failed to match community needs, largely as a result of weak administrative capacity, a lack of transparency and accountability in the use of public funds, the disconnect between the decision-makers and beneficiaries, and the lack of project-based planning." (O'Rourke 2003, p. 2) And

> "popular participation and grassroots demand for a political voice have grown, but the country remains a one-party state, centrally driven for the most part. Although the country has moved forward with its decentralization framework, the implementation is uneven." (World Bank 2011c)

2.2 Introduction of the Case Study Site: The Old Quarter of Hanoi

Hanoi is the most ancient capital city in Southeast Asia, having celebrated its millennium in 2010. It is the second largest city in Vietnam (after Ho Chi Minh City) and an important socio-cultural and politico-economic center of the country. Hanoi has rich traditional streetscapes and cultural heritage sites, and comprises a mixture of traditional settlements and new developments. During its long urban evolution, Hanoi was alternately ruled by different foreign regimes, through which many exotic cultural elements were brought in. However, indigenous elements have always remained and flourished, particularly in the Old Quarter (OQ) – the root of the city. This 100 ha quarter (also commonly called "36 Old Streets" or sometimes "Ancient Quarter") has been serving as an administrative center, a highly dense residential area (app. 660 residents/ha in late 1990's) as well as a trade center for many centuries (To 2008, p. 457; see Figure 3 and Figure 4).

With regard to cultural properties, the popular dwelling form called a "tube house" is the most significant housing form here. Additionally, there are a number of religious buildings like temples and pagodas.

Although Hanoi has a long history of urban development, it is only after the "Doi Moi" (Economic Reform) in 1986 that urbanization became remarkable, making drastic changes in urban fabrics (see Figure 5).

> "The OQ is not an exception. Under rising modernization processes, many old tube houses (especially those over 100 years old) were torn down for new commercial-oriented constructions." (To 2008, p. 458; see Figure 6)

Figure 3: Map of Central Hanoi (dotted line shows the OQ)

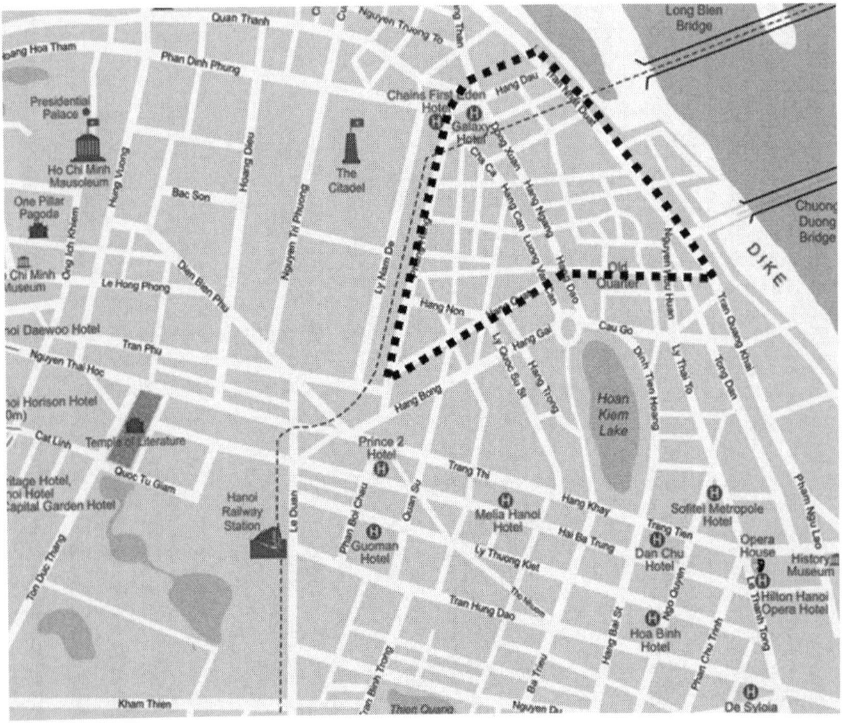

Author's archive

Figure 4: Panoramic View of Hang Buom Street (Formerly a Chinatown), an East-West Arterial Busy Street during Off-Pick Hour

Author's archive

Figure 5: Comparison of Different Factors on Hanoi before and after Economic Reform

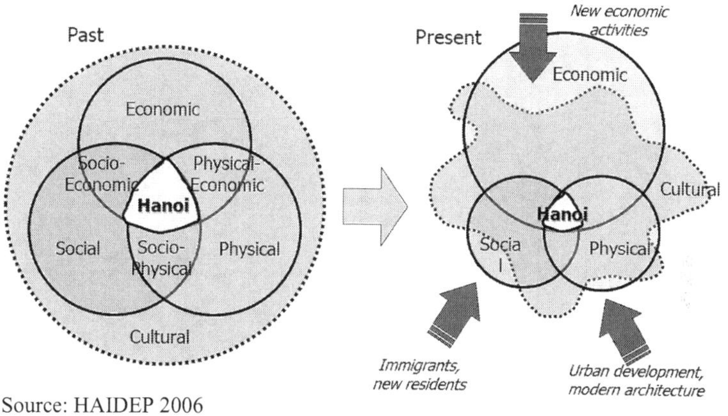

Source: HAIDEP 2006

Many temples and pagodas have also been destroyed, occupied, modified, or reconstructed. Thus, it has become a pressing task to preserve, reclaim and restore those cultural properties (Figure 7 shows my effort for preservation through a virtual restoration project). Therefore, the OQ was officially recognized as a National Heritage site for preservation in 2004, which should be compliant with the Heritage Act.

The biggest challenge now is how to balance new development with the preservation task. The OQ has three dominant roles:

(1) a vibrant central business district,
(2) a very high density neighborhood and
(3) the most popular sightseeing spot in Hanoi.

From the tourism industry aspect, a large part of the community gets benefits from the industry (e.g. hotels, restaurants, travel agencies, shops, etc.) Tourists come to the OQ for both tangible and intangible properties (see Figure 8). So tourism boosts up the need for more and better services. Consequently, more cultural properties have been invaded. But this physical modernization ruins the tangible and intangible values. This is the "Preservation-Development" dilemma in the OQ.

Figure 9 shows the complexity of the dilemma from the system dynamics viewpoint. The "plus" and "minus" arrows respectively indicate the "reinforcing" and "balancing" impacts. In this diagram, we can see that both phenomena that influence the strength of "traditional values", "international integration" and "commercialization & modernization", are incompatible with it. The diagram reflects the paradox of preservation and development happening in many touristic old towns like Hanoi and it is not easy to solve it.

Figure 6: A Tube House Located at Gateway to the OQ (Arrow) was being Reconstructed to Become a Restaurant (2006)

Author's archive

Figure 7: Virtual Restoration Project of the Tube House at #47 Hang Bac Street, Accomplished in 2008

Author's archive

Figure 8: Traditional Values of the OQ

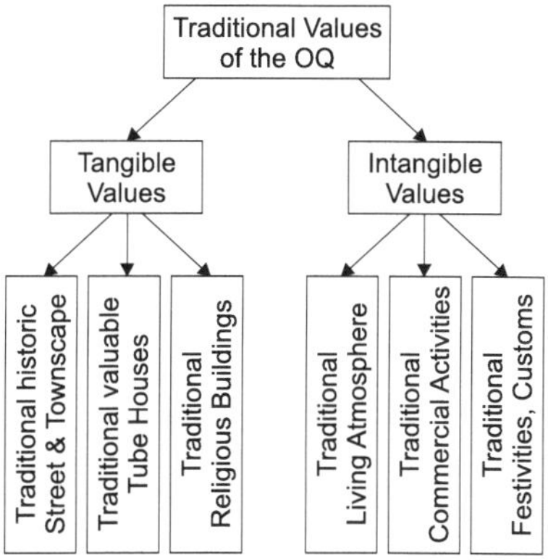

Author's archive

Figure 9: Complexity of "Preservation-Development" Dilemma in the OQ from the System Dynamics Viewpoint

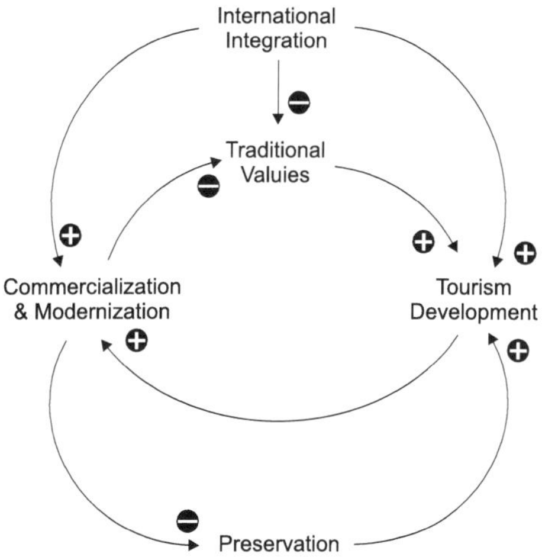

Author's archive

Figure 10 shows a comparison of schemes of all stakeholders in the OQ preservation before 1990 and now. In the past, there were three stakeholders: The Old Quarter Management Board (OQMB) founded in 1996, ward authorities, and domestic experts. The community had no role in the process. Nowadays there are 3 more stakeholders, i.e. the community, foreign experts and foreign funding bodies.

In terms of community cohesion, the OQ still retains strongly connected communities. The communities have retained good common activities, living customs and particular lifestyles such as group morning exercise, occasional cleaning days, and hanging around at sidewalk food and/or tea stalls (stalls as community spots; see Figure 11).

Figure 10: Comparison of Schemes of all Stakeholders in Preservation of OQ before 1990 (left) and Now (right)

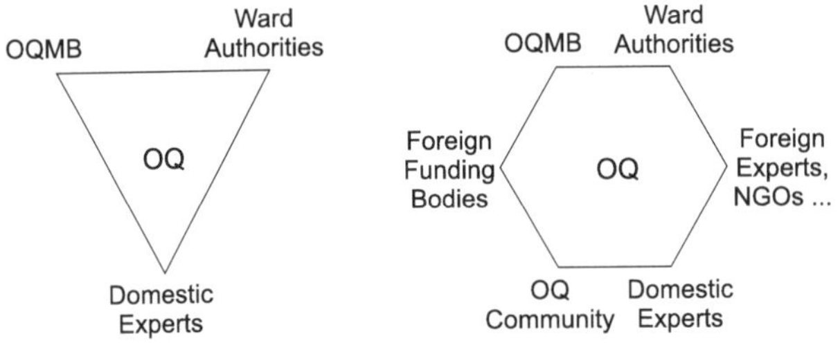

Author's archive

Figure 11: Tea/Food Stalls as Community Spots (left) and Foreign Tourists Enjoying Local Styled Street Beer (right)

Author's archive

2.3 Autonomy and Communal Committee

As mentioned earlier, although governance in Vietnamese cities is very much top-down oriented, there are rising signals of bottom-up community autonomy. For instance, each community appoints their own communal steering committee consisting a head, vice-heads and councilors, etc., who (mostly retirees) are very active to social activities. The committee comprises different sectors and plays a key role in management, mobilization and reconciliation of the community.

2.4 SC Initiative: Hang Buom Ward Pilot Project

This project was conducted within the framework of the pilot project "Sustainable Development of the Ancient Quarter" implemented within "Hanoi Integrated Development and Environmental Program" (HAIDEP). This is a collaboration program between Hanoi People's Committee and the Japan International Cooperation Agency (JICA, the main foreign partner). The project established standardized procedures and steps to guide local people on how to take part in the decision-making process. It established platforms for participation, such as local consultation meetings to identify the core values of the OQ or necessary infrastructure, and take part in small-scale local development projects. Hang Buom Street was selected to implement the community participation pilot project.

Since September 2005, the pilot project task force comprising JICA and local experts conducted several comprehensive field surveys on socio-economic, cultural and physical aspects in the OQ. The detailed reports on the socio-economic situation as well as assessment and proposals for preserving and promoting the core values of the OQ were presented to the local authorities and people through multiple "all-stakeholders meetings" (see Figure 12).

The study team used assessment methods with community participation to identify activities to be piloted. Hang Buom St. and one block (Hang Buom, Hang Giay, Luong Ngoc Quyen, Ta Hien) in Hang Buom Ward was selected as a pilot site. With support from the project, local authorities and residents implemented some pilot activities such as improving environmental and commercial conditions in some houses (#53 and #93 Hang Buom St.), cleaning the street, installing public dustbins and moveable pent-roofs, restoring conferring materials, introducing historic values of Bach Ma temple (cf. JICA 2006).

The highlight of the activities was "The Event Week in Hang Buom Street" which lasted from 17th to 26th June 2006 at Hanoi Cultural House at #88 Hang Buom St. and Bach Ma temple (see Figure 13).

Figure 12: An All-Stakeholder Meeting (April 2006) with Representatives of Residents of Hang Buom Ward where Residents had Chance to Brainstorm Ideas and Discussion Group for the Project[a]

a – Left: The Author sat in Middle; right: The Author stood leading a Group

Author's archive

Figure 13: Dragon Dance on the Opening of Event Week (left) and a Scene of Photovoice Exhibition

Source: Viet Bao Newspaper, 19 June 2006

The program included the introduction of traditional well-known food in Hang Buom St., the presentation of anthropological films on the cultural values of the OQ, the exhibition of preservation and re-development models of some pilot streets, and particularly the "Photovoice" exhibition.

Photovoice (originally "Photo Novella", cf. Wang/Burris 1994) is a method by which people can identify, represent, and enhance their community through a specific photographic technique (cf. Wang/Burris 1997, p. 369).

> "It also promotes critical discussion about important issues through the dialogue about photographs they have taken. Their concerns may reach policy makes through public forums and the display of their photographs. By using a camera to record their concerns and needs, it permits individuals who rarely have contact with those who make decisions over their lives to make their voices heard." (Compilation by Pranee Liamputtong; cf. Liamputtong 2010, p. 197).

Within reason, the Photovoice method was used in the project. As a subproject ("My life – My view"), it involved 20 volunteer residents. They were provided with digital cameras by the taskforce, and were taught how to use them. Then they were requested to take photographs of their neighborhood's tangible and intangible cultural values as well as their concerns and needs based on their point of view.

> "After 3 months, around 6,000 photos were taken, reflecting various aspects of the life in the OQ. This activity not only aimed to preserve and introduce the OQ but also helped the residents understand and love their neighborhood more. Mr. Nguyen Van Sam, 71, living at # 85 Hang Buom St., who took photos of the night market said, 'There are markets in the OQ during the day, but without the night market, the quarter would be so humdrum'. Dr. Iwata Shizuo, the head of the taskforce team said: 'With the community participation, the project will help Hanoi City find out suitable solutions for the preservation and renovation of the OQ in the future'." (LDN 2006)

3 Case Study in Indonesia

3.1 Overview of Community-related Urban Issues in Indonesia

> "In 1998, Indonesia faced political upheaval and financial crisis. The country was marred by its graft-ridden political and administrative systems and poverty had increased tremendously. [...] With 17,000 islands and millions of villages across the archipelago, Indonesia had to reach out to its poorest areas to ensure that these populations enjoy an equal opportunity to grow and develop. [...] Therefore, poverty alleviation has become a priority for Indonesia. [...] To accelerate government efforts to reduce poverty and to ensure equity and inclusiveness, on August 16, 2006, the President of Indonesia [...] announced the National Program for Community Empowerment (Program Nasional Pemberdayaan Masyarakat – PNPM) as the policy and operational umbrella for all community empowerment programs in the country. The PNPM builds primarily upon the previous ten years of successful experience with the Kecamatan Development Program (KDP) and the Urban Poverty Project (UPP), now the PNPM-Rural and PNPM-Urban, respectively. Adopting a community-driven development approach and with technical and financial assistance from the International Bank for Reconstruction and Development, the PNPM is now a national program covering all villages and cities in the country. The overall PNPM objectives are being achieved through: (a) communities participating in an open planning process; (b) the provision of grants to communities directly and transparently to finance an open 'menu' of poverty-alleviation activities; and (c) enhancing the capacity of central and local governments to partner with community organizations in the provision of services.

> Community participation in PNPM-Rural and PNPM-Urban is high. The participation of women in PNPM meetings averaged 45%. Nearly 60% of those who attend these meetings are from the poorer segments of the community. The 2008 impact evaluation and gender review found, however, that the PNPM could do much more to promote the participation of women and vulnerable groups." (World Bank 2011d; see Figure 14)

Figure 14: PNPM Pilot Program

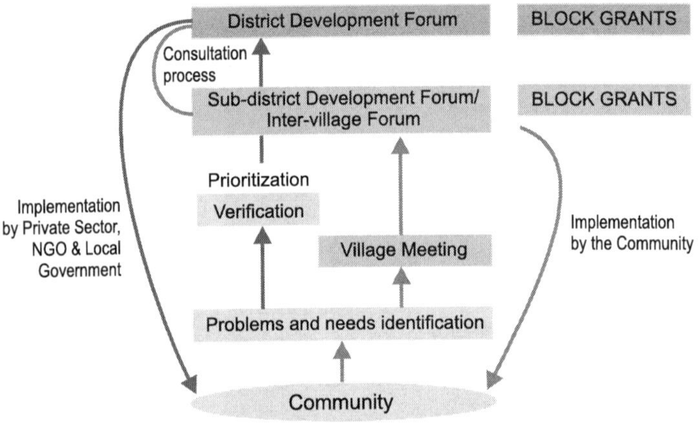

Source: World Bank 2011e

Therefore, it can be said that post-Suharto Indonesia is moving towards more participatory development planning.

> "Decentralization process has been opening chances for local government to develop new planning mechanism as shown in various localities such as in Bima and Dompu regencies under GTZ's 'Support for Decentralization Measures' project, 35 municipalities and regencies in various provinces under USAID's 'Performance Oriented Regional Management' project and budget planning in Bandung regency." (Widianingsih 2005, p. 69)

Although the whole country is moving toward decentralization, there are many differences in practice depending on the social, cultural, and political backgrounds of the localities. Among others, successful community initiatives could be found in Yogyakarta's urban municipalities, which adopted participatory planning approach.

3.2 Introduction of the Case Study Site in Yogyakarta City

With a population of about 400.000, Yogjakarta City (also Jogja, Jogjakarta) can be classified as a small and medium city in the Yogyakarta Special Region, Indonesia (see Figure 15, left). The area of the province is 3,185 km^2, which is Indonesia's second smallest next to Jakarta Capital Province. In the local administration, the province is composed of four regencies and one city. Yogyakarta City, capital of the province, is geographically located in the center of the province (compilation from Shima et al. 2006, p. 5). The city is one of the most important tourist destinations in Indonesia and renowned as a center of classical Javanese culture. It is also famous as a center for Indonesian higher education accommodating a number of universities.

Figure 15: Location of Yogyakarta City (left) and Map of the Area of conducted Field-survey

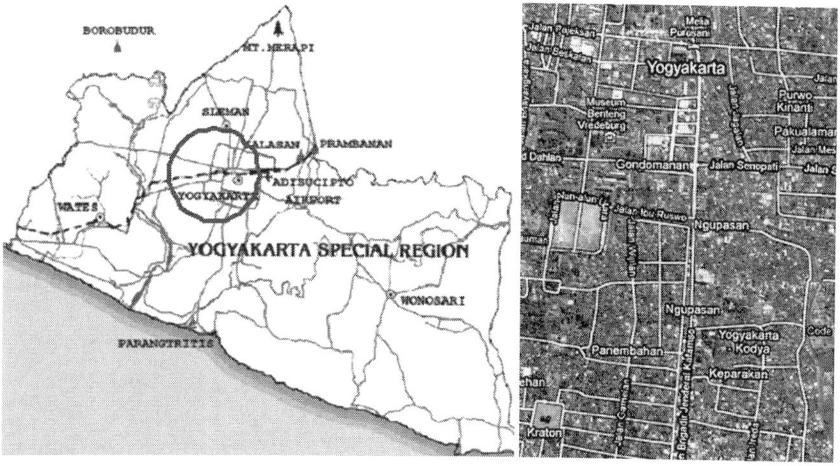

Source: Google Earth

Along with urban growth, the city is undergoing rapid development and transformation. This includes the displacement, consolidation, and transformation of kampong (urban village) on the urban fringe. After the 1998 national crisis, the government provided less fund allocation for kampong physical development, yet self-help kampong development rose. Interestingly, Yogyakarta was recognized as the only city in Indonesia that succeeded to handle slum areas in 2005. In addition, Yogyakarta gained the predicate of City of Tolerance on the national and international levels. The mayor of Yogyakarta also enacted the Kampong Based City Development Program in 2005 as the basis for sustainable development. The issue of Yogyakarta as a special province with the special privilege to manage its land and cultural assets (including having special government structure) has been lively debated until nowadays" (Murti 2010, pp. 7f.).

Table 1 shows the Indonesian terms for urban administration in Indonesia.

Table 1: Hierarchy of Urban Administration Level in Indonesia

Administration Level	Number of Households	Population
City – Kota	50,000–300,000	300,000–1,000,000
District – Kecamatan	10,000–50,000	50,000–125,000
Neighborhood – Kelurahan	1,000–10,000	2,500–7,500
Sub-neighborhood – RW[a]	50–500	500–1,000
Block – RT[b]	20–50	50–250

a – RW – Rukun warga (section of Kelurahan); b – RT: Rukun tetangga
Source: After Taylor 2009

3.3 SC Activities and Initiatives

My team and I conducted a field survey (October 2010) in the Southern part of Yogyakarta, along the North-South axial Jalan Wijilan Road down to Jalan Gamelan and on both sides of the axis (see Figure 15, right). From the fieldtrip, we could observe a number of community activities and initiatives toward SC and sustainability. With support of local assistants for arranging meetings and interpretation, we could interact with some community leaders and residents to understand more about their communities and their activities. The following are some good SC initiatives and lessons learned from the field trip.

"DIY Green and Clean" Program

In 2008, Daerah Istimewa Yogyakarta (DIY) (or Yogyakarta Special Region) in cooperation with PT Unilever Indonesia launched the "DIY Green and Clean" Program with the purpose to encourage good environmental waste management. The program was very successful from 2008 through 2010. In 2010, more than 300 RWs and hamlets were involved, with a target of 500 for this year (2011).

According to Mr. Asri Wahyuni, Chairman of PT Unilever Indonesia, "with this program people as actors can feel the benefits and economic value of waste management". And "in addition to assistance to the community, this program is expected to transmit an understanding of the love of the environment, both in terms of cleanliness and greening." Besides, "this program is getting tremendous response from the DIY community and able to drive change in people's behavior to create a clean and green environment". Followed the program was the "training of facilitators" for the 300 RWs in the districts of Sleman and Yogyakarta as well as over 250 "refreshing facilitators" in Kulon Progo, Bantul and Gunungkidul districts"[2] (see Figure 16).

Figure 16: Gateway to a Semifinalist RW of the Program (2010)

Author's archive

One of the very impressive outcomes of the program was the urban art works found throughout Yogyakarta.

> "A range of sites were made available for transformation in collaboration with mural artist Samuel Indratma. Handrails of the bridge were painted by the children and a prominent retaining wall was painted with a mural scene." (Dovey/Raharjo 2007, p. 13)

Through the art works, dirty ugly walls were turned into beautiful colorful graffiti walls, which look very vibrant and can carry meaningful messages (see Figure 17).

Community Leaders

Small communities have good autonomy for their development and management. Community leaders are usually motivated activists appointed by the community. They are often retirees with much time for community work, keep big responsibilities, and work voluntarily without salary. We interacted with two

2 Cf. Krjogja.com, 10 May 2011 (URL: http://www.krjogja.com/news/detail/83065/DIY.Green.and.Clean.Target.500.RW.html)

very active and creative leaders of the Gadjah Wong community (RT45/RW08) which contains approximately 30 households (see Figure 18).

Figure 17: Graffiti Art Work at a Common Playground with the Message "Green Village Pioneer for Green Justice"

Author's archive

Figure 18: Two Leaders of RT05/RW08 Community

Author's archive

Community House and Community Playground

The Community house has a 45 m^2 multi-purpose room. It has a small library set up in 2003 (books donated by residents and kept by a volunteer), a table-tennis set, TV set, and a community photo exhibition (see Figure 19). The common playground is facilitated with a badminton court, fitness machines, a pavilion and many plants (see Figure 17).

Figure 19: The Community House (in the area RT05/RW08)

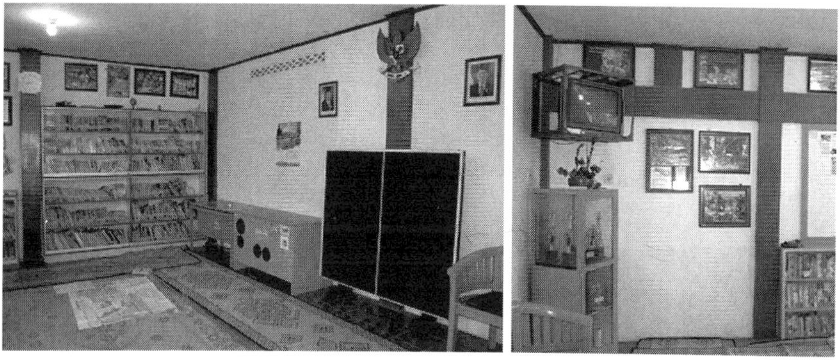

Author's archive

Open Space

There is a wide range of small open spaces in the community. Many open spaces are ambiguous in the way that they are widely used for both internal and public needs. Figure 20 shows a very good example of a 5,000 m^2 open space reserved for new development. When we visited, the community leaders expressed their idea to build on it an "Environmental Education Park for Kids", and consulted us on design and development ideas.

Figure 20: Open Space to Build an Environmental Education Park (RT05/RW08)

Author's archive

Semi-public Semi-private Space

The public/private status of pathways is often unclear to outsiders. Pathways with the presence of private stuff may be publicly accessible while others are not. Figure 21 shows a typical case where the originally private yard of a housing complex was converted to be a semi-public pathway.

Figure 21: A Semi-public Pathway within a Community

Author's archive

Waste Management

The waste/garbage management system in the area was surprisingly well-organized. We walked around several small communities (RTs), and everywhere where suitable, we could find a set of three sort-out trash bins (for metal, paper and plastic). Some residents even self-created their own extra garbage sorting bags hung on their houses' fences. Moreover, there were garbage storage shelters for the residents to gather, sort out, and orderly store garbage until it is regularly collected by the city (see Figure 22).

Night Watch Shelter

A small shelter known as a *gardu ronda* (night watch shelter) is built at the main entrance to each RT. It is used for purposes of security night watch and surveillance. They are designed and built in a very simple way, mostly unfurnished and there is no wall or gate. The designs are also not standardized among them (see Figure 23).

Figure 22: Very Good Waste Management System: Sort-out Bins provided by City (top-left), Residential Self-made Sort-out Bags (bottom-left), and Sort-out Garbage Storage Shelter (right)

Author's archive

Figure 23: Two Examples of Night Watch Shelters

Author's archive

Pathway Paving

Most of the vehicle pathways are paved in concrete tiles or asphalt. Many of the smaller paths are unpaved and at times covered with rubble. Paving formalizes public space, and thus, it is often done by the state. For some small pathways deep inside the community, however, paving is financed by the residents themselves who use it. Figure 24 shows a pathway which is being paved, and the site is well managed for the safety of the people passing by.

Figure 24: A Pathway is being Asphalted and the Site is Well Managed

Author's archive

4 Conclusions

This paper first discussed the emergent opinion that culture is integral to sustainability as the fourth pillar, particularly with respect to community. The most significant contribution was the novel development of the four-pillar scheme of sustainability. Next, it discussed the theoretical discourse and issues of community participation, CBP as well as SC with focus on developing countries.

The body of the paper focused on two study cases: Hanoi, Vietnam and Yogyakarta, Indonesia. By conducting a comprehensive field survey with a combination of observation, participation and interview methods, the paper explored new community initiatives toward SC in terms of autonomous development and management initiatives as well as policies and practical activities, and gave an insight into some good SC initiatives of the two cases to share lessons and experiences.

From the two case studies, it can be concluded that

- CBP is an innovative approach, as decentralization to the grass-roots level has never happened before in those countries.
- CBP has a number of benefits, such as:
  - Increased participation and active involvement of citizens in the development process.

  - More effective and realistic planning, including more integrated development planning.
  - Greater and more flexible, efficient, innovative administrative capability for local government.
  - Increased inter-municipal solidarity, human resource management and law enforcement.
- The key to the success of CBP is not just the planning results, but the whole planning process. Key elements to be focused on include: planning methodology, facilitation, training, monitoring and evaluation, and the linkage to the local government planning system.
- CBP is the right direction for the future, and should be expanded to more communities.

In the case of Hanoi, the following fundamental transitions toward SC can be recognized:

- From inactive to active, unconcerned to concerned.
- From merely top-town to partly bottom-up, from merely bureaucracy to partly democracy.

From the case of Yogyakarta, we could learn that:

- Competition among communities and municipalities is a very effective mechanism toward great self-improvement and social solidarity.
- Small-sized communities with good given autonomy can be very creative and sustainable.
- The importance of facilitators as multipliers for good trends and movements.

*

Acknowledgement

I would like to express my sincere gratitude to Japan Society for the Promotion of Science (JSPS) and German Academic Exchange Service (DAAD) in collaboration with Forum for Urban Future in Southeast Asia for their generous financial supports for the field surveys in Vietnam and Indonesia respectively. I wish to thank Florida Institute of Technology (FIT) for the kind invitation to present this research at the "Sustainability: Is it Worth It?" conference, FIT, March 8–10, 2011. My special thanks go to Professor *Atsushi Deguchi,* my host scholar at Kyushu University, for his great academic inspiration on the sustainability theme during my academic stay at the university. My gratefulness is extended to *Jonathan S. Krones* for the thorough proofreading and insightful comments of this paper.

References

Brills, M. (2001): Problems with Mistaking Community Life for Public Life. In: Places, Vol. 14/No. 2, pp. 48–55

Cheema, G. S.; Rondinelli, D. A. (1983): Decentralization and Development: Policy Implementation in Developing Countries. Beverley Hills/CA

Dovey, K.; Raharjo, W. (2007): Informal Settlement Fieldtrip – Yogyakarta (URL: http://www.placeresearch.net/publications-pdfs/informal-settlements.pdf)

Dréo, J. (2007): Illustration of Sustainable Development (URL: http://en.wikipedia.org/wiki/File:Sustainable_development.svg)

Duxbury, N.; Gillette, E. (2007): Culture as a Key Dimension of Sustainability. Exploring Concepts, Themes and Models (URL: www.cultureandcommunities.ca/downloads/WP1-Culture-Sustainability.pdf)

HAIDEP – Hanoi Integrated Development and Environmental Program (2006): HAIDEP's material collected by the Author

Hawkes, J. (2001): The Fourth Pillar of Sustainability. Culture's Essential Role in Public Planning. Melbourne/Australia

JICA – Japan International Cooperation Agency, Vietnam Office (in Hanoi) (2006) (URL: http://www.jica.go.jp/vietnam/english/office/others/media/2006/jun_02.html)

LDN (2006): The Event Week in Hang Buom Street: Opening an orientation for upgrading the Old Quarter. In: Lao Dong Newspaper, 19 June, Hanoi page

Liamputtong, P. (2010): Performing Qualitative Cross-Cultural Research. Cambridge/MA

Midgley, J. (1986): Community Participation, Social Development, and the State. London

Murti, Y. F. K. (2010): From Yogyakarta: Unfinished Story of Contesting Identities and Creating Negotiation Space on The History of Urban Development (URL: http://ypr.or.id/pdf_oleh-oleh_babad-kampung-dari-yogyakarta-cerita-yang-belum-selesai_id.pdf)

O'Rourke, D. (2003): Community-driven Regulation. Balancing Development and the Environment in Vietnam. Cambridge/MA

SDRI – Sustainable Development Research Institute (1998): Social Capital Formation and Institutions for Sustainability. Workshop Proceedings Prepared by Asoka Mendis, November 16–17. Vancouver (URL: www.williambowles.info/mimo/refs/soc_cap.html)

Shima, N.; Kidokoro, T.; Onishi, T.; Leksono, P. S. (2006): Challenges and Scopes Toward the Decentralized Regional Development Framework in Southeast Asian Countries. Several Lessons from Yogyakarta Special Province, Indonesia. 42nd ISoCaRP Congress, 2006 (URL: http://www.isocarp.net/Data/case_studies/768.pdf)

Taylor, J. (2009): Building on Understanding of Solo's Neighbourhood. Solo Citywide Indicator Projects. Data collected by the Author

To, K. (2008): Conservation Pressing Task and New Documentation of Old Tube Houses in Hanoi Old Quarter through the Case of No. 47 Hang Bac Street House. In: Journal of Architecture, Planning and Environmental Engineering (Transactions of Architectural Institute of Japan), No. 624, pp. 457–463

UN – United Nations (2005): World Summit Outcome. Resolution A/60/1, adopted by General Assembly. New York (URL: http://www.johannesburgsummit.org/html/documents/summit_docs/131302_wssd_report_reissued.pdf)

UN – United Nations (2005): World Summit Outcome. Resolution A/60/1, adopted by General Assembly. New York (URL: http://unpan1.un.org/intradoc/groups/public/documents/un/unpan021752.pdf)

UNESCO – United Nations Educational, Scientific and Cultural Organization (1995): The Cultural Dimension of Development: Towards a Practical Approach. Paris

Wang, C.; Burris, M. (1994): Empowerment through Photo Novella. Portraits of Participation. In: Health Education and Behavior, Vol. 21/No. 2, pp. 171–186

Wang, C.; Burris, M. (1997): Photovoice. Concept, Methodology, and Use for Participatory Needs Assessment. In: Health Education and Behavior, Vol. 24/No. 3, pp. 369–387

WCED – World Commission on Environment and Development (ed.) (1987): Our Common Future. Oxford

Widianingsih, I. (2005): Local Governance, Decentralization and Participatory Planning in Indonesia. Seeking a New Path to a Harmonious Society. In: Network of Asia-Pacific Schools and Institutes of Public Administration and Governance (NAPSIPAG) Annual Conference 2005, Beijing, December. pp. 69–90

Widianingsih, I. (2006): Local Governance, Decentralization and Participatory Planning in Indonesia. Seeking a New Path to a Harmonious Society. In: Ahmad, R.; Asian Development Bank (eds.): The Role of Public Administration in Building a Harmonious Society. Mandaluyong City/Philippines, pp. 69–89

World Bank (2011a): Urban Development (URL: http://go.worldbank.org/PQE9TNVDI0)

World Bank (2011b): Vietnam: Community Based Rural Infrastructure Project. Report (URL: http://go.worldbank.org/W2X3GA6BH0)

World Bank (2011c): East Asia Decentralizes – Vietnam (URL: http://go.worldbank.org/H0BTZLQA90)

World Bank (2011d): Results Profile: Indonesia's Community-Driven Development (URL: http://go.worldbank.org/CE4BSHHAA0)

World Bank (2011e): Indonesia. Support for Poor and Disadvantaged Areas Project (URL: http://go.worldbank.org/OQPKSLJKK0)

Perspectives of Cultural Interplays in Sustainability Research

Caroline Y. Robertson-von Trotha, Oliver Parodi, Robert Hauser

1 Introductory Remarks

On the basis of the interdisciplinary discussions of the topic of culture and sustainability in the present volume, the following will present a few of the – in our view – essential research tasks for the future, as well as possible goals for the future.

The scholarly discourse on sustainability that has been going on for some 20 years has been interdisciplinary from the very beginning. The topic of sustainable development has thus always cut across various fields: It is located at the intersection of theoretical and practical scholarly research and normative and political objectives. It has increasingly influenced political and social decision processes and is thus extending into the realm of real life. By observing the "cultural dimension" through the perspective of sustainable development, this area of knowledge and action is expanded and takes on many new and complex facets. The cultural dimension is not uncoupled from this process, but rather has its own effects, in turn, on the scholarly debate surrounding sustainability. The international and interdisciplinary contributions collected in this volume clearly show the diverse implications and points of contact between sustainable development and culture, from the perspective of different disciplines, theoretical backgrounds and the diverging cultural contexts of the nations represented herein. From these contributions, i.e., their scholarly and cultural perspectives, the research tasks of the future prove to be just as diverse. The workshop and the present volume represent the next steps of a continuous long-term dialogue on cultural and intercultural aspects of sustainable development. The continuation and intensification of this dialogue – with regard to both theoretical and practical implications – is necessary in order to concretely name the future tasks of global research on sustainability. Here, we can only highlight the future tasks that emerge particularly clearly against the backdrop of the discussions that have been conducted, and against the backdrop of the articles in this volume. It should here be noted that this act of highlighting is itself informed by a specific disciplinary and cultural background, and is also observed from that background. In our opinion, the following inadequacies can be identified with regard to the interactions between culture and sustainable development, allowing us to pinpoint areas that require further research.

2 Sustainability and Cultural Reference

The preparatory work for this book at two conferences as well as the contributions itself have made clear that although established sustainability concepts do indeed target sustainable social development, they have hitherto demonstrated no references to culture, or only very weak and implicit ones. Furthermore, the discussion showed that various connections between sustainability programmes and culture are conceivable. Here, the type of connection between the two depends largely on the objective at hand. For theoretical considerations, it is necessary to be able to integrate the cultural perspective into existing sustainability concepts. For the perspective that seeks practical guiding principles, the question of how a culture of sustainability can be established comes to the fore. These two points of view do not exclude one another, but rather are directly bound up with one another: It is only when cultural factors are accordingly taken into consideration in sustainability concepts that strategies and (political) control mechanisms can be identified, or rather developed, strategies and mechanisms with which a more sustainable culture can be established or promoted successfully. For the HGF Integrative Sustainability Concept mentioned in this book, for example, this could mean defining cultural goals by using a modern and theoretically well-founded cultural concept.

3 Normative Questions – Basic Assumptions

Implicit and partially inadequately thought-out "Western" assumptions form the basis of existing sustainability concepts, since these concepts are generally practical ones that seek guiding principles for action.

Questions about normative assumptions and the engagement with ethical issues – and specifically with implicit value conceptions and constructions – form an indispensable foundation for a "culturally sensitive" theory of sustainability. A more intensive engagement with these questions is a fundamental condition for establishing a theoretically grounded and well-founded sustainability programme that can be applied to other cultural spaces. In the field of cultural studies, this debate occurred quite early on. The Western or Eurocentric basic assumptions of early cultural theory were uncovered and critically examined by cultural studies and the debates surrounding postcolonialism. Contemporary cultural theories thus consider cultural practices to be value-neutral. Sustainability concepts have yet to undergo a similar process. Toward this end, we need to reflect critically on basic normative assumptions and the clear labelling (e.g. in self-description) of these assumptions. Many implicit normative assumptions became obvious in the debate surrounding growth, or rather degrowth: While American, European and Hispanic debates see degrowth as a viable path toward sustainable development, representatives from nations with greater relative poverty indeed concretely refused this perspective. It became apparent that degrowth suggestions emerge implicitly from saturated markets and high levels of widespread affluence, as is typical of most Western industrialised nations. For countries with greater poverty – which have experienced nothing other than stagnant or negative economic growth for at least the past few decades, if not longer – it is hard to understand how a global degrowth movement can be the recommended path toward sustainable development, for this recommendation is made with reference to Western sustainability conceptions alone. On the whole, more research is needed with regard to economic "growth aspects" to determine which roles growth and degrowth play under different basic cultural and economic conditions. Which subjects of growth are important (economy, population, civilisation, wealth, happiness ...)? How exactly does growth relate to development, and what are the supposed dependencies that factor into this? And what about growth as a cultural programme, one that has been at work for ages in Occidental cultural history? How is this development to be ethically evaluated from a global perspective?

4 Methodological Questions – Distinct Perspectives

Sustainability programmes and theories are devoted to large social contexts, and are applicable on the collective level (e.g. suggestions for laws, political regulations, economic regulations, etc.). The perspective and significance of the individual is generally disregarded or negated. If one intends for sustainability programmes and theories to actually be applicable, then it is impossible – from a cultural-theoretical point of view – to avoid bringing the individual into (a second) focus, in addition to the focus placed on collective aspects. Contemporary cultural theories (c.f., for example, Hansen 2003) view culture as an interplay between the collective and the individual (enculturation/individuation). In this respect, a comprehensive theory of sustainability is still largely lacking the half devoted to the individual. Furthermore the linkage and interdependences between the collective and the individual must be taken into account. This brings up the question of how we can empirically grasp the complex decision-making processes and calculations of individuals either for or against sustainable actions and ways of living. In order to be able to answer this question, we must first develop approaches that allow us to conceptually grasp the implicit – yet guiding – norms and values that underlie these complex decision-making processes and calculations.

In addition to this, with regard to conceptually grasping cultural diversity and sustainability on the meso-level, considerable research tasks become apparent. Cultural pluralism on the local level is an indispensable resource, yet one that has thus far received far too little consideration in these debates, on account of concepts and programmes that inadequately describe the meso-level. These concepts and programmes have hitherto related the distinct perspectives of the macro-level and the micro-level to one another, allowing meaningful inferences to be made about both levels, but in doing so have largely bypassed the meso-level.

5 Education for Sustainable Development – What Opportunities for Educating are there?

In addition to the problem areas mentioned above, a further problem area can be identified, albeit one that is located less on the scholarly level and more at the junctures between research and government (organisational administration and management). For example, in order to structure organisational – or rather institutional – cultures to be more sustainable, it is necessary to raise awareness in new ways. This process can be encouraged and promoted through specific course offerings and further education. In both research and teaching, even when there is an underlying general understanding of sustainability, the organisation and infrastructure of educational and research institutions are often only not very sustainable, or not sustainable at all. Approaches like that of the Karlsruhe School of Sustainability, which organises a comprehensive approach for sustainable work and living (including "personal sustainability") through special offerings of further education, lend great support to the process of raising awareness, and can lead to new perspectives on one's own work and life. Such processes of reflection and awareness can in turn lead to changes in actions and behaviour-changes that, in the best of cases, result collectively in more sustainable ways of living and working. A further goal can then be to identify and analyse weak points in one's own organisational and institutional culture, on the basis of a general model of sustainability, and to look for solutions that would lead to a more sustainable work culture and organisational culture. These solutions should then be implemented consistently in a common discursive process. Holistic sustainable management – to give only a small impression of its scope – extends from: forms of communication and manners; to dealing with resources such as paper, electricity, water, etc.; all the way to structural and infrastructural questions.

Since such a rethinking and the changes that accompany it represent intrusions into the existing cultural structure, resistance is to be expected here. In time, every culture creates firm models of communication, thinking, and action-models that can also be described as conventions. Here, tried and tested value structures find expression as successful – or rather, practicable – models of action, and are established for the long run; this guarantees the long-term preservation of complex social structures. In institutions and organisations as well, e.g., in those engaged in research and teaching, corresponding conventions are formed over long periods of time and constitute a specific institutional or organisational culture. The paradigm shift toward more sustainable ways of life and modes of work therefore requires a rethinking on the part of the employees (and/or students) on all hierarchical and professional levels, since the new paradigm – in itself, and in its implementation – goes, as a rule, against accustomed principles and practices that have long been ingrained in people. The attempt should therefore be made to convince, on all levels, the older employees in particular of the new paradigm – i.e., those employees who have long been active in the institution or organisation and who have helped form the existing culture. These long-standing employees often represent "social institutions" in their sphere of influence and have the status of opinion leaders. A mental shift needs time and can only be achieved when one succeeds in convincing the (informal) opinion leaders that changes make sense. This process can be advanced by, among other things, individual conversations, coaching sessions, and concomitant training and further education.

References

Hansen, K. P. (2003): Kultur und Kulturwissenschaft (3rd ed.). Tübingen, Basel (in German)

The Authors

Banse, Gerhard, Professor Dr.; Karlsruher Institut für Technologie (KIT), Institut für Technikfolgenabschätzung und Systemanalyse (ITAS)/Karlsruhe Institute of Technology (KIT), Institute for Technology Assessment and Systems Analysis (ITAS), Karlsruhe, Germany (gerhard.banse@kit.edu)

Damodaran, Appukuttan N., Professor Dr.; Indian Institute of Management Bangalore, Bangalore, India (damodaran@iimb.ernet.in)

Füle, Miklós, Dr.; Budapesti Műszaki és Gazdaságtudományi Egyetem, Környezetgazdaságtan Tanszék/Budapest University of Technology and Economics, Department of Environmental Economics; Budapest, Hungary (fulem@eik.bme.hu)

Graupe, Silja, Professor Dr.; Alanus Hochschule für Kunst und Gesellschaft, Institut für philosophische Bildung/Alanus University of Arts and Social Sciences, Institute of Philosophical Education; Alfter, Germany (silja.graupe@alanus.edu)

Grunwald, Armin, Professor Dr.; Karlsruher Institut für Technologie (KIT), Institut für Technikfolgenabschätzung und Systemanalyse (ITAS)/Karlsruhe Institute of Technology (KIT), Institute for Technology Assessment and Systems Analysis (ITAS) & Büro für Technikfolgenabschätzung beim Deutschen Bundestag (TAB)/Office of Technology Assessment at the German Bundestag; Karlsruhe & Berlin, Germany (armin.grunwald@kit.edu)

Hauser, Robert, Dr.; Karlsruher Institut für Technologie (KIT), Zentrum für Angewandte Kulturwissenschaften (ZAK)/Karlsruhe Institute of Technology (KIT), Centre for Cultural and General Studies (ZAK); Karlsruhe, Germany (robert.hauser@kit.edu)

Holz, Verena, MA; Leuphana Universität Lüneburg, Institut für integrative Studien (infis)/ Leuphana University of Lueneburg, Institute of Integrative Studies (infis); Lüneburg, Germany (verena.holz@uni.leuphana.de)

Hübner, Renate, Ass.-Professor Dr.; Alpen-Adria-Universität Klagenfurt, Institut für Interventionsforschung und Kulturelle Nachhaltigkeit/University of Klagenfurt, Department of Intervention Research and Cultural Sustainability; Klagenfurt, Austria (renate.huebner@uni-klu. ac.at)

Krainer, Larissa, Professor Dr.; Alpen-Adria-Universität Klagenfurt, Institut für Interventionsforschung und Kulturelle Nachhaltigkeit/University of Klagenfurt, Department of Intervention Research and Cultural Sustainability; Klagenfurt, Austria (larissa.krainer@uni-klu.ac.at)

Kopfmüller, Jürgen, Dipl.-Volkswirt; Karlsruher Institut für Technologie (KIT), Institut für Technikfolgenabschätzung und Systemanalyse (ITAS)/Karlsruhe Institute of Technology (KIT), Institute for Technology Assessment and Systems Analysis (ITAS); Karlsruhe, Germany (juergen.kopfmueller@kit.edu)

Lindeman, Kenyon C., Professor Dr.; Florida Institute of Technology, Department of Education & Interdisciplinary Studies; Melbourne, FL, U.S. (lindeman@fit.edu)

Metzner-Szigeth, Andreas, PD Dr.; Westfälische Wilhelms-Universität Münster, Institut für Soziologie/WestphalianWilhelms-University of Münster, Institute of Sociology; Münster, Germany (metzner@uni-muenster.de)

Müller, Eduard, Professor Dr.; Rector of the University for International Cooperation, San José, Costa Rica (emuller@uci.ac.cr)

Muraca, Barbara, Dr.; Ernst-Moritz-Arndt-Universität Greifswald, Institut für Philosophie/ Ernst Moritz Arndt University of Greifswald, Institute of Philosophy; Greifswald, Germany (barbara.muraca@uni-greifswald.de)

Nelson, Gordon L., Professor Dr.; Florida Institute of Technology, Vice President for Academic Affairs; Melbourne, FL, U.S. (nelson@fit.edu)

Parodi, Oliver, Dr.; Karlsruher Institut für Technologie (KIT), Institut für Technikfolgenabschätzung und Systemanalyse (ITAS) und KIT-Schwerpunkt „Mensch und Technik" (MuT)/ Karlsruhe Institute of Technology (KIT), Institute for Technology Assessment and Systems Analysis (ITAS) and KIT Research Focus „Humans and Technology" (MuT); Karlsruhe, Germany (oliver.parodi@kit.edu)

Robertson-von Trotha, Caroline Y., Professor Dr.; Karlsruher Institut für Technologie (KIT), Zentrum für Angewandte Kulturwissenschaften (ZAK)/Karlsruhe Institute of Technology (KIT), Centre for Cultural and General Studies (ZAK); Karlsruhe, Germany (caroline. robertson@kit.edu)

Sharma, Virender K., Professor Dr.; Florida Institute of Technology, Department of Chemistry; Melbourne, FL, U.S. (vsharma@fit.edu)

Shenker, Jonathan M., Associate Professor; Florida Institute of Technology, Department of Biological Sciences Melbourne, FL, U.S. (shenker@fit.edu)

Szlávik, János, Professor Dr.; Eszterházy Károly Főiskola, Gazdaság- és Társadalomtudományi Főiskolai Kar tudományos adatbázisa/Eszterházy Károly College, Faculty of Economic and Social Sciences, Eger; Hungary (szlavikj@eik.bme.hu, szlavik@ektf.hu)

Tapia Uribe, Medardo, Professor Dr.; Universidad National Autónoma de México, Centro Regional de Investigaciones Multidisciplinarias/Mexico's National University, Regional Centre for Multidisciplinary Research; México, Méxiko (medardo@servidor.unam.mx, medardo-tapia@gmail.com)

Tautscher, Gabriele, Dr.; Universität Wien, Institut für Südasien-, Tibet- und Buddhismuskunde/University of Vienna, Department of South Asian, Tibetan and Buddhist Studies; Vienna, Austria (gabriele.tautscher@gmail.com)

To, Kien, PhD; Singapore University of Technology and Design, Singapore-MIT International Design Centre; Singapore (tokien@sutd.edu.sg or tokien98@yahoo.com)

Tulbure, Ildiko, Professor Dr.; Universitatea 1 Decembrie 1918 Alba Iulia, Topografie si Cadastru/University "1. December 1918", Department Topography and Cadastre; Alba Iulia, Romania (ildiko.tulbure@tu-clausthal.de)

Voget-Kleschin, Lieske, Diplom-Landschaftsökologin; Ernst-Moritz-Arndt-Universität Greifswald, Institut für Botanik und Landschaftsökologie und Institut für Philosophie/Ernst-Moritz Arndt University of Greifswald, Institute of Botany and Landscape Ecology and Institute of Philosophy; Greifswald, Germany (lieske.voget-kleschin@uni-greifswald.de)

Yang, Ge, Professor Dr.; Shanghai University of Finance and Economics, The School of Economics, Shanghai, China (gyang16@sina.com)

The Editors

Professor Dr. sc. phil. *Gerhard Banse*
Researcher at Research Center Karlsruhe (KIT), Institute for Technology Assessment and Systems Analysis (ITAS), professor of general technology at Brandenburg University of Technology, Cottbus, Germany

Professor *Gordon L. Nelson*, PhD
Vicepresident for academic affairs of Florida Institute of Technology , Melbourne, FL, U.S., and professor of chemistry

Dr. phil. Dipl.-Ing. *Oliver Parodi*
Senior scientist at Research Center Karlsruhe (KIT), Institute for Technology Assessment and Systems Analysis (ITAS), administrative manager of the KIT research focus "Humans and Technology" (MuT)